Agriculture, Price Stabilisation and Trade Rules

# World Trade Institute Advanced Studies



VOLUME 3

The titles published in this series are listed at *brill.com/wtia*

# Agriculture, Price Stabilisation and Trade Rules

*A Principled Approach*

*By*

Irene Musselli

BRILL
NIJHOFF

LEIDEN | BOSTON

The opinions expressed in this book are those of the author and are not to be taken as the official views of the UNCTAD secretariat or its member states.

Library of Congress Cataloging-in-Publication Data

Names: Musselli, Irene, author.
Title: Agriculture, price stabilisation and trade rules : a principled approach / by Irene Musselli.
Description: Leiden ; Boston : Brill Nijhoff, 2017. | Based on author's thesis (Doctoral - Faculty of Law of the University of Bern, within the program of the World Trade Institute), 2016. | Includes bibliographical references and index.
Identifiers: LCCN 2017021293 (print) | LCCN 2017022381 (ebook) | ISBN 9789004350540 (E-book) | ISBN 9789004314238 (hardback : alk. paper)
Subjects: LCSH: Foreign trade regulation. | Agricultural prices--Government policy.
Classification: LCC K3943 (ebook) | LCC K3943 .M874 2017 (print) | DDC 338.1/3--dc23
LC record available at https://lccn.loc.gov/2017021293

Typeface for the Latin, Greek, and Cyrillic scripts: "Brill". See and download: brill.com/brill-typeface.

ISSN 2405-9331
ISBN 978-90-04-31423-8 (hardback)
ISBN 978-90-04-35054-0 (e-book)

*To Mirco and Chiara Luna*

# Contents

# Series Editor Foreword

Agricultural commodities traded internationally are subject to changing production patterns in terms of climatic conditions. At the same time, they are of key importance for food security in all countries alike. Varying conditions often result in price fluctuations which strongly affect developing, and in particular least developed countries. More than 40 percent of them depend upon agricultural exports, and 38 of 48 least developed countries are reported to be net food importers. The instability and variations introduced by fluctuating conditions induced government intervention to stabilise commodities both in terms of prices and supply. These efforts, implemented by means of International Commodity Agreements (ICAs), largely failed to stabilise markets and prices. More recent times witnessed a return to a market-oriented approach. Realities, however, are more complex, and the evidence shows that this approach equally failed to deliver stability in terms of prices and supply, nor did it assist developing countries effectively to develop in a sustainable manner.

The underlying problems are of enormous complexity, both in economics and law. Dr Musselli, using her extensive practical experience in UNCTAD as a background, offers a comprehensive analysis of the history of ICAs, and of the underlying and competing regulatory approaches. The analysis includes a thorough assessment of relevant WTO law, in particular the nature and implications of the Agreement on Agriculture and of Article XI GATT. Finding her with contradictory entanglements, the author takes a step back and reflects upon the underlying normative principles which should inform the field of law. Expounding the principles of food security, rural development and livelihood and sustainable development, she lays the foundation of policy tools assisting the realisation of these goals. The thesis offers a fresh look at the tool box of managed trade in agricultural commodities and developed new and refined solutions which take into account the legal role of equity and of graduation.

The book thus offers new insights and is able to invigorate a debate which currently still is caught in overly ideological entanglements between market oriented and interventionist schools. Her proposals offer a careful and viable balance. The book is characterised by a thorough understanding both of the law and the economics of commodities, but also of the wider societal and development background within which the two unfold. It assembles a wide spread literature on the subject in law and economics and offers a truly comprehensive review and discussion of the subject matter.

The book resulted from a PhD written within the doctoral programme of the World Trade Institute. It was a pleasure to supervise the thesis, jointly with

Professor Michael Hahn, writing the second report. The doctoral thesis, entitled *Agricultural, Price Stabilisation and Trade Rules – A Principled Approach,* was approved and adopted summa cum laude by the Faculty of Law of the University of Bern on 26 May 2016. It was an enriching pleasure to work with Irene Musselli. In the process of research and work on a complex and controversial topic, she combined experience in the field and a critical analytical mind. Both of which provided the background for new insights the reader will be able to find in this volume.

*Thomas Cottier*
Bern, March 2017

# Preface

This study was driven by two motives: a compelling research interest and some discontent with the state of play in agricultural trade and its framework conditions in international law.

The regulation of agricultural commodity trade is a fascinating area of inquiry. In a complex way, it stands at the junction of law, economics and politics; eclectically mixes technical complexities and principled decisions; and is contextually rich, firmly grounded in real-world particulars. The regulation of commodity trade does have texture, of a special kind: a complex fabric of dry technicalities and vital socio-economic concerns, twisted together. It is up to the researcher to disentangle this thread, and draw out the essential elements involved. Ultimately it is an absorbing and rewarding endeavour.

Discontentment is, like interest, a strong research driver; as it carries a quest for change. On matters of agricultural, and broadly commodity price dynamics, a personal concern arises from the perceived disconnect between law and justice. Positive law has progressively disengaged from an assessment of the fairness of distributional outcomes. The 'rule of the market' and efficiency have become the cognitive categories, the main analytical framework within which policy makers can think upon and act upon the global commodity economy. There is a pressing need for expanding again the boundaries of legal action, by creating normative parameters within which agricultural market price dynamics can be contained and managed, and not only facilitated. Eventually, this prompts a move beyond a formalist, technically-oriented and allegedly politically-neutral conception of the law, towards a more 'substantive' rationality: commodity trade regulation involves principled decisions, rooted in value systems, and value systems are not neutral.

This research endeavour tries to articulate these concerns. It reflects the experience of a trade policy analyst, lawyer by background, who has worked in a policy environment largely dominated by economists.

# Acknowledgements

This book is a revised version of my doctoral thesis submitted to the University of Bern in 2016, within the framework of the doctoral programme of the World Trade Institute in Bern. I would like to express my special appreciation and thanks to my supervisor, Professor Thomas Cottier, who encouraged my research and taught me to think critically and rigorously with an open mind. Professor Cottier advice has been invaluable. I would also like to thank Professor Michael Hahn for letting my PhD defense be an enjoyable moment, and for his essential comments and suggestions. Furthermore, I am indebted to Professor Lucius Caflisch, for his encouragement and advice. I would like to thank Christian Häberli, Elisabeth Bürgi, Ilaria Espa and Miho Shirotori for valuable insights on trade and agriculture policy, Guillermo Valles, for encouraging synergies between my research and professional work, and Samuel Gayi, for facilitating interviews with commodity stakeholders. Special thanks to my family. I am grateful to my husband, Mirco, for his understanding and encouragement, and to my daughter, Chiara Luna, for her cheerful indulgence towards a distracted mother. Finally I thank my mother and my father for the stimulating intellectual environment in which I grew up.

# List of Abbreviations

AA Agricultural Act
AAA Agricultural Adjustment Act
AB Appellate Body
ACP African, Caribbean and Pacific
ADM Archer Daniels Midland
AGP Agreement on Government Procurement
AMS Aggregate Measurement of Support
AoA Agreement on Agriculture
ASCM Agreement on Subsidies and Countervailing Measures
BCC Bourse du Café et du Cacao
CACP Commission for Agricultural Costs and Prices
CAISTAB Caisse de Stabilisation et de Soutien des Prix des Productions Agricoles
CAP Common Agricultural Policy
CCFF Contingency and Compensatory Financing Facility
CERDS Charter of Economic Rights and Duties of States
CFC Common Fund for Commodities
CFF Compensatory Financing Facility
CIF cost, insurance & freight
CMC Ghana Cocoa Marketing Company Limited
COCOBOD Ghana Cocoa Board (est. 1947)
CWB Canadian Wheat Board
DDA Doha Development Agenda
DSB Dispute Settlement Body
DSU Dispute Settlement Understanding
EC European Communities
ECOSOC Economic and Social Council
EEC European Economic Community
EPA Environmental Protection Agency
EU European Union
EUI European University Institute
FAO Food and Agriculture Organization
FFD International Conference on Financing for Development
FOB free on board
G33 Group of 33
GA General Assembly
GATT General Agreement on Tariffs and Trade

| | |
|---|---|
| GCF | Global Commodities Forum |
| GDP | gross domestic product |
| HLPE | High Level Panel of Experts on Food Security and Nutrition |
| ICA | International/Intergovernmental Commodity Agreement/ Arrangement |
| ICCA | International Cocoa Agreement |
| ICCICA | Interim Co-ordinating Committee for International Commodity Arrangements |
| ICCO | International Cocoa Organization |
| ICESCR | International Covenant on Economic, Social and Cultural Rights |
| ICO | International Coffee Organization |
| ICoA | International Coffee Agreement |
| ICTSD | International Centre for Trade and Sustainable Development |
| IEA | International Energy Agency |
| ILO | International Labour Office |
| IMF | International Monetary Fund |
| INRA | International Natural Rubber Agreement |
| IPC | Integrated Programme for Commodities |
| ISA | International Sugar Agreement |
| ITA | International Tin Agreement |
| ITO | International Trade Organization |
| IWA | International Wheat Agreement |
| LDC | least developed country |
| MAFF | Ministry of Agriculture, Forestry & Fisheries |
| MFN | Most Favoured Nation |
| MIFAFF | Ministry for Food, Agriculture, Forestry and Fisheries |
| MSP | minimum support prices |
| MTN | multilateral trade negotiations |
| MYEM | Multi-year Expert Meeting |
| NCCR | National Centres of Competence in Research |
| NFA | National Food Authority |
| NFSA | National Food Security Act |
| NIEO | New International Economic Order |
| NY | New York |
| OECD | Organisation for Economic Co-operation and Development |
| OPEC | Organization of the Petroleum Exporting Countries |
| OTC | over-the-counter |
| OTDS | overall amount of trade-distorting support |
| PBS | price band system |
| PPP | public-private partnership |

| | |
|---|---|
| PPS | public procurement system |
| S&DT | special and differential treatment |
| SACA | Special Agreement on Commodity Arrangements |
| SDGS | Sustainable Development Goals |
| SIC | Standard Industrial Classification |
| SITC | Standard International Trade Classification |
| STABEX | Stabilisation of Export Earnings |
| STAX | Stacked Income Protection |
| STE | state trading enterprise |
| SVE | small and vulnerable economy |
| TPDS | Targeted Public Distribution System |
| TRIPS | Trade-related Aspects of Intellectual Property Rights |
| TxRQ | tax-rate quota |
| UN | United Nations |
| UNCTAD | United Nations Conference on Trade and Development |
| UNDP | United Nations Development Programme |
| US | United States of America |
| $ | United States Dollar |
| VCLT | Vienna Convention on the Law of Treaties |
| WFP | World Food Programme |
| WTI | World Trade Institute |
| WTO | World Trade Organization |
| WWII | World War II |

CHAPTER 1

# Introduction

## 1.1 Scoping the Research

This study considers the use of trade policy instruments for price stabilisation in agriculture, and their regulation by trade law (Box 1). The book traces the evolution from interventionist regimes to neoliberal policies and back to managed approaches in recent, post financial crisis and food crisis periods. Drawing and combining insights from the underlying and competing regulatory approaches, it proposes a synthesis that seeks to outline a forward agenda in commodity regulation.

### Box 1: Trade policy to manage prices

In spite of scepticism from economic quarters, market intervention to calm commodity prices has remained pervasive, particularly in developing countries. Most notably, countries increasingly resorted to trade policy to manage prices through 2007–11, in a context of major disturbances and uncertainty in commodity markets. A 2011 survey covering 105 countries found that 33 countries, or 31 percent of the sample, had resorted to one or more export restrictive measures through 2007–11 in an effort to calm consumer price spikes.[1] Countries are also increasingly using trade policy, and direct price intervention, to stabilise producers' prices, often at above the market-clearing level. In India, for example, the 2013 National Food Security Act (NFSA) scaled-up procurement and distribution operations of rice and wheat at administered prices. Côte d'Ivoire, which had fully liberalised its cocoa sector in 1999, is reintroducing publicly managed forward sales, to stabilise intra-year and inter-year cocoa prices.[2] There is also renewed interest in concerted price action to 'tame' commodity markets. Proposals have been tabled to set up global buffer stocks – physical, virtual, or a combination of

1 Ramesh Sharma, *Food Export Restrictions: Review of the 2007–2010 Experience and Considerations for Disciplining Restrictive Measures*, FAO Commodity and Trade Policy Research Working Papers, no. 32 (Rome: FAO, 2011).

2 H.E. Amb. Guy-Alain Emmanuel Gauze, former Permanent Representative of the Permanent Mission of Côte d'Ivoire in Geneva, "Reform of the Cocoa Sector in West Africa" (presentation delivered at UNCTAD, Global Commodities Forum 2015, Geneva, 13–14 April 2015).

 DOI 10.1163/9789004350540_002

both.[3] Resources have been mobilized for strategic reserves at the regional level.[4] Finally, there have been concerted efforts to revive supply management schemes such as for rice and natural rubber.[5] As discussed in chapter 2, these stabilisation arrangements involve a mixture of trade policy instruments (tariff protection, price support, state trading, etc.), which are complexly interlocked. This complex fabric of intersecting policies is to be scrutinised under the dissecting scope of discrete WTO disciplines.

While the topic area is vast, the research question is narrowly framed. The focus is on stabilisation policies in their interface with trade law. The key question concerns the 'normative' orientation of trade law in this issue area, whether it should follow a trade liberalisation paradigm or a trade regulation paradigm that also embraces stabilisation concerns. The analysis assesses competing regulatory approaches and reflects upon the normative values that

3 At the global level, the most articulated proposal for physical and virtual food reserves has been advanced by Joachim von Braun and Maximo Torero of IFPRI. The proposal combined emergency food reserves and a hypothetical international buffer stockholding scheme to stabilise international wheat prices. See Joachim von Braun and Maximo Torero, *Physical and Virtual Global Food Reserves to Protect the Poor and Prevent Market Failure*, International Food Policy Research Institute, IFPRI Policy Brief 4 (Washington, D.C., 2008); Joachim von Braun and Maximo Torero, *Implementing Physical and Virtual Food Reserves to Protect the Poor and Prevent Market Failure*, International Food Policy Research Institute, IFPRI Policy Brief 10 (Washington, D.C., 2009). On food reserves, see generally Institute for Agriculture and Trade Policy, *Grain Reserves and the Food Price Crisis: Selected Writings from 2008–2012* ([Minneapolis]: IATP, 2012) and Thomas Lines, *The Potential Establishment of Emergency Food Reserve Funds*, UNCTAD Special Unit on Commodities Working Paper Series on Commodities and Development, Discussion Paper 3 (Geneva, 2011).

4 The most accomplished regional scheme is the ASEAN Plus Three Emergency Rice Reserve (APTERR). APTERR was set up under an agreement signed by the Ministers of Agriculture and Forestry of the ASEAN member countries plus China, Japan and the Republic of Korea in October 2011. Note that the APTERR is a strategic stock/emergency food reserve, not a buffer stock to stabilise prices. Stocks are released to meet emergencies that threaten food availability at the national level (Tier 1 and Tier 2 earmarked stocks) and to deal with acute humanitarian crises (Tier 3 stockpiled emergency rice reserves). See *ASEAN Plus Three Emergency Rice Reserve Agreement*, downloaded from the ASEAN site http://www.asean.org/communities/asean-economic-community/category/agreements-declarations-5 on 7 May 2015.

5 In 2008, Thailand, Vietnam, Burma, Laos, Cambodia considered a cartel-type output restraint scheme in rice to sustain prices. The scheme was never implemented, due to international pressure rooted in food security concerns. The same year, Thailand, Malaysia and Indonesia orchestrated cutbacks in natural rubber to inflate prices under the International Rubber Consortium.

should inform this field of law. Its central thrust is towards the establishment of a 'principled approach' to trade rules. Its ultimate gist is to integrate considerations of social justice into the framework of multilateral trade governance. The perspective is by large *de lege ferenda*; and one that complexly intertwines law, economics and politics.

The analysis moves beyond the dichotomy between 'market' and 'authority' in commodity trade regulation, and steers a middle course in between. In the author's view, the specificity of agricultural commodities invites regulation. This is not to say that markets should be eschewed in setting pricing patterns, as market prices are an inescapable signalling device. What is meant is that commodity market dynamics, and extreme price swings in particular, should be constrained within some normative perimeters. Trade law is called upon to play a twofold role in this field. First, it should set the normative parameters to be 'factored' into the working of markets. Second, trade law should set principles, techniques and procedures to manage trade-offs. In particular, it should strike a balance between stabilisation policies and liberal trade interests; and between the right of a country to stabilise its farm sector and the right of farmers elsewhere to compete on fair terms at home or abroad.

The analysis reflects upon the underlying normative principles which should inform the field of law. It expounds the principles of food security, sustainable rural livelihood and environmental sustainability as normative benchmarks against which to assess the legitimacy of price stabilisation policies in agriculture. It then outlines a framework capable of weighing and balancing trade and stabilisation concerns, expounding the concept of cosmopolitan multilateralism and equity as conceptual foundations. The first one depicts a dedication to multilateralism, but also entails legal responsibilities on the part of the global community and 'price setters'. Equity is introduced as a foundation for fairness, distributive justice, and modulation of the law, in line with modern functions the principle assumes in international law. These principles are then employed to bring about an appropriate balance with trade and provide the basis for detailed operational proposals developed in the book.

Why are considerations of principles and objectives so important to deserve separate in-depth treatment? The answer requires two sets of reasons, of both a practical and a theoretical nature.

First, principles are normatively important. They are bound to become increasingly so within the 'post-2015' normative framework.[6] Their relevance can be ascertained in two respects: as a possible 'material source' of international law; and through the process that shapes the emergence of legal rules ('formal

6 See *infra* text accompanying notes 717–21.

sources' of international law).[7] This distinction is analytically convenient but somewhat artificial, as the two pathways are complexly interlocked.

In 'material' terms, goals and objectives set the "aspirational basis for rules of law",[8] the moral and political grounds for specific legal provisions.[9] They act, in this respect, as 'material sources' of international law.[10] Moral and political in character, they precede law; they are upstream to it, as is politics.[11] Yet, they also feed into the law-making process, including through 'formal' venues, as discussed below.

In 'formal' terms, principles that are not given sufficient expression in legal form[12] do not themselves amount to a source of legal obligations. Yet, they assist in interpreting and applying legal rules. They are formally relevant in the interpretation of WTO treaty law. They are relevant as 'context', pursuant to Article 31 (3) of the Vienna Convention on the Law of Treaties (VCLT), if they find expression in a discernible pattern of acts and pronouncements. They can also be relevant as a supplementary means of interpretation, under Article 32 of the VCLT, particularly when a consistent pattern is not discernible. Furthermore, statements of principles may have normative value in ascertaining the emergence of new customary rules, particularly when enshrined in Resolutions of the UN General Assembly.[13]

Overall, through material or formal venues, statements of objectives and principles help to shape new norms and standards. Aspirational and transformative, they contribute to the gradual formation of the rules through the political law-making process.[14] They are an ingredient in the largely procedural

---

7 As described in Pellet, 'material sources' are defined as "the political, sociological, economic, moral or religious origins of the legal rules", while 'formal sources' refer to "the processes through which international law rules become legally relevant" (Alain Pellet, "Article 38", in *The Statute of the International Court of Justice: A Commentary*, ed. Andreas Zimmermann, Christian Tomuschat, and Karin Oellers-Frahm (Oxford: Oxford University Press, 2006), 714).

8 As acknowledged by the International Court of Justice (ICJ) with respect to humanitarian considerations and generally moral principles. See *South West Africa,* ICJ Reports (1966), 6, 34 (paras. 49–50).

9 Pellet, above n 7, at 714–16.

10 Ibid, at 714.

11 Ibid.

12 Through treaty or customary practice, or as general principles of law distilled from municipal systems.

13 They can be used to ascertain the existence of *opinio juris*, or state practice, or both.

14 For important insights into the gradual formation of international law, Georges Abi-Saab, "Les sources du droit international: essai de deconstruction", in *Liber Amicorum Eduardo*

alchemy that transmutes political claims into legal rights and obligations. Interestingly, a combination of goals, targets and indicators, rather than legally binding norms, has driven progress under the Millennium Development Goals (MDGs) framework; and is likely to shape the 2030 Agenda for Sustainable Development.[15]

Second, turning to legal theory, a discussion of normative principles and objectives is valuable in rediscovering the distinctiveness of legal reasoning and legal contents *vis-à-vis* economics. In international economic law, the particularity of legal thought has traditionally relied on the capacity to weigh competing policy objectives and principles and strike a balance between social concerns (equity) and economic rationality (efficiency). Trade law thus moves beyond purely economic rationale. Its thrust is not, or not only, allocative efficiency. In Professor Cottier's words, "[...] there is more to international economic law than implementing economics".[16] What "lawyers bring to the table" is: "a principled approach to problems combined with case by case assessment, the ability to deal with exceptions and irregularity, the relevance of values and justice, the relevance of human experience and psychology, the expertise in institutional design and in due process decision making with fairness and transparency."[17]

It is an expressed aim of this study to revive this 'principled approach' to trade rules in the issue area of agricultural stabilisation. The objective is to rediscover the aspirational basis of the rules of law; to give sufficient expression in legal form to the moral considerations that should inform international trade law. This rediscovery starts from a reflective exercise on the normative purpose, objectives and principles of trade rules in their bearing on agricultural stabilisation arrangements.

The regulation of agricultural stabilisation policies lends itself well to this inquiry into the moral (*versus* 'economistic') foundations of trade law. Indeed,

---

*Jiménez de Aréchaga* (Montevideo: Fundación de cultura universitaria, 1994), 29–49; Marcelo G. Kohen and Magnus Jesko Langer, *Georges Abi-Saab. Le développement du droit international. Réflexions d'un demi-siècle*, vol. 1 (The Graduate Institute Publications, PUF, 2013).

15 On the transformative significance of a 'goal framework', see: High Level Panel of Eminent Persons on the Post-2015 Development Agenda, *A New Global Partnership: Eradicate Poverty and Transform Economies through Sustainable Development* (New York: United Nations, 2013), 13.

16 Thomas Cottier, "Challenges ahead in International Economic Law," *Journal of International Economic Law* 12, no. 1 (2009): 12.

17 Ibid, at 12.

as briefly outlined below, this subject matter engages critical ethical concerns in addition to economic considerations. It is important to specifically identify the moral and political sensitivities involved, before turning to the design of this research.

## 1.2 Agricultural Price Stabilisation: Why Does It Matter

Agricultural commodity prices, it should be recalled, are inherently volatile, and are generally subject to greater fluctuations than the prices of manufactured products. This volatility, whether 'natural' or man-made, is problematic. It is problematic in so far as it impacts human welfare as a pre-eminent good. It is worth recalling why agricultural commodity markets are inherently volatile; and then draw attention to the humanitarian costs, particularly in the most vulnerable economies, of such instability. The analysis concludes by enquiring about whether a regulatory response to curb volatility is needed.

### 1.2.1 *The Inherent Volatility of Agricultural Commodity Prices*

There are multiple drivers behind price movements in agricultural commodity markets. Some are 'natural', or fundamental, and refer to imbalances of supply and demand that stem from natural shocks, seasonality or cyclical crop factors. They are inherent to the functioning of the market. Others refer to complex dynamics of interdependence and transmission between agricultural markets and other markets such as energy markets, or monetary and financial markets. They are systemic in nature. Others are artificially engineered, or behavioural such as panic buying or speculation. They present instances of market imperfection or failure. These drivers are often mutually interdependent and complexly intertwined. Which among them matters most is a matter of controversy.

#### 1.2.1.1 'Natural' Factors

Major supply price shocks in agriculture stem from climatic and environmental factors. Weather risks, such as droughts and floods, as well as the incidence of pests and diseases may translate into major supply shocks, both within season and from year to year. In this volatile context, stocks-to-use ratio is also critically important. With stocks down to levels not seen since the early 1970s, the impacts of capricious weather conditions cannot be effectively smoothed through the manipulation of reserves.

For most agricultural commodities, price variability also 'naturally' stems from seasonality. Reference is here to price fluctuations within the season, or intra-year price volatility. There are quite discernible seasonal price patterns for most crop commodities. At harvest, prices drop, as supply is abundant. They then rise steadily with the progressive depletion of stocks, to peak before harvest. Private storage and temporal arbitrage is critical to smooth this type of intra-season volatility.

In the medium-run, some agricultural commodities exhibit a cyclical price pattern, with boom and bust cycles. These price dynamics essentially reflect delayed and unsynchronised adjustments in supply and demand. This is notably the case for tree crops with relatively long gestation periods such as cocoa. As new plants take several years to produce maximum yields (in cocoa, up to 10 years), increased demand cannot be met in the short run by increased production, which puts upward pressure on prices. Sustained high prices encourage new planting, which, after a relatively long time lag, results in oversupply and downward price pressure. In tree crops like cocoa, this age-dependent yield factor is to be assessed alongside high entry and exit costs. For poor farmers, investment in new plants or the grafting of existing plantation is hardly recoverable. This means that farmers will not invest, unless there is some prospect for sustained high prices; and that they will continue to produce as long as prices cover the cost of labour. The time-lag factor, coupled with entry and exit barriers, reduces the short-term price elasticity of demand and supply, and magnifies price movements. In the long-run, the same dynamics of investment 'time lag' may also explain some long-term cycles in the price of annual crops such as cereals. This occurs when sustained strong prices favour research and development (R&D) investment that spurs major technological advances.

#### 1.2.1.2 Systemic Factors

The inherent tendency of agricultural commodity prices to fluctuate widely is further exacerbated by the link with energy markets, either through energy consumed directly in production, or through energy-related inputs such as fertilizer. For staple food commodities that are used to make biofuels, biofuel policies also count towards price movements.

Exchange rate movements add to the inherent volatility of agricultural prices. As international commodity prices are denominated in US dollars, exchange rate movements *vis-à-vis* the dollar affect the dollar-denominated commodity price. Commodity prices increase when the dollar depreciates as exporters need to offset the exchange rate loss, and *vice versa*.

Beyond the strong inverse correlation between the dollar and commodity prices, there are other complex interactions between commodity markets and financial and monetary markets. These include: interest rate fluctuations;

sovereign credit spreads; and trading in commodity derivatives.[18] Altogether, these dynamics refer to the so-called 'financialisation of commodity markets', with reference to "the increasing role of financial motives, financial markets and financial actors in the operation of commodity markets".[19]

#### 1.2.1.3 Policies

Unilateral policies can also trigger or magnify price movements. Important man-made triggers include export restrictions, especially if coupled with hoarding or 'panic buying' by public actors, as well as stocking and de-stocking policies by large players in the trade. Export restrictions on rice by Vietnam and India in 2007–08, coupled with panic buying by the Philippines and Indonesia, are held liable for the disastrous price spike in rice of May 2008.[20] Likewise, the 2010 Russian wheat export ban exerted upward pressure on prices, and led to short-term contract defaults and supply disruptions.[21] In some cases, such as rice, unilateral trade restrictions likely triggered the price surge.[22] In other instances, such as wheat, they exacerbated a price surge that was rooted in exogenous shocks (weather, the weak dollar, high oil prices, etc.).

Together, these drivers define complex patterns of short-term price volatility and short- to medium-run boom and bust episodes in agricultural markets.

### 1.2.2 *Socio-economic Costs of Agricultural Price Volatility in Poor Countries*

Agricultural price volatility carries acute sensitivities. These sensitivities relate to key social concerns and involve questions that are highly political in nature. They touch upon elementary considerations of equity and justice.

From a moral standpoint, what is perhaps most problematic is the 'anti-poor' bias of agricultural price instability. Both across and within countries,

---

18 For an outline of these transmission mechanisms, Yilmaz Akyuz, "Managing Boom-Bust Cycles in Commodity Dependent Economies" (presentation given at UNCTAD, Global Commodities Forum 2015, Geneva, 13–14 April 2015, downloadable at http://unctad.org/meetings/en/Presentation/SUC%20GCF2015%20Yilmaz%20Aky%C3%BCz.pdf).

19 UNCTAD, *Price Formation in Financialized Commodity Markets: The Role of Information* (New York; Geneva: United Nations, 2011), 13.

20 World rice prices trebled within less than four months and reached a 30-year inflation-adjusted high. For a detailed review, Tom Slayton, *Rice Crisis Forensics: How Asian Governments Carelessly Set the World Rice Market on Fire*, Center for Global Development, CGD Working Paper 163 (Washington, D.C.: 2009).

21 The World Bank and FAO, *The Grain Chain Food Security and Managing Wheat Imports in Arab Countries* (Washington, D.C.: The World Bank, 2012), at 4.

22 Slayton, above n 20.

the instability of agricultural prices is primarily a matter of concern for the poor. The costs tend to be disproportionately borne by the poor, who are the least equipped to handle them. This social unfairness can be appreciated at the macro and micro levels, and at the producer and consumer ends of the price spectrum.

In low-income countries, agricultural commodity trade and poverty are complexly entangled.[23] Developing countries, and particularly the poorest ones, are still largely agrarian societies. In countries classified as 'least-developed' (LDCs),[24] about 70 percent of the population still lives in rural areas,[25] and agriculture continues to occupy an estimated 63 percent of the labour force.[26] This has important ramifications. It translates in accrued exposure, for the poor, to agricultural price fluctuations.[27]

At the macro level, developing countries' exposure to agricultural price volatility is two-fold. It comes from both the export and import sides of the trade equation. In both respects, developing countries are more concerned with the effects of agricultural price instability than are developed economies.

On the export side (the production end), developing countries are comparatively more reliant on agricultural export proceeds than their developed countries counterparts (Table 1 and Appendix 2). Specifically, of 48 LDCs, 21, close to half, derive the bulk of their export proceeds from agricultural exports. These exports are highly concentrated in a few major products, typically agricultural raw materials (like cotton, timber and natural rubber) or tropical beverages (cocoa, coffee and tea). They represent a major source of foreign currency for the purchase of imports, including staple foods. They also represent an

---

23 For some illustrative facts of the extent of the least developed countries' dependence on commodities: UNCTAD and CFC, *Global Crises and the Commodity Dependence of the Least Developed Countries: Impacts, Challenges and the Way Forward*, UNCTAD/ALDC/MISC/2011/6, 28 April 2011, 2. Specifically on agriculture, UNCTAD, *Least Developed Countries Report 2015: Transforming Rural Economies* (New York; Geneva: United Nations, 2015).

24 Classification criteria are detailed at http://www.un.org/en/development/desa/policy/cdp/ldc_info.shtml (accessed on 11 May 2015).

25 World Bank, World Development Indicators, "Rural population (% of total population)", 2013 (downloaded 18 September 2014).

26 UNCTAD, UNCTADstat, "Total labour force and agriculture labour force, annual", 2013 (downloaded 17 June 2014).

27 On the impact of price volatility on low-income countries, see especially Hannah Bargawi et al., "Low-Income Countries and Commodity Price Volatility", in *The Prospects of International Trade Regulation: From Fragmentation to Coherence*, ed. Thomas Cottier and Delimatsis Panagiotis (Cambridge: Cambridge University Press, 2011), 452–82.

TABLE 1 *Computation of countries more heavily reliant on agricultural exports than on other product groups (% of 2011–13 avg merchandise exports), by economic group*

| Economic group | Sample (no. of countries*) | Agr. exports as main product group (no. of countries*) | % of countries with agr. exports as main product group |
|---|---|---|---|
| LDC | 48 | 21 | 43.8 |
| Developing, excluding LDC* | 108 | 24 | 22.2 |
| Transition | 17 | 0 | 0.0 |
| Developed* | 40 | 3 | 7.5 |

* 'Developed' and 'developing' includes sovereign States and other territories.
Note: Merchandise trade by trading partner and product based on SITC, Rev.3. Country economic groups as used in UNCTAD statistics (http://unctadstat.unctad.org/EN/Classifications.html). Products groups include: "Agricultural exports" (categories "All food items" (SITC 0 + 1 + 22 + 4) + "Agricultural raw materials" (SITC 2 less 22, 27 and 28)); "Fuels" (SITC 3); "Ores, metals, precious stones and non-monetary gold" (SITC 27 + 28 + 68 + 667 + 971); "Manufactured goods" (SITC 5 to 8 less 667 and 68).
SOURCE: AUTHOR'S COMPUTATION. DATA FROM UNCTADSTAT, MERCHANDISE TRADE MATRIX – PRODUCT GROUPS, EXPORTS IN THOUSANDS OF DOLLARS, ANNUAL, 1995–2013 (DATA RETRIEVED ON 16 FEBRUARY 2015).

important source of government revenue through export taxes, direct taxes on income in the export sector, and, in the case of government-controlled sectors, the contribution of state trading enterprises (STEs) to the Treasury.

On the import side of the trade equation (the consumption end), it is important to recall that most of the LDCs (38 out of 48) are net-food importers,[28] and heavily exposed to price spikes in staple food commodities.

The exposure of developing countries, and especially LDCs to agricultural price volatility is thus two-fold. On the export side, they are exposed to fluctuations in export proceeds from their 'core' agricultural exports, typically agricultural raw materials or cash crops. On the import side, they are exposed, given their heavy reliance on international markets to satisfy their food requirements. It follows that developing countries, particularly the poorest, tend to have higher levels of vulnerability to agricultural price instability than their

28 Data from UNCTADstat, Merchandise trade matrix (retrieved on 16 February 2015). All food items (SITC Rev 3, groups 0 + 1 + 22 + 4). The WTO list of net food-importing developing countries is detailed in WTO Doc. G/AG/5/Rev.10, 23 March 2012.

developed counterparts. The countries less able to cope with or manage the effects of agricultural price instability are thus those that are most affected by this instability.

At the micro or individual level, the socio-economic impacts of agricultural price volatility are likewise disproportionately borne by the poor. Again, this can be appreciated at both the producer and consumer ends of the price spectrum.

At the producer end (farmgate price instability), recall that, in the developing world, the rural poor still outnumber the urban poor. There are an estimated 1.4 billion poor people living on less than US$1.25 a day; 1 billion, above 70 percent of these poor, live in rural areas and rely on agriculture as their means of living.[29]

In poor countries, the interests of the poor are also vitally at stake on the consumer end. In developing countries, the poor spend between 50 and 80 percent of their income on food.[30] Sudden price spikes in food commodities thus translate for poor consumers in a substantial loss of entitlements to food, which may lead to irreversible nutritional damage, especially among children.

To sum up, agricultural price volatility carries acute political sensitivities in low-income countries. In contexts of extreme rural and urban poverty, agricultural price swings hinder livelihood security, absent adequate safety nets. They encroach on the enjoyment of basic needs and frustrate efforts to secure lives with dignity. In extreme cases, they are a matter of life or death. This is the background against which to assess the prospective role of trade law *vis-à-vis* agricultural stabilisation policies in contexts of extreme poverty.

### 1.2.3 *The Need for Regulatory Responses*

In light of the above, shall the tendency for agricultural commodity prices to fluctuate widely be countered by purposive policy intervention? Two fundamental differences of attitudes and creeds have emerged in this respect and continue to polarise the debate.

On the one hand are those who treat commodity price volatility as problematic, either as an instance of market imperfection or failure, or as a normal attribute of markets that nonetheless entails too high human costs. Government

---

29 IFAD and UNEP, *Smallholders, Food Security, and the Environment* (Rome: IFAD, 2013), 6. See also World Bank, *World Development Report 2008: Agriculture for Development* (Washington, D.C.: The World Bank, 2007), 26. According to the World Bank Report, three out of four poor people in developing countries lived in rural areas in 2002; most depended on agriculture for their livelihoods.

30 WFP, *World Hunger Series: Hunger and Markets* (London: Earthscan, 2009), 39.

intervention is needed, it is argued, to redress market malfunctions or to channel market dynamics towards socially acceptable outcomes. This policy stance stems from a variety of theoretical perspectives. 'Structuralist' perspectives link commodity price fluctuations to structural patterns of production and consumption.[31] They call for purposive policy action to stabilise prices at levels remunerative to producers (Section 3.2.1.1 b). Underlying this is a 'positive conception' of economic policy, in the sense of a "deliberate design for influencing economic forces" for redistributive purposes.[32] The 'stabilisation' approach rejects the structuralist desire to use trade and pricing policies for income redistribution purposes. Yet, it calls for some degree of market intervention to stabilise prices around the market trend.[33] Its main contention is that mainstream economic models do not fully capture the costs of price volatility; and that if these costs were factored-in, the welfare gains from price stabilisation would often outweigh the costs governments incur to stabilise prices. Rent-seeking behaviour is limited by using competitive private agents for marketing activities, but within government-set price bands.[34]

---

31 Structuralist economics originated in the 1960s with the work of the Economic Commission for Latin America (ECLA or CEPAL). Primarily associated with the work of Raúl Prebisch and of Celso Furtado, it emphasises the importance of structural patterns of production and trade when undertaking economic analysis. As discussed in Chapter 3, structuralist perspectives furnished the underpinning of UNCTAD's policy stance on commodities.

32 UNCTAD, *Towards a New Trade Policy for Development*, report by the Secretary-General of the Conference, in *Proceedings of the United Nations Conference on Trade and Development*, vol. II (New York: United Nations, 1964), at 7.

33 Pursuant to the 'stabilisation' approach, optimal efficiency requires market intervention to offset short-term price fluctuations (sources of efficiency losses), while allowing domestic prices to reflect long-term price trends. The central analytical question addressed is to demonstrate that the efficiency losses associated with short-term price instability are quantitatively more significant than the costs incurred to alleviate them. For an introduction C. Peter Timmer, "Food Price Policy: The Rationale for Government Intervention," *Food Policy* 14, no. 1 (1989) (also, from the same author, *Getting Prices Right: The Scope and Limits of Agricultural Price Policy* (Ithaca: Cornell University Press, 1986) and "Getting Agriculture Moving: Do Markets Provide the Right Signals?" *Food Policy* 20, no. 5 (1995)). On the design of 'optimal' intervention policies, see also Christophe Gouel, *Food Price Volatility and Domestic Stabilization Policies in Developing Countries*, National Bureau of Economic Research, NBER Working Papers, no. 18934 (Cambridge, M.A., 2013) and "Food Price Stabilization Policies: Lessons from Economic Theory" (presentation delivered at UNCTAD, Seventh Multi-year Expert Meeting on Commodities and Development, Geneva, 15–16 April 2015).

34 Timmer, "Food Price Policy," n above, at 18.

A different school of thought, informed by the 'neo-classical' paradigm, contends that price intervention is neither efficient nor effective. It challenges the welfare gains from price stabilisation relative to its pervasive efficiency costs, and highlights the opportunity costs of stabilisation policies compared to market-based alternatives.[35] The optimal approach to stabilise prices, it is argued, is to leverage market dynamics. Spatial and temporal arbitrage by traders will transfer supplies from years of high production to years of low production, and from surplus to deficit areas. More fundamentally, volatility is acknowledged as an inherent feature of well-functioning agricultural markets. To ease adjustment costs, it is argued, emphasis should shift from the stabilisation of prices to the mitigation of the effects of price instability. The focus is on market-based risk-management instruments such as futures, derivatives and swaps, along with insurance schemes and targeted safety net interventions.[36] These instruments do not reduce price volatility, but the income effects of price changes.

In the author's view, the answer is contextual. Certainly, the optimal approach, in so far as instability is 'natural',[37] is to manage the effects of price instability by means of targeted safety nets. Likewise, the first-best policy would be to leverage market dynamics for price stability, for example, by enabling and stimulating efficient private storage. Yet, particularly in the context of the LDCs, there are intractable trade-offs and insurmountable barriers in the way of conventionally efficient solutions. In many developing countries, safety nets may not be in place, may be imperfect, or may be difficult to adjust conjuncturally.[38] Likewise, the most basic market infrastructures (storage facilities

35 A review from a neo-classical perspective is contained in Theodore W. Schultz, ed., *Distortions of Agricultural Incentives* (Bloomington: Indiana University Press, 1979). For a reassessment, David M.G. Newbery and Joseph E. Stiglitz, *The Theory of Commodity Price Stabilization: A Study in the Economics of Risk* (Oxford: Oxford University Press, 1981). The World Bank added an institutional voice, emphasising the welfare losses associated with agricultural pricing policies: World Bank, *World Development Report 1983* (New York: Oxford University Press, 1983); World Bank, *World Development Report 1985* (New York: Oxford University Press, 1985).

36 What Galtier terms 'B instruments' (market-based risk management instruments and insurance schemes) and 'D instruments' (public transfers, producer and consumer subsidies). For a comprehensive overview, Franck Galtier, *Gérer l'instabilité des prix alimentaires dans les pays en développement* (Paris: AFD, 2012), 165–85 and 228–49.

37 Instability is deemed 'natural' when it stems from fundamental supply and demand imbalances.

38 See Gouel, "Food Price Stabilization Policies," above n 33. Safety nets involve high transaction and monitoring costs, and are institutionally complex. Furthermore, safety nets are more financially costly than countercyclical trade policies. Paradoxically, the poorer the

and feeder roads) may be highly under-developed. In this setting, price and countercyclical trade policies[39] may offer the only effective way to deal with price instability. First-best policy options, and particularly safety nets, may not provide a viable alternative, at least in the short run. This is particularly true when vulnerable stakeholders represent the majority of the population, government resources are meagre, and price instability is essentially imported from abroad.[40]

As stated by a commentator in the late 1960s, "in an imperfect world, imperfect policies intelligently applied may produce more desirable results than theoretically perfect policies applied only in fragmentary fashion".[41] The key issue is then how to optimise the design of price stabilisation schemes so as to make them more administratively transparent and genuinely pro-poor. This research moves in this direction, by considering underlying legal principles and approaches to 'optimal' stabilisation policies.

## 1.3 Research Design and Method

### 1.3.1 *Research Outline*

The study consists of four chapters (Chapters 2 to 5), and is completed by a conclusion.

Chapter 2 sets the stage for the following analysis. To inform and delimit the scope of the inquiry, the analysis in Section 2.1 outlines the notion of 'agricultural price stabilisation'. Section 2.2 takes a cursory look at major price stabilisation arrangements, at both the international and domestic level. Section 2.3 examines their interface with trade rules. This introductory part is intended to provide non-specialist readers with an overview of agricultural price stabilisation arrangements, in their interface with trade rules. It can be skipped by readers familiar with the issue.

Chapters 3 to 5 engage more deeply in the core subject matter of this study: the normative objectives and 'principles' of trade law in its regulation of price stabilisation arrangements in agriculture.

---

country, the more costly the scheme would be, as it would need to cover a large segment of the population.

39 Trade policies that move in the opposite direction to changes in world prices (e.g. a variable import levy scheme, providing for tariff increases when world prices decrease and tariff decreases when prices increase).

40 See, in this direction, Galtier, above n 36.

41 Harry J. Johnson, *Economic Policies toward Less Developed Countries* (Washington, D.C.: The Brookings Institution, 1967), 42.

Chapter 3 takes stock of major past attempts to set multilaterally agreed principles and procedures for the regulation of international commodity prices. Attention is focused on three post-war endeavours: negotiations leading to Chapter VI of the Havana Charter for an International Trade Organization; discussions during the 1954–1955 review of the General Agreement on Tariffs and Trade (GATT); and UNCTAD's Integrated Programme for Commodities (IPC). The analysis therefore looks backward, but with a view to generating insights that may be valuable in the present context.

Chapter 4 considers changes of attitude towards commodity control in the late 1980s and 1990s, and the major implications involved in terms of trade law and policy. It then turns to explore the scholarly and policy debate on trade rules and agricultural stabilisation policies in the aftermath of the 2007–08 and 2010–11 commodity crises. Eventually, the analysis points to a 'crisis in law legitimacy',[42] out of which a new normative approach can emerge.

Drawing and combining insights from the previous chapters, Chapter 5 proposes a synthesis that seeks to outline a forward agenda in commodity regulation. The analysis is three-fold. Section 5.1 brings to light a set of normative objectives and principles against which to benchmark stabilisation policies in agriculture. In the light of the expounded principles, Section 5.2 seeks to reappraise some areas of convergence and tension between liberal trade rules and agricultural price stabilisation policies. Finally, Section 5.3 considers possible litigation and decision making avenues through which to promote a 'principled' reading of WTO law, instructed into a coherent set of normative objectives and principles.

The Conclusion restates the issue being researched, summarises the research findings and claims, and presents deductions and implications of a wider nature.

### 1.3.2 *Interdisciplinary Aspects and Legal Approaches*

The regulation of commodity markets stands at the interface of law, economics and politics. Accordingly, the analysis interweaves three strands of analysis: legal, economic and political/institutional.

The legal analysis involves consideration of regulatory issues that come within the purview of international trade regulation, domestic public law, and general international law; and freely combines legal technicalities and broad theoretical issues.

42 In the sense that legal norms are no longer aligned with social needs and expectations. On this notion, Gunther Teubner, "Substantive and Reflexive Elements in Modern Law," *Law & Society Review* 17, no. 2 (1983): 258–59.

The economic analysis limits itself to a review of some tenets of the economic debate on commodity price stabilisation. The justification for this review is essentially to expose the lack of conclusiveness in the economic debate. In commodities, evidence for and against price regulation is contradictory and view-dependent. This means that regulation is bound to be inherently biased, under inevitable pressure from a variety of sectional interests.

This leads on to the last dimension: the political one. The focus is here on the factional pressure behind commodity price stabilisation. In fact, any attempt at stabilising commodity prices involves decisions as to the level at which prices ought to be stabilised; and a transfer of resources from consumers to producers, or the other way round. The acknowledgement of this political dimension sheds light onto the distributional struggle underlying commodity trade policy reform, and provides insights into potential political constraints that may arise when implementing schemes to manipulate commodity prices.

### 1.3.3 *Information Sources*

The legal analysis borrows from diverse sources and eclectically combines different methodologies.

#### 1.3.3.1 Agricultural Price Stabilisation Arrangements

The analysis of commodity price stabilisation arrangements involved the review of major intergovernmental commodity arrangements (ICAs) and of a sample of domestic price stabilisation schemes.

With regard to ICAs, 51 intergovernmental commodity agreements were reviewed – 36 post-Second World War arrangements and 15 inter-war arrangements. This assessment covered all the most important dual-interest ICAs, involving both consumers and producers. The post-war treaties were searched through the United Nations Treaty Series Online Collection.[43] For earlier material, the analysis relied on a collection of early agreements by the International Labour Office,[44] as well as on material retrieved from online archives.

As for domestic price stabilisation arrangements, the analysis was based on a review of farm support policies in the European Union (EU); rice price stabilisation policies in South and South-East Asia (India, Thailand, Indonesia, Vietnam and the Philippines); export crop marketing boards and *caisses de stabilisation* in West Africa (Ghana, Côte d'Ivoire and Cameroon); dairy and wheat boards in Canada; family farming price support policies in Brazil; and

43 Searchable at https://treaties.un.org/.

44 International Labour Office, *Intergovernmental Commodity Control Agreements* (Montreal, 1943).

managed tariff schemes in Chile and Peru. Details on country's commodity price stabilisation policies were obtained from the WTO Secretariat's Trade Policy Reviews,[45] relevant GATT and WTO cases, government documents, and technical analysis by commodity and trade specialists.

Beyond desk research, the author has drawn extensively upon primary sources (in the social science sense), including: personal exchanges with commodity stakeholders; in-country assessments of commodity marketing structures and related institutional settings; as well as insights gained from participation in intergovernmental commodity bodies (ICBs). The analysis also reflects discussions and interactions during a number of public meetings hosted at UNCTAD, including: UNCTAD's Multi-year Expert Meeting (MYEM) on Commodities and Development; UNCTAD's Global Commodities Forum (GCF); and UNCTAD Secretary-General's Multi-Stakeholder Consultations on Trade and Development issues relating to commodities. Information is presented in the book at a level of aggregation that prevents the disclosure of sensitive data.

#### 1.3.3.2 Trade Regulation

The focus of this study is on multilateral trade rules. Bilateral and plurilateral arrangements have not been examined in their bearing on commodity price stabilisation policies.

Two sets of provisions have come into focus through the study. Each includes rules evolved within and outside the WTO framework, and elements of enabling and constraining regulation.

The first set of rules consists of provisions that lay down substantive and procedural criteria for *international* action on commodity prices. This special commodity trade regime was largely elaborated outside of the GATT framework, under the aegis of the Havana Conference and within the framework of UNCTAD. It was then 'grafted' onto the GATT through the GATT Article XX(h) exemption.[46] Major instruments include Chapter VI of the Havana Charter for

---

45 Retrieved through the WTO Trade Policy Reviews Gateway at http://www.wto.org/english/tratop_e/tpr_e/tpr_e.htm.

46 Provisionally applied since 1 January 1948, the General Agreement on Tariffs and Trade (GATT) was negotiated and agreed during 1946–47, in parallel to the negotiations for the Havana Charter. The text of the GATT 1947 is reproduced in: WTO Secretariat, *The Legal Texts: The Results of the Uruguay Round of Multilateral Trade Negotiations* (Cambridge.: Cambridge University Press, 1999), 423. For the drafting history of the relevant provisions, see WTO Secretariat, *GATT Analytical Index – Guide to GATT Law and Practice* (Geneva, 2012), 589 [online edition of the 1995 updated sixth edition, available at http://www.wto.org/english/res_e/booksp_e/gatt_ai_e/gatt_ai_e.htm].

an International Trade Organization (hereafter, the Havana Charter), as formally adopted in 1948,[47] and the Integrated Programme for Commodities, agreed upon at the final plenary of UNCTAD IV on 30 May 1976.[48] The Havana Charter provisions were interpreted in the light of the preparatory work of the Charter.[49] Important insights were also derived from relevant GATT Discussions on the Havana principle during the 1954–1955 Review Session.[50] UNCTAD's IPC provisions were read in light of statements by Heads of Delegation and records of Plenary Meetings.[51] Havana Charter and GATT documents were retrieved through the GATT online database. UNCTAD Proceedings were retrieved from the UNCTAD website.

The second set of rules lays down requirements for *domestic* agricultural stabilisation arrangements. As discussed in Section 2.3, the relevant rules are countless, and straddle across discrete areas of international trade regulation. They include, among other: disciplines on subsidies laid down in the WTO

47 Havana Charter for an International Trade Organization [hereafter, Havana Charter], done at Havana, 24 March 1948. The text of the Havana Charter is annexed to the Final Act of the United Nations Conference on Trade and Employment, held at Havana, Cuba, from 21 November 1947 to 24 March 1948. See United Nations Conference on Trade and Employment, *Final Act and Related Documents*, E/CONF.2/78, United Nations publication, Sales No. 1948.II.D.

48 Resolution 93 (IV), Integrated Programme for Commodities, adopted by the United Nations Conference on Trade and Development on 30 May 1976, in *Proceedings of the United Nations Conference on Trade and Development, Fourth Session, Nairobi, 5–31 May 1976* (New York: United Nations, 1977), vol. I, *Report and Annexes*, at 6.

49 Relevant reports and records included: the 'London Report' (*Report of the First Session of the Preparatory Committee of the United Nations Conference on Trade and Employment* (UN Document E/PC/T/33 dated October 1946)); the 'Geneva draft' (*Report of the Second Session of the Preparatory Committee of the United Nations Conference on Trade and Employment* (UN Document E/PC/T/186 dated 10 September 1947)); Summary records of the Fifth Committee of the Havana Conference, charged with the examination of the Geneva draft of Chart VI at Havana (Documents E/CONF.2/C.5/SR/1-15); and the Secretariat's Reports relating to the Fifth Committee (the 'Havana Reports') (*Reports of Committees and Principal Sub-Committees* (ICITO I/8 dated September 1948)).

50 Materials consulted included the reports of the Review Working Party IV on Organizational and Functional Questions and summary records and reports of the Working Party on Commodity Problems (Ninth, Tenth and Eleventh Sessions).

51 For the summaries of these statements, see *Proceedings of the United Nations Conference on Trade and Development, Fourth Session, Nairobi, 5–31 May 1976* (New York: United Nations, 1977), vol. I (*Report and Annexes*), Part two (*Summary of Proceedings*), and vol. II (*Summary of Statements by Heads of Delegation and Summary Records of Plenary Meetings*).

Agreement on Agriculture (AoA)[52] and the WTO Agreement on Subsidies and Countervailing Measures (ASCM);[53] rules on agricultural exporting STEs under the GATT and the AoA; tariff disciplines as provided for in the GATT and the AoA; and disciplines on export restrictions (under the GATT and the AoA). These sets of rules are not discussed comprehensively nor in detail. They come into focus for their potential constraining role *vis-à-vis* agricultural stabilisation policies in developing countries.

## 1.4 Reach of This Inquiry

The assessment of the interface between commodity price stabilisation schemes and trade rules is fraught with difficulty. The two terms of the equation, 'trade rules' and 'commodity price stabilisation', are intricate, compound notions, as also discussed in the following Chapter. *A fortiori*, the analysis of their interface is somewhat elusive, and perplexingly entangled, possibly too much so. This complexity sets the limits of this research endeavour: some elusiveness in scope; and the non-exhaustive, often cursory treatment of too many legal issues that would deserve each monographic attention, especially in Chapter 5. Yet, these shortfalls somewhat follow from the purpose of this research, and from what it seeks to do. The aspiration is to engage in a 'framing' exercise that dwells on considerations of normative objectives and principles, behind the positivist assessment of rules. It is an effort to move beyond the narrowly framed, functional boundaries of discrete trade provisions, an exercise in policy coherence, beyond fragmentation.[54]

---

52 The text of the WTO Agreement on Agriculture is reproduced in: WTO Secretariat, *The Legal Texts*, above n 46, at 33.

53 The text of the ASCM is reproduced in: WTO Secretariat, *The Legal Texts*, above n 46, at 231.

54 This effort resonates through the work of Professor Thomas Cottier. See, in particular: Thomas Cottier and Delimatsis Panagiotis, eds., *The Prospects of International Trade Regulation: From Fragmentation to Coherence* (Cambridge: Cambridge University Press, 2011). The institutional dimension of policy coherence is discussed in detail in Marina Foltea, *International Organizations in WTO Dispute Settlement: How Much Institutional Sensitivity?* (Cambridge: Cambridge University Press, 2012).

CHAPTER 2

# Setting the Stage: Key Concepts and Issues

Definitions for 'agricultural commodities' and 'price stabilisation' are essential to both inform and delimit the study. It is also important to map major price stabilisation schemes in agriculture, and grasp their interface with trade rules. Only a brief summary of the main aspects will be attempted here. The discussion will bring into focus those dimensions that are relevant for the following analysis.

## 2.1 Agricultural Price Stabilisation: Unpacking the Notion

This analysis will first specify what is meant by 'primary agricultural products', or 'agricultural commodities'. It will then outline the contours of the notion of 'price instability' in agricultural commodity markets. It concludes with some summary observations.

### 2.1.1 *Agricultural Commodities*

#### 2.1.1.1 The Notion Outlined

Primary agricultural products, or agricultural commodities can be loosely described as unprocessed (raw) or semi-processed materials derived from agriculture, as opposed to industrially manufactured products. This definition may serve as a rough guide. Yet, it does not exactly locate the external boundaries of the term 'agricultural commodities'.

The degree of processing is indeed relevant, but to some extent only. Certainly, a few agricultural commodities (such as cocoa and coffee beans or coconuts) are exportable fairly near the raw state, though some processing for example via fermentation and drying is done at farmgate. Yet, most commodities require factory processing before they are exportable as commercial items. Cereals have to be threshed to separate the grains from the husks and straw. Cotton is ginned to detach the seed from the lint. Sugarcane is crushed and milled to extract raw sugar, and so on.[55] What is traded, then, is not the raw produce of the peasant farmer such as green tea leaves, but the product conditioned for export, which may have a significant degree of processing such as

55 See in this direction John W.F. Rowe, *Primary Commodities in International Trade* (Cambridge: Cambridge University Press, 1965), 2.

 | DOI 10.1163/9789004350540_003

made tea. In other words, export commodities do not situate at the farm gate level, but at the ex-factory or wholesale level.[56] This also reflects in the product coverage of the most important ICAs (Appendix 1).

Eventually, if we want to capture the essence of what agricultural commodities are, we should introduce the notion of 'tradability'; and define agricultural commodities as the product of nature as "dealt with in the way of trade".[57] The distinctive character of agricultural commodities thus lies in their commercial nature, their merchandise character as articles of trade. Gathered or harvested from nature, agricultural products are 'commoditised', turned into commercial items "valued only, or almost entirely, for their cash returns when traded or exchanged".[58] In some respects, the very notion of agricultural commodities is thus linked to the introduction of "profit-oriented motives", trade and the cash economy, against "communitarian notions of stewardship and responsibility".[59] This process is socially constructed and historically contingent. Accordingly, the content and scope of the notion of 'commodities' is neither exhaustive, nor enduring.[60] Thus, items currently dealt with in the way of trade

---

56 The Havana Charter itself was quite broad in defining the product scope of the disciplines laid down in Chapter VI. Article 56 of the Havana Charter covered primary *and related* commodities, defined as products "[...] which are so closely related, as regards conditions of production or utilization, to the other commodities in the group, that it is appropriate to deal with them in a single agreement" (Article 56 (2), Havana Charter, supra n 47). Processed products, beyond raw materials, have fallen to varying extents within the purview of ICAs negotiated within the Havana Charter and UNCTAD's frameworks. Relevant GATT and WTO jurisprudence is along the same line. For example, within the framework of GATT 1947, the panel report on French Assistance to Exports of Wheat and Wheat Flour considered wheat as well as wheat flour to be primary products, for specific legal purposes. GATT Panel Report, *French Assistance to Exports of Wheat and Wheat Flour*, L/924, adopted 21 November 1958, BISD 7S/46, 52, para. 14; as reported in WTO Secretariat, *GATT Analytical Index*, above n 46, at 452.

57 "tradable, adj.," *OED Online* (Oxford University Press, 21 November 2013) (http://www.oed.com/view/Entry/204272?redirectedFrom=tradable). Rowe, above n 55, at 2.

58 Michael Lipton, "Staples Production: Efficient 'Subsistence' Smallholders Are Key to Poverty Reduction, Development, and Trade" (presentation delivered at UNCTAD, Global Commodities Forum 2013, Geneva, 18–19 March 2013), at 5, available at http://unctad.org/meetings/en/Presentation/SUC_GCF2013_18-03-2013_Michael-LIPTON_Study.pdf (visited 17 September 2014).

59 The language is from Agnar Helgason and Gísli Pálsson, discussing the expansion of market relations to new areas of social life. See Agnar Helgason and Gísli Pálsson, "Contested Commodities: The Moral Landscape of Modernist Regimes," in *Journal of the Royal Anthropological Institute* 3, no. 3 (1997): 454.

60 Just to give an example, the rise of commerce in food staples, and the notion of food as a commodity, is itself historical. As summarised by Lipton (Lipton, above n 58, at 5),

can be 'decommoditised'; while others that are non-commercial in character can be 'commoditised'. This process is still unfolding, most often through incremental, indirect changes; which eases the tensions of abrupt adjustments. For example, water, which many are reluctant to openly treat as a commodity, is in fact increasingly being commoditised by means of water supply concessions and land leases. Some argue that even air has been turned into a commodity through tradable pollution rights.[61] The list is open, with the prospect that human organic materials may be ultimately commoditised. In all these areas, we are witnessing "the replacement of values and meanings that formerly excluded a thing from the sphere of commodity exchange, with the more homogenized field of significance of the market, that has at its core a single standard of commensurability".[62] The 'single standard of commensurability' is the market price, revealing of the balance between demand and supply. How far can this go? This ultimately depends on how far the ethical boundaries of human conscience can be stretched; which in turn appeals to the role of law as a "repository of meanings and values".[63]

#### 2.1.1.2 The Notion Unpacked

The aggregate focus on agricultural commodities masks important distinctions. The notion broadly covers the produce of farm (crops and livestock), forests (timber and non-timber forest products) and fisheries (capture and culture) (Figure 1). Each of these groups and sub-groups is complexly branched within. This Section brings into focus only a few distinctions that have specific bearing on the following analysis. The main focus is on crop commodities.

---

human food started by being hunted or gathered by each small kin-group for its own use (hunter-gatherer society); from about 7,500–5,000 B.C., food was farmed increasingly by settled agriculturalists, consisting of scattered, small-scale, largely subsistence farmers (agricultural stage); with development, food supply increasingly concentrated in the hands of large-scale 'farmer specialists', trading staple crops and other farm products to others (commercial stage of development). In this evolutionist approach, environmental goods formerly taken to be commonly owned were progressively 'commoditised'.

61 For an overview, Sharon Beder, "Trading the Earth: The Politics behind Tradeable Pollution Rights," *Environmental Liability* 9, no. 2 (2001). On the triple commoditisation of food, water and air: José Luis Vivero Pol, "Food as a Commodity, Human Right or Common Good? Implications for Hunger Eradication" (presentation given at UNRISD, Seminar Series, Geneva, 9 April 2013), available at http://www.unrisd.org/80256B3C005BD6AB/(httpEvents)/CB6BD3C8531F7087C1257B5F003151D2?OpenDocument.

62 Helgason and Pálsson, above n 59, at 454.

63 On the role of law as a "repository of meanings and values", David Nelken, "Is There a Crisis in Law and Legal Ideology?" *Journal of Law and Society* 9, no. 2 (1982): 184.

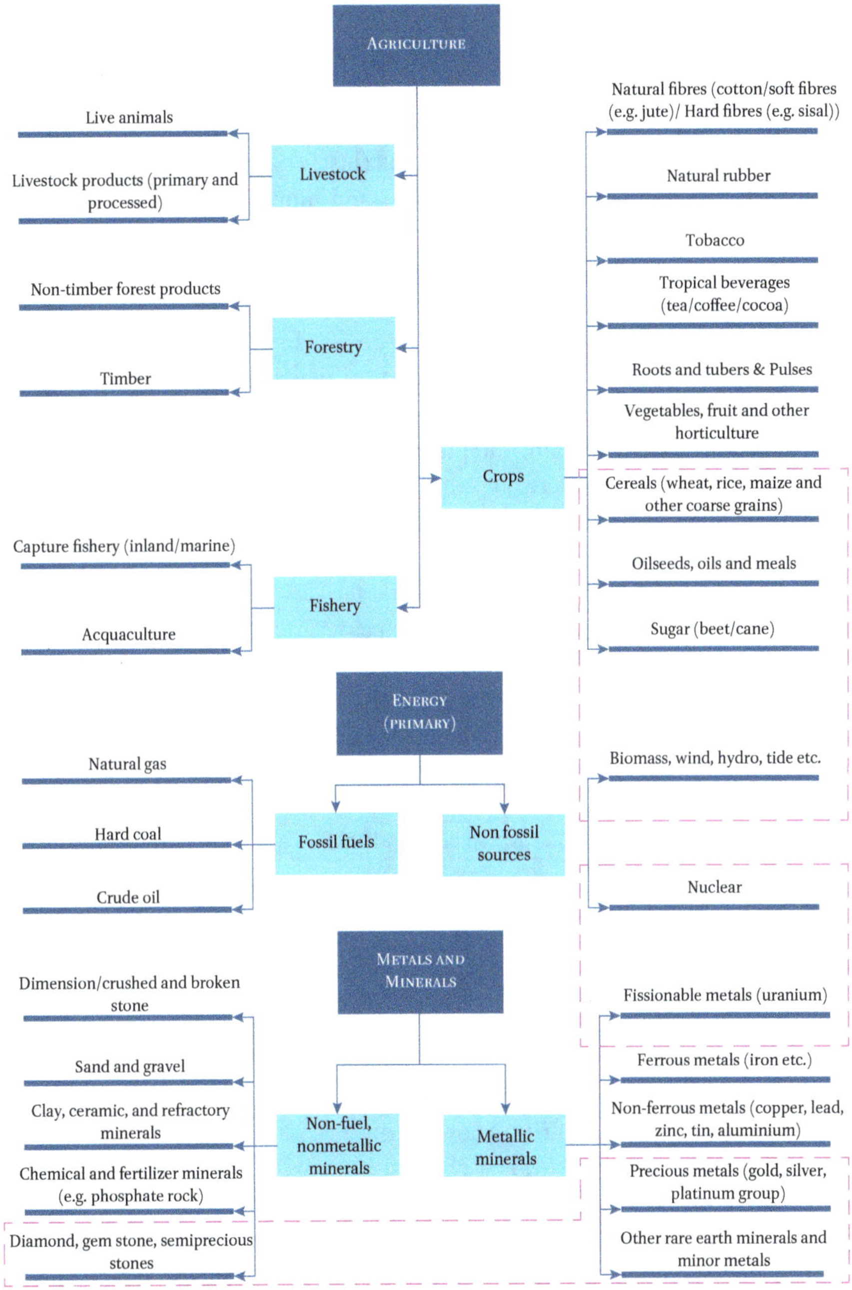


FIGURE 1 *Agriculture and other commodity aggregates*
Source: Elaborated by the author, based on the following trade and industry classifications: Standard International Trade Classification (SITC) Revision 3 and FAOSTAT aggregates (for agricultural commodities); OECD/IEA/Eurostat, Energy Statistics Manual 2005 (definition of primary energy resources); and Standard Industrial Classification (SIC) codes 10 and 14 (for metals and minerals).

### a) *Export Cash Crops and Traditional Staple Foods*

In the context of developing countries, a line is to be drawn between export cash crops and traditional staple food commodities. Export cash crops are mainly produced and marketed for export. In developing countries, they include both 'traditional' export cash crops (historical exports generally of colonial origin, such as cocoa and coffee) and 'non-traditional' export crops (relatively new, dynamic export sectors, such as flowers). Traditional staple food crops, in WTO language, refer to "primary agricultural products that are predominant staples in the traditional diet of a developing country".[64] The group is complexly branched within. It covers staple foods that are widely traded internationally (such as rice, wheat or maize), as well as 'minor' traditional staples mainly grown by peasant farmers for self-consumption or local marketing (like cassava, yam, and plantains).

In several respects, the two groups overlap. For example, in countries like India and Thailand, rice is the major export cash crop and at the same time the traditional staple food. Likewise, the distinction between subsistence (for own consumption) and commercial (marketed) crops is, at best, artificial. Certainly, traditional subsistence staples such as cassava are mainly produced for local or self-consumption by peasant farmers in low-income countries. Yet, even these traditional staples are traded. This mainly occurs via highly informal trade across porous borders with neighbouring countries – a buzzing track of largely informal cross-border exchanges partially unaccounted for in official trade statistics.

Both product categories are of 'special' interest to developing countries, based on criteria of food security, livelihood security and rural development.[65] Yet, each category raises different price issues. Tropical export crops raise issues of capturing more value in producing countries and stabilising prices at levels remunerative to producers. The focus is on price support and stabilisation at the producer end of the spectrum. With staple food commodities, the analysis is more nuanced. The emphasis shifts to the need to smooth price spikes that adversely affect food security in vulnerable economies on the consumer end, while also ensuring a fair return to peasant producers in producing countries on the producer end.

---

64 World Trade Organization, Ministerial Decision of 7 December 2013 on Public Stockholding for Food Security Purposes, WT/MIN(13)/38, WT/L/913.

65 For an illustrative list of these criteria, see WTO Committee on Agriculture, Revised Draft Modalities on Agriculture, WTO document TN/AG/W/4/Rev.4 of 6 December 2008 [hereafter, December 2008 revised draft modalities], Annex F.

### b) *Tradability and Export Orientation*

A related distinction concerns the degree of tradability and export orientation. It is important to observe in this respect that not all products of farm, forest or fishery are commercialised. Even fewer varieties are marketed in substantial volumes in international trade. For example, although there are many species in the cereal family, only a few are commercially cultivated; and even fewer, wheat, rice, maize, sorghum, barley, oats, and millet, are internationally traded in substantial volumes. Table 2 shows the major internationally traded agricultural commodities, by direction of trade flows.

TABLE 2 *Top ten most internationally traded agricultural commodities (Harmonised System, four-digit level), by direction of trade flows (2012)*

| | South-South (US$440 billion total) | | South-North (US$296 billion total) | | North-South (US$313 billion total) | | North-North (US$612 billion total) | |
|---|---|---|---|---|---|---|---|---|
| 1 | palm oil | 7.0 | coffee | 6.7 | wheat and meslin | 7.1 | wine | 3.8 |
| 2 | soya beans | 5.6 | natural rubber | 3.8 | soya beans | 7.1 | meat (pork) | 3.4 |
| 3 | cane or beet sugar | 4.6 | crustaceans | 3.6 | milk and cream | 4.1 | cheese and curd | 3.4 |
| 4 | natural rubber | 4.0 | oil cake | 3.5 | cotton | 3.2 | bread, pastry, cakes | 3.0 |
| 5 | rice | 4.0 | fish fillets | 3.5 | prepared food | 2.8 | cigars, cigarettes, etc. | 2.7 |
| 6 | maize | 3.6 | bananas | 3.0 | alcohol, spirits, liqueur | 2.7 | alcohol, spirits, liqueur | 2.6 |
| 7 | wheat and meslin | 3.2 | palm oil | 2.7 | synthetic rubber, etc. | 2.7 | chocolate | 2.5 |
| 8 | oil cake | 2.7 | prepared fish | 2.5 | maize | 2.7 | wood, sawn or chipped | 2.4 |
| 9 | cotton | 2.5 | fruit juices | 2.1 | waste and scrap paper | 2.5 | prepared food | 2.4 |
| 10 | fish, frozen | 2.1 | soya beans | 2.1 | wood, sawn or chipped | 2.4 | meat (beef) | 2.4 |
| Total | | 39.4 | | 33.6 | | 37.3 | | 28.4 |

Source: Reproduced from UNCTAD, *Evolution of the International Trading System and its Trends from a Development Perspective* (document TD/B/61/2, 7 July 2014), at 5. Data source: United Nations Comtrade database, available at http://comtrade.un.org/.

A distinct, though related issue is a sector's 'export-orientation', defined as the export-to-production ratio, the share of production which is exported. Internationally traded commodities exhibit different degrees of export-orientation (Figure 2).

Some tropical crops, such as coffee and cocoa, are essentially grown as cash crops for export. Domestic consumption, including consumption for processing is limited. These commodities are internationally traded in substantial volumes and exhibit high degrees of export orientation.

Other agricultural commodities, for example cereals and livestock products, are manly produced for domestic consumption, though their export volume is large in absolute terms. They enter trade in substantial volumes, though their export-orientation is limited.

Other staple crops are mainly produced by peasant farmers for local or self-consumption (traditional subsistence staple crops). The amount that enters into international trade via formal channels, as officially recorded in trade statistics, is small, almost negligible, both in absolute terms and relative to total production. Export volumes and export orientation are low.

Finally, some products do not have appreciable significance in international trade, so trade volumes are low. Yet, their export-orientation is high, as they are typically grown and harvested for export. This category generally refers to high-value, low-volume specialty niche products. These include a range of traditional medicinal plants and other non-timber forest products (NTFPs), typically for use in cosmetics and pharmaceuticals; as well as natural resources that have acquired commercial interest as feedstock for the manufacture of biofuels and bio-products (such as algae for biodiesel, or pyrethrum for bio-plastics).

### c) *Agronomic Conditions and Farming Systems*

Other important distinctions cut across the cash crop – staple crop divide. For example, a line is to be drawn between strictly tropical commodities (e.g. cocoa, coffee, tea, natural rubber, bananas and palm oil) and commodities that are widely grown across climatic zones (cereals, but also cotton, tobacco and citrus fruit, just to name a few).

Tropical crops can be further sub-divided according to farming system:[66] export crops suitable for small-scale peasant-type farming (typically, cocoa and coconuts); crops that are mostly plantation grown (tea and sisal, just to name some); and crops suited to peasant and plantation agriculture (coffee

66 For an informative overview of tropical estate and peasant crops, Vernon D. Wickizer, "The Smallholder in Tropical Export Crop Production," *Food Research Institute Studies* 1, no. 1 (1960).

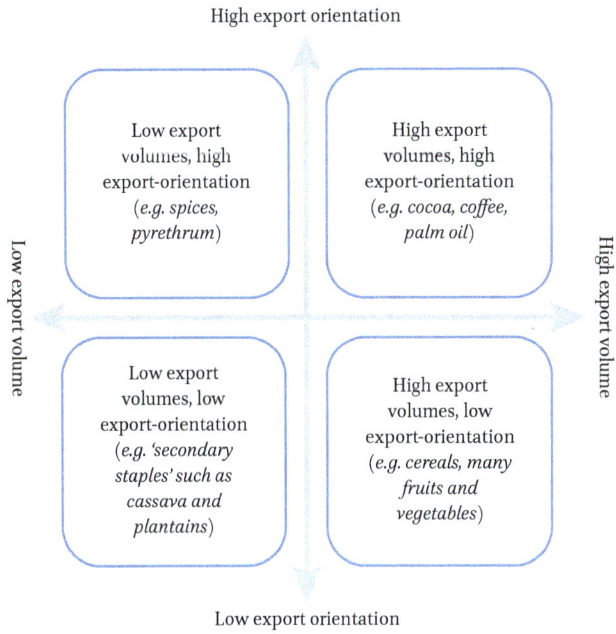


FIGURE 2 *Selected agricultural commodities, trade volumes and export-orientation* (2011)
Source: Elaborated by the author, based on export and production volume data from FAOSTAT, retrieved on 24 November 2013.

and natural rubber being the most notable examples). Note however, that no definite or permanent line can be drawn across these categories. In tea and coconuts, for example, estate and smallholder crops coexist in many contexts.

Other distinctions that bear importantly on price dynamics stem from a crop's agronomic and post-harvest characteristics. A line can be drawn between annual crops, for example, cereals, and perennial crops with a longer gestation period (e.g. tropical tree crops such as cocoa and natural rubber). It is also important to distinguish between storable commodities with long shelf life (like cereals and most agricultural raw materials) and perishable commodities (such as fruits and vegetables).

These and other important distinctions come into focus when discussing tools and approaches to commodity price stabilisation.[67] As discussed in Chapter 5, they should matter for legal purposes. They are among the factors that should be taken into account when modulating regulatory response

67 For example, the inherent characteristics of the commodity influence the choice of the market intervention mechanism: non-perishable and standard commodities are suitable

according to factual differences. This aspect will be discussed at length later. It is important at this stage to clarify the second term of the subject at stake: that of price volatility.

### 2.1.2 *Agricultural Price Instability*

#### 2.1.2.1 The Notion Outlined

In a purely descriptive sense, price instability, or volatility, refers to price variation over time: how much and how quickly prices change on a period of time.[68] While this concept may seem obvious, a precise definition of its contours is elusive, and prone to subjectivity. It is important to unravel the various threads of the definition; and disentangle the different levels of analysis and approaches involved.

#### 2.1.2.2 The Notion Unpacked

The contours of the notion of 'agricultural price stabilisation' is blurred as we add granularity and differentiation with the following questions.[69]

- Is the focus on domestic prices, to various extent insulated from international markets, or on international (border) commodity prices?
- Where does the primary concern lie? Is it with the protection of consumers against price spikes, or with assuring to producers a price floor?
- Furthermore, is the focus on mitigating price fluctuations or on managing the effects thereof on consumers and producers?
- Besides, which time horizon should be considered? Should the focus be on short-term price fluctuations (intra-month, weekly, or even intra-day

---

for public stockholding or buffer stock intervention; for the non-storable commodity, price stabilisation is to be sought by different means, which in principle do not involve the physical handling of the commodity.

68 FAO et al., *Price Volatility in Food and Agricultural Markets: Policy Responses* (n.p., 2011) [hereafter, *Inter-agency Report on Price Volatility*], at 6.

69 Technical complexities in gauging commodity price volatility were extensively discussed at the 3d session of UNCTAD's Multiyear Expert Meeting on Commodities and Development, Geneva, 23–24 March 2011. See, in particular, the following presentations: Bernard Valluis, "Policy Actions about Agricultural Commodity Market Volatility" (available at http://unctad.org/Sections/wcmu/docs/MYEM2011_Valluis_en.pdf, accessed 19 September 2014); Eugenio Díaz Bonilla, "Price Volatility and Commodity-Dependent Countries" (http://unctad.org/sections/wcmu/docs/MYEM2011_Bonilla_en.pdf, accessed 19 September 2014), and David Hallam, "Developments and Challenges in Agricultural Commodity Markets: Situation and Outlook" (http://unctad.org/sections/wcmu/docs/MYEM2011_Hallam_en.pdf, accessed 19 September 2014).

price volatility); seasonal, or intra-year price variability; price fluctuations between years, possibly over several years; or long-term price patterns? In a related vein, are we assessing variability around the trend or variability of the trend; and how do we measure the trend?
- And lastly, in a related vein, what is the key trade policy issue at stake: price instability or price levels? Price stabilisation or price support?

It is useful to explore these thorny issues in some detail, and then move on to discuss major price stabilisation arrangements.

### a) *Time Horizon and Price Objectives*

#### i Price Fluctuations and Price Levels

At the outset, a distinction needs to be made between approaches to moderate excessive short-term price fluctuations around a given trend, and approaches to influence the price trend itself. This translates into the distinction between policies to stabilise prices and policies to support prices.

As discussed in the following Section, domestic and international efforts to regulate commodity markets have had either or both of these two distinct, although related, objectives. Attempts at moderating short-term fluctuations in prices have, in principle, given rise to less controversy than agreements aimed at maintaining prices at certain levels, as they were considered less market distortive.

It should be stressed, however, that the two objectives are in practice complexly intermingled, as much of the debate on price stabilisation ultimately revolves around the level at which prices should be stabilised.[70] Even when the stated objective is price stabilisation at market levels, the setting of the reference price triggers some degree of arbitrariness and subjectivity. This is the case whatever the methodology used to track market price levels, whether a moving average of market prices, a base-period average, or the production costs of the 'most-efficient producer'. The distinction between stabilisation and support is analytically useful, yet, as a matter of fact, intractable. Indeed, at some point one needs to set the level at which prices are to be stabilised; which almost inevitably has redistributive implications, and entails discretionary choices.

Price stabilisation and price level concerns are tightly entangled in the forthcoming analysis. Behind concerns about commodity price instability are concerns about the level at which prices ought to be stabilised; and behind both lies the quest for 'just' prices in commodity markets.

---

70 As also noted in the *Inter-agency Report on Price Volatility*, above n 68, at 6.

### ii Price Volatility and Long Price Cycles

A partially overlapping distinction is the one that lies between price volatility, within season or inter-year; and mid- to long-term commodity price cycles.

Evidence points to a cyclical boom-bust trend in commodity prices, characterised by long depressed periods, punctuated by periodic bursts of volatility. Economic historians point to cycles that last for periods of between 20 to 30 years, with very significant price tensions for 5 to 10 years, followed by around 20 years of falling and flat prices.[71] These cycles are explained by fundamental supply-demand factors. Specifically, they are the result of a gap between supply and demand due to investment 'time lag'.[72]

Price cycles differ from short-term fluctuations in a number of respects. First, the time-frame is different. Cycles tend to span a much longer period of time, typically over 20 to 30 years. Second, they are observed over a broad range of commodities, and often reflect macro-economic cycles.[73]

Long price cycles raise systemic structural issues that go beyond the reach of this research.

### iii Seasonal Price Variability and Inter-year Price Variations

With regard to commodity price instability, an important line is to be drawn between stabilisation of producer prices intra-year, within the season; or between seasons, inter-year.

From a policy perspective, intra-year stabilisation is an attainable policy goal. A few governments have managed to effectively stabilise prices within the season. This, for example, has been done by means of forward selling by marketing boards, such as with cocoa in Ghana; or through financial hedging, as with sovereign oil hedging in Mexico. Physical and financial pledges are a means to lock-in minimum selling prices, and offer a price insurance to producers against falling export prices. Some revenue insurance crop schemes have also re-oriented from inter-year to intra-year stabilisation. For example, the Stacked Income Protection (STAX) scheme under the 2014 US Farm Bill only provides short-term revenue insurance, for price falls within a season, between planting and harvest. So far as prices fall from the current to the next season, there will be no indemnity for that.

---

71 Philippe Chalmin, "What is the New Normal in Commodity Markets?" (presentation delivered at UNCTAD's Global Commodities Forum 2015, Geneva, 13–14 April 2015).

72 High prices stimulate investment, but the time frame of investment is a long one. Between the moment investment is undertaken and full exploitation, 10 or 15 years can easily elapse.

73 Bilge Erten and José Antonio Ocampo, *Super-Cycles of Commodity Prices since the Mid-Nineteenth Century*, DESA Working Paper 110 (New York, 2012), at 1.

Inter-year commodity price stabilisation raises more intractable issues in agriculture. As mentioned above when discussing price volatility and longer cycles, agricultural markets tend to be characterised by long flat periods, punctuated by violent boosts of volatility. In this setting, stabilisation is difficult. For example, international buffer stocks tend to go out of stocks in the attempt to calm price spikes, or out of cash in the attempt to sustain prices during prolonged low-price crises. Inter-year price stabilisation is feasible, but the stabilisation band must be periodically adjusted to reflect market trends.

Reference hereafter is to both intra-year and inter-year price stabilisation arrangements. They are here subsumed, alongside farm income stabilisation arrangements, under the working notion of 'agricultural stabilisation policies'.

### b) *Stabilisation Approaches*

#### i Price v. Income Stabilisation

In terms of stabilisation approaches, an important distinction is the one between price and income stabilisation. It is important to observe, in this respect, that farmers' incomes are not only determined by the price the farmers receive for their produce. Input costs for seeds, fertilizers, gasoline, electricity or water, as well as taxes, may also significantly impact producers' income margins. Likewise, the amount received is not only a matter of prices, but also of volume. Polices to mitigate price volatility do not insure against a sharp fall in output or a decline in demand.

At the country level, it is likewise important to distinguish between export price volatility on the one hand, and export earning instability on the other. The former describes price fluctuations and the latter refers to variations in export proceeds. This latter notion is broader than that of price volatility, as it also covers shortfalls in export earnings that arise from fluctuations in export volumes, beyond fluctuations in export prices.[74]

As discussed in the following Chapter, price and income or revenue stabilisation entails different policy instruments and approaches. It is important to note, however, that the dividing line between the two sets of policy instruments is hardly precise. For example, some income support measures have

74 While the main, direct objective of intergovernmental commodity agreements was to stabilise prices, alternative or complementary schemes have been operated to compensate commodity exporting countries for export shortfalls. The best-known examples of compensatory finance are the Contingency and Compensatory Financing Facility (CCFF) of the International Monetary Fund (IMF), preceded by the Compensatory Financing Facility (CFF); and the European Union's Stabilisation of Export Earnings (STABEX) scheme. Commodity export compensation schemes are often perceived as a preferable alternative to price stabilisation/support schemes, since, in principle, they do not involve direct intervention in the market. For a brief discussion, refer to Section 2.2.1.

discernible price support effects.[75] This blurs the distinction between direct action on prices and efforts to manage the effects of price instability.

### ii Managing Prices and Managing the Effects of Price Instability

A partially overlapping distinction is that between managing prices and managing the effects of price instability (Table 3). This is an analytical useful way of 'taxonomising' stabilisation policies at both the international and domestic level.

As discussed in Chapter 4, the orthodox policy prescription is that countries should avoid trade intervention for purposes of commodity price stabilisation. Instead, they should turn to non-trade instruments to cope with or mitigate the effects of commodity price volatility. These coping and mitigation alternatives include social protection policies such as safety nets and market-based risk-management instruments. These instruments may entail public intervention (targeted public safety nets), market-based instruments (commodity derivatives, or private insurance), or a combination of both (as with

TABLE 3 *Managing prices and managing the effects of price changes*

| **Market price intervention tools (managing prices)** | | |
|---|---|---|
| *Domestic* | Internal measures (direct) | Price controls<br>Domestic marketing boards / Stabilisation funds<br>Buffer stock intervention<br>Public stockholding<br>Supply management (acreage restrictions, market withdrawals etc.) |
| | Border measures (indirect) | Import measures (price bands, variable import levies, minimum import prices, quotas, import licences or other measures to enforce domestic price controls)<br>Export measures (variable export taxes and other export restrictions to stabilise domestic prices) |

75 For example, 'coupled' payments, such as commodity loan programmes or counter-cyclical payments in the US under the Farm Security and Rural Investment Act were acknowledged to have discernible influence on production decisions. See WTO Secretariat, *Trade Policy Review: United States* (WT/TPR/S/200, 5 May 2008), at 85.

| | | |
|---|---|---|
| **Market price intervention tools (managing prices)** | | |
| | *International* | International commodity stocking arrangements<br>Harmonisation of stocking policies and the setting up of co-ordinated national stocks<br>Internationally agreed negotiated price ranges<br>Internationally agreed supply management measures, including export quotas and production policies<br>Multilateral long-term supply and purchase commitments at agreed prices |
| **Alternative policy options (managing the effects of price changes)** | | |
| Income/ revenue support | *Domestic* | Direct payments to offset output price fluctuations (≠ target and market price)<br>Payments based on input used (subsidies reducing the costs of variable inputs, fixed capital, on-farm services)<br>'Decoupled' income support (direct payment / revenue foregone / reimbursement of taxes / gratuitous service in kind, if decoupled from output/prices) |
| | *International* | Compensatory finance (CFF, CCFF, STABEX) |
| Market-based risk management instruments & credit | *Domestic* | Insurance tools, including weather index products<br>Commodity derivatives (futures, options, swaps) |
| | *International* | International Task Force on Commodity Risk Management |
| Social protection, including safety nets | *Domestic* | Contributory schemes<br>Non-contributory (cash / in-kind transfers; school feeding and public work programmes; targeted subsidisation of staple food / direct food transfers) |
| | *International* | International safety nets (e.g. emergency food reserves) |

Source: Compiled by author.

subsidised revenue insurance for farmers). More efficient and effective than price intervention, direct transfers tend to be costly and institutionally complex, and difficult to implement in contexts of widespread poverty, limited budgetary resources and weak institutions.[76]

### c) *Domestic and International Price Stabilisation*

For analytical purposes, another key distinction lies between domestic and international prices; and between domestic price stabilisation arrangements and international price stabilisation. Both arrangements come within the purview of this study.

Domestic price stabilisation is concerned with domestic, or internal, prices at the farm, wholesale, or retail stages of the domestic marketing chain. It seeks to cushion the impact upon domestic producers and/or consumers of internal and external price fluctuations.

International price stabilisation is concerned with international prices, typically assessed by reference to 'benchmark' prices, which reflect trading in major physical or futures markets.[77] It tries to manipulate prices at the global level.

Though this distinction may seem at first clear, it is all the more artificial. In fact, there is a complex interaction between domestic and international factors; which blurs the line between internal and external policies.

### d) *The Price Spectrum and Price Transmission Dynamics*

#### i The Consumer and Producer Ends of the Price Spectrum

Price developments have distributive implications: they transfer resources within and between societies. Hence, there is inherently some distributional struggle, or factional pressure, behind commodity price stabilisation. This can be appreciated at both the domestic and international level.

At the domestic level, commodity price support and stabilisation tend to have discrete welfare effects across groups, and are highly divisive issues. Price defence policies in staple food commodities will likely benefit farmers, to the extent of their surplus production; hit net consumers, with a disproportionate

---

76 As specified at the outset, this research is not concerned with these first-best policy options, which are relatively uncontroversial. Note, however, that they do raise trade policy issues, if subsidies are involved.

77 For example, the f.o.b. price of Thai 5-percent broken white rice is a common benchmark for Asian rice prices. Benchmark prices are then adjusted for usual import costs (such as freight, insurance, credit costs, agents' fees, unloading, transport to the plant and wastage costs), to set reference prices on a c.i.f. basis.

effect on the urban poor; and have mixed impacts on agricultural labourers.[78] These distributional outcomes are highly sensitive and may spur social and political tensions, or even class rivalries.[79]

Regarding international prices, the distributional struggle is not within countries, but between them. When prices are stabilised at above market prices, the transfer is from consuming (importing) to producing (exporting) countries; when they are set at below market levels, resources flow from producing to consuming countries. In some instances, the transfer is redistributive, from the relatively affluent to the poorer. For example, high cocoa prices are expected to benefit peasant farmers in West African countries, while they may possibly hit relatively rich consumers in Europe. In other instances, the distributional struggle is between unprivileged constituencies, across developing countries. Thus, sustained rice prices may benefit poor smallholder producers in South and South East Asia, but severely hit the urban poor in net-rice importing countries – Côte d'Ivoire, Nigeria, Senegal, to name a few examples.

These distributional outcomes should have specific normative relevance, as discussed in Chapter 5.

### ii Commodity Price Transmission

Last but not least, it is important to consider price transmission dynamics within the domestic chain. A few observations are in order, with respect to both commodity producers and consumers.

With regard to producers, it has been observed that the benefits from high prices will not automatically feed through to farmers. Much depends on domestic production and marketing structures.[80]

---

78 For a detailed assessment of the distributive outcomes of high food prices, Will Martin and Maros Ivanic, "The Food Price Crisis, Poverty and Agricultural Trade Policy," in *Food Crises and the WTO*, ed. Bariş Karapinar and Christian Häberli (Cambridge: Cambridge University Press, 2010), 25–48; Todd Benson et al., *Global Food Crises: Monitoring and Assessing Impact to Inform Policy Responses* (IFPRI, 2008).

79 In Thailand, for example, the Pheu Thai party's rice pledging scheme catalysed long-standing tensions between two constituencies: Bangkok's commercial districts, on the one hand, and rural constituencies, on the other.

80 This analysis was integral part of the US Congressional Budget Office (CBO) revision of UNCTAD's IPC. Among other, the CBO pragmatically assessed the potential beneficiaries of the IPC, in order to clarify whether the programme would benefit the poorest people. See Congress of the United States, Congressional Budget Office, *Background Paper: Commodity Initiatives of Less Developed Countries: U.S. Responses and Costs* (Washington, D.C.: US Government Printing Office, 1977), 19–21.

In tropical smallholder agriculture, the peasant farmer may well reap the benefits of remunerative and stable export prices. Yet, this depends on the pass-through of improved prices from the point of export to farm-gate. Indeed, as already mentioned, export prices are not fully captured by the peasant producer: important marketing margins need to be deduced. These include the costs of processing, transportation and handling, captured by other interveners in the domestic chain, such as traders and processors. These intermediaries may realise all the benefits of improved prices. This is likely to occur when scattered peasant farmers sell their produce to a small number of buyers who dominate the trade.

When production or marketing is controlled by the Government through marketing boards, the local government ultimately determines whether benefits in fact accrue to the poorest. It is important to note, in this respect, that marketing boards have frequently set producer prices at below market levels. For example, through the 1970s and early 1980s, cocoa farmers in Ghana had to sell their crop to government-designated agents for as little as a twentieth of the world price.[81] In the early 2000s, the government of Ecuador set the local farmgate price for bananas at US$2.90 per box, whereas the export price was as high as US$17 per box.[82] Bureaucracies and middlemen captured most of the export price.

Finally, in the case of estate (plantation) agriculture, benefits from sustained prices will certainly accrue to the capital owner (local or foreign business interests), but might or might not go to labourers (waged estate workers). The outcome depends on whether higher profits for the company translate into either improved wages or higher taxes and public spending for the benefit of the poor. Ultimately, this engages the responsibility of the enterprises involved (a matter of corporate responsibility) and of the host state (through labour law, taxation and public spending decisions).[83]

In all cases, the pass-through to the neediest and most vulnerable, i.e. the peasant smallholder or the estate labourer, is neither automatic nor straightforward. This warrants caution when assessing the pro-poor impact of high cash crop prices, in terms of accrued benefits to peasant farmers.

Similar qualifications are in order when turning to the consumption side of the equation. It is important to acknowledge in this respect that the 'first'

---

81 "Ghana as Economic Model: Good, but not at Election Time," *The Economist* (25 April 2002), online: <http://www.economist.com/node/1103646>, 44.

82 "Ecuador's Economy: Banana Skins," *The Economist* (25 April 2002), online: <http://www.economist.com/node/1101652>, 54

83 Congress of the United States, above n 80.

consumers of primary commodities are, most often, traders or processors and should not be equated with the final, or end consumer. Agricultural raw materials such as cotton, rubber or timber are used as industrial inputs in manufacturing.[84] In importing countries, their 'first' consumers are intermediate processors or manufacturers of consumer goods. With regard to tropical beverages and oilseeds, there are notable variations across countries and commodities. Coffee and cocoa, for example, are sold internationally near to their raw form: to roasters, in the case of coffee; and to grinders or directly chocolate manufacturers, in the case of cocoa. The price of the 'core commodity' is just a fraction of the retail price of the final consumer product. Tea, to the contrary, is locally processed and exported as end product, made tea. Even in this case, the export price is a far proxy of the final consumer price. Important costs are to be added, including freight forwarding, international trader margins, and import charges, as well as wholesale and retail mark-ups in consuming countries. As regards other major staple food commodities such as grains, these are either self-processed and consumed, or sold locally to traders and millers, for domestic consumption or export.[85] In all cases, the pass-through of farmgate price developments to end consumers is complex, mediated by the intermediate nodes.

### 2.1.3 *Assessment*

A few considerations arise from this brief, almost sketchy review of definitional issues.

First, given the extremely complex texture of agricultural commodity markets, there is a danger of overly fine categorisation, or excessive 'granularity' in defining key issues and concepts in agricultural commodities. And yet to avoid it is to run the risk of oversimplifying the intricate characteristics of many commodity markets. Indeed, the commodity price problematique is a complex fabric of twisted strands. For example, it is difficult to separate the price stabilisation dimension from concerns about the level at which 'just prices' ought to be set. Though analytically distinct, these threads are in practice tightly intertwined and cannot be easily disentangled. Similarly, it is very difficult to disentangle domestic and international perspectives. Domestic price intervention

84 For example, the tire manufacturing industry (giants like Bridgestone, Michelin and Goodyear) is the major consumer of natural rubber.

85 In the industrial economies, the bulk of farm and animal husbandry products is sold on to industrial consumers: 'first handlers' of milk and meat are processors or manufacturers; the main market outlets for wheat are the flour milling industry, including production of starch and bioethanol, and the brewing, malting and distilling industry.

often has a major bearing on international markets; which raises issues of accountability in a multilateral context.

Second, on matters of commodity prices, it is important to avoid excessive ideological polarisation, and to treat things pragmatically. This is not to say that the debate should be de-politicised. To the contrary, the terms of the debate necessarily involve some ideological posturing. As discussed, commodity price policies entail subjective choices as to 'just' price levels, and invite principled decisions rooted in value systems. Yet, this ideological posturing should be intellectually rigorous and eschew simplistic generalisations. In fact, the picture is nuanced. The social welfare implications of commodity price dynamics are complex, both within countries and between countries, and tend to be commodity specific. Any normative discussion about commodities is thus particular and circumstantial, grounded in the assessment of underlying industry structures, farming systems and direction of trade flows.

## 2.2 Agricultural Price Stabilisation Arrangements: An Overview

This Section provides a snapshot of the different kinds of existing price stabilisation arrangements in agriculture. A distinction is drawn between international and domestic price stabilisation arrangements. At either level, discrete attention is paid to price stabilisation arrangements *stricto sensu*, on the one hand, and export earnings or income stabilisation schemes, on the other. It is not the purpose here to detail the wide spectrum of these stabilisation arrangements. The objective is to coarsely outline their major features, map external boundaries and define areas of overlapping. For a more detailed review of individual schemes, the reader is referred to the rich literature that exists on the topic.[86] Appendix 3 also provides a brief overview of the major ICAS.

86 For a review of early commodity control arrangements (pre-World War I and inter-war period), Rowe, above n 55.; International Labour Office, *Intergovernmental Commodity Control Agreements*, above n 44; United Nations Interim Co-ordinating Committee for International Commodity Arrangements, *Review of International Commodity Arrangements* (E/CA/2), United Nations, 16 September 1947. A concise but insightful assessment is also provided in Joseph S. Davis, "Experience under Intergovernmental Commodity Agreements, 1902–45," *Journal of Political Economy* 54, no. 3 (1946). For a comprehensive, useful matrix of 'modern' commodity price stabilisation arrangements (and alternative options): Galtier, above n 36. See also: Richard N. Gariepy, "International Commodity Agreements," *International and Comparative Law Quarterly* 25, no. 3 (1976); Alain Coret, "Les accords internationaux relatifs aux produits de base: l'evolution depuis 1965," *Clunet* 1969; James E.S. Fawcett, "The Function of the Law in International Commodity Agreements," *British*

### 2.2.1 *International Schemes*

This Section provides a scant overview of intergovernmental efforts to stabilise agricultural markets. It covers concerted action geared to stabilise global prices in agricultural commodity markets. The analysis also briefly considers major multilateral and plurilateral efforts aimed at revenue stabilisation in agriculture, as distinct from price stabilisation.

It is important to bear in mind the economic background against which these efforts took place.

Historically, particularly for tropical crops, emphasis has long been on the producer end. Indeed, the dominant long run characteristic of agricultural commodity prices in the past was their steady decline in real terms, accompanied by large short-term price swings. This was the economic background against which major experiments in commodity control took place. The ultimate objective was to raise agricultural commodity prices from unsustainably low levels, in addition to smoothing price volatility around downward trends.

In recent years, there has been some reversal in this situation. The pace of decline in commodity prices has slowed down since the mid-1990s, and if the timeframe of the analysis is limited to the last decade, the downward trend

---

*Year Book of International Law* 47 (1970); [Charles R. Johnston, Jr.] "Access to Supplies and Resources: Commodity Agreements – Remarks by Charles R Johnston, Jr." *American Society of International Law Proceedings* 71 (1977); Kabir-Ur-Rahman Khan, *The Law and Organization of International Commodity Agreements* (The Hague: M. Nijhoff, 1982); Kenneth Klein, "International Commodity Agreements," *Georgia Journal of International & Comparative Law* 6 (1976); Christian Tomuschat, "International Commodity Agreements," in *International Encyclopedia of Comparative Law*, ed. Ernst-Ulrich Petersmann, Christian Tomuschat, and Albert Bleckmann, vol. 17, *State and Economy*, chap. 25, *Universal Economic Organizations* (Mohr Siebeck, 1997); Paul Donovan Reynolds, *International Commodity Agreements and the Common Fund: A Legal and Financial Analysis* (New York: Praeger, 1978); Geoffrey L. Goodwin and James Mayall, *A New International Commodity Regime* (London: Croom Helm, 1979); Mohamed Bennouna, "Le droit international relatif aux matières premières," *Collected Courses* 177 (1982); B.S. Chimni, *International Commodity Agreements: A Legal Study* (London: Routledge, 1987); UNCTAD, *Intergovernmental Producer-Consumer Cooperation in Commodities in Mid 1990s: A Handbook on International Commodity Agreements, Arrangements and Study Groups* (Geneva: United Nations, 1998). For an exhaustive overview of the various stabilisation mechanisms deployed at the international level and their performance: Christopher Gilbert, "International Commodity Agreements: Design and Performance," *World Development* 15 (1987): 596; Christopher Gilbert, "International Commodity Agreements: An Obituary Notice," *World Development* 24 (1996); Christopher L. Gilbert, "International Commodity Agreements and Their Current Relevance for Grains Price Stabilization," in *Safeguarding Food Security in Volatile Global Markets*, ed. Adam Prakash (Rome: FAO; 2011).

seems to have partially reversed, at least for some food commodities.[87] A few agricultural commodities appear to have been transformed from low-priced commodities in chronic oversupply to high-priced commodity in relative scarcity. At least for these commodities, the very rationale for intervention has then been called into question. Emphasis has shifted on smoothing out price spikes, while continuing to address the need to raise prices from 'unsustainably' low levels for those commodities for which the issue remains important.

For the time being, the possible 'end of the super-cycle'[88] may re-focus attention to the need to attain some balance between demand and supply, and sustain prices.

#### 2.2.1.1 Price Stabilisation

Concerted efforts to stabilise commodity prices essentially entailed ICAs of a restrictive nature, involving regulation of production, trade or prices (commodity 'control' arrangements, in the Havana Charter jargon). In their most mature form, in post-Second World War arrangements, they consisted of dual-interest ICAs, involving both consuming and producing countries. These most recent arrangements are to be assessed against the background of their inter-war antecedents from the 1920s and 1930s; and in interplay with the intensified drive towards commodity cartelisation in the 1960s and 1970s.

---

87 Hallam, above n 69. Since the mid-2000s, there has been a trend of steeply rising and increasingly volatile agricultural commodity prices. Until recently, most analysts endorsed the view that real food prices could remain sustained in the long-term, on account of "strong consumer demand in emerging markets, policy-driven demand for biofuels, and long lead-time for a supply response by farmers worldwide" (International Food & Agricultural Trade Policy Council, *High Food Prices and Food Price Volatility: What Role for Policy?* IPC Alert (4 April, 2011), available at http://www.agritrade.org/pressroom/documents/FoodPricesandPriceVolatilityroleforpolicy.pdf (accessed 17 September 2014)). The OECD-FAO Agricultural Outlook 2011–2020 projected agricultural commodity prices to average in real terms over the 2011–20 period up to 20 percent higher for cereals (maize) and up to 30 percent higher for meats (poultry), compared to the last decade (OECD/FAO, *OECD-FAO Agricultural Outlook 2011–2020* (OECD Publishing and FAO, 2011), 14).

88 Some analysts argue that, after a ten-year upward trend, the peak of a commodity 'super-cycle' has been attained, and we are now entering the descending phase of the super-cycle. For a discussion on the end of the super-cycle in commodities, UNCTAD, Global Commodities Forum 2015, Plenary session 5. Presentations downloadable at http://unctad.org/en/pages/MeetingDetails.aspx?meetingid=647 (last accessed 31 May 2015).

### a) *Early Control Arrangements in the 1920s and 1930s*

Multilateral post-war efforts to stabilise agricultural commodity markets are to be assessed in the light of their inter-war antecedents: the early control schemes of the 1920s (on tin, rubber and tea) and 1930s (tin, rubber, sugar and wheat).[89]

These early arrangements were, in essence, 'restrictionist'. They consisted of cartel-type schemes for the regulation of supply.[90] The 1920 arrangements had originated in post-war conditions, the large excess stocks and depressed prices following the First World War.[91] Later arrangements in the 1930s mainly arose from the Great Depression economic downturn. The 1929 Wall Street crash subsequently shattered commodity markets, resulting in a dramatic fall in prices for virtually all primary commodities. That vigorously stimulated new governmental efforts in commodity supply management, at both the domestic and international levels.[92]

In terms of underlying price objectives, the prime concern was price maintenance or support, in the face of oversupply, or threat of oversupply, and depressed prices. To sustain prices, the early 1920 arrangements mainly involved

89 A few international control agreements were established in the 1930s. The most important included: the 1931 Agreement on the International Tin Control Scheme, superseded by the 1933–36 and the 1937–41 Agreements, and complemented in 1934 by the Agreement for the Tin Buffer Stock Scheme (renewed in 1938); the 1931 International Sugar Agreement among sugar producers associations (the so-called Chadbourne Plan), followed by the 1937–42 Agreement concerning the Regulation of the Production and Marketing of Sugar (International Sugar Agreement); the International Tea Agreement 1933–38; the First International Wheat Agreement of 1933; the 1934 Agreement for the Regulation of Production and Export of Rubber; and the 1936 copper control scheme. Other highly specialised agreements, quite heterogeneous in character, included: the short-live 1933 Silver Agreement, pressed by silver-mining interests to boost the price of silver; the 1937 Scheme to Regulate the Supply of Beef to the United Kingdom market; as well as schemes for the orderly marketing of the accumulated wool stocks owned by the British government. For a detailed assessment, Rowe, above n 55 and Davis, above n 86.

90 A few (arrangements on rubber, tin and tea) managed to secure tight monopolistic control in the 1930s, covering 80–90 percent, or even more, of exportable production. Carmine Nappi, *Commodity Market Controls* (Lexington, Mass.: D.C. Heath, 1979), 34; Rowe, above n 55, at 137.

91 These arrangements were put to an abrupt end by the Wall Street crash in 1929, though some continued to exist on paper: Rowe, above n 55, at 129–36.

92 The Wall Street crash resulted in a dramatic fall in prices for virtually all primary commodities, much more significant than for industrial products; the steady decline in process continued though the 1930–33, followed by a short-live price boom and subsequent fall through 1936–39. Rowe, above n 55, 129–36.

the use of production and export restrictions.[93] A few resorted to commodity stockpiling, involving holding back surpluses, to be sold when quotations were more favourable.[94] Later arrangements in the 1930s continued to rely primarily on production and export restrictions.[95]

As to their form, several of the early 1920 arrangements consisted of private arrangements between producing associations.[96] Yet, a few took the form of official government intervention, sometimes arising out of early private schemes.[97] Most of the later 1930s arrangements were intergovernmental in form,[98] with some notable variations and exceptions, though.[99] However, formal distinctions should not be overemphasised. Private arrangements were frequently officially backed, if not instigated by governments.[100] Arrangements

93 As in rubber, tin and copper.

94 Brazil's coffee 'valorisation' scheme, the 'Bandoeng Pool' on tin and the Canadian wheat pools.

95 The case of rubber, sugar, tea and wheat; though arrangements in tin also involved a buffer stock.

96 The most notable examples included: voluntary restriction schemes by British rubber estate companies (1917–18 and 1920–21); the international cartel of the principal copper exporters (1926–29); attempts by the Canadian wheat pools to control the price of wheat (1928); efforts by the Tin Producers' Association to restrain output (1929–30); and partial restriction of output schemes for petroleum, lead and zinc (1927, 1928). Rowe, above n 55, at 77–85.

97 Examples of direct governmental intervention in commodity production and prices included: the 'Stevenson' Rubber Restriction Scheme (1922–28); the 'Bandoeng Pool' by the Governments of the Federated Malay States and the Netherlands Indies (1929–30); the Brazilian coffee valorisation schemes (1907, 1923–29); and sugar output restrictions by the Cuban authorities (from 1926). Rowe, above n 55, at 77–85.

98 The case of rubber, tin, wheat and sugar.

99 Arrangements in tea and the early 1930 schemes on sugar (the International Tea Agreement (1933–38) and the Chadbourne Agreement among sugar producers' associations (1931–35)) were private in form, yet officially backed by the Governments concerned; the copper agreement of 1936 was, in form and in practice, an international business arrangement, free of government intervention.

100 For example, the International Tea Agreement 1933–38, signed by private associations of tea exporters, was officially backed by the Governments of the three producing countries (India, Ceylon and the Netherlands East Indies). These latter undertook to implement enforcing legislation, and were represented on the controlling committee. Similarly, the Chadbourne Agreement among sugar producers' associations (1931–35), though a private arrangement in form, was officially backed by the Governments of the participating associations, including Cuba and Java (major sugar cane producers), as well as by the Governments of a number of sugar beet producing countries. It then evolved into an intergovernmental agreement – the International Sugar Agreements of 1935.

that were intergovernmental in form typically originated from powerful industry groups. Some even explicitly provided for the representation on their controlling committees of producing and trading interests, associated to civil servants and diplomats as advisers.[101] Overall, there was a visible interlocking of public and private interests.

Finally, in terms of membership, the tin, rubber and tea agreements were all concluded under Anglo-Dutch leadership. They initially involved only the two 'metropolitan' states (the United Kingdom and the Netherlands) and their Empire dependencies in South and South-East Asia, with no representation of consumers' interests.[102] Through the 1930s, their membership was enlarged to other producing interests, notably, dependencies and other territories under French or Belgian jurisdiction. In some cases, the dependent territories participated in their own capacity. In other circumstances the metropolitan state signed on behalf of its dependent territories. The 1930 arrangements in wheat and sugar were more comprehensive and ambitious in terms of membership. Consuming countries were members of the 1933 wheat agreement, and they also participated in the sugar arrangements.

Overall, the trajectory from the 1920s to the late 1930s seems to indicate a progressive shift from unilateral producer action to agreements more international in scope, as a way to secure tighter monopolistic control and to 'police' export restrictions. This would progressively lead to the "modern post-war creed" that consuming interests must be adequately represented,[103] and to the concerted approaches discussed below.

### b) *Post-War Dual-Interest ICAs*

Five agricultural commodities have been the object of concerted action on prices by producers and consumers (dual-interest ICAs) after the Second

---

101 Formal arrangements on rubber, tin and tea in the 1930s were pressed by powerful industry groups, respectively: the Rubber Growers' Association, formed by British owners of estates in Ceylon and Malaya; the Tin Producers' Association, with British, Dutch and Bolivian (Patino) mining interests; and tea producers' associations in India, Ceylon and London.

102 The tin agreement was signed by the British dependencies of Malaya and Nigeria, the Netherlands East Indies, Bolivia, and later, Siam – with the official British and Dutch endorsement; parties to the rubber agreements were the United Kingdom, the Netherlands and France (on behalf of their dependent territories), Indian and Siam; the tea agreement was signed by the tea producing associations involved, backed by their respective Governments (India, Ceylon, the Netherlands East Indies and their 'mother' governments – the United Kingdom and the Netherlands).

103 Rowe, above n 55.

World War: sugar, coffee, wheat, cocoa and natural rubber.[104] Some schemes (natural rubber, sugar and cocoa) continued a tradition of market intervention that traced back to the former colonial administrations. In sugar and wheat, commodity agreements were negotiated against a background of State trading, as international commerce in these commodities was essentially on an intergovernmental basis.[105] As discussed in detail in Chapter 3, in form, ICAs were open, multilateral treaties, with broad membership. All agreements were dual-interest arrangements, with equal representation of producers and consumers. Their stated price objective essentially referred to price stability, with an emphasis on assurance of supplies in wheat.

Institutionalised multilateral cooperation in cocoa traces back to 1972, with the adoption of the first International Cocoa Agreement (ICCA) by the United Nations Conference on Cocoa.[106] Successor agreements were adopted in 1975 (second ICCA),[107] 1980 (third ICCA),[108] 1986 (fourth ICCA),[109] 1993 (fifth ICCA),[110] 2001 (sixth ICCA)[111] and 2010 (seventh ICCA).[112] Only the first four Agreements (1972, 1975, 1980 and 1986) included price control mechanisms.

The history of coffee control goes back as far as the early 1900s, though the first open, multilateral commodity agreement on coffee was elaborated and approved only in 1962, within the framework of the United Nations Conference on Coffee.[113] Since then six successor agreements have been adopted.

---

104 Stabilisation provisions were also enshrined in plurilateral agreements on bovine meat and dairy products established within the GATT framework. Refer to Section 3.1.2.4.

105 OECD, Working Party on Agricultural Policies and Markets, *An Assessment of Commodity Agreements for Commodity Price Stabilisation*, TAD/CA/APM/WP(2010)36/FINAL (19 May 2011), at 15.

106 The first ICCA was adopted on 21 October 1972 at Geneva and entered into force provisionally on 30 June 1973. The Agreement expired in accordance with its provisions on 30 September 1976. 882 UNTS 67.

107 1023 UNTS 253.

108 1245 UNTS 221; 1276 UNTS 520 (procès-verbal of rectification of the original English, French and Russian texts); and 1288 UNTS 437 (rectification of the authentic Russian text).

109 1446 UNTS 103.

110 1766 UNTS 3.

111 2229 UNTS 2.

112 The Seventh ICCA was adopted on 25 June 2010 at Geneva by the United Nations Cocoa Conference for the Negotiation of a Successor Agreement to the International Cocoa Agreement, 2001. 2871 UNTS.

113 Concluded at New York on 28 September 1962, the Agreement entered into force provisionally on 1 July 1963. It expired in accordance with its provisions on 30 September 1968. 469 UNTS 169 and 515 UNTS 322 (procès-verbal of rectification of the authentic Russian

These include the International Coffee Agreement (ICoA) 1968, and its two extensions,[114] the ICoA 1976, with one extension,[115] the 1983 Agreement, and its four extensions,[116] ICoA 1994, with one extension[117] and the 2001 Agreement, with three extensions.[118] The text of the latest Agreement, the ICoA 2007, was adopted by the Council in September 2007.[119] Price control was suspended in 1989.

Rubber was the subject of more than one experiment in control in the inter-war period.[120] Early control arrangements, which had involved the metropolitan territories and their dependent territories, laid the foundation for successor arrangements based on cooperation between producing and consuming countries. The first 'modern' dual-interest ICA, the International Natural Rubber Agreement (INRA), was concluded in 1979 under the auspices of UNCTAD.[121] It was then renegotiated in the mid-1980s (INRA, 1987)[122] and during 1994–1995 (INRA, 1994).[123]

Institutionalised multilateral cooperation in sugar resulted in the International Sugar Agreement (ISA) 1953,[124] followed by six successor agreements

text of the Agreement). The predecessor instruments had included producer-only agreements, or agreements limited in their geographic scope.

114 647 UNTS 3.

115 1024 UNTS 3.

116 1333 UNTS 119.

117 2086 UNTS 147.

118 2161 UNTS 308.

119 2734 UNTS 101.

120 For an authoritative account, International Rubber Regulation Committee, *The History of Rubber Regulation: 1934–1943*, ed. Sir Andrew McFadyean (London: G. Allen & Unwin, 1944). See also Peter T. Bauer, "The Working of Rubber Regulation," *The Economic Journal* 56, no. 22 (1946).

121 1201 UNTS 191. Adopted at Geneva on 6 October 1979, the Agreement entered into force provisionally on 23 October 1980, in accordance with article 61(2) and definitively on 15 April 1982, in accordance with article 61(1). It was extended until 22 October 1987, and was terminated in accordance with its provisions on 22 October 1987.

122 International Natural Rubber Agreement, 1987. 1521 UNTS 3 and doc. TD/RUBBER. 2/EX/R.1/Add.7 and depositary notification C.N.82.1988.TREATIES-2 of 26 May 1988 (procès-verbal of rectification of the original Arabic, Chinese, English, French and Russian texts).

123 International Natural Rubber Agreement, 1994. 1964 UNTS 3 and depositary notification C.N.466.1995.TREATIES-5 of 8 February 1996 (procès-verbal of rectification of the authentic text).

124 258 UNTS 153.

(the ISA 1968,[125] the 1973 Agreement (extended in 1975, 1976 and 1977),[126] the ISA 1977 (extended once),[127] the ISA 1984,[128] the ISA 1987,[129] and the 1992 Agreement).[130] From 1984 onward, ISA did not contain price stabilising clauses.

Multilateral grains cooperation traces back to the 1934 International Wheat Agreement (IWA), which essentially operated through an export quota system.[131] A new IWA was concluded in 1949.[132] The 1949 Agreement envisaged a system of multilateral contracts between wheat exporting and importing countries, involving long-term supply and purchase commitments and mandatory price ranges. Similar agreements were negotiated in 1953,[133] 1956,[134] 1959[135] and 1962.[136] Stabilisation arrangements have been absent from 1971.[137]

The post-war ICAs have used three types of devise: export restrictions; buffer stock intervention; and multilateral contracts.[138]

ISA and ICoA essentially operated through output and export restraints. Supply management was also used for cocoa in the ICCA, but as a complement to buffer stock stabilisation. Output and export quotas are typically used to sustain and defend prices. They may also be used to stabilise prices around a

125 654 UNTS 3.

126 906 UNTS 69 and 958 UNTS 279 (rectification of authentic texts).

127 1064 UNTS 219; 1102 UNTS 355; 1103 UNTS 398; 1119 UNTS 388; 1122 UNTS 391; 1132 UNTS 444; 1157 UNTS 459 (procès-verbaux of rectification of the original French and Russian, French and Spanish, Russian, French, and French, Spanish and Russian, respectively).

128 1388 UNTS 3.

129 1499 UNTS 31.

130 1703 UNTS 203.

131 Final Act of the Conference of Wheat Exporting and Importing Countries (25 August 1933). Reprinted in International Labour Office, *Intergovernmental Commodity Control Agreements*, above n 44, 1.

132 International Wheat Agreement. Done at Washington, on 23 March 1949. 203 UNTS 179.

133 Agreement revising and renewing the International Wheat Agreement. Done at Washington, on 13 April 1953. 203 UNTS 242.

134 International Wheat Agreement, 1956. Formulated at the United Nations Wheat Conference which ended at London on 25 April 1956, and open for signature at Washington until 18 May 1956. 270 UNTS 103.

135 International Wheat Agreement, 1959. Opened for signature at Washington from 6 April 1959 until and including 24 April 1959. 349 UNTS 167.

136 International Wheat Agreement, 1962. Opened for signature at Washington from 19 April 1962 until and including 15 May 1962. 444 UNTS 3.

137 International Grains Council, at http://www.igc.int/en/downloads/brochure/gen08094rev6.pdf.

138 For a comprehensive and detailed review: Bennouna, Gilbert, above n 86.

trend: participants in the scheme seek to raise prices by restricting supply; and to contain upward price pressure by expanding quotas. These arrangements were mainly criticised on efficiency grounds, as they tended to 'freeze' production and trade patterns, to the detriment of efficient producers. Major practical problems included difficulties in allocating quotas, an incentive to renege on the part of cartel members, and free-riding by non-members.

ICCA and INRA have relied wholly or partly on buffer stock intervention. The first two ICCAs, 1972, and 1975, envisaged an export quota system and a buffer stock arrangement. The third and fourth ICCAs, 1980, and 1986, entirely operated through buffer stock mechanisms, though the Council could institute supplementary measures in order to further the price stabilisation objectives of the Agreement. The 1979 INRA operated entirely through buffer stock intervention. Buffer stocks are essentially instruments to reduce price fluctuations around a known long-run level. When the price exceeds or falls below a specified range, the manager of the buffer stock attempts to restore the reference price by buying or selling on the open market. Buffer stock stabilisation can work well so long as price volatility remains low. It is more problematic in turbulent times, as the buffer stock, unless huge, would run out of stocks or cash to calm abrupt price movements.[139] It is also deemed unsuitable to face long-term or cyclical trends, for the same reasons.

Wheat Agreements have traditionally relied on long-term supply and purchase commitments. As summarised in Gilbert, IWA exporting members guaranteed assured supplies of wheat subject to a maximum price while importing countries guaranteed purchases subject to a minimum price.[140] Thus, the multilateral contract mechanism acts like a forward contract,[141] setting a permissible price range. This arrangement, first elaborated in the 1949 IWA, was maintained in the 1953, 1956, 1959 and 1962 IWAs. Contractual floor and ceiling prices were absent from IWAs after 1971.[142] Multilateral contracts involved contracts between governments, in a context of government to government sales and state trading. As pointed out by Gilbert, in the present context of a private merchandise order, they would need to be enforced by means of export taxes and subsidies, which may pose issues of WTO compatibility, among other issues.[143]

139 See, on this point, Gilbert, "International Commodity Agreements and Their Current Relevance for Grains Price Stabilization," above n 86.

140 Ibid, at 218.

141 Ibid, at 219.

142 Ibid, at 218–19.

143 Ibid.

In practice, the operation of ICAs was fraught with considerable difficulties; none of them successfully stabilised prices for more than relatively short periods. Eventually, all the five agricultural price-stabilising ICAs have either collapsed or lapsed between 1985 and 1999 (for an assessment, refer to Section 4.1.2.1). As discussed in Gilbert, they were possibly more effective in defending floor than ceiling prices; and more successful in sustaining than stabilising prices.[144]

c) *Post-War Cartel-type Arrangements*

Multilateral intervention coexisted with and was stimulated by the drive towards commodity cartelisation in key extractive industries in the 1960s and 70s.

The early 1970s witnessed a proliferation of formal cartel organisations, sparked by the success of the Organization of the Petroleum Exporting Countries (OPEC).[145] Formal cartels were established in a number of key industries, including: copper, the Intergovernmental Council of Copper Exporting Countries; bauxite, International Bauxite Association; iron ore, Association of Iron Exporting Countries; mercury, the Mercury Group; lead, the Lead Group; and tungsten, the Tungsten Group; these, in addition to petroleum.[146] As reported in Clarfield et al., by the mid-1970s, cartels with anywhere from four to 12 members controlled from under 20 percent to over 90 percent of the annual production of selected minerals.[147]

Unilateral producer action gained new momentum in the aftermath of the 2007–08 commodity crisis, including in agriculture. In 2008 Thailand, Vietnam, Burma, Laos, Cambodia envisaged a cartel-type output restraint scheme to sustain rice prices which eventually was not implemented due to food security

144 Christopher Gilbert, *International Agreements for Commodity Price Stabilisation: An Assessment*, OECD Food, Agriculture and Fisheries Papers, no. 53 (Paris: OECD Publishing 2011), 21–23; Rowe, above n 55, at 209.

145 In 1973 a group of oil-producing developing countries grouped under OPEC withheld supplies of oil to raise prices. The success of the 1973 oil embargo sparked considerable debate about the prospects for producer cartels to enhance developing countries' export earnings. Many believed that a new era had commenced, whereby developing producer countries would force their requests through the strength of their economic leverage in key markets.

146 For a review, Nappi, above n 90, at 103–75; Robert S. Pindyck, "The Cartelization of World Commodity Markets," *American Economic Review* 69, no. 2 (1979); Kenneth W. Clarfield et al., *Eight Mineral Cartels: The New Challenge to Industrialized Nations* ([New York]: Metals Week, 1975).

147 Clarfield et al. above n 146.

concerns. Likewise, Thailand, Malaysia and Indonesia orchestrated cutbacks in natural rubber to inflate prices, which encouraged foreign competitors, such as Vietnam, to expand their exports.

Most of these cartel efforts were unsuccessful in their attempts to raise prices above the market level, due to organisational problems such as cheating on the part of cartel members,[148] or because of limited room to raise prices above market levels when the demand facing the cartel is highly elastic.[149]

#### 2.2.1.2 Revenue Stabilisation

While the main, direct objective of ICAs and cartels was to stabilise or defend prices, alternative or complementary schemes have operated to compensate commodity exporting countries for export shortfalls. The best-known examples of compensatory finance are the Contingency and Compensatory Financing Facility (CCFF) of the International Monetary Fund (IMF), preceded by the Compensatory Financing Facility (CFF); and the European Community's Stabilisation of Export Earnings (STABEX) scheme. The latter, which is agriculture-specific, deserves some consideration.[150]

STABEX was established under the first Lomé Convention on 1 February 1975.[151] It ended in 2000. The scheme was revised three times, under the second,[152] third[153] and fourth[154] Lomé Conventions. The countries covered by the system were the African, Caribbean and Pacific (ACP) States signatory to the Lomé Convention. The products covered were mostly tropical products of agricultural origin, including fishery and forestry, and were chosen "as much

148 Cheating on the part of cartel members coexisted with difficulties to agree on price and production levels or the division of revenue. See Pindyck, above n 146, at 155. Cartels tend to work better when they can be 'policed' by a dominant member – the case of Saudi Arabia in OPEC.

149 Due for example to the existence of substitutes or of alternative sources of supply. Pindyck, above n 146, at 155.

150 For a comparison of the IMF and STABEX schemes, John Ravenhill, "What Is to Be Done for Third World Commodity Exporters? An Evaluation of the STABEX Scheme," *International Organization* 38, no. 3 (1984), Table 4, at 569–70.

151 ACP-EEC Convention of Lomé. Signed at Lomé on 28 February 1975. Complete text. The Courier No 31, Special Issue, March 1975 [hereafter, the Lomé I Convention].

152 The Second ACP-EEC Convention signed in Lomé on 31 October 1979. Complete text reproduced from The Courier No. 58, Special Issue, November 1979 (the Lomé II Convention).

153 Third ACP-EEC Convention signed at Lomé on 8 December 1984. Complete text. The Courier No 89, Special Issue, January-February 1985 (the Lomé III Convention).

154 Fourth ACP-EEC Convention signed in Lomé on 15 December 1989. Complete Text. The Courier No. 120, March-April 1990 (the Lomé IV Convention).

for political as economic reasons",[155] to satisfy various political constituencies in the beneficiary countries. Processed products and mineral exports were excluded, with the exception of iron ore under Lomé one.[156]

STABEX was established as a politically acceptable alternative to price stabilisation arrangements. Its rationale was inherently conservative: to counter pressures within the European Economic Community (EEC) and from former colonies towards a revival of price stabilisation arrangements in producing countries.[157] Its avowed objectives were twofold. At the micro and sector level, it aimed to stabilise farmers' income and channel resources to the affected industry. At the macro level, it aimed to stabilise a country's export revenue.[158]

STABEX was a form of insurance against instability of export earnings. Through offsetting transfers, it insured against a decline in export proceeds. The transfer of STABEX funds was triggered by a fall of export receipts from specific products below a reference level. Two thresholds had to be met: a dependency threshold and a fluctuation threshold.[159] As for the former, under Lomé I the product in question must account for at least 7.5 percent of a country's total merchandise exports to all destinations during the year preceding the year of application.[160] For the fluctuation threshold, export proceeds from the concerned product ought to have decreased by at least 7.5 percent below the reference level.[161] This latter was calculated as the average exports to

155 Note, for example the addition of iron ore under the first STABEX scheme, to accommodate the concerns of Mauritania, then chairing the STABEX negotiating committee. Ravenhill, above n 150, at 545.

156 A complementary scheme was set up for specified mineral products (copper, phosphates, manganese, bauxite and aluminium, tin and iron ore) under Lomé II (see n 152 above), articles 49–56. The scheme, known as SYSMIN, involved concessional aid granted from a special financing facility. Possible recourse to the facility was open to countries that experienced, in one of the covered products, substantial fall in production or export capacity owing to accidents or political events.

157 Ravenhill, above n 150, at 540–41.

158 Ibid, at 541.

159 For a detailed description, Hamisi S. Kibola, "Stabex and Lomé III," *Journal of World Trade* 18, no. 1 (1984), at 33–41; Ravenhill, above n 150, at 549–58.

160 The dependency threshold was lowered to 5 percent in the case of sisal and 2.5 percent in the case of the least-developed landlocked and island countries (LDLICs). Lomé I, above n 151, article 17 (2).

161 The fluctuation threshold was 2.5 percent in the case of LDLICs. Lomé I, above n 151, article 19 (1) and (2).

the EEC of the product in question over the preceding four years. These thresholds were lowered under Lomé II and IV.[162]

It is widely acknowledged that the scheme's impact was limited. This is on account of a number of shortfalls in its design, largely the product of political choices, more than of technical constraints.[163] As discussed in Ravenhill, major limitations included: the limited product coverage;[164] the trigger thresholds;[165] the calculation of the reference period;[166] limited resource available; and some arbitrariness in the administration of the scheme. It has also been highlighted that STABEX did not succeed in transferring resources to its intended beneficiaries, peasant producers and farm sectors. In the absence of conditionality, transferred funds were allotted to the general account and spent in line with overall spending priorities.[167]

### 2.2.2 *Domestic Schemes*

While concerted price action attempts to manipulate global prices, domestic price stabilisation seeks to cushion the impacts of external and internal price fluctuations upon domestic producers and consumers. It is worth recalling the main features of domestic price stabilisation, at least in terms of policy tools involved (Section 2.2.2.1), while also recalling some policy alternatives, in the form of direct transfers (Section 2.2.2.2).

Again, some preliminary observations are in order, to put the analysis in perspective.

First, it is important to acknowledge that market price intervention in agriculture has for long been the norm, rather than the exception in the advanced

162 The 7.5 percent dependency threshold was lowered to 6.5 percent (2 percent in the case of LDLICs) under Lomé II and 5 percent (1 percent for LDLICs) under Lomé IV. The fluctuation threshold was lowered to 6.5 percent (2 percent for the LDLICs) under Lomé II.

163 Ravenhill, above n 150, at 572.

164 Minerals were excluded (until the setting up of an *ad hoc* facility under Lomé II), as were processed products – as these latter would compete with European production. This limitation significantly hindered the developmental potential of the STABEX scheme, by freezing production patterns and discouraging downstream investment.

165 This resulted in a situation where large percentage drops in export proceeds from a minor export were compensated even if small in absolute terms, whereas small percentage falls from a major commodity were not compensated, even if significant in absolute terms. It follows that countries were incentivised not to diversify their exports, to meet the dependency threshold.

166 The 4 year moving average precluded transfers where a rising trend was interrupted. Drops were assessed in nominal terms.

167 Ravenhill, above n 150, at 573.

market-based economies. There are here some discernible historical patterns in agricultural pricing policies, from taxing to subsidising the farm sector, and from direct price intervention to less distortive forms of income stabilisation. The history of farm stabilisation policies in the most advanced economies illustrates these developments.

Agricultural price stabilisation, as a permanent form of State intervention in the economy, is a policy that historically emerged regionally from the first economies to industrialise: Britain, other parts of Western Europe, Japan and the US.[168] The history of commodity price control here interweaves with the long history of government intervention in the farm sector, which goes back much earlier than the 20th century.[169] Price intervention was at that time aimed at stabilising domestic food prices and at raising revenue for those in authority, with a transfer of resources from the rural to the urban dwellers. In Britain, other parts of Western Europe, as well as Japan, industrialisation then prompted a switch from taxing to subsidising the farm sector; and domestic price stabilisation became inextricably linked with farm price support policies.[170] Similar patterns, from taxing to subsidising the farm sector, are now evident in other contexts, in particular in some large developing economies.[171]

---

168 For a historic review, Kym Anderson, ed., *The Political Economy of Agricultural Price Distortions* (Cambridge: Cambridge University Press, 2010).

169 Kym Anderson, "Understanding Government Interventions in Agricultural Markets," in *The Political Economy of Agricultural Price Distortions*, e.d Kym Anderson (Cambridge: Cambridge University Press, 2010), 3–24.

170 Ibid, at 13. Pursuant to this account, shifts in demography and intersectoral terms of trade – i.e. the decline of agriculture relative to industry – are the main variables that explain the shift from taxing to subsidising the farm sector. With industrialisation, as comparative advantage shifts from agriculture to industry, the focus of public policy protection shifts from industry to agriculture. According to the logic of collective action, farmers were able to demand protection in part because their shrinking numerical strength, paradoxically, became an organisational advantage. See also Kym Anderson and Yujiro Hayami, *The Political Economy of Agricultural Protection: East Asia in International Perspectives* (Sydney; London; Boston: Allen & Unwin, 1986). For a critical perspective on this approach: Robert Paarlberg, "The Political Economy of American Agricultural Policy: Three Approaches," *American Journal of Agricultural Economics* 71, no. 5 (1989): the actual level of protection granted to US farmers from the 1930s onward responded to macro shocks (depression, war, inflation, recession) more than to shifts in comparative advantages of industry and agriculture.

171 In nominal terms, farm support – as captured by the OECD Producer Support Estimate (PSE) – has increased appreciably in key emerging economies, including China, Turkey and Russia. Most remarkably, since the late 1990s, there has been a steady rise in farm support in China, with a rapid increase since 2008. In 2010, China reportedly spent $147 bn

In the advanced, market-based economies, agricultural price intervention has continued to be a central feature of the post-war commodity order up to present days (Appendix 4 and Appendix 5).[172] In the US, during the Great Depression the Federal Government stepped-in vigorously to relieve critical

---

on agricultural subsidies, outranking the EU as the top subsidiser. This rising trend in subsidies reflects a policy shift from taxing to supporting the farm sector, in response to pressing equity and food security concerns. For a detailed assessment, Fuzhi Cheng, *China: Shadow WTO Agricultural Domestic Support Notifications*, International Food Policy Research Institute, IFPRI Discussion Paper 00793 (Washington, D.C., 2008).

172 A rich literature exists on farm support policies in the US, the EU and Japan. For a compendium of resources on US farm policies, including an agricultural law bibliography, updated quarterly: The National Agricultural Law Center (http://nationalaglawcenter.org/about-the-center/). A selection of key readings is also available at http://www.ers.usda.gov/topics/farm-economy/farm-commodity-policy/analysis-of-previous-farm-bills.aspx (United States Department of Agriculture, Economic Research Service). For a historical overview, see, in particular, Carolyn Dimitri and Anne Effland, "Milestones in U.S. Farming and Farm Policy," *AmberWaves* (June 2005), 10; Anne B. Effland, "U.S. Farm Policy: The First 200 Years," *Agricultural Outlook* (March 2000), 21; Douglas E. Bowers et al, "History of Agricultural Price-Support and Adjustment Programs, 1933–84: Background for 1985 Farm Legislation," *Agriculture Information Bulletin* 485 (Economic Research Service, US Department of Agriculture, 1984). For major retrospective analyses of the CAP since its inception, Robert Ackrill, *Common Agricultural Policy* (Sheffield: Sheffield Academic Press, 2000); Rosemary Fennell, *The Common Agricultural Policy: Continuity and Change* (Oxford; Clarendon Press, 1997); Christopher Ritson, and David Harvey, eds., *The Common Agricultural Policy*, 2d ed. (New York: CABI Publishing, 1997). On the original CAP design: J.H. Richter, "Agricultural Policy in the European Common Market," *Journal of Farm Economics* 43, no. 3 (1961); "The EEC's Farm Policy," *The Economist*, 1 April 1978, 60–62; Werner J. Feld, "Implementation of the European Community's Common Agricultural Policy: Expectations, Fears, Failures," *International Organization* 33, no. 3 (1979). For interesting insights into the changing rationale of support under the CAP: Martin Petrick, "The Co-Evolution of Semantics and Policy Paradigms: 50 Years of Europe's Common Agricultural Policy," *Intereconomics* 43, no. 4 (2008). For a review of the CAP reform, refer to EUROPA [European Union's web site], Agriculture and Rural Development pages, http://ec.europa.eu/agriculture/index_en.htm. For a snapshot of the CAP: David Stead, "Common Agricultural Policy," *EH.Net Encyclopedia*, ed. Robert Whaples, 21 June 2007 (http://eh.net/encyclopedia/common-agricultural-policy/); "The common agricultural policy (CAP) and agriculture in Europe – Frequently asked questions," (European Commission memo, Brussels, 26 June 2013), at http://europa.eu/rapid/press-release_MEMO-13-631_en.htm. On policy reform in Japan: OECD, *Evaluation of Agricultural Policy Reforms in Japan* (Paris: OECD Publishing, 2009). For up-to-date information on agricultural policy developments, refer to the OECD's Agricultural Policy Monitoring and Evaluation (http://www.oecd.org/tad/agricultural-policies/monitoring-and-evaluation.htm) and the WTO's Trade Policy Reviews (at https://www.wto.org/english/tratop_e/tpr_e/tpr_e.htm).

conditions for primary commodity producers in the 1930s, including through intervention purchases and acreage controls.[173] These New Deal programmes laid the groundwork for the US 'permanent' farm stabilisation law:[174] the Agricultural Adjustment Act (AAA) of 1938,[175] along with the Agricultural Act (AA) of 1949.[176] In Europe, agricultural market intervention became an even more prominent feature of the farm economy in the early 1960s, when the broad outline of a uniform Community system for the marketing of agricultural products within the European Community (EC) took shape in the Common Agricultural Policy (CAP) (see Box 2).

Through the 1970s and 80s, policies towards agriculture in the developed market-based economies continued to be essentially interventionist – involving, among other policies, volume control regulation, price setting provisions, intervention purchases, border protection, export subsidies, and variable rate payments. Only recently, since the mid-1990s, have most of these policies been rolled-back, with a shift in support towards less distortive forms of income stabilisation such as insurance schemes and fixed rate payments. Underlying this move were budgetary pressures, the economic inefficiencies associated with market intervention, and the perverse distributive effects of price support (see below).

While agricultural pricing policies are no longer important among the traditional subsidisers, they are gaining momentum elsewhere. In particular, some

173 Price support measures included heavy government purchases of wheat by the Federal Farm Board through the Grain Stabilisation Corporation (1930); successive schemes of voluntary subsidised acreage control in wheat and cotton (since 1933); as well as the bail-out of bankrupt growers' cooperative societies (1930). Rowe, above n 55, at 89–90 and 130.

174 Failure to enact a new Farm Bill would imply a reversion to the 1949 AA and to the applicable provisions of the 1938 AAA regarding permanent law. The permanent law provisions of the 1938 Act regard acreage allotments (quotas, to sustain prices) for wheat and upland cotton. Under the Agricultural Act of 1949, the Secretary is instructed to "make available through loans, purchases, or other operations" permanent price support for defined commodities – wheat, corn, rice, upland cotton, honey and milk. For details: Jim Monke et al., "Expiration and Extension of the 2008 Farm Bill," Congressional Research Service Report, December 2013, at https://fas.org/sgp/crs/misc/R42442.pdf; USDA memorandum, "The Effects of Failure to Enact a New Farm Bill: Permanent Law Support for Commodities and Lapse of Other USDA Programs," February 2008, at https://www.agri-pulse.com/ext/resources/pdfs/p/e/r/m/o/Permanent_Law_Authorization_memo.pdf.

175 7 U.S.C. 1281 et seq.

176 7 U.S.C. 1421 et seq.

large developing economies are now implementing the type of policies that the EU and US had implemented in the 1970s and 1980s.[177]

An overview of these developments is well beyond the reach of this study. They have been recalled here to stress that commodity price intervention had been the norm, rather than the exception, in the first economies to industrialise.

Second, it is important to keep in mind the highly sensitive distributional outcomes of domestic stabilisation arrangements. As mentioned, commodity price support and stabilisation tend to have discrete welfare effects across groups, and are highly divisive. Some general patterns are discernible, across developed and developing counties.

Modern agricultural stabilisation policies in high-income countries have traditionally given broader consideration to producer interests. Price stabilisation in industrialised countries has involved substantial transfers from consumers to producers, and in some instances carried an anti-poor bias. For example, in the mid-2000, the CAP cost consumers and taxpayers around €100 billion per year, half from taxpayers via taxes, and half from consumers via higher food prices.[178] The €50 billion annual cost to consumers fell disproportionately on the poorest in society, who spend a larger share of their income on food.[179] Likewise, in the late 1980s, most of all US commodity program budget outlays went to the prosperous 22 percent minority of US farmers in the $100,000 sales class and above.[180] As detailed in Paarlberg, "[t]he average government payment to each of these farmers in 1986 was $42,000, well above the $27,735 median family income of the not-so-wealthy average taxpayers who are asked to pay for the benefit".[181] This 'producer-bias' was largely the outcome of pressure group politics. As pointed out in a 70s review of the Common Agricultural

177 According to OECD data, this path is being followed by China, Turkey and Russia (countries that report data to the OECD). Agricultural market price intervention is also a key policy feature in a few Asian and South-east Asian countries, including India, the Philippines and Indonesia.

178 UK HM Treasury, *A Vision for the Common Agricultural Policy* (London: HM Treasury, 2005), 4. On the distributive effects of the CAP, see: Cristiano Perugini, "Who Bears the Burden of Common Agricultural Price Policy? The Distributive Effects of Market Price Support in the Agricultural Sector," *Rivista internazionale di scienze sociali* 112, no. 4 (2004).

179 UK HM Treasury, above, at 5.

180 US Department of Agriculture 1987, p. 3, cited in Robert Paarlberg, "The Political Economy of American Agricultural Policy," *American Journal of Agricultural Economics* 71, no. 5 (1989), at 1161.

181 Paarlberg, above n 180, at 1161.

Policy (CAP) by The Economist, farmers "have traditionally wielded more political clout than housewives".[182]

In developing countries, domestic commodity price arrangements have focused on either or both of the consumer and produce ends. In many contexts, the bias reflected the personal adherences and allegiance, whether rural or urban, of the ruling establishment. Some schemes tended to give broader consideration to consumer interests, and essentially aimed to stabilise or set ceilings on domestic consumption prices. Yet, others were operated to sustain and stabilise producer prices, especially when rural constituencies had strong political leverage.[183] Finally, several pursued the 'schizophrenic policy' of high producer and low consumer prices, by keeping procurement prices high, while setting wholesale or retail prices at relatively low levels, often incurring large losses.[184]

With these considerations in mind, it is important to review some major price stabilisation arrangements, before briefly considering available alternative policy options.

#### 2.2.2.1 Price Stabilisation

Domestic price stabilisation policies are geared to mitigate the domestic impacts of external and internal price fluctuations. These fluctuations may be 'exogenous', originating from outside, on foreign markets; but they may also arise from domestic, or internal sources of instability, such as localised yield drops.[185] In the first case, international trade channels domestic price volatility. In the latter, it can smooth out domestic price shocks.[186]

---

182 "The EEC's Farm Policy," *The Economist*, 1 April 1978, 60–62.

183 William O. Jones, "Food-Crop Marketing Boards in Tropical Africa," *The Journal of Modern African Studies* 25, no. 3 (1987): 380.

184 Odin Knudsen and John Nash, "Commodity Price Stabilization Schemes in Developing Countries," *Economic Development and Cultural Change* 38, no. 3 (1990): 544–48. See also Anne O. Krueger, *The Political Economy of Agricultural Pricing Policy*, vol. 5, *A Synthesis of the Political Economy in Developing Countries* (Baltimore: Johns Hopkins University Press, 1992).

185 Committee on World Food Security. High Level Panel of Experts on Food Security and Nutrition, *Price Volatility and Food Security. A Report by the High Level Panel of Experts on Food Security and Nutrition of the Committee on World Food Security* (Rome: Secretariat HLPE c/o FAO, 2011), 43–48.

186 When domestic price volatility arises from outside, the transmission of international price developments to domestic prices is not linear: the extent of the pass-through depends, among other, on a country's trade openness, as well as on its domestic policies to decouple domestic prices from international prices. HLPE, above, at 45–46.

Domestic price stabilisation and support is effected through a mixture of trade policy instruments, which are complexly interlocked. Administered price schemes, statutory marketing and variable levies and taxes have been routinely used and combined to mitigate price volatility, or the effects thereof. For example, India has stabilised domestic prices for major agricultural commodities through a mix of border and internal measures: a *de facto* variable import levy,[187] the setting of minimum support prices, and guaranteed purchases by government-designated agencies. Likewise, as originally conceived, the CAP maintained for years producer prices at above the market trend by a combination of policy instruments: minimum guaranteed prices and purchases, variable import levies and export subsidies. Canada too in the past stabilised its dairy sector through a system involving production quotas, regulated prices and border measures, administered by marketing boards.

As discussed in Section 2.3, this multifaceted, entangled set of policies is scrutinised under the dissecting scope of separate WTO disciplines. What matters, for purposes of legal analysis, is not the integrated whole (the policy), but its discrete components (the policy measures). These are individually assessed in their trade distorting potential. The following analysis will thus lay bare the main policy instruments involved in the stabilisation of domestic prices, and examine them separately. The focus is on five set of stabilisation policies: price controls; supply management; variable import levies and price bands; variable export taxes and stabilisation funds; and statutory marketing through state trading. These policies involve direct and indirect forms of price stabilisation. Note that state trading is not per se a stabilisation arrangement, but a venue for the administration of agricultural pricing policies (refer to Section e) below).

### a) *Administered Prices*

Direct price stabilisation entails price regulation. This can be effected by various means, including: the setting of output prices at various stages of the marketing chain (farmgate, wholesale and retail prices; selling / buying prices); administered input prices (price controls on fertilizers, irrigation water, electricity rates, diesel prices, and seeds); and regulated costs or margins through the marketing chain. All these measures are a matter of internal, beyond the border regulation. They are almost inevitably coupled with border restrictions to insulate domestic prices from international prices. Price controls have been extensively used in both developed and developing countries.

187 India tends to modify its import tariffs frequently, using the spread between applied and bound tariffs, to offset the variability of import prices. For a review, WTO, *Trade Policy Review: India – Revision* (WT/TPR/S/249/Rev.1, 20 October 2011).

i) Agricultural Pricing Policies in the Advanced Economies

Since the mid-1990s, farm stabilisation and support policies in the largest subsidising market-based economies have re-oriented towards less-trade distortive forms notably, income support. Yet, price controls and other intervention measures had been a prominent feature of the advanced economies' farm policies up to the late 1980s. These developments are well illustrated by the CAP (Box 2). Set up in 1962, the CAP had one major policy objective: producer support. This was defined at the micro level to sustain farmers' incomes; at the macro level to equalise incomes between poor, farming, regions and rich, industrial, ones. And, indeed, prices would be maintained for years at above the market trend. This by a combination of policy instruments: minimum guaranteed prices and purchases; variable import levies to offset the competitive edge of imports; and export subsidies to dispose of accumulated surpluses.

**Box 2: Price controls under the CAP (1962–1992)**

Within the CAP framework, the EEC administered three sets of prices:

i) 'target prices', or domestic support prices, based on prices in area of shortest supply (e.g. for wheat, the target price was set for Duisburg, in the Ruhr valley);
ii) 'intervention prices', or the prices at which national intervention agencies would buy in all the surplus produce that could not otherwise be sold at the target price. Intervention prices were usually set at a specified percentage below the target price; and
iii) 'threshold prices' at the border, or fixed minimum import prices, set slightly lower than target prices so that once storage and transport costs from the port of import were added (such as marketing costs from Rotterdam to Duisdburg), the product would sell at the target price. The threshold price was in practice a minimum import price administratively set at a level that would allow the sale of EEC output at the target price.

Price controls were complemented by two sets of border measures: variable levies and restitution payments. These counter-cyclical trade policies were a central feature of the CAP architecture. Internal prices were maintained in the face of low world prices by the use of a sliding-scale tariff, a variable levy, while surplus exports were assured through the use of sliding-scale export subsidies, restitution payments.[188] The variable import levy, paid by the

188 Gary P. Sampson and Richard H. Snape, "Effects of the EEC's Variable Import Levies," *Journal of Political Economy* 88, no. 5 (1980).

EEC importer to the Community, corresponded to the difference between the 'threshold price' and the adjusted cost, insurance and freight (c.i.f.) (delivered EEC port) price, the lowest landed price. It kept domestic prices relatively insulated from international prices, in a two-price system. To allow otherwise non-competitive exports from the EEC to third countries, export refunds (restitutions) were paid by the Community to bridge the gap between the Community and world market prices.

Since the early 1990s, policy emphasis in Europe has progressively shifted from price to income support (see Appendix 4). This entailed a move away from the most trade-distortive policy instruments (price fixing, variable levies and export subsidies) to allegedly less-trade distortive income support measures (direct transfers to producers). Transfers were initially 'coupled', i.e. related to current price or output parameters, and countercyclical in nature. They were then increasingly 'decoupled', based on historical or fixed entitlements.[189] The shift from price to income support was initiated by the 1992 MacSharry reform.[190] The reform process was deepened and completed under the Agenda 2000 Reforms (further reduction of intervention prices),[191] the 2003 mid-term

189 For a short bibliography, above n 172. See also: Commission of the European Communities, *Communication of the Commission to the Council: The Development and Future of the CAP: Reflections Paper of the Commission*, CoM(91) 100 final, Brussels, 01/02/1991, http://ec.europa.eu/agriculture/cap-history/1992-reform/com91-100_en.pdf; Commission of the European Communities, *Communication of the Commission to the Council and to the European Parliament: The Development and Future of the Common Agricultural Policy: Follow up to the Reflection Paper – Proposals of the Commission*, CoMC(91) 258 final, Brussels, 22/07/1991, http://ec.europa.eu/agriculture/cap-history/1992-reform/com91-258_en.pdf.

190 Commission of the European Communities, *Reform of the Common Agricultural Policy – Legal texts (arable crops, sheepmeat, beefmeat)*, CoMC(91) 379 final, Brussels, 18 October 1991. The Reform entailed substantial reduction of intervention prices (cereal guaranteed prices were lowered by 35 percent, and beef prices by 15 percent). Direct payments were introduced in order to compensate for the decrease of the price support. Compulsory set-aside and other accompanying measures (agri-environment programmes, afforestation, early retirement, and diversification) were also introduced. For key documents and explanations, refer to EUROPA [European Union's web site], Agriculture and Rural Development pages (History of the CAP, The 1992 reform (MacSharry reform)), at http://ec.europa.eu/agriculture/cap-history/index_en.htm.

191 Support prices were further reduced (by 15 percent in two annual steps for cereals); direct payments were correspondingly increased.

review of the CAP, or Fischler's reform ('decoupling' of income support),[192] the 2009 'Health Checker' (further 'decoupling' of support)[193] and the June 2013 reform ('greening' of the CAP).[194]

A similar pattern of 're-instrumentalisation' of support was observable through the 1990s and 2000s for other major subsiding OECD countries, including Switzerland, the US, Japan and Norway though with notable variations. Across the developed economies, the focus is now on revenue, as distinct from price, stabilisation, and on direct transfers.[195]

ii) Price Intervention in the Developing Economies

While the most advanced economies have reoriented towards direct transfers, the setting of intervention prices remains a key stabilisation tool in a number of developing countries. This issue is complexly entangled with that of state trading, addressed separately in Section e) below.

In staple food commodities, a few governments still maintain minimum support prices, generally under public stocks or food reserve arrangements. These schemes generally involve the setting of minimum prices, guaranteed purchases by government-designated agencies, and subsidised releases for targeted segments of the population. Notable examples are the price control and stocking schemes implemented in most of the rice-growing countries in East-Asia and South-East Asia (Box 3). All of these arrangements involve guaranteed purchases from farmers at a set procurement price. They vary widely in their specifics. Under some schemes, the designated agencies procure all the rice offered by farmers at the announced support price (for example, under the

---

192 Council Regulation (EC) No 1782/2003 of 29 September 2003 (OJ L 270, 21.10.2003, p. 1) (amended on several occasions; repealed and replaced by Council Regulation (EC) No 73/2009 of 19 January 2009 establishing common rules for direct support schemes for farmers under the common agricultural policy and establishing certain support schemes for farmers, amending Regulations (EC) No 1290/2005, (EC) No 247/2006, (EC) No 378/2007 and repealing Regulation (EC) No 1782/2003 of 19 January 2009 (OJ L 30, 31.1.2009, p. 16)). The reform introduced a Single Farm Payment (SFP) Scheme, based on historical receipts.

193 Council Regulation (EC) N° 73/2009, which replaced Regulation 1782/2003.

194 30 percent of direct payments were linked to European farmers' compliance with sustainable agricultural practices; at least 30 percent of the rural development programme budget is to be allocated to agri-environmental measures, organic farming, and environmentally friendly investment or innovation measures.

195 For a review of agricultural policy developments in the OECD economies, the OECD Agricultural Policy Monitoring and Evaluation reports provide an up-to-date source of information. Downloadable at: http://www.oecd.org/tad/agricultural-policies/monitoring-and-evaluation.htm.

Thai mortgage scheme[196] and the Indian public procurement system (PPS)). Others procure only the amount needed for building up and replenishing a strategic reserve (like China's purchases to build strategic reserves[197]). Another critical aspect is the level at which the intervention price is set relative to the market price: well above market levels (Thai mortgage scheme, Indian PPS, and purchases by the National Food Authority (NFA) in the Philippines);[198] or in line with market prices.

**Box 3: Price intervention in rice, East and South-East Asia**

Price control schemes have been implemented in most of the rice-growing countries in East-Asia and South-East Asia as part of intervention purchase schemes and other farm support policies.

In India, the Government maintains minimum support prices (MSPs) for major agricultural commodities.[199] MSPs are set by the Government following the recommendations of the Commission for Agricultural Costs and Prices (CACP). They aim at covering the actual expenses incurred by the farmer, both in cash and kind, including imputed value of wages of un-paid family workers.[200] When market prices fall below the MSP, government-designated agencies can intervene in the market to purchase, at the MSP, "any amount of produce that farmers offer".[201] Guaranteed purchases from

196 Sam Mohanty, "Why does everyone hate the Thai rice mortgage scheme?" (blog entry, 5 November 2012, http://irri.org/blogs/sam-s-rice-price-and-market-blog/why-does-everyone-hate-the-thai-rice-mortgage-scheme).

197 China also does have minimum purchase prices schemes for rice and wheat. Refer to WTO, *Trade Policy Review: China – Revision* (WT/TPR/S/264/Rev.1, 20 July 2012), at 106.

198 Domestic price support schemes often entail that domestic prices are higher than border prices. In the Philippines, for example, as reported in the Philippines' Trade Policy Review, "[i]n 2007, estimated nominal protection rates (NPR) (i.e. domestic prices are higher than border prices) were 26 percent for beef, 27 percent for chicken and rice, 32 percent for maize, 80 percent for sugar, and 94 percent for pork. Coconut was an exception as NPRs were negative for coconut oil and copra" (WTO, *Trade Policy Review: The Philippines – Revision* (WT/TPR/S/261/Rev.2, 9 May 2012), at 67).

199 For a review, WTO, *Trade Policy Review: India*, above n 187, at 102–03 and 134–35.

200 Ibid, at 134. Several factors are taken into account to fix MSPs, including, as reported in the Trade Policy Review: "[...] the cost of production, changes in input prices, trends in market prices, inter-crop price parity, effect on industrial cost structure, effect on cost of living, effect on general price level, international prices, and parity between prices paid and prices received by the farmers and the effect on issue prices and implications for subsidy" (at 134, footnote 27 and accompanying text).

201 Ibid, at 134.

farmers were used to set up and replenish public stocks for food security under the Targeted Public Distribution System (TPDS). This system is being scaled up under the National Food Security Act (see *infra*, Section 5.2.1.1).

In Thailand, producers could obtain a low-interest loan from the Government against the pledge of rice as collateral. After harvest, they had the option of either repaying the loan or deliver the commodity in full settlement of the loan (forfeiture). The amount of the loan was determined by the 'loan rate' (the government-determined price), expressed in local currency per unit of output.[202] The scheme was discontinued in 2014.

In the Philippines, the NFA procures paddy from farmers at an administratively set price recommended by the Inter Agency Committee on Rice, composed of representatives from different government agencies. The NFA is not the sole purchaser: farmers may sell directly to millers and traders. Under the Farmers Option Buy Back scheme, they can buy-back the same amount sold to the NFA within six months and resell it, to benefit from price increases above the NFA support price.[203]

In Indonesia, the Government is involved in stabilising the price of rice through the state logistics agency, Perum BULOG. The scheme involves guaranteed purchase of rice from farmers at a set procurement price.[204]

Price intervention was likewise commonplace in tropical export cash crops. In Côte d'Ivoire, for example, private agents operated within an official cost schedule (the *barème*) that set prices, marketing costs and margins through the chain, from farmgate to the point of export. The *barème* was set at the beginning of each season by a regulatory board, the *Caisse de Stabilisation et de*

202 On the Thai mortgage scheme, Mohanty, above n 196; Samarendu Mohanty, "Thailand's Rice Mortgage Program," *AsiaSentinel*, 27 September 2011, http://www.asiasentinel.com/society/thailands-rice-mortgage-program/; "Thai rice. Less paddy power. Populist politics mess up Thailand's biggest crop," *The Economist*, 14 July 2012; Sara Forssell, *Rice Price Policy in Thailand: Policy Making and Recent Developments*, Department of Economics at the University of Lund, Minor Field Study Series, no. 189, 2009, at https://liveatlund.lu.se/intranets/LUSEM/NEK/mfs/MFS/189.pdf (accessed 16 May 2014); "Thailand Rice Mortgage Scheme," http://oryza.com/tags/thailand-rice-mortgage-scheme#; USDA Foreign Agricultural Service, *Thailand. Grain and Feed. Cabinet Approval of Rice Mortgage Scheme 2008*, GAIN Report TH8095, 13 June 2008, at http://apps.fas.usda.gov/gainfiles/200806/146294908.pdf (accessed 16 May 2014).

203 WTO, *Trade Policy Review: The Philippines*, above n 198.

204 WTO, *Trade Policy Review: Indonesia – Revision* (WT/TPR/S/278/Rev.1, 16 July 2013), at 65.

*Soutien des Prix des Productions Agricoles* (CAISTAB).[205] Price fixing was also an essential feature of the export monopoly marketing boards most common in English-speaking African countries. These boards stabilised producer prices by fixing a single price paid to the producer for the entire season. These pricing policies, effected through stabilisation funds or marketing boards, are discussed at greater length in Section e) below.

### b) *Supply Management*

Supply management aims to manage supply of a commodity relative to demand in order to influence prices. Management of supply is typically effected through a combination of mechanisms, including production or marketing quotas, manipulation of stocks, and border restrictions. The scheme can be state-controlled or private (farmer-driven or corporate).[206]

Supply management has been one of the most widely used tools to stabilise commodity prices, in both developed and developing countries. The advanced market-based economies made extensive use of supply management schemes in the past; they continue to do so for some commodities. For example, since the early 1970s, Canada has managed the supply of all its domestically produced raw milk (Box 4). A similar system was operated in the EU: milk quotas were first introduced in 1984, and eventually dismissed in 2015.[207] In the United States, the Agricultural Marketing Agreement Act of 1937 authorises the Secretary of Agriculture to administer industry-driven supply management schemes (marketing agreements and orders) for fruit, vegetable, and specialty crops.[208] Marketing orders are also permissible in the dairy sector.[209] Note also

205 For a detailed assessment, Panos Varangis and John McIntire, *Reforming Côte d'Ivoire's Cocoa Marketing and Pricing System*, The World Bank, Policy Research Working Papers, no. WPS2081 (Washinton, D.C., 1999).

206 Thomas Lines, *Supply Management: Options for Commodity Income* (Winnipeg, Manitoba: International Institute for Sustainable Development, 2007).

207 Milk quotas were introduced by the EEC under the Dairy Produce Quota Regulations of 1984 (SI 1984 no. 1047). The milk quota system was extended many times, before being dismissed in 2015.

208 US Code of Federal Regulations (CFR) annual edition, Title 7, Subtitle B, Chapter IX (http://www.ecfr.gov/cgi-bin/text-idx?sid=285d017562453496d60f218d5fbe932f&c=ecfr&tpl=/ecfrbrowse/Title07/7cfrv8_02.tpl). US Department of Agriculture, Guidelines for Fruit, Vegetable & Specialty Crop Marketing Orders, January 1982.

209 US CFR annual edition, Title 7, Subtitle B, Chapter X (http://www.ecfr.gov/cgi-bin/text-idx?SID=7b93b3a582d5bfa790270c8639e838c5&tpl=/ecfrbrowse/Title07/7chapterX.tpl).

that 'set-aside' requirements under WTO Blue Box measures involve some form of supply management.

**Box 4: The Canadian milk supply management scheme**

All milk produced in Canada is subject to supply management. Farmers can sell only through milk marketing boards or agencies; sales outside the system trigger sanctions. The supply management scheme, administered by the Canadian Dairy Commission (CDC), entails two segments: the 'fluid milk' segment (raw milk processed into table milk and fresh cream), administered at the provincial level; and the 'industrial milk' segment (raw milk processed into dairy products), under joint federal-provincial programmes. For 'fluid milk', each Province makes an estimate of the anticipated demand and individual fluid milk quotas are allocated to farmers; returns are pooled in a 'fluid' pool account, and paid to the farmer net of costs. The industrial milk market is administered nationally. The Canadian Milk Supply Management Committee (served by the CDC) sets the national industrial milk production target, or Market Sharing Quota (MSQ) (an estimate of the anticipated domestic demand plus planned exports minus anticipated imports). The MSQ is shared among provinces who in turn allocate the provincial share to farmers.

Source: GATT Panel Report, *Canada – Import Restrictions on Ice Cream and Yoghurt*, L/6568, adopted 5 December 1989, BISD 36S/68; Canadian Dairy Commission, Supply Management section (http://www.cdc-ccl.gc.ca/CDC/index-eng.php?id=3806, accessed 4 December 2015); Dairy Farmers of Canada, Supply Management section (http://www.dairyfarmers.ca/what-we-do/supply-management, accessed 4 December 2015).

Supply management has also been extensively used in developing countries. Domestic and international supply management schemes were here complexly intertwined. In tropical commodities, international commodity price stabilisation schemes typically involved domestic adjustment programmes in producing countries. This was notably the case of ICAs reliant on production/export quotas. Their terms required supply management enforcement at the domestic level in producing countries, by means of planting restrictions, acreage idling, production allotments, market withdrawal etc.

Note that supply management systems rely on the interrelationship of various components, including production controls, price supports and levies, and import controls. These components trigger separate WTO disciplines.

### c) *Variable Levies, Minimum Import Prices and Price Bands*

Domestic price controls are generally accompanied by border restrictions in the form of variable levies, price bands and minimum import prices, among other arrangements. These border measures typically disconnect domestic market prices and border prices. They tend to shield domestic producers and consumers from price fluctuations on foreign markets.

Variable levies represent the difference between two price parameters: a threshold, or minimum import entry price based on the domestic market price or an administratively set price; and the import price, the actual transaction value of the imports, or a reference import price, typically the lowest c.i.f. price for the product concerned.[210] The variable levy changes with movements in either or both of these price parameters. When world market prices decrease relative to the threshold price, the levy rises. It declines with increases in world market prices. Variable levies thus have protective, as well as stabilisation effects. Variable import levies were a central feature of the CAP architecture (see above Box 2).

A subtle line is drawn between variable import levies and *de facto* variable levies. For WTO purposes, to qualify as a variable import levy, "the measure itself – as a mechanism – must impose the variability of the duties".[211] This "inherent variability" distinguishes variable levies from *de facto* variable levies which are ordinary customs duty subject to occasional changes in applied

---

210 These are the characteristics of variable import levies as distilled from the pre-Uruguay Round notifications by a WTO Panel. See: Panel Report, *Chile – Price Band System and Safeguard Measures Relating to Certain Agricultural Products*, WT/DS207/R, adopted 23 October 2002, as modified by Appellate Body Report WT/DS207/AB/R [hereafter, *Chile – Price Band System*], para. 7.36 (a) to (d), at 130–31. For the appeal case: Appellate Body Report, *Chile – Price Band System and Safeguard Measures Relating to Certain Agricultural Products*, WT/DS207/AB/R, adopted 23 October 2002, DSR 2002:VIII, p. 3045 (Corr.1, DSR 2006:XII, p. 5473).

211 As stated by the Appellate Body, "[v]ariability is inherent in a measure if the measure incorporates a scheme or formula that causes and ensures that levies change automatically and continuously". See Appellate Body Report, *Chile – Price Band System*, above n 210, para. 233. See also Panel Report, *Peru – Additional Duty on Imports of Certain Agricultural Products*, WT/DS457/R and Add.1, adopted 31 July 2015, as modified by Appellate Body Report WT/DS457/AB/R [hereafter Panel Report, *Peru – Agricultural Products*], paras. 7.287, 7.288 and 7.320. For the Appellate Body Report: Appellate Body Report, *Peru – Additional Duty on Imports of Certain Agricultural Products*, WT/DS457/AB/R and Add.1, adopted 31 July 2015.

tariff rates.[212] A number of countries still keep *de facto* variable import levies.[213] These are controversial grey area measures, likely to amount to a circumvention of WTO obligations.

Minimum import prices are similar to variable levies in many respects, but their operation is generally simpler.[214] Variable import levies are usually based on the difference between a governmentally determined threshold price and the lowest world market offer price, while minimum import price schemes typically operate in relation to the price of an individual consignment.[215] If the actual transaction value of the import is below a defined minimum import price, an additional charge is levied corresponding to the difference.[216] A notable example, which was challenged under the GATT, was the minimum import price for tomato concentrates, which prohibited tomato concentrate importation into the EEC below a certain price.[217]

Price band systems (PBS) have been described as a "hybrid instrument, which has most, but not all, of its characteristics in common with either or both a variable import levy and a minimum import price".[218] The price band results in a system of import duty increases and rebates. When import prices drop below a floor, a surcharge (the PBS duty) is applied. When they exceed a threshold, importers receive a rebate. As for its mode of operation, the PBS involves the setting of the price band, a lower and upper price threshold, and of a reference price. The price band thresholds are generally derived yearly from a moving average of benchmark international prices. The reference price is generally determined weekly or infra-weekly, and is most often an administratively determined lowest world market offer price. Thus, differently from either

---

212 As put by the Appellate Body, "[t]he level at which ordinary customs duties are applied can be varied by a legislature" (Appellate Body Report, *Chile – Price Band System*, above n 210, para. 233). This is the case of India, where import tariffs are frequently adjusted using the spread between applied and bound tariffs to offset the variability of import prices. For a review, WTO, *Trade Policy Review: India*, above n 187.

213 As pointed out through the Trade Policy Review mechanism, India tends to modify its import tariffs frequently, using the spread between applied and bound tariffs, in order to offset the variability of import prices. For a review, WTO, *Trade Policy Review: India*, above n 187.

214 Panel Report, *Chile – Price Band System*, above n 210, para. 7.36 (a) to (d), at 130–31

215 Ibid.

216 Ibid, para. 7.36 (e), at 131

217 GATT Panel Report, *EEC – Programme of Minimum Import Prices, Licences and Surety Deposits for Certain Processed Fruits and Vegetables*, L/4687, adopted 18 October 1978, BISD 25S/68.

218 Panel Report, *Chile – Price Band System*, above n 210, para. 7.46.

a variable levy or a minimum import price, all the price parameters are derived from or linked to international prices. Domestic prices and the actual transaction price of import play no role in the formula.[219] Price band schemes have been widely used in countries like Colombia, Ecuador, Peru and Chile to establish price floors and ceilings on import prices.[220] Chile's and Peru's scheme have been challenged before the WTO Dispute Settlement Body (DSB).[221]

### Box 5: Chile's price band system (PBS)

Chile's PBS covered the following product categories: wheat and wheat flour, edible vegetable oils, and sugar. Its stated purpose was to ensure "a reasonable margin of fluctuation" of domestic prices for such products in relation to their international prices.

For each covered product, the price band set an upper and a lower price threshold and a 'reference price'. The upper and lower price thresholds were set once a year through Decrees issued by the Executive. These floors and ceilings were based on a 5 year (10 for sugar) moving average of international benchmark prices.[222] The resulting values were then converted to a c.i.f. basis, by adding "usual import costs" such as freight, insurance, credit costs, agents' fees, unloading, transport to the plant and wastage costs. Chilean customs authorities also determined weekly 'reference prices' every Friday for the following week for each of the product covered by the PBS. These prices corresponded to the lowest free on board (f.o.b.) price for the product on foreign "markets of concern to Chile" (e.g. with respect to wheat, Argentina, Canada, Australia and the US). The same weekly reference price applied for each product regardless of the origin of the goods and the transaction

219 Panel Report, *Chile – Price Band System*, above n 210, paras. 4.49 and 4.51.

220 Brian Wight and Adam Prakash, "The Fallacy of Price Interventions: A Note on Price Bands and Managed Tariffs," in *Safeguarding Food Security in Volatile Global Markets*, ed. Adam Prakash (Rome: FAO, 2011), 231–41, at 238–39. Unlike variable import tariffs, triggered by import price movements relative to a domestic support price, price bands are based on an international reference price – a moving average, a base-period price average, or other.

221 Panel Report, *Chile – Price Band System*, above n 210; Panel Report, *Peru – Agricultural Products*, above n 211.

222 Hard Red Winter No. 2, f.o.b. Gulf, quoted on the Kansas Exchange, in the case of wheat; the price of crude soya bean oil, f.o.b. Illinois, on the Chicago Exchange, for edible vegetable oils. These averages where adjusted for inflation using an external price index calculated by Chile's Central Bank. The compiled monthly prices where then arranged in descending order, with cut-off of bandwidth peaks and lows (up to 25 percent of the highest and lowest values).

value of the shipment. The determination of the reference price depended on the date of shipment from the exporting country.

The PBS operated as follows. When a shipment arrived at the border, customs authorities applied the *ad valorem* duty. The appropriate weekly reference price was then determined according to the date of the shipment, as per bill of lading. When the reference price was below the lower threshold of the price band, an additional, specific, PBS duty was levied, equivalent to the difference between the lower threshold and the reference price. *Ad valorem* plus specific duties could not exceed the tariff rate bound in Chile's WTO schedule. If the reference price fell between the lower and upper threshold, only the *ad valorem* duty applied. When the reference price was higher than the upper band threshold, the customs authorities granted a rebate on the *ad valorem* duty, equal to the difference between the reference price and the upper threshold.

The operation of the Chilean PBS came under scrutiny for lack of transparency and predictability. In particular:

- No legislation or regulation in Chile specified which international markets were used for the calculation of the Reference Price (the lowest f.o.b. price on "markets of concern to Chile")
- No published legislation or regulation in Chile set out the "usual import costs" which were added to the f.o.b. prices for the determination of the PBS values on a c.i.f. basis
- Unlike with the PBS values, the weekly reference price was not converted from an f.o.b. basis to a c.i.f. basis. This was likely to inflate the amount of specific duties applied under Chile's PBS, equal to the difference between Chile's annual price band thresholds, based on higher c.i.f. prices, and Chile's weekly reference prices, based on lower f.o.b. prices.

As the result of these and other technical shortfalls, the process of determining the relevant values and the amount of the applied duties was found to be non-transparent and not predictable for traders.

Source: Based on Panel Report, *Chile – Price Band System and Safeguard Measures Relating to Certain Agricultural Products*, WT/DS207/R, adopted 23 October 2002, as modified by Appellate Body Report WT/DS207/AB/R.

### d) *Variable Export Taxes and Buffer Funds*

Export restraints are a controversial policy measure. In stabilisation terms, they act as a double edge sword: they tend to aggravate world price fluctuations in a bid to smooth domestic price spikes. Export restraints have been routinely used as part of domestic price stabilisation schemes. In particular, export restrictions have been widely used as a policy tool to dampen domestic price rises at times of rising inflation or perceived shortages. This had occurred in the 1970s, through the 1995–2002 period and during the 2003–09 period.[223] They came to prominence again during the 2007–11 commodity crises. Thus, for example, in Vietnam and India rice has been subject to a minimum export price to ensure prices and availability in the domestic market.[224] In India, export prohibitions and export quotas have been notified, among other products, for non-basmati rice, wheat, pulses, edible oils, milk powder, casein and casein derivatives, and onions.[225]

Less controversial are variable export levies and buffer funds. Under variable export taxes, the applied rate varies with the world market price: the higher the world price, the higher the tax. One variation of the variable tariff is the buffer, or stabilisation fund. Unlike buffer stocks and marketing boards, buffer funds do not physically handle the commodity, but stabilise prices by means of variable tariffs and subsidies. When export prices are high, an export tariff is levied, the tax proceeds are put into a revolving fund, and paid out as an export subsidy to cushion the fall of export prices later. These arrangements were maintained by the *caisses de stabilisation* in the former French African countries. This kind of fund has also been used in Papua New Guinea for coffee, cocoa, copra, and palm oil; and South Korea for wheat.[226] Variable export levies are still used in some contexts. For example, the Ghana Cocoa Board has sought to ensure some inter-year price stability through the manipulation of the export tax component.[227]

#### e) *State Trading*

State trading in agriculture covers a large variety of entities. They range from governmental departments, to quasi-governmental entities, to private companies with special trading rights. They may have exclusive trading rights (monopoly rights over foreign trade, or a domestic monopsony), or concur with private traders. They may have jurisdiction generally, or in respect of specific products, in canalising agencies. They may participate in the market directly or through private operators. And they may operate domestically, internationally, or on both sides. Another important distinction runs across statutory

---

223 Giovanni Anania, *Agricultural Export Restrictions and the WTO: What Options do Policy-Makers Have for Promoting Food Security?* International Centre for Trade and Sustainable Development, ICTSD Issue Paper 50 (Geneva, 2013).

224 See USDA Foreign Agricultural Service, *Vietnam Grain and Feed Annual 2013*, GAIN Report Number VN3016, 3 April 2013, at 18 and WTO, *Trade Policy Review: India*, above n 187, at 77.

225 WTO, *Trade Policy Review: India*, above n 187, at 131.

226 Knudsen and Nash, above n 184, at 542.

227 Refer to note 251 below.

marketing boards and regulatory boards. The former engage in trade. The latter do not transact goods, but set and administer the trade regime through allocation of import licences, by setting prices and traded quantities, or through the specification of standards.

Whatever their institutional form, STEs have been a key vehicle for stabilising agricultural commodity prices in both developed and developing countries. They were the pivot of complex architectures, including stabilisation funds and marketing boards, aimed at stabilising prices intra- and/or inter-annually. These schemes are briefly discussed below, with discrete attention to their configuration in developed and developing countries.[228]

#### i) Agro-STEs in Developed Economies

In the past, state trading had been a traditional feature of the marketing of agricultural products in a few developed economies with significant agricultural trading interests (Australia, New Zealand, Canada, among other countries).[229] In Australia and New Zealand, for example, statutory marketing arrangements were set up for all major agricultural export commodities.[230] The dominant architecture was based on marketing boards. A few combined monopsonistic and monopolistic powers as the sole purchaser and seller of the domestic produce. Their primary objectives were to increase returns to producers and to stabilise prices, production and incomes. The arrangements involved compulsory acquisition of all farm produce by the Board, price and marketing cost pooling from all the product sales, contributions to or withdrawals from a stabilisation fund, and price controls. Most of these boards have been restructured and their monopsony and monopoly powers lifted.[231]

---

228 For a more comprehensive overview, Christopher B. Barrett and Emelly Mutambatsere, "Marketing Boards," in *The New Palgrave Dictionary of Economics*, 2d ed., ed. Steven N. Durlauf and Lawrence E. Blume (London: Palgrave Macmillan, 2008).

229 For a review, Peter T. Bauer, "A Review of the Agricultural Marketing Schemes," *Economica* 15 (1948).

230 In Australia, for example, statutory marketing arrangements were set up for dairy products, wheat, sugar, rice, wool, coarse grains and oilseeds, apples and pears, dried fruits, and tobacco. For a review, Industry Commission, *Statutory Marketing Arrangements for Primary Products*, Report 10 (Canberra: Australian Government Publishing Service, 1991). In New Zealand, exclusive or special trading privileges were granted in respect of apples and pears, hops, dairy products, raspberries, kiwifruit, meat, wheat and flour, citrus fruits, bananas, pineapples and grapes, honey, eggs, and potatoes (WTO, *Trade Policy Review: New Zealand* (G/STR/N/4/NZL, 5 May 1999)).

231 Reform policies have included: the unbundling of regulatory and marketing functions; increased commercial orientation of the marketing vehicle; and removal of government-funded concessional credits to the marketing entity.

In the advanced market-based economies, far fewer statutory marketing arrangements exist than previously. Yet, in a few cases, exclusive or special trading privileges continue to be granted in respect of specific agricultural exports. In Canada, for example, the Canadian Wheat Board (CWB) is solely responsible, on behalf of producers, for the domestic (inter-provincial) and export marketing of wheat and barley grown in the 'designated' area of Western Canada (Box 6). The CWB accounts for the bulk of wheat exports from Canada,[232] or about 13 percent of world wheat exports.[233] In New Zealand, the Zespri Group Limited, successor to the New Zealand Kiwifruit Marketing Board, has "automatic but not sole right to export kiwifruit".[234] Zepri accounts for 98 percent of kiwifruit exports from New Zealand, with over 20 percent of the world market share.[235] These STEs are still pivotal in stabilising prices by means of price pooling.

**Box 6: The Canadian Wheat Board**

The CWB was established under the *Canadian Wheat Board Act* in 1935. Its statutory objective is the orderly marketing, in inter-provincial and export trade, of Canadian grain. The CWB enjoys the exclusive right to purchase and sell Western Canadian wheat and barley for export and domestic human consumption. The Board pools the returns from wheat and barley sales over the crop year. Producers participating in the pool receive an initial payment, fixed for an entire marketing year, when they deliver grain to a primary elevator. The initial price is generally equal to 65 to 70 percent of the estimated final market value of the grain. Farmers receive a final payment at the end of a crop year, after all grain has been sold and all costs, including CWB's marketing costs, have been deduced. CWB's export prices are benchmarked against relevant US futures exchange prices and those of competing suppliers from other origins; domestic prices are a function of the relevant US prices. Export sales of western Canadian wheat and barley are effected by the CWB directly or through its accredited exporters.[236]

232 A notified 90 percent of wheat and 100 percent of barley exports from Canada in 2010/11. Canadian notification G/STR/N/14/CAN, 6 July 2012.

233 UNCTADstat, Merchandise trade matrix – detailed products, exports in thousands of dollars, annual, 2013, SITC Rev. 3 [041] "Wheat (including spelt) and meslin, unmilled".

234 Notification to the WTO by New Zealand (G/STR/N/15/NZL of 22 May 2014).

235 Notification to the WTO by New Zealand (G/STR/N/15/NZL of 22 May 2014), statistical appendix, UN Comtrade data (2012), and Zespri company information at http://www.zespri.com/companyinformation/faqs.

236 Notification to the WTO by Canada (G/STR/N/14/CAN of 6 July 2012).

To perform its statutory objective, the CWB enjoys special trading rights that make it unlike most 'commercial' grain traders. These special and exclusive rights include: monopoly rights to purchase and sale Western Canadian grain; the right to establish the initial payment price to producers, even if below full market value, with any remaining income disbursed through 'pool' payments; and government guarantees of the initial purchase price paid to producers, of CWB borrowings, and of certain CWB credit sales to foreign buyer.[237] It has been asserted that these privileges translate in significant competitive advantages for the CWB.[238] In particular, the exclusive right to purchase grain, together with the right to set the initial purchase price paid to producers, would give the CWB a stable supply of wheat at a cost of acquisition below its market value. Likewise, government backing of CWB borrowings would translate into lower interest rates, while public guarantee of certain CWB credit sales would allow the CWB to extend credit to high-risk buyers.

Sources: WTO Doc. G/STR/N/14/CAN of 6 July 2012; Panel Report, *Canada – Measures Relating to Exports of Wheat and Treatment of Imported Grain*, WT/DS276/R, adopted 27 September 2004.

In some contexts, state trading continues to feature importantly on the import side of the trade equation. For example, Japan's Ministry of Agriculture, Forestry and Fisheries (MAFF) has exclusive rights to the importation of in-quota rice,[239] as does the Ministry for Food, Agriculture, Forestry and Fisheries (MIFAFF) in Korea.[240]

---

237 Panel Report, *Canada – Measures Relating to Exports of Wheat and Treatment of Imported Grain*, WT/DS276/R, adopted 27 September 2004, upheld by Appellate Body Report WT/DS276/AB/R, DSR 2004:VI, p. 2817 [hereafter, *Canada – Wheat Exports and Grain Imports*]. For the appeal case, Appellate Body Report, *Canada – Measures Relating to Exports of Wheat and Treatment of Imported Grain*, WT/DS276/AB/R, adopted 27 September 2004, DSR 2004:VI, p. 2739.

238 The United States challenged on these grounds the CWB export regime, claiming its inconsistency with the obligations of Canada under Article XVII:1 of the GATT 1994. Panel Report, *Canada – Wheat Exports and Grain Imports*, above n 237.

239 Rice imports under the minimum access opportunities and wheat and barley imports under the current access opportunities, both of which are established in Schedule XXXVIII-JAPAN in the WTO Agreement. WTO, *Trade Policy Review: Japan – Revision* (WT/TPR/S/276/Rev.1, 18 June 2013).

240 Within the limit of quotas on rice as established in Korea's Schedule. WTO, *Trade Policy Review: Republic of Korea* (WT/TPR/S/268/Rev.1, 8 November 2012).

### ii) Agro-STEs in Developing Countries

State trading has been a key feature of the marketing of export cash crops in the developing economies.[241] Even in this context, all but a few marketing boards and stabilisation funds have been dismantled or deprived of trading privileges. Yet, there are calls for their reinstatement. Statutory marketing continues to feature importantly in staple foods, at least in some contexts, notably, Asia. In some countries such as India, it is becoming increasingly prominent. In a rather subtle way, this is occurring through entities that handle strategic food reserves, which are stepping back into statutory marketing.

#### *Export Cash Crops*

Export monopoly marketing boards and stabilisation funds (*caisses de stabilisation*) had in the past been a prominent feature of developing countries' export trade for key tropical cash crops. This was notably the case in tropical Africa, for such export cash crops as cocoa, coffee, cotton, tea, palm oil and ground-nuts.[242] In the 1980s, the bulk of agricultural export trade of African countries was conducted under the control of such boards and funds.[243] Their origin lies in the colonial period.[244] In 1947–1949, statutory monopolies were established over the export of all major agricultural crops from British West Africa (Nigeria, the Gold Coast, Sierra Leone, and the Gambia).[245] Similar

241 For comprehensive reviews, Krueger, above n 184; Takamasa Akiyama et al., *Commodity Market Reforms : Lessons of Two Decades*, World Bank Regional and Sectoral Studies (Washington, D.C., 2001).

242 Jones, above n 183, at 379.

243 John C. Abbott, "Agricultural Marketing Boards in the Developing Countries," *Journal of Farm Economics* 49, no. 3 (1967): 709, 706.

244 See Peter T. Bauer, "Origins of Statutory Export Monopolies of British West Africa," *The Business History Review* 28, no. 3 (1954); David Meredith, "State Controlled Marketing and Economic "Development": The Case of West African Produce during the Second World War," *The Economic History Review* 39, 1 (1986); David Meredith, "The Colonial Office, British Business Interests and the Reform of Cocoa Marketing in West Africa, 1937–1945," *The Journal of African History* 29, 2 (1988); Gavin Williams, "Marketing Without and With Marketing Boards: The Origins of State Marketing Boards in Nigeria," *Review of African Political Economy* 12, no. 34 (1985).

245 Bauer, "A Review of the Agricultural Marketing Schemes," above n 229: 197. For an assessment of the establishment of marketing boards in British West Africa in the 1940s: Bauer, "Origins of Statutory Export Monopolies of British West Africa," above n 244: 205; Meredith, "State Controlled Marketing," above n 244: 77–91; Meredith, "The Colonial Office," above n 244: 285–300; Williams, above n 244. Marketing Boards in British West Africa originated in the Second World War. They were set up to assure supplies of strategic agricultural commodities to Britain and were perpetuated after. Before their establishment,

marketing systems were then introduced throughout British Africa and in other British colonies.[246] The *caisses de stabilisation* in the former French African colonies were likewise inherited from the colonial period.

Marketing boards and stabilisation funds differed in their functions and institutional set-up, though both set and fixed producer prices (Box 7). Marketing boards such as the Ghana Cocoa Board (COCOBOD) consisted of parastatals with a monopoly over domestic and external marketing. They handled the crop at all stages of the domestic and external marketing chain, typically through several subsidiaries or through closely controlled private agents. The funds, such as Côte d'Ivoire's *Caisse de Stabilisation et de Soutien des Prix des Produits Agricoles*, (CAISTAB), did not transact goods, but set and administered the trade regime. This typically occurred through allocation of trading licences and through a schedule of prices, costs and margins throughout the marketing chain. In spite of these differences, both marketing boards and stabilisation funds set and fixed producer prices and engaged in intra-year and inter-year price stabilisation.

### Box 7: COCOBOD and CAISTAB

Until the 1992/93 marketing year, the Ghana Cocoa Board (COCOBOD) controlled the marketing chain from farmgate through export. COCOBOD's domestic marketing subsidiary (the Produce Buying Company (PBC)) was the sole purchaser of cocoa. It bought the crop at farmgate (at 2,000 village-level buying centres), arranged and paid for transport and storage, and sold on to the COCOBOD's exporting subsidiary. Producer prices were administratively fixed for the entire crop year by the Producer Price Review Committee, consisting of COCOBOD representatives, government officials and private stakeholders. The cocoa takeover price (i.e. the PBC selling price to the COCOBOD's exporting subsidiary) was also administratively set to cover producer prices and the PBC marks-up. COCOBOD's exporting company had the monopoly on cocoa exports (and of sales to local processors). Around 60–70 percent of Ghana's cocoa was sold forward over the counter. The difference between export (f.o.b.) and producer prices covered marketing costs, including domestic marketing costs and so-called 'fobbing' costs (maritime freight and insurance), COCOBOD's operating and administrative expenses, the explicit export tax, and a stabilisation margin (used to stabilise prices between seasons). In 1992/93, domestic procurement and transportation

British merchant firms had dominated the trade through purchase cartels. The marketing Boards eventually replaced the merchant firms at the top of the system.

246 Bauer, above.

were opened to private operators. Since 2000/01, licensed buying companies are allowed to export up to 30 percent of their cocoa purchases.

Côte d'Ivoire's *Caisse de Stabilisation* (CAISTAB) did not handle the crop, though it licensed the traders, and authorised each individual export shipment. Furthermore, CAISTAB regulated the entire marketing chain through an official schedule of prices, costs and margins (the *barème*). The schedule was set annually at the beginning of each season. It started with CAISTAB's assessment of the reference export (c.i.f.) price for the coming season, based on the price obtained in forward sales and the projected spot price for the remaining crop during the current season. The c.i.f. price was then expressed on a f.o.b. basis (guaranteed export price), by deducing estimated 'fobbing' costs. The farmgate price was administratively set by deducing domestic marketing costs, the explicit export tax (the *droit unique de sortie*) and CAISTAB's operating costs from the f.o.b. price. All these costs and prices were set and fixed at the beginning of the marketing year. The stabilisation margin (the difference between the export price and world prices) was used to stabilise prices across seasons. CAISTAB's pricing and licensing system was eventually abandoned in 1999.

Forward sales of cocoa (covering about 60–70 percent of next year's crop) were the cornerstone of both the Ghanaian and Ivorian systems, in that they permitted COCOBOD and CAISTAB to lock-in intra-annual prices (and, in the Ivorian case, margins) along the chain.

Sources: COCOBOD; Akiyama et al., above n 241; Varangis and McIntire, above n 205.

These statutory arrangements faced serious financial difficulties and major operational inefficiencies. In particular, marketing boards crowded out private actors and ended up absorbing a significant share of the export price.[247] All but a few schemes were eventually dismantled, under domestic and external reform pressure.

Yet, there are pressures for their reinstatement. In Côte d'Ivoire for example, the Government envisages reintroducing publicly managed forward sales of cocoa.[248] Note also that while most of the African export marketing boards and buffer funds have now been dismantled or deprived of their trading rights, their importance continues to be conspicuous in some contexts. This

247 Akiyama et al., above n 241.

248 The Government envisages selling forward between 70 and 80 percent of Côte d'Ivoire cocoa harvest, so as to lock-in prices within the season for approximately 800,000 cocoa farmers. Gauze, above n 2.

is notably the case of India,[249] and Ghana.[250] Some schemes have managed to effectively stabilise prices within the season by mans of publicly managed forward sales as with cocoa in Ghana,[251] or in non-agricultural commodities, through financial hedging as with sovereign oil hedging in Mexico.[252] Physical

249 In India, STEs are granted special privileges to export, among other, some agricultural and minor forest products, grown or harvested by large numbers of small farmers or tribal farmers.

250 The Ghana Cocoa Board (COCOBOD) still controls the export trade of cocoa in Ghana.

251 Ghana's cocoa is still sold forward by the trading arm of Ghana's Cocoa Board (the Ghana Cocoa Marketing Company Limited (CMC)) through forward contracts (typically, 12 months forward contracts). Forward selling is based on production forecasts: 70 percent of the previous year volume is sold forward (historical forecast); the amount is then adjusted through actual forecasts. The selling price is based on international price benchmarks (futures prices on the London terminal market or at NYSE/LIFFE, closest delivery date), plus a premium (about 10 percent). The trade is not conducted in an organised marketplace or exchange: forward contracts are privately negotiated between the Cocoa Marketing Company and buyers. Branch offices in London and other consuming countries receive bids from buyers for transmission to Accra for decision and then the sale is bilaterally agreed off-exchange. There are about 17 big buyers, with established long-term relationship. Forward selling offers cocoa farmers in Ghana an insurance policy against price risk. The farmgate (producer) price of cocoa is set at the beginning of the harvest season for the entire crop year (stabilisation of seasonal prices). The price is based on the export price (futures prices plus Ghana premium (10 percent)), less the 'fobbing costs' (insurance and freight), to arrive at what is called 'net f.o.b. price': 70 percent of this price goes to the farmer; 30 percent is left to cover the Board's operating costs, internal marketing (local buying) and storage costs, quality control, and the export tax. The export tax component is flexibly adjusted, to keep nominal producer prices constant across seasons, to the extent possible.

252 Sovereign hedging has been used mainly for non-agricultural commodities (oil). In 2009, Mexico hedged all its net oil exports for 2010 through put options – thus setting a price floor on its future oil sales, without giving away potential upside. In the past, Ecuador, Colombia, Algeria, Texas and Louisiana have likewise hedged their oil exports through derivative contracts. There are several obstacles to sovereign hedging in developing countries: high upfront costs, significant political risks, and the likelihood of speculative attacks, if traders learn that a big producer is forward selling its output, or is buying put options against low prices. Yet, sovereign hedging remains an attractive policy option to insure against falling prices (export cash crops) or rising prices (cereals imports in NFIDCs). If upfront costs (insurance premium and broker commissions) were covered by donor money through well-designed technical assistance projects, significant political obstacles could be eased. Gregory Meyer, "Mexico Hedges Against Falling Oil Prices," *Financial Times*, 8 December 2009; Javier Blas, "Mexico's Big Gamble on Oil Pays Off," *Financial*

and financial pledges are a means to lock-in minimum selling prices, and offer price insurance to producers against falling export prices. They entail a move from direct price control to more sophisticated, market-based approaches. Financial hedging also involves a shift in policy emphasis, from price stabilisation to managing the effects of price instability.

*Domestic Staple Foods*

A few stabilising STEs have essentially intervened in the internal marketing of basic consumption items. The operational schemes involved domestic buffer stocks, marketing boards and strategic reserves. In most cases, government control of imports and/or exports through the STE was, and is, an integral part of the domestic price stabilisation arrangement.

The buffer stocks, operated by either government agencies, or 'parastatal' entities, purchase, hold, and release stocks at trigger prices to counter market price movements. Buffer stocks trade on their own account, in competition with commercial actors. Stocks are maintained through domestic procurement, at set or market prices, or through imports. They essentially deal with basic consumption items, such as cereals, meat and dairy products.[253] Domestic buffer stocks have been widely used in Latin America, South and Southeast Asia, and the Near-Eastern countries. They are still in use in many contexts. Notable examples include the rice stocking intervention by Perum Bulog in Indonesia[254] and by the NFA in the Philippines.[255]

Like buffer stocks, domestic monopoly marketing boards engage in internal and external marketing. This can occur directly, through the boards own purchasing and selling stations and agents, or through licenced private companies. Differently from buffer stocks, domestic monopoly marketing boards often have exclusive trading rights and typically set prices at various stages of the domestic chain. Common in East and Central Africa (for example, the National Marketing Corporation in Tanzania and the National Cereals and Produce Board in Kenya), the boards were primarily intended to overcome technical deficiencies in internal marketing, and assure adequate supply of basic foodstuff.

---

*Times*, 7 September 2009; Javier Blas and Adam Thomson, "Mexico Hedges Oil Exports for 2009," *Financial Times*, 11 November 2008.

253 For a review of buffer stock schemes in developing countries, Knudsen and Nash, above n 184.

254 WTO, *Trade Policy Review: Indonesia*, above n 204, at 61.

255 WTO, *Trade Policy Review: The Philippines*, above n 198.

Strategic food reserves serve food security purposes, rather than price objectives. They should thus be kept distinct from price stabilising buffer stocks and marketing boards. In practice, however, the line is not easy to draw. In a few developing countries, price stabilisation, support, and food security objectives have traditionally been complexly interlaced. For example, the statutory purpose of Perum BULOG, as notified by Indonesia, is: "to support domestic rice producers, to stabilise the price of rice at consumer and producer levels, and to enhance food security".[256] In the Philippines, the NFA has a two-fold mandate: "ensure food security in staple cereals in times and places of emergency, both natural or man-made" thus, food security; and "ensure farmgate price levels that enable farmers to derive reasonable returns on their production investment on the one hand, and ensuring reasonable retail prices" thus price stabilisation and support.[257] In a number of countries, large-scale food procurement from farmers at administered prices to set up or replenish food stocks has turned into a key price stabilisation and support measure. These schemes, which vary widely in their design and price objectives, have been discussed in some detail in Box 3.

Domestic grain boards and buffer stocks have faced significant organisational challenges in the past. A few entailed substantial financial losses and generated sizeable public liabilities. In many contexts especially in Africa, the inefficiency of their operations brought the boards under attack and led to their dismantlement.[258] In other settings especially in Asia, their importance continues to be momentous.

#### 2.2.2.2 Income Stabilisation

Domestic farm stabilisation policies are not confined to market (price) intervention, whether direct or indirect. As mentioned, income support measures in the form of direct transfers have emerged as a key policy alternative to price intervention, particularly in the advanced economies. More recently, farm revenue insurance and other risk-management tools have been suggested as a less costly way than governmental direct payments to stabilise incomes.

256 Notification to the WTO by Indonesia (G/STR/N/11/IDN, G/STR/N/12/IDN, 9 February 2009), at 1.

257 Notification to the WTO by the Philippines (G/STR/N/4/PHL, G/STR/N/5/PHL, G/STR/N/6/PHL, G/STR/N/7/PHL, 24 September 2002), at 2.

258 Akiyama et al., above n 241.

Direct payments to producers involve a variety of schemes.[259] In WTO terms, some fall under the Amber and Blue Boxes of trade-distorting support, while others are exempted Green Box subsidies.[260]

The most trade-distorting schemes involve variable rate payments to farmers based on current prices, income, or cost. These schemes in effect stabilise the price producers receive, though by other means than market price intervention. They include compensatory or deficiency payments to farmers, triggered when current market prices fall below a reference level (typically, a moving average of market prices).[261] Another recurrent scheme is that of commodity loan schemes such as the US marketing assistance loan scheme, or Thailand's rice mortgage scheme (now discontinued), whereby producers obtain a loan by pledging the crop as collateral.[262] Producers have then the option of either repaying the loan, capital plus interests, or deliver the collateral. All of these income support measures tend to have discernible price support effects[263] and are to be notified in the WTO under the trade-distorting Amber Box.[264] The dividing line between income and price support is here hardly precise.

---

259 The OECD provides the following taxonomy: payments with or without current commodity production limits and/or limits to payments; with variable or fixed payment rates; with or without input constraints; based on area, animal numbers, receipts or income; based on a single commodity, group of commodities or all commodities; with or without commodity exceptions. See OECD, "Producer Support Estimate and Related Indicators of Agricultural Support: Concepts, Calculations, Interpretation and Use," July 2008 [hereafter, *The PSE Manual*].

260 In WTO terminology, Green Box subsidies, defined in Annex 2 of the WTO AoA, are non or minimally trade distorting subsidies, unconstrained; Amber Box subsidies (Articles 6 and 7 of the AoA and Annex 3) are trade distorting subsidies, subject to limits; Blue Box subsidies (exempted) are also linked to production, but under production-limiting schemes (Article 6.5 of the AoA).

261 The amount received may depend on marketed quantities (current output) (e.g. payments under the Agricultural Stabilization Act in Canada), or historical acreage / yields (e.g. deficiency payments under the Price Loss Coverage (PLC) programme in the US, introduced under the 2014 Farm Bill).

262 The amount of the loan is determined by the loan rate, governmentally set, multiplied by the quantity produced.

263 For example, 'coupled' payments, such as commodity loan programmes or counter-cyclical payments in the US under the Farm Security and Rural Investment Act were acknowledged to have discernible influence on production decisions. See WTO, *Trade Policy Review: United States* (WT/TPR/S/200, 5 May 2008), at 85.

264 The Trade Policy Review of the United States endorsed research by the US Department of Agriculture pointing to the fact that "[...] payments under some commodity programmes (e.g. marketing assistance loans) provide incentives for resource use that may be

Other schemes involve direct payments at fixed rates unrelated to prices, income or cost. If decoupled from production, they can be notified in terms of Green Box under the WTO Agreement on Agriculture.[265] While described as 'non-distorting', these arrangements, in fact, provide a fixed revenue floor for producers. It has been argued, in particular, that they may well have a bearing on output and prices by providing incentives for resource use that may be inconsistent with market signals.[266] An increasing body of theoretical and empirical literature points in this direction.

All the above schemes transfer price and income risks to the public sector and involve direct subsidies. Other instruments leverage market dynamics and transfer risk to the private sector. This is the case of farm revenue insurance and market-based risk management tools. Revenue insurance protects farmers against income fluctuations caused by price or production variability. In exchange for this protection, farmers pay an annual premium that reflects their individual risks. Some schemes are purely private. Others involve a high degree of subsidisation (governmentally subsidised private insurance schemes). The most commercially-oriented farmers can also use commodity derivatives such as futures, options and swaps to hedge price risks (see *infra*, Section 4.1.2.2).

inconsistent with market signals and may affect trade when supported output finds its way into world markets" (WTO, *Trade Policy Review: United States*, at 79). In particular, "[…] marketing assistance loans provide an incentive to plant more than would be the case in their absence" (ibid, at 85) and "[…] counter-cyclical payments may provide for the reduction of price-related revenue risk, and could also have some influence on production decisions" (ibid).

265 Notable examples include Direct Payments (DP) and their predecessor (Production Flexibility Contract (PFC) payments) in the US, a key instrument of US agricultural farm support until the 2014 Farm Bill. DP and PFC were eliminated at the end the 2013 crop year.

266 In this direction: Ricardo Meléndez-Ortiz et al., eds., *Agricultural Subsidies in the WTO Green Box* (Cambridge: Cambridge University Press, 2009); Apelu Tielu and Ivan Roberts, *Farm Income Support: Implications for Gains from Trade of Changes in Methods of Support Overseas*, ABARE Current Issues 98, no. 4 (1998); Rashmi Banga, *Impact of Green Box Subsidies on Agricultural Productivity, Production and International Trade*, Unit of Economic Cooperation and Integration among Developing Countries, UNCTAD, Background Paper No. RVC-11 (Geneva, 2014); *Agreement on Agriculture: Green Box / Annex 2 Subsidies – Proposal to the June 2000 Special Session of the Committee on Agriculture by Cuba, Dominican Republic, Honduras, Pakistan, Haiti, Nicaragua, Kenya, Uganda, Zimbabwe, Sri Lanka and El Salvador* (WTO Document G/AG/NG/W/14, 23 June 2000). Even the most undisputed schemes, namely, general services, have an obvious bearing on the famous 'level-playing field' between countries, as a country's agricultural competitiveness is proactively shaped by the extent and quality of its supply-side services.

Overall, direct payments to producers, along with other arrangement such as revenue insurance, can provide a viable alternative to direct or indirect price intervention. Yet, they may involve huge budgetary outlays. Furthermore, they entail high transaction costs and efficient administrations. Their workability in a context of weak governance, high informality and widespread poverty is open to question.

### 2.2.3 *Assessment*

A few considerations arise from the above cursory review of major price stabilisation arrangements at the international and domestic levels.

First, stabilisation policies are multifaceted and entangled. They entail a variety of measures, typically, a combination of border and domestic measures, in practice intertwined. As discussed in the following analysis, this entangled set of policies raise discrete regulatory issues that come under the purview of trade law.

Second, commodity price stabilisation is multi-layered. There is much history to look at, beyond concerted intergovernmental action on prices by producing and consuming countries. First, dual-interest arrangements are to be set against the background of producers' cartel-type arrangements, and particularly the intensified drive towards commodity cartelisation in the 1960s and 70s. Second, they coexist with domestic policies (stockpiling, variable tariffs and subsidies and so on) to cushion the domestic impact of international price fluctuations. It is important to grasp the complexity of this multi-layered order, in order to appreciate correctly the limits, but also the significance and distinctiveness of multilateral action on prices.

Third, it is difficult, in this area, to delineate the boundaries between what is genuinely domestic and what raises international concerns. Domestic stabilisation schemes most often are a matter of international concern. On the import side, they routinely involve some form of tariff protection to offset the competitive edge of imports, which restricts market access. On the export side, internal efforts to stabilise domestic producer prices at relatively high levels, if not coupled with output restrictions, may stimulate oversupply and result in large exportable surplus. If aggressively disposed of on export markets, potentially by means of export subsidies, this surplus can severely depress world market prices, displace other countries' exports, and, in a vicious circle, exert downward pressure on domestic farmgate prices elsewhere. This was the case of Community sugar exports enhanced through the use of subsidies,[267] and

267 Subsidised Community sugar exports severely depressed world market prices and displaced other countries' exports (see GATT Panel Report, *European Communities – Refunds*

of subsidised US cotton exports.[268] Similar concerns have been raised more recently in connection with stocking arrangements by large developing economies (India, Thailand and China, among others). Overall, particularly for countries whose supply and demand are large, the so-called 'price-makers', it is very difficult to disentangle domestic and international perspectives. Unilateral action on domestic prices almost inevitably entails important repercussions beyond the border. This complicates the dichotomy between domestic and international policies, and between areas of domestic policy discretion and of international concern.

Finally, it is important to acknowledge that, on matters of commodity prices no country held consistently to its neoliberal creed. Countries that preached free trade abroad were intervening massively in their farm economy and those same countries that most opposed international commodity agreements (the US and Germany, *in primis*) were using the world market as a 'safety valve' for their own stabilisation operations.[269] In Hager's words, in dealing with agricultural commodities, "almost at every turn political reality thwarts economic rationality".[270]

## 2.3 Agriculture, Price Stabilisation and Trade Rules: Seizing the Interface

How are stabilisation policies apprehended and regulated by trade law? A line is drawn between ICAs and domestic stabilisation schemes. The former are comprehensively carved out from key multilateral trade disciplines, with some qualifications. The latter are not regulated as such, but in their discrete policy tools, in so far as they distort trade.

---

*on Exports of Sugar – Complaint by Brazil*, L/5011, adopted 10 November 1980, BISD 27S/69, paras. 79–80).

268 US price-based support measures for upland cotton were found to have contributed to depress world cotton prices, causing 'serious prejudice' to the trade interests of other cotton exporting countries (Panel Report, *United States – Subsidies on Upland Cotton*, WT/DS267/R, Add.1 to Add.3 and Corr.1., adopted 21 March 2005, as modified by Appellate Body Report WT/DS267/AB/R, DSR 2005:II, p. 299).

269 In what has been termed the "duplicity of the free trade dogma". Michael L. Hager, "Commodity Agreements and the Developing Countries: A Collective Bargaining Approach," *International Lawyer* 7, no. 2 (1973): 311.

270 Ibid, at 313.

This Chapter provides and overview of the regulatory issues at stake and clarifies the relationship between the main relevant WTO Agreements (Section 2.3.1). This sets the overall context for the following analysis, which separately examines the regulation of international (Section 2.3.2) and domestic (Section 2.3.3) price stabilisation schemes.

### 2.3.1 *The Regulatory Framework*

Price stabilisation schemes raise regulatory issues that come within the purview of international trade law. The legal issues involved are many and multifaceted. Yet, as discussed through this Chapter, they essentially revolve around three key areas of regulatory concern: non-discrimination; market access; and subsidisation, both internal (domestic support) and external (export subsidies). As discussed, the relevant trade rules are countless, and straddle across discrete areas of international trade regulation. They include, among other: disciplines on subsidies laid down in the WTO AoA and the WTO ASCM; rules on STEs under the GATT; as well as market access disciplines as provided for in the GATT and the AoA. Before considering in depth some of the regulatory issues involved, it is important to clarify some aspects of the complex relationship between the GATT and the AoA, and between the AoA and the ASCM, so as to lay the groundwork for the following analysis.

#### 2.3.1.1 GATT and AoA

With specific reference to agricultural price stabilisation, how do GATT provisions relate to the AoA? Specifically, to what extent does the AoA supersede conflicting GATT disciplines? This question has specific relevance to the issue area under consideration, that is, the regulation of farm stabilisation policies. In this area, the provisions of the GATT and of the AoA complement each other, but also stipulate somewhat contradictory obligations. Regulatory coherence is restored through conflict clauses in the AoA. Note that mutual exclusiveness only applies in case of conflict, but not generally. WTO Panels and the Appellate Body seek to bring about mutually supportive interpretations and to avoid conflict of rules. It is worth exploring these issues in some detail.

On matters of agricultural price stabilisation policies, GATT and the AoA are complementary and mutually supportive, in a number of key respects. First, concessions and commitments framed by the AoA are incorporated into the GATT. Specifically, country-specific commitments on domestic support, export subsidies and market access, as framed by the AoA, are incorporated in a Member's Schedule and made integral part of the GATT. Second, the GATT still complements existing AoA rules. In particular, it lays down basic trade rules, such as the non-discrimination obligation and the prohibition of quantitative restrictions, which apply to stabilisation schemes, unless exceptional clauses come into play (see below). Furthermore, it establishes key disciplines in specific areas, such as state trading, that are not *per se* specifically addressed by the AoA. Finally, mutual supportiveness is sought through the interpretative process: in interpreting WTO rules, Panels and the Appellate Body use their discretion to bring about mutually supportive interpretations and to avoid conflict of rules.

Yet, some grey areas remain, particularly with respect to whether some exceptional clauses enshrined in the GATT are still operative, or have been superseded by the AoA. Reference is here to the 'managed economy' provisions of the GATT. Two sets of disciplines come into focus. The first set of rules consists of provisions that lay down criteria for international action on commodity prices: GATT Article XX (h), and the relevant provisions contained in Articles XXXVI and XXXVIII of the GATT (see below, Section 2.3.2). This special commodity trade regime was largely elaborated outside of the GATT framework, under the aegis of the Havana Conference and within the framework of UNCTAD. It has been 'grafted' onto the GATT through the GATT Article XX(h) exemption. A second set of controversial provisions are enshrined in Article XI:2(c) of the GATT. This latter exempts certain domestic supply management schemes from the general prohibition of quantitative restrictions under the GATT. This exemption, as discussed in Section 2.3.3.2, is subject to stringent requirements.

The exceptions in GATT Articles XX (h) and XI:2(c) are particularly important in the context of agricultural price stabilisation. They provide significant room, particularly at the international level, for otherwise GATT inconsistent price stabilisation arrangements. When the exempted schemes involve measures proscribed under the AoA, questions remain as to whether these GATT exceptions have been superseded by the AoA.

The AoA provides guidance on how to reconcile these GATT provisions and the AoA market access disciplines, while leaving some issues open to interpretation. As a general rule, if conflicts cannot be avoided, the AoA prevails over the GATT, pursuant to Article 21 of the AoA and as *lex specialis* or *lex posterior* under general conflict rules.[271] Yet, there are instances where the AoA

271 AoA Article 21.1 states: "The provisions of GATT 1994 and of other Multilateral Trade Agreements in Annex 1A to the WTO Agreement shall apply subject to the provisions of this Agreement."

specifically exempts measures otherwise inconsistent with the AoA, if maintained under GATT rules. In detail, footnote 1 to Article 4.2 of the AoA exempts certain measures maintained under general GATT exceptions from the prohibition on non-tariff measures established by Article 4.2 of the AoA.[272] Specifically, the text of the note allows border measures other than ordinary customs duties[273] if "maintained under balance-of-payments provisions or under other general, non-agriculture-specific provisions of GATT 1994 or of the other Multilateral Trade Agreements in Annex 1A to the WTO Agreement".[274] This exemption has been interpreted quite narrowly in jurisprudence.[275] It has been held to cover measures maintained under general safeguards and exception provisions of the GATT (in essence, Articles XII, XVIII, XIX, XX and XXI), but not under other substantive GATT rules.[276] One relevant case seems to point in the direction that measures maintained under agriculture-specific exceptions (like supply management schemes under GATT Article XI:2(c)) could still be challenged under the AoA's market access disciplines.[277] The same would hold for measures consistent with general GATT rules, but proscribed by Article 4.2 of the AoA (for example, variable import tariffs within a Member's bound rate, i.e consistent with GATT Article II:1(b)).[278]

In line with this interpretation, stabilisation arrangements, if maintained under general exception provisions of the GATT such as Article XX (h) would be excluded from the scope of the AoA's market access obligations. Yet, they could be challenged as under other AoA relevant disciplines. Conversely, stabilisation arrangements maintained under agriculture-specific exceptions (like supply management schemes under GATT Article XI:2(c)) could still be challenged under the AoA's market access disciplines. The same would hold for measures consistent with general GATT rules, but proscribed by Article 4.2 of the AoA (for example, variable levies within a Member's bound rate, if held consistent with GATT Article II:1(b)).[279]

---

272 In addition, certain members could maintain, through the implementation period, import restrictions compliant with the requirements of Annex 5 to the AoA.

273 Specifically, "quantitative import restrictions, variable import levies, minimum import prices, discretionary import licensing, non-tariff measures maintained through state-trading enterprises, voluntary export restraints, and similar border measures other than ordinary customs duties".

274 Note 1 to Article 4.2 of the AoA.

275 See in particular Panel Report, *Chile – Price Band System*, above n 210.

276 Ibid, paras 7.71 to 7.73.

277 See in particular Panel Report, *Chile – Price Band System*, above n 210, paras 7.71 to 7.73.

278 Ibid.

279 Ibid.

#### 2.3.1.2 AoA and ASCM

As extensively discussed *infra*, price regulation and other stabilisation approaches raise issues of subsidisation. Relevant disciplines are laid down in the AoA and the ASCM. Can subsidies maintained under the AoA be challenged under the ASCM?

Until the end of 2003, agricultural subsidies otherwise permitted under the AoA could not be challenged under other WTO Agreements, including the ASCM. This pursuant to a 'Peace Clause' enshrined in Article 13 of the AoA ('Due Restraint'). More specifically, there was complete exemption from Green Box subsides.[280] Blue Box subsidies and permitted Amber Box subsidies (within a country's Aggregate Measurement of Support (AMS) ceiling or *de minimis* levels) remained actionable if injury could be proved, but countries were instructed to exercise 'due restraint' in initiating any countervailing duty investigations, so long as support levels did not exceed 1992 levels. They were also exempted from actions based on non-violation nullification or impairment, if support levels did not rise above 1992 levels.[281] Export subsidies committed under the AoA were moved from the ASCM prohibited category to the actionable category, with the warning to exercise due restraint in challenging them.[282] As a matter of fact, the 'due restraint' admonition effectively discouraged countries from challenging agricultural subsidies under the ASCM.

The Peace Clause expired at the end of 2003. Agricultural subsidies otherwise permitted under the AoA can now be challenged under the ASCM. More specifically, domestic subsidies are subject to challenge under the ASCM on the basis of a determination of injury to the interests of another country, regardless of their status under the AoA. Three types of damage are envisaged: to import-competing farmers in the importing country; to exporters from another country in third markets; and to exporters trying to compete in the subsidising country's domestic market. Export subsidies are prohibited, unless permitted under the AoA.[283]

Having clarified the complex relationship between the main relevant Agreements, it is now possible to turn to the regulation of international and domestic stabilisation arrangements, from a trade law angle.

### 2.3.2 *International Schemes*

As mentioned (Section 2.3.1.1), 'control' ICAs can find legal cover under the 'managed economy' provisions of the GATT in particular, GATT Article XX (h)

280 Article 13(a) of the AoA.

281 Article 13(b) of the AoA.

282 Article 13(c) of the AoA.

283 ASCM, Article 3.1.

and the relevant provisions contained in Articles XXXVI and XXXVIII of the GATT. GATT Article XX(h), by way of exception, exempts ICAs from GATT disciplines, when either of two conditions is met: the intergovernmental commodity control arrangement conforms to multilaterally agreed disciplines (the Havana principles, or other criteria agreed upon by the WTO 'legislator'); or the 'control' arrangement is as such "submitted and not so disapproved" by the WTO members. The second provides an escape clause: ICAs that contravene to multilaterally agreed principles could nonetheless find legal cover under the GATT, if notified to and not 'disapproved' by the WTO membership (for a discussion see below). Also relevant are the guidelines for joint action under Article XXXVIII to further the objectives set forth in Article XXXVI, and Article XXXVI. Article XXXVIII (2) (a) allows WTO Members to take "joint action" including through international arrangements for ensuring "stable equitable and remunerative prices" for exports of primary commodities of particular interest to developing countries. The objective "to attain stable, equitable and remunerative prices" is also enshrined in Article XXXVI.

These disciplines are quite vague and open, in at least two important respects. First, the legal status of ICAs that contravene to the Havana principles remains uncertain. This is with regard to both restrictive agreements entered into by producing countries only and plurilateral arrangements between a few producers and consumers.[284]

---

284 Outside the WTO framework, the legitimacy of unilateral producer action was acknowledged in a number of 'soft law' instruments adopted within regional and multilateral frameworks. Public assertions about 'going alone' were recorded at Third World meetings, such as the Dakar meeting of the non-aligned countries in February 1975 and the Third Ministerial Meeting of the Group of 77 in Manila (26 January – 7 February 1976). The G7 Meeting in Manila adopted a proposal for a detailed integrated programme for commodities, the Manila Declaration and Programme of Action, which emphasised, among other, unilateral producer action (*Proceedings of the United Nations Conference on Trade and Development, Fourth Session, Nairobi, 5–31 May 1976* (New York: United Nations, 1977), vol. I, Annex V). The developing countries reiterated and furthered their stance in the UN General Assembly, pressing for concessions that they had not been able to obtain in more technically oriented discussions, within and outside UNCTAD (J. Robert Vastine jr, "United States International Commodity Policy," *Law and Policy in International Business* 9 (1977)). The 1974 Declaration on the Establishment of a New International Economic Order (NIEO) (UN General Assembly Resolution No. 3201, 1 May 1974) officially sanctioned the role of producers' associations in the pursuit of economic development in developing countries. Similarly, the Charter of Economic Rights and Duties of States (CERDS), among other things, confirmed the right of all states to associate in organisations of primary commodity producers in order to develop their national economies (Charter of Economic Rights and Duties of States, GA Res. 3281 (xxix), 12 Dec. 1974, Article 5). Note, however, that these Resolutions were firmly opposed by a few influential countries that

GATT Article XX (h) does not settle the issue of the permissibility of these arrangements. Producers' only and plurilateral commodity control arrangements run counter two basic tenets of the Havana principles: producer-consumer cooperation; and multilateralism. In this respect, they do not conform to what may be taken as multilaterally agreed principles; and accordingly are not immune from challenge as to their legality under the first part of sub-paragraph (h) of Article XX. Yet they could find legal cover under the GATT, if, in GATT language, 'submitted' and not 'disapproved' (second part of sub-paragraph (h) of GATT Article XX).[285]

Questions arise as to the meaning of the second part of sub-paragraph (h) of GATT Article XX (h). The requirement to 'submit' and not 'disapprove' appears to trigger the waiver process under Article IX (3) of the WTO Agreement. In the current system, there are no cases where a country can seek political approval of an exception invoked; this will be a matter for litigation, if contested. Producers' only and plurilateral restrictive ICAs would need to be justified by means of waiver. As discussed in Section 5.3, the WTO's waiver competence is one of the law-making venues through which the WTO 'legislator' can try to balance trade and stabilisation interests. The waiver procedure may 'legalise' non-compliant ICAs taken by individual members in concrete situations (*ad hoc* waver). Waivers could also be granted to justify producers' only and/or plurilateral control ICAs that comply with abstractedly defined criteria. These collective waiver decisions would contribute towards the definition of multilaterally agreed criteria against which to benchmark the legitimacy of stabilisation arrangements, pursuant to the first part of sub-paragraph (h) of GATT Article XX.[286]

More flexible procedures could possibly be envisaged, in a perspective *de lege ferenda*. Attention is drawn to the information exchange procedures in the

---

clearly stated their opposition to producers' arrangements. Specifically, though the Declaration on the Establishment of a NIEO was eventually adopted, the US, together with several other developed countries, submitted a number of reservations on the texts. The CERDS was adopted by 115 votes to 6, with 10 abstentions. Eventually, little guidance can be drawn from the 'external context', outside the WTO framework, on the legitimacy of unilateral producer action.

285 In the WTO context, by way of waiver, unless more flexible approaches can be envisaged, by leveraging the notification and peer review mechanisms within the Committee on Agriculture.

286 For a discussion of collective waiver decisions in the WTO context and of the role of waivers as rule-making instruments, Isabel Feichtner, "The Waiver Power of the WTO: Opening the WTO for Political Debate on the Reconciliation of Competing Interests," *European Journal of International Law* 20, no. 3 (2009).

WTO Committee on Agriculture, and the associated processes of notification, contestation and justification. Through these venues, the Committee could elaborate on the opened ended language of GATT Article XX (h), and set procedures and possibly substantive norms to pragmatically deal with producers' only and plurilateral ICAs.[287]

In both cases, whether formal waiver or Committee procedures, the legitimacy of producers' arrangements and other plurilateral control schemes remains a political decision, rather than a rule-based one.

Second, questions remain as to the relationship between the managed economic provisions of the GATT and other substantive disciplines under the Annex 1A Agreements. In particular, can GATT-compliant ICAs be challenged under the AoA?

On the import side, these arrangements, if maintained under Article XX (h), may possibly find legal cover under footnote 1 to Article 4 of the AoA. As interpreted in the Chile's PBS case, footnote 1 is to be read "as excluding from the scope of Article 4.2 [of the AoA] those measures which Members are allowed to maintain in accordance with the provisions in GATT 1994 laying down exceptions to the general obligations of GATT 1994".[288] If this interpretation is maintained, ICAs conforming with GATT Article XX(h) could not be challenged under the AoA's market access provisions, Article 4.2.

Eventually, tensions are more likely to arise under the domestic support and export competition pillars of the AoA. It has been observed, for example, that price commitments under multilateral contracts would need to be enforced through export subsidies and export taxes, where the trade is conducted by private merchants, rather than STEs.[289] The AoA provisions on export subsidies do not include conflict clauses similar to footnote 1 to Article 4.2. If conflicts cannot be avoided, the AoA would prevail over the GATT, pursuant to Article 21 of the AoA and as *lex specialis* or *lex posterior* under general conflict rules.

These interpretative issues have not yet been fully addressed in the WTO context. As mentioned, all price-stabilising ICAs have collapsed or lapsed. A legacy of the past, the 'managed economy' provisions of the GATT have not been invoked due to the abolishment of corresponding policies. However, this neglect in practice does not mean termination on grounds of desuetude. Though dormant, the provisions of GATT Article XX(h) and Article XXXVIII are still there, and may be re-activated by new state practice. As with a recessive

287 For a discussion on the possible normative functions of Committee work, refer to Section 5.3.2.

288 Panel Report, *Chile – Price Band System*, above n 210, at para. 7.71.

289 Gilbert, "International Agreements for Commodity Price Stabilisation," above n 144.

gene, they can surface again, even in more radical forms. And certainly renewed intervention in commodity markets is likely to make these GATT flexibilities relevant again. It may act as a 'wake up' call for quiescent disciplines. Interestingly, the December 2008 revised draft modalities[290] contain text that would clarify the permissibility of international action on commodity prices, exempting not only dual-interest ICAs, but also producer agreements.

### 2.3.3 *Domestic Arrangements*

As outlined in the previous Section, agricultural price stabilisation policies typically involve a mixture of trade policy instruments (tariff protection, price support, state trading, etc.), which are complexly interlocked. This complex fabric of intersecting policies is to be scrutinised under the dissecting scope of discrete WTO disciplines. This Section offers only passing reference to some areas of discipline involved. Each would deserve monographic attention, far beyond the reach of this cursory overview.

#### 2.3.3.1 Agricultural Price Controls

From a trade law perspective, governmentally determined prices are not controversial *per se*, nor are trade monopolies, as discussed in Section 2.3.3.5. The critical aspect is the level at which the intervention price is set relative to market prices, assessed by reference to a base-period price. The difference between the acquisition price and the external reference price is accounted for as trade-distorting, or Amber Box support, and is subject to limits.

Under current disciplines (AoA Articles 6.3 and 7.2(b)), price support[291] can be used up to a threshold: either the Member's Bound Total AMS, or the statutory *de minimis* level. As a matter of fact, few developing countries set AMS commitments:[292] for the overwhelming majority of them, including all

---

290 December 2008 revised draft modalities, above n 65.

291 Price support is determined differently for different legal purposes. Under the AoA, price support is calculated using the gap between a fixed external reference price and the applied administered price, multiplied by the quantity of production eligible to receive the applied administered price (AoA, Annex 3, para. 8). The fixed external reference price "shall be based on the years 1986 to 1988 and shall generally be the average f.o.b. unit value for the basic agricultural product concerned in a net exporting country and the average c.i.f. unit value for the basic agricultural product concerned in a net importing country in the base period" (AoA, Annex 3, para. 9). Under the ASCM, the issue is defined in terms of "adequate remuneration", determined with reference to the "prevailing market conditions for the good or service in question in the country" (ASCM, Article 14 (d)).

292 These include: Thailand, Brazil, Argentina, Colombia, Costa Rica, Korea, Mexico, Morocco, Papua New Guinea, Chinese Taipei.

the LDCs, price support is evaluated against the *de minimis* level. The *de minimis* threshold for developing countries allows governments to spend up to 10 percent[293] of the total value of agriculture in a given year on general, trade-distorting support to the agriculture sector; plus a further 10 percent of the production value of each crop, which can be spent on support specific to that crop.[294] As to the way forward, the Doha commitment is to attain further "substantial reductions in trade-distorting support".[295] Yet, significant leeway is made to accommodate policy sensitivities.[296]

It has been observed that current, Uruguay Round, spending thresholds on price and other forms of trade-distorting support are relatively high for developing countries;[297] in most cases well above actual spending levels on domestic support. As a matter of fact, no LDC has fully exploited its flexibility under either the *de minimis* threshold or the AoA Article 6.2 exemption.[298]

Yet, for a few developing economies, the current flexibilities enshrined in multilateral disciplines are under strain. In particular, a number of countries are at risk of exceeding their product-specific AMS limits.[299] In a few countries,

293 Newly acceding countries have negotiated specific terms (e.g. 8.5 percent for China and 5 percent for Chinese Taipei ad South Africa).

294 Developing countries have significant room to resort to other policy instruments. In particular, input subsidies in developing countries are unrestricted, if "generally available to low-income and resource poor producers" (under Article 6.2 of the AoA).

295 World Trade Organization, Ministerial Declaration of 14 November 2001, WT/MIN(01)/DEC/1, para. 13.

296 The latest negotiating text (December 2008 revised draft modalities, above n 65) sets tightened limits on permitted *de minimis* support: for developing countries, this type of support would be capped at 6.7 percent of the average value of production (down from the current 10 percent) (paras. 30–31). However, LDCs and some categories of recently-acceded members would be exempted from these reduction commitments (para. 33); as would be developing countries that allocate almost all their *de minimis* support for "subsistence and resource-poor producers" (para. 32). The second exemption would also cover a few large developing economies (India, Thailand, Indonesia, etc.), as their rural production base is largely composed of peasant farmers.

297 For example, given a total agricultural production of 5,777 billion RMB in 2010, China (8.5 percent *de minimis*) could virtually provide price support up to a maximum 982 RMB billion (product-specific and non-product-specific combined). India also has high overall spending thresholds.

298 As a matter of fact, price support is fiscally burdensome. Particularly in the least-developed countries the *de facto* policy space for support is constrained by budgetary pressures.

299 India, China, Pakistan, Egypt, Turkey, and the Philippines, among other countries, face compliance problems, as reported in a few studies based on publicly available data. Note that different computation methods (e.g. to account for deflation /exchange rate

including India, this is the result of massive public procurement schemes at support price, part of large public stockholding programmes allegedly for food security purposes.[300] Note also that the *de minimis* exemption could be meaningless when the starting point, in the form of the current agricultural output, is low.[301] In cereal-dependent low-income countries that wish to 're-localise' cereals production, current levels of output are negligible, and the *de minimim* threshold of permissible price support, 10 percent of the value of that crop production, is meaningless. As pointed out in Murphy: "10 percent of zero is still zero".[302] Technical flaws add to current strictures. Under existing price support disciplines, administered prices are not assessed against current market prices,

---

movements) lead to different results. Cf. Panos Konandreas and George Mermigkas, *WTO Domestic Support Disciplines: Options for Alleviating Constraints to Stockholding in Developing Countries in the Follow-up to Bali*, FAO Commodity and Trade Policy Research Working Papers, no. 45 (Rome: FAO, 2014); DTB Associates, *Domestic Support and WTO Obligations in Key Developing Countries* (n.p., 2011); DTB Associates, *Agricultural Subsidies in Key Developing Countries: November 2014 Update* (n.p., [2014]); Sudha Narayanan, *The Balance: The National Food Security Act vis- à -vis the WTO Agreement on Agriculture*, Indira Gandhi Institute of Development Research (Mumbai, 2013); Lars Brink, *Support to Agriculture in India in 1995–2013 and the Rules of the WTO*, International Agricultural Trade Research Consortium, IATRC Working Paper 14-01 (2014).

300 India has notified product-specific AMS within its *de minimis* ceiling (G/AG/N/IND/10 of 10 September 2014). The method used by India to calculate support departs from other countries' approach in two important respects. First, India uses a US$-denominated external reference price (ERF), rather than the fixed ERP from its AGST, denominated in Indian Rupees (a departure from the methodology outlined in AoA Article 1(a)(ii)). It has been observed, in this connection, that the India's USD$-denominated ERP is increased by currency depreciation, which reduces the price gap. In this latter respect, there is some ambiguity in the AoA disciplines as to the possibility to adjust the price gap by inflation or exchange rate movements (by means of inflating the fixed ERP, or deflating the support price, or accounting for currency depreciation in foreign-exchange denominated ERP). The second deviation concerns the understanding of 'eligible production': in the case of India, the price gap is multiplied by the actual quantity procured, rather than the total/marketed production. This approach departs from the DSB ruling in *Korea– Various Measures on Beef* (Appellate Body Report, *Korea – Measures Affecting Imports of Fresh, Chilled and Frozen Beef*, WT/DS161/AB/R and WT/DS169/AB/R, adopted 10 January 2001). In the case of India, alternative calculation methods produce different results. Cf. DTB Associates, *Agricultural Subsidies in Key Developing Countries: November 2014 Update*, at 34; Konandreas and Mermigkas, above n 299, at 12–13; Narayanan, above n 299, at 7–8; and Brink, above n 299.

301 Sophia Murphy, *Trade and Food Reserves: What Role Does the WTO Play?* (Institute for Agriculture and Trade Policy, 2010).

302 Ibid, at 9.

but against a base-period price, generally, the average 1986–1988 international price for the product in question.[303] In a number of cases, this external fixed reference price tends to be lower than current market prices, which results in inflated figures on domestic support.[304]

To sum up, in some instances there is a case for more policy space. Yet, this is to be assessed on a case-by-case basis, taking into account the spending capacity of the country concerned.

To provide temporary lee-way for some countries, an interim solution was found in Bali in the form of a peace clause, temporarily shielding certain stockpile programmes (notably, India's scheme under the NFSA) from legal action under the WTO AoA.[305] The Bali 'peace clause' was reaffirmed in Nairobi, where

303 The average export (f.o.b.) price notified for 1986–88, in the case of a net exporters; and the average import (c.i.f.) price in the case of a net importer. AoA Annex 3 (Calculation of Aggregate Measurement of Support).

304 A few countries have argued for a revision of the price gap methodology to account for inflation. In October 2013, two interim options were brought to the table by some G-33 members for consideration at Bali: a revision of the external reference price, to reflect changing market conditions (e.g. based on a moving average of market prices, or the previous year reference price); the possibility to deflate the administered price at which foodstuffs are procured. See Submission by the G-33, *G-33 Non-paper*, JOB/AG/25 (3 October 2013).

305 World Trade Organization, Ministerial Decision of 7 December 2013 on Public Stockholding for Food Security Purposes, WT/MIN(13)/38, WT/L/913. The Ministerial Decision temporarily shields certain public stockholding schemes from subsidy complaints under the WTO AoA. In legal terms, the Decision does not amend existing WTO disciplines. It amounts to a political commitment by members to refrain from challenging as trade-distortive food stockpile programmes implemented in developing countries. The Decision is narrowly framed in more than one respect. First, in terms of product coverage, it only covers stockpile purchases of "traditional staple food crops" which excludes, for example, dairy products, or crops that are not "predominant staples in the traditional diet of a country" (para. 2 and footnote 2). Second, it only extends to programmes existing as of the date of the Decision, December 2013. New programmes would fall under general disciplines. Third, it only shields existing programmes from legal challenges under the WTO AoA. It is unclear whether the peace clause also extends to the ASCM. Finally, it sets stringent notification and transparency requirements, and the obligation for the benefiting country not to distort trade. The reach of this anti-circumvention/safeguard is unclear. On the export side, it means no surplus dumping on foreign markets. The focus is here on the disposal on foreign markets of exportable surpluses generated by the stocking programme. On the import side, it could mean that domestic food stockpile programmes in one country cannot jeopardise the WTO-enshrined market access rights of countries trying to compete in the subsidising country's domestic market. For a review, and on the post-Bali scenario, Christian Häberli, *After Bali: WTO Rules Applying to Public*

WTO Members restated their commitment to achieve a permanent solution on the issue of public stockholding for food security purposes.[306]

#### 2.3.3.2 Supply Management

From a trade law angle, the legal issue involved is the permissibility of import restrictions to enforce domestic supply management schemes. In other words, supply management does not come under legal scrutiny *per se*. At the domestic level, countries are free to enforce planting restrictions, acreage idling, production allotments, market withdrawal etc. What come under scrutiny are the import restrictions associated with domestic supply management. These border controls are an essential feature of supply management. In fact, there is little purpose in restricting supplies domestically if imports can be freely brought in.

Import restrictions necessary to enforce domestic supply management schemes in agriculture were permissible under Article XI:2(c) of the GATT, though permissibility was narrowly framed. Article XI:2(c) of the GATT continues to be relevant for fisheries products, as they fall beyond the scope of the AoA. It has been observed that it is now inoperative as regards agricultural products, in respect of which it has been superseded by the AoA.[307] The following analysis recalls the requirements set down in GATT Article XI:2(c) and its interpretative note, in the light of the relative drafting history and relevant GATT panel reports. It then moves on to quickly consider key disciplines on supply management under Article 4.2 of the AoA.

---

*Food Reserves*, FAO Commodity and Trade Policy Research Working Paper, no. 46 (Rome: FAO, 2014); Eugenio Díaz-Bonilla, *On Food Security Stocks, Peace Clauses, and Permanent Solutions After Bali*, International Food Policy Research Institute, IFPRI Working Paper ([Washington, D.C.], 2014); Alan Matthews, *Food Security and WTO Domestic Support Disciplines Post-Bali*, ICTSD Programme on Agricultural Trade and Sustainable Development (Geneva: International Centre for Trade and Sustainable Development, 2014); Raul Montemayor, *Public Stockholding for Food Security Purposes: Scenarios and Options for a Permanent Solution*, International Centre for Trade and Sustainable Development, Issue Paper 51 (Geneva, 2014).

306 World Trade Organization, Ministerial Decision of 19 December 2015 on Public Stockholding for Food Security Purposes, WT/MIN(15)/44, WT/L/979.

307 See the explanatory note by the WTO Secretariat on market access disciplines in agriculture, and specifically the section on the prohibition of non-tariff border measures, at https://www.wto.org/english/tratop_e/agric_e/ag_intro02_access_e.htm#prohibition (accessed on 28/10/2016).

### a) *Article XI:2(c) of the GATT*

Article XI.2(c) of the GATT 1947 permitted the use of import restrictions "necessary" to enforce domestic supply restrictions and surplus disposal schemes.[308] This provision, subject of significant litigation in the GATT,[309] was narrowly construed in jurisprudence. It was interpreted to set stringent requirements to be met cumulatively.[310] These conditions significantly narrowed the applicability of the exemption to price stabilising arrangements, in key respects. First, under the exception, as interpreted, it was possible to restrict imports only in connection with domestic measures which operated to 'restrict' domestic production or market. Price stabilisation schemes were covered only if they kept output below the level that would have existed in the absence of restrictions.[311] In practice, the domestic product concerned ought

308 Article XI.2(c) of the GATT 1947 permitted the use of import restrictions "on any agricultural or fisheries product, imported in any form [...]necessary to the enforcement of governmental measures which operated to [...]": "restrict the quantities of the like domestic product permitted to be marketed or produced, or, if there is no substantial domestic production of the like product, of a domestic product for which the imported product can be directly substituted" (sub-paragraph (i)); or "to remove a temporary surplus of the like domestic product, or, if there is no substantial domestic production of the like product, of a domestic product for which the imported product can be directly substituted" (sub-paragraph (ii)).

309 See, in particular, GATT Panel Report, *EEC – Minimum Import Prices*, above n 217; GATT Panel Report, *Japan – Restrictions on Imports of Certain Agricultural Products*, L/6253, adopted 2 February 1988, BISD 35S/163 [*Japan – Agricultural Products I*]; GATT Panel Report, *Canada – Import Restrictions on Ice Cream and Yoghurt*, L/6568, adopted 5 December 1989, BISD 36S/68 [*Canada – Ice Cream and Yoghurt*].

310 First, the challenged measure must constitute an import restriction (and not an import prohibition). Second, it must be on an agricultural or fishery product (quite broadly defined to encompass, for example, ice cream or tomato concentrates). Third, there must be a governmental measure that operated to 'restrict' (and not only 'regulate') domestic supply. Fourth, the import and the domestic supply restrictions must apply to 'like' or 'directly substitutable products'. If the import restrictions concerned processed products, additional requirements were set (the processed product must be "in an early stage of processing", still "perishable", "compete directly" with the fresh product, and if freely imported would "make the restriction on the fresh product ineffective"). Fifth, the import restriction must be "necessary" to the enforcement of the domestic supply restriction. Sixth, applied quotas should specify the quantity or value permitted to be imported. Seventh, the restricting country should maintain a minimum proportion of imports relative to domestic production. GATT Panel Report, *Japan – Agricultural Products I*, above n 309, para. 5.1.3. On GATT practice in respect of these requirements, see *GATT Analytical Index*, above n 46, at 327.

311 Proposals to include governmental measures to stabilise prices had been rejected in the sub-committee which considered these provisions during the Geneva session of the

to be in surplus supply. Second, the exception was not meant to apply to processed products that competed *indirectly* with the fresh product, in the sense that their imports displaced the raw product which would have been processed in these products. As stated by a GATT Panel, "the concept of displacement was apparently not intended by this provision".[312] The exception could only be extended to processed products in an early stage of processing, of a perishable kind that competed *directly* with the fresh product.[313] Third, under the second paragraph of Article XI:2(c), the scheme should not "reduce the total of imports relative to the total of domestic production, as compared [...] with the proportion prevailing during a previous representative period". This paragraph was interpreted to set a rigid formula of proportional reduction: the proportion between imports and domestic production was fixed as the one prevailing before the implementation of the scheme. The burden of proving the proportionality requirement, which lay fully with the state invoking the exception, was particularly onerous, as it involved counter-factual conditions. In particular, to meet the proportionality requirement, a country should establish the proportion between imports and domestic supplies that would prevail in the absence of restrictions. When this could no longer be determined, Article XI:2(c)(i) could in practice not be invoked.[314]

To sum up, Article XI:2(c) of the GATT provided some flexibility for the border enforcement of supply management schemes, but did not open the door too wide.[315] The *raison d'être* of this provision was the problem of dealing with an unmanageable surplus. Article XI:2(c) was not meant to be an exception for price stabilisation.

---

Preparatory Committee in 1947. For a discussion, Second session of the Preparatory Committee of the United Nations Conference on Trade and Development, Verbatim Report, Nineteenth Meeting of Commission A held on Friday, 27 June 1947 (EPCT/A/PV/19 p. 14–33).

312 GATT Panel Report, *Canada – Ice Cream and Yoghurt*, above n 309, para. 73. The Panel found that ice cream and yoghurt did not compete directly with raw milk, and that their free importation would not render ineffective the domestic supply management scheme for raw milk. Cf. GATT Panel Report, *EEC – Minimum Import Prices*, above n 217, where the Panel considered that tomato concentrate was perishable and could compete directly with fresh tomatoes.

313 Interpretative note ad Article XI:2(c)(i).

314 Panel Report, *Japan – Agricultural Products I*, above n 309, para. 5.1.3.7.

315 Eventually, countries sought country-specific waivers to exempt their supply-management schemes. The US obtained such a waiver in 1955 for key commodities.

b) *Article 4.2 of the AoA*

It has been observed that Article XI:2(c) of the GATT is now inoperative as regards agricultural products, as it has been superseded by Article 4.2 of the AoA, which prohibits the use of agriculture-specific non-tariff measures.[316]

Article 4.2 of the AoA does not provide much leeway for the border enforcement of supply management in agricultural markets. It prohibits the use of import restrictions other than "normal customs duties". Such non-tariff import restrictions include quantitative import restrictions, variable import levies, minimum import prices, discretionary import licensing, non-tariff measures maintained through state-trading enterprises.[317] These and all similar border measures other than ordinary customs duties are no longer permitted.

As discussed (Section 2.3.1.1), measures maintained under general, non-agriculture-specific provisions of GATT 1994 are exempted from Article 4.2 of the AoA. However, this exemption has been interpreted to only cover non-agriculture-specific WTO provisions, including restrictive measures maintained under balance-of-payments provisions (Articles XII and XVIII of GATT), general safeguard provisions (Article XIX of GATT and the related WTO agreement), and general exceptions (Article XX of GATT). Instead, measures maintained under agriculture-specific exceptions (like supply management schemes under GATT Article XI:2(c)) could still be challenged under the AoA's market access disciplines.[318]

2.3.3.3 Variable Import Levies and Price Bands

The measures at stake include variable import levies, minimum import prices and price band schemes. Relevant multilateral trade disciplines, as applied, are quite stringent.

Variable import levies and minimum import prices are proscribed by Article 4.2 of the WTO AoA. Note, however that these border restrictions can be maintained, if they fall "under [...] other general, non-agriculture-specific provisions of GATT 1994 [...]" (pursuant to footnote 1 to Article 4.2). As discussed, this exemption has been held to cover measures maintained under general safeguards and exception provisions of the GATT (in essence, Articles XII, XVIII, XIX, XX and XXI), but not under other substantive GATT rules.[319] In

316 See the explanatory note by the WTO Secretariat on market access disciplines in agriculture, above n 307.

317 Note 1 to Article 4.2 of the AoA.

318 See Panel Report, *Chile – Price Band System*, above n 210 and Section 2.3.1.1 above.

319 Ibid, paras 7.71 to 7.73.

line with this interpretation, variable import levies would be prohibited under Article 4.2 of the AoA, unless maintained under general exception provisions of the GATT such as under Article XX (h). Conversely, schemes compliant with other specific GATT provisions would nonetheless be proscribed under Article 4.2 of the AoA. For example, countries could not maintain or resort to variable levies, even if the overall duty, *ad valorem* plus specific, does not exceed a Member's bound rate (i.e. the measure is consistent with GATT Article II:1(b)).

Price band schemes are not textually included in the illustrative list of measures that cannot be maintained under Article 4.2 of the AoA. If considered as "ordinary customs duties", price bands could be maintained, provided that they do not exceed a country's tariff bindings (GATT Article II:1(a)).[320] If held to be border measures "other than ordinary customs duties", they could not be maintained or resorted to under Article 4.2 of the AoA, unless covered by general GATT exceptions.[321] As other duties or charges levied on bound tariffs, they would also be contrary to GATT Article II:1(b), second sentence, if unrecorded in a Member's schedule of concessions.[322] This interpretative issue has been settled in relevant cases. The 2002 WTO ruling in the case brought by Argentina against Chile's PBS significantly locked-in policy space to use price bands to offset import price variations. The Panel found that Chile's price band was a measure similar to a variable import levy or a minimum import price, within the meaning of footnote 1 to Article 4.2 of the AoA.[323] This finding was upheld by the Appellate Body[324] and supported by following jurisprudence.[325] In line with this judicial interpretation, countries shall not maintain, resort to, or revert to price band systems.

#### 2.3.3.4 Variable Export Taxes and Stabilisation Funds

'Stabilisers' enjoy comparatively more flexibility on the export side of the trade equation. In particular, the use of variable export taxes is largely unrestrained under current disciplines.[326] GATT Article XI, which prohibits quantitative

320 In particular, for the product concerned, the specific PBS duty added to the applied *ad valorem* tax shall not exceed the base tariff rate bound by a country under the WTO.

321 Footnote 1 to AoA Article 4.2.

322 GATT Article II:1(b), second sentence and Understanding on the Interpretation of Article II:1(b) of the General Agreement on Tariffs and Trade 1994 (paragraph 1), as interpreted in Panel Report, *Chile – Price Band System*, above n 210, paras. 7.105–7.108).

323 Ibid, paras. 7.47, 7.65 and 7.102.

324 Appellate Body Report, *Chile – Price Band System*, above n 210, para. 262.

325 Panel Report, *Peru – Agricultural Products*, above n 211, paras. 7.371 and 7.372.

326 For a detailed assessment of WTO disciplines on export restrictions, Baris Karapinar, "Export Restrictions and the WTO Law: How to Reform the 'Regulatory Deficiency',"

restrictions, specifically does not cover export taxes or charges, which are largely unregulated, whatever their level. However, countries cannot discriminate in the levying of export taxes, as the most-favoured-nation (MFN) treatment laid down in Article I also applies to export taxes or charges. Furthermore, some countries have bound their export taxes in their GATT Schedules and Accession Protocols. Finally, to the extent that stabilisation funds or variable export tax schemes involve export subsidies, they would come under the purview of Articles 9 and 10 of the AoA.

#### 2.3.3.5 Agro-STEs

As discussed, state trading is an integral part of many domestic price stabilisation schemes. WTO law is relatively flexible towards STEs.[327] It recognises Member's right to establish and maintain STEs, including trade monopolies (e.g. under Articles II:4, XVII and XX:d of the GATT and Article 6.7(b) of the ASCM). Yet, it requires that such enterprises do not engage in discriminatory conduct, in their "purchases or sales involving either imports or exports".[328] A description is hereafter given of the essential features of this complex regime as it bears on price-stabilising STEs. The analysis concisely addresses the following questions: What are the specific measures at issue? What are the legal issues involved, from a trade law angle? And in what way does WTO law regulate marketing boards?

##### a) *Measures at Issue*

When assessing the trade restrictive and distorting impacts of STEs, two sets of measures are at stake: the legal framework of the STE, and procedures and policies of the STE. The former encompasses the laws and regulations that establish and govern the conduct of the STE. It includes the special privileges provided by the government to the STE, such as monopoly and monopsony rights, the right to set producer prices, or government backing of certain

---

*Journal of World Trade* 45, no. 6 (2011); Baris Karapinar, "Defining the Legal Boundaries of Export Restrictions: A Case Law Analysis," *Journal of International Economic Law* 15 (2012); Ilaria Espa, "The Appellate Body Approach to the Applicability of Article XX GATT In the Light of *China – Raw Materials*: A Missed Opportunity?," *Journal of World Trade* 46, no. 6 (2012); Ilaria Espa, *Export Restrictions on Critical Minerals and Metals: Testing the Adequacy of WTO Disciplines* (Cambridge: Cambridge University Press, 2015).

327 For a thorough assessment of the WTO legal framework for STEs, Thomas Cottier and Petros C. Mavroidis, eds., *State Trading in the Twenty-First Century* (Ann Arbor, MI: University of Michigan Press, 2000).

328 Article XVII:1(a). Appellate Body Report, *Canada – Wheat Exports and Grain Imports*, above n 237, para. 85.

transactions by the STE. The latter covers procedures and policies of the STE with respect to purchases and sales involving imports and exports. What is at stake in this second respect are not governmental measures, but restrictive business practices by STEs, in the form of purchase and sale decisions, pricing decisions, allocation of business quotas, holding and disposal of stocks, and so on.[329] This complex set of laws and regulations, procedures and policies form the STE trade regime. It comes under the purview of WTO law, in its entirety. When the measure at issue is a "law, regulation, or requirement" (i.e. a governmental measure), it comes straightforwardly under WTO scrutiny. The procedures and policies of STEs can likewise come within the reach of WTO law, even if a governmental measure is not directly at stake. First, STE practices could trigger WTO rules when expression of market regulatory functions vested in the STE by the government.[330] Second, procedures and policies of a STE can be taken "as a whole" with laws and regulations to constitute the measure under challenge.[331]

b) *Legal Issues Involved*

With specific reference to the operation of price-stabilising STEs, trade concerns arise in particular as regards three issue areas: non-discrimination, market-access, and competitiveness/subsidisation.

---

329 For an overview of agro-STEs restrictive practices, Ernst-Ulrich Petersmann, "GATT Law on State Trading Enterprises: Critical Evaluation of Article XVII and Proposals for Reform," in *State Trading in the Twenty-First Century*, above n 327, 71–96, at 72.

330 In *Canada – Dairy*, for example, the Panel found that the provision by the Canadian Dairy Commission and the provincial marketing boards of discounted milk to processors/exporters involved export subsidies within the meaning of AoA Articles 9.1(a) and 9.1(c). In its analysis under AoA Article 9.1(a), the Appellate Body upheld the Panel's findings that the dairy marketing boards constituted agencies of the government for purposes of AoA Article 9.1(a), while reversing the Panel's interpretative approach with regard to 'direct subsidies'. See Panel Report, *Canada – Measures Affecting the Importation of Milk and the Exportation of Dairy Products* [hereafter, *Canada – Dairy*], WT/DS103/R, WT/DS113/R, adopted 27 October 1999, as modified by Appellate Body Report WT/DS103/AB/R, WT/DS113/AB/R, DSR 1999:VI, p. 2097.

331 In *Canada – Wheat Exports and Grain Imports*, the United States challenged the Canadian Wheat Board (CWB) Export Regime "as a whole". At stake were Canadian laws and regulations that establish and govern the conduct of the CWB, exclusive and special privileges provided by the Government of Canada to the CWB, as well as procedures and policies of the CWB with regard to setting the terms of sale for wheat exports. These three elements taken collectively constituted the measure under challenge, alleged to be inconsistent with the obligations of Canada under Article XVII:1 of the GATT 1994. See Panel Report, *Canada – Wheat Exports and Grain Imports*, above n 237, paras. 6.12 – 6.17.

Purchase, holding and re-sale of farm produce by STEs for price stabilisation and support purposes are inherently discriminatory. STEs generally purchase from domestic producers notwithstanding possibly more competitive offers from foreign suppliers – a departure from the national treatment (NT) clause (GATT Article III). Subject to Article VII GATT discussed below, they may also choose to ignore commercial considerations and favour particular exporting countries through their resale decisions, circumventing the MFN commitment (GATT Article I:1).[332]

STEs, particularly import monopolies, have also come under scrutiny as they could undermine Members' market access commitments (GATT Articles XI and II). For example, an import monopoly could simply refuse to import or import limited quantities, thus effectively enforcing a quota. It may also domestically re-sell imports at high prices, thus offsetting a tariff concession.[333]

A third set of concerns relate to subsidies and competitiveness issues. Price-stabilising STEs can easily come under scrutiny as recipients and providers of subsidies. This raises issues of export and domestic subsidisation. On the export side, STEs set up for the 'orderly' marketing of peasant cash crops may well involve some degree of export subsidisation. Turning to domestic support, stabilisation boards subsidise producers when they purchase at support prices.

### c) *Relevant Disciplines*

As mentioned, WTO law recognises that Members may establish or maintain marketing boards or other STEs. Yet, it requires that Members do not use such enterprises to circumvent their WTO obligations.[334] Indeed, as observed, states can easily circumvent or evade their key trade obligations through STEs. This can notably occur when STEs enjoy special trading privileges such as when they operate as the sole buyer in the domestic market (domestic monopsony), and/or as the sole importer or exporter (import/export monopoly).[335] The WTO "basic balance" with regard to STEs (i.e. permissibility, qualified by anti-circumvention provisions) is hereafter considered with regard to the three areas of concern previously outlined.

---

332 William J. Davey, "Article XVII GATT: An Overview," in *State Trading in the Twenty-First Century*, above n 327, 17–36, at 21–22. Imports / purchases of goods by STEs "for immediate or ultimate consumption in governmental use and not otherwise for resale or use in the production of goods for sale" are comprehensively carved out from non-discrimination obligations, as specified in Articles XVII:2 and III:8 of the GATT.

333 Davey, above n 332, at 22; Petersmann, above n 329, at 72.

334 As restated in the Ministerial Decision of 19 December 2015 on Export Competition, WT/MIN(15)/45, WT/L/980.

335 See, on this aspect, Davey, above n 332, at 21–22; Petersmann, above n 329, at 72–73.

i) Non-Discrimination

Can STEs discriminate, in the terms of their commercial sales or purchases,[336] between different export markets, or between domestic and export markets? In other words, can STEs run counter general principles of non-discriminatory treatment, as enshrined in GATT Article I:1 (MFN treatment) and Article III (NT)?

Key disciplines in this regard are laid down in Article XVII:1 of the GATT 1994 and its *ad* Note. Specifically, subparagraph (a) of Article XVII:1 requires that marketing boards and other STEs "in their purchases or sales involving either imports of exports, act in a manner consistent with the general principles of non-discriminatory treatment". Subparagraph (b) clarifies the scope of the requirement not to discriminate.[337] The first clause of subparagraph (b) requires that STEs make their sales or purchases "solely in accordance with commercial considerations"; the second clause requires that STEs allow the enterprises of other Members "adequate opportunity [...] to compete for participation in such purchases or sales". The non-discrimination obligation is relaxed under the *ad* Note to Article XVII:1, which allows STEs to differentiate between export markets for commercial reasons, to meet conditions of demand and supply.

It is well established that the non-discrimination obligation under GATT Article XVII:1 includes general principles of MFN treatment as enshrined in GATT Article I:1:[338] STEs cannot discriminate in their sales between different export markets, unless for commercial reasons. It is not clear, however, if the obligation also refers to national treatment. In other words, there is disagreement over whether STEs can discriminate in their sales/purchases between domestic and foreign markets. As pointed out in Davey, there is some uncertainty in this respect: the drafting history may suggest that only MFN treatment is required; this interpretation is corroborated by two panel reports.[339] More

336 Other than for "immediate or ultimate consumption in governmental use". This latter would be a matter of government procurement, rather than state trading.

337 Appellate Body Report, *Canada – Wheat Exports and Grain Imports*, above n 237, paras. 89 and 100.

338 Panel Report, *Canada – Wheat Exports and Grain Imports*, above n 237, para. 6.48.

339 Davey, above n 332, at 26. Cf. Petersmann, above n 329. See also the GATT Panel Report, *Belgium Family Allowances*, G/32, adopted 7 November 1952, BISD 1S/59, para. 4 ("[a]s regards the exception contained in paragraph 2 of Article XVII, it would appear that it referred only to the principle set forth in paragraph 1 of that Article, i.e. the obligation to make purchases in accordance with commercial considerations and did not extend to matters dealt with in Article III") and GATT Panel Report, *Canada – Administration of the Foreign Investment Review Act*, L/5504, adopted 7 February 1984, BISD 30S/140, para. 6.16 ("[t]he Panel saw great force in Canada's argument that only the most-favoured-nation and

recent cases have left the issue unresolved.[340] However, this "definitional uncertainty"[341] only exists with respect to policies and practices of STE that do not involve governmental measures. This is the case, for example, when a marketing board discriminates between domestic and foreign markets through its purchasing and pricing decisions. If the discriminatory action involves a "law, regulation or requirement", it can always be challenged under GATT Article III.

#### ii) Market Access

As mentioned, STEs provided with special privileges, such as monopoly rights of purchase and sale, can effectively restrict market access through their purchasing decisions and pricing policies. A number of provisions can be relied upon to constrain similar conducts. GATT Article XVII:1(b) requires that STEs, including import and export monopolies, make their import and export purchases and sales "solely in accordance with commercial considerations". Broadly interpreted, this provision could be read to preclude STEs from restricting market access through their purchasing and pricing decisions.[342] Yet, the provision has been interpreted narrowly in jurisprudence, as a specification of the non-discrimination provision under subparagraph (a).[343] As such, it does not establish a legal basis to challenge purchasing practices that in fact enforce a quota or pricing decisions that nullify tariff concessions. As summarised by Davey, other rules can be invoked to this effect.[344] If a STE's restrictive practices involve laws, regulations or requirements, GATT Articles II and XI would apply directly.[345] Otherwise, their operations could be challenged

---

not the national treatment obligations fall within the scope of the general principles referred to in Article XVII:1(a). However, the Panel did not consider it necessary to decide in this particular case whether the general reference to the principles of non-discriminatory treatment referred to in Article XVII:1 also comprises the national treatment principle [...]").

340 In *Canada – Wheat Exports and Grain Imports*, the Panel decided that it did not need to take a position on this issue. Panel Report, *Canada – Wheat Exports and Grain Imports*, above n 237, para. 6.50.

341 Davey, above n 332, at 26.

342 Ibid, at 27.

343 Ibid.

344 Ibid.

345 In *India – Quantitative Restrictions*, the Panel for example found that "canalisation" of certain imports through STEs ("canalising" agencies) violates Article XI:1 (Panel Report, *India – Quantitative Restrictions on Imports of Agricultural, Textile and Industrial Products*, WT/DS90/R, adopted 22 September 1999, upheld by Appellate Body Report WT/DS90/AB/R, DSR 1999:V, p. 1799, paras. 5.132–136).

under the Article II:4 provisions on import monopolies[346] and the interpretative note ad Articles XI, XII, XIII, XIV and XVIII.[347] Note also that Article 4.2 of the AoA prohibits non-tariff border measures, including "non-tariff measures maintained through state-trading enterprises".[348]

iii) Competitiveness and Subsidies

As discussed, STEs can come under scrutiny as recipients and providers of subsidies. This raises issues of competitiveness and subsidisation.

A first set of concerns revolves around the competitive advantages that these enterprises might gain from their special rights and privileges. These privileges give STEs more flexibility with regard to pricing and other terms of sale than 'commercial' actors. For example, monopoly rights of purchase, together with the right to fix the purchase price, result in assured supplies and price certainty.[349] Likewise, government guarantees of borrowings translate in more favourable credit terms. These privileges give STEs a competitive advantage over 'commercial' traders that do not benefit from similar conditions.

Does WTO law, and specifically GATT Article XVII:1 require Members to level the playing field between STEs and 'commercial' traders? This view resonates in

---

346 Pursuant to GATT Article II:4, import monopolies "shall not [...] operate so as to afford protection on the average in excess of the amount of protection provided for" in a member's Schedule. This provision has been interpreted to prevent import monopolies from imposing prices in excess of costs plus a reasonable profit margin. In particular, mark-ups which are higher on imported than on like domestic products (differential mark-ups) can only be justified to the extent that they cover additional costs necessarily associated with marketing of the imported products. Specifically, the differential mark-up should allow the recovery of costs directly associated with the handling of imported products (variable costs), plus charges for fixed assets employed in proportion to the use of these assets by the imported product. See GATT Panel Report, *Canada – Import, Distribution and Sale of Alcoholic Drinks by Canadian Provincial Marketing Agencies*, L/6304, adopted 22 March 1988, BISD 35S/37 [*Canada – Provincial Liquor Boards* (*EEC*)], paragraph 4.19 and GATT Panel Report, *Canada – Import, Distribution and Sale of Certain Alcoholic Drinks by Provincial Marketing Agencies*, DS17/R, adopted 18 February 1992, BISD 39S/27 [*Canada – Provincial Liquor Boards* (*US*)], paras. 5.17–5.22.

347 The note ad Articles XI, XII, XIII, XIV and XVIII of the GATT states explicitly that "the terms 'import restrictions' or 'export restrictions' include restrictions made effective through state-trading operations". This would cover the purchase/resale and pricing decision of STEs.

348 Note 1, Article 4.2 of the AoA.

349 As asserted by the United States in its claim against the CWB. For a summary, Panel Report, *Canada – Wheat Exports and Grain Imports*, above n 237, para. 6.110.

the United States' claim against the Canadian Wheat Board. The United States maintained that the special privileges enjoyed by the CWB gave the Board a competitive advantage towards 'commercial' actors, with regard to pricing and other terms of sale. This was alleged to be inconsistent with the obligations of Canada under Article XVII:1 of the GATT 1994. Specifically, it run counter the requirement that STEs make purchases or sales solely in accordance with commercial considerations (first clause of Article XVII:1(b) of the GATT 1994), and to allow the enterprises of other Members an adequate opportunity to compete (second clause of Article XVII:1(b) of the GATT 1994).[350] The Panel did not uphold this view. According to the Panel, the "commercial considerations" requirement (first clause of Article XVII:1(b)) "is simply intended to prevent STEs from behaving like 'political' actors";[351] the second clause of subparagraph (b) requires that a STE "afford its customers, and not its competitors, adequate opportunity to compete for participation in its wheat sales".[352] The Appellate Body upheld the Panel position:

> [...] we cannot accept that the first clause of subparagraph (b) would, as a general rule, require STEs to refrain from using the privileges and advantages that they enjoy because such use might 'disadvantage' private enterprises. STEs, like private enterprises, are entitled to exploit the advantages they may enjoy to their economic benefit. Article XVII:1(b) merely prohibits STEs from making purchases or sales on the basis of non commercial considerations.[353]

Overall, Article XVII provides significant room for price pools and other price-stabilising marketing techniques by STEs. These arrangements are not *per se* inconsistent with Article XVII:1 of the GATT, if non-discriminatory.[354]

A distinct, tough overlapping area of concern relates to 'hidden' or implicit subsidies associated with certain STE activities. This raises issues of export and domestic subsidisation.

---

350 US views as summarised in Panel Report, *Canada – Wheat Exports and Grain Imports*, above n 237, para. 4.180.

351 Panel Report, *Canada – Wheat Exports and Grain Imports*, above n 237, para. 6.94

352 Ibid, para. 6.150.

353 Appellate Body Report, *Canada — Wheat Exports and Grain Imports*, above n 237, para. 149.

354 Panel Report, *Canada — Wheat Exports and Grain Imports*, above n 237, paras. 6.126, 6.130, 6.133 and Appellate Body Report, *Canada — Wheat Exports and Grain Imports*, above n 237, para. 149.

On the export side, STEs set up for the 'orderly' marketing of peasant cash crops may well involve some degree of export subsidisation. At issue are direct and indirect forms of government subsidies to the board (e.g. subsidies to cover operational deficits, transportation/marketing subsidies, favourable interest rates, etc.), as well as the ability of STEs to cross-subsidise export sales from the proceeds of monopolistic rents.[355] Relevant disciplines are framed by the interaction of the AoA and the ASCM.

Export subsidies are prohibited under the ASCM, "except as provided in the Agreement on Agriculture" (ASCM Article 3). The AoA provided two inroads for export subsidies. First, Article 9.4 established a temporary exemption for developing countries, allowing them to subsidise marketing and transport costs during the Uruguay Round phase-in period. Subsidies to export marketing boards for the 'orderly marketing' of peasant crops may be possibly justified under this exemption, if extended.[356] Second, Members with scheduled export subsidy commitments could still use notified export subsidies, though within their bound levels.[357] If the subsidisation scheme was included in a Member's export subsidy reduction commitment, the subsidy was not actionable at the WTO level.[358] These export subsidy entitlements have been eliminated or are

355 FAO, *Agricultural State Trading Enterprises and Developing Countries: Some Issues in the Context of the WTO*, FAO Papers on Selected Issues Relating to the WTO Negotiations on Agriculture (Rome: FAO, 2002). For an assessment of export marketing boards in the grain and dairy sector, United States General Accounting Office, *Report to Congressional Requesters – Canada, Australia, And New Zealand: Potential Ability of Agricultural State Trading Enterprises to Distort Trade*, GAO/NSIAD-96-94, June 1996.

356 Yet, some developed countries argue that, absent legally-binding decision by the WTO to extend the application of Article 9.4 of the Agreement of Agriculture, there is no longer legal basis for the provision of these export subsidies.

357 At the tenth WTO Ministerial Conference in Nairobi, developed countries undertook to immediately eliminate their remaining scheduled export subsidy entitlements. Yet, an exception was provided for notified subsidies on processed products, dairy products, and swine meat, to be eliminated by the end of 2020. Developing countries agreed to eliminate their export subsidy entitlements by the end of 2018. They retained the right to use export subsidies for transport and marketing (covered by Article 9.4 of the Agreement on Agriculture) until the end of 2023 (LDCs and NFIDCs until the end of 2030). World Trade Organization, Ministerial Decision on Export Competition of 19 December 2015, WT/MIN(15)/45, WT/L/980.

358 Gary N. Horlick and Kristin Heim Mowry, 'The Treatment of Activities of State Trading Enterprises under the WTO Subsidies Rules', in *State Trading in the Twenty-First Century*, above n 327, 97–119 at 101. The subsidy would however be countervailable at the domestic level. The interaction of the AoA and the ASCM was also considered in *Canada – Dairy*

to be phased out under the terms of the Ministerial Decision of 19 December 2015 on Export Competition.[359]

Turning to internal support, stabilisation boards subsidise producers when they purchase at support prices.[360] Under the AoA, this is a matter of domestic support, previously discussed. Under the ASCM, it may involve actionable subsidies when the action (subsidy) of the STE causes 'injury' to: exporters trying to compete in the country's domestic market; a domestic industry in an importing country; or rival exporters from another country when the two compete in third markets.[361]

To curb abuse through STEs, the disciplines being negotiated in the Doha framework, as laid down in the December 2008 revised draft modalities,[362] set relatively stringent disciplines on agricultural exporting STEs. In particular, the new rules, if approved, would preclude the granting of trade monopoly powers to STEs, as well as their government financing, whether direct or indirect. To preserve policy space for development, the draft modalities also envisage significant special and differential treatment (S&DT) for developing countries. In particular, agro-STEs in developing countries shall be permitted to maintain or use export monopoly powers if: they enjoy special privileges to preserve domestic consumer price stability and to ensure food security; or the entity's share of world exports of the product or products concerned does not exceed 5 percent in three consecutive years; or they are based in LDCs or 'small, vulnerable economies' (SVEs).[363] It is open to question whether these flexibilities preserve lee-way for price-stabilising STEs in a number of developing countries.[364]

### 2.3.4 *Assessment*

The analysis of the interface between price stabilisation arrangements and trade rules is somewhat inconclusive. This is on account of a number of difficulties.

---

(above n 330), were the Panel found that export subsidies permissible under the AoA could not be challenged under Article 3 of the ASCM (paras 7.18–31).

359 See above, n 357.

360 On the definition of support prices, above n 291.

361 For an assessment, Horlick and Mowry, above n 358, at 97–113. Under the "peace clause", now expired, domestic support, if within a member's *de minimis* or AMS threshold under the AoA, was not actionable under the ASCM unless it granted product-specific support "in excess of that decided during the 1992 marketing year" (WTO AoA Article 13 (b) (ii)).

362 December 2008 revised draft modalities, above n 65.

363 Ibid, Annex K, paras. 4–6.

364 An issue further discussed in Section 5.2.3.

First, stabilisation policies are multifaceted and entangled, while trade rules are discrete, specific and fragmented. As extensively discussed, domestic price stabilisation is accomplished through a variety of measures, typically, a combination of domestic procurement, buffer stock releases and trade policy. These measures in practice intertwine and their separate assessment is all the more artificial. Yet, for purposes of legal analysis, this entangled set of policies is unbundled in its discrete components. These are individually assessed in their trade distorting potential under the dissecting scope of separate WTO disciplines. What is eventually lost is the stabilisation policy dimension.

Second, price stabilisation arrangements trigger provisions of different historic origin and rationale that stipulate somewhat contradictory obligations. For example, on matters of price stabilisation policies, frictions may arise between the GATT 'managed economy' provisions (GATT Articles XI (c), XX (h) and (i), XXXVI (4) and XXXVIII (3) (a)) and relevant 'liberal' disciplines under the AoA such as market access commitments under Article 4.2. Underlying these two sets of rules are two different attitudes towards commodity 'control'.[365] These reflect the continuing nature of the WTO Treaty, and some "subjectivity of legal values",[366] with the embodiment in the same body of rules, WTO law, of particular traditions of thought that are historic and contingent in nature.

Finally, each set of rules is complexly articulated within. Even the most liberal provisions laid down in the AoA consist of commitments and escapes, rules and exceptions. They proscribe, while allowing lee-way. This ambivalence reflects some uncertainty, if not inconsistency, in terms of the legal principles underlying agricultural trade regulation. Overall, as a matter of *lex generalis*, agricultural commodities are subject, on equal footing with other goods categories, to multilateral trade disciplines, as these disciplines apply with no distinction between kinds of goods. On the other hand, agricultural commodities continue to be segregated under special rules and arrangements, on account of the sensitivities involved.

---

365 The 'managed economy' provisions enshrined in the GATT are a legacy of the past: Article XXXVIII (and generally Part IV) brought into the GATT UNCTAD's quest for "a new trade policy for development"; the Article XX (h) exemption provided room for the special commodity trade regime laid down in Chapter VI of the Havana Charter. The WTO AoA disciplines reflect commodity policy developments in the late 1980s and 1990s, and the shift in policy paradigm from commodity 'control' to 'market-based' regulation.

366 For a critical perspective on this notion, see David Jabbari, "From Criticism to Construction in Modern Critical Legal Theory," *Oxford Journal of Legal Studies* 12, no. 4 (1992): 534.

In the face of this fragmentation and complexity, it is important to go back to the basics, to the broad underlying motives, the normative objectives and principles of trade law in its regulation of farm stabilisation policies. The remainder of this study will seek to untangle these underlying normative values.

CHAPTER 3

# A Historical Review of Multilaterally Agreed Criteria for Action on Commodity Prices (1947–1989)

Having clarified some background concepts and issues also relating to the multilateral trading system, the analysis turns to the research question as defined: the proper and underlying role of trade law and policy in agricultural price stabilisation. This Chapter takes stock of major past attempts to set multilaterally agreed principles and procedures for the regulation of international commodity prices. The analysis looks backward, but with a view to generating insights that may be valuable in the present context. Attention is focused on three post-war endeavours: negotiations leading to Chapter 6 of the Havana Charter; discussions during the 1954–1955 review of the GATT; and UNCTAD's IPC. The narrative first provides a descriptive account of the main negotiation settings. It then outlines the special regime therein laid down for commodities. The focus is on the varying rationales, objectives and principles of multilateral action on commodity prices. The analysis looks at areas of agreement, while also pointing to major divergences and disagreements.

The scope of the analysis is limited, in two important respects. First, attention is exclusively focused on concerted multilateral action on commodity prices by producing and consuming countries. This only covers dual-interest commodity agreements of which all interested producing and consuming countries were parties. Second, the analysis focuses on multilateral commodity control in its post-Second World War form. The narrative starts with the Havana Charter in the 1940s and ends with the establishment of the Common Fund for Commodities in 1989. As discussed, the history of commodity price control is richer than this account suggests. First, it traces back to much earlier times.[367] Second, multilateral action ought to be assessed in interplay with other forms of commodity price intervention, including producers' cartel-type arrangements, domestic price stabilisation arrangements, as well as private cartels. Due to the limited space available, in the following sections, these important aspects cannot be brought sufficiently into focus.

367 For an overview of early commodity control arrangements, refer to Section 2.2.1.1.

 | DOI 10.1163/9789004350540_004

## 3.1 A Descriptive Account: Havana, Geneva and Nairobi

This Section reviews efforts to lay down multilaterally agreed criteria for action on commodity prices. The analysis, fairly descriptive, brings into focus three major endeavours: negotiations leading to Chapter 6 of the Havana Charter; proposals for a Special Agreement on Commodity Arrangements (SACA), during the GATT Review Session of 1954–1955; and UNCTAD's Resolution 93 (IV), agreed upon at the final plenary of UNCTAD IV on 31 May 1976. The objective is to introduce these commodity policy frameworks, and briefly review the outcome of negotiations, so as to set the stage for the following discussion.

### 3.1.1 *The Havana Charter Framework*

Attempts by the international community to develop a concerted approach to commodity regulation go back as far as the 1927 World Monetary and Economic Conference.[368] However, it was not until the Havana Charter that an enduring framework for the organisation of the post-war commodity regime came into existence. Called by the Economic and Social Council of the United Nations (ECOSOC) in the aftermath of the Second World War, the United Nations Conference on Trade and Employment was held at Havana, Cuba, from 21 November 1947 to 24 March 1948.[369] The Conference ended with the

368 For a review of early attempts to develop a concerted approach to commodity regulation, United Nations Interim Co-ordinating Committee for International Commodity Arrangements, *Review of International Commodity Arrangements*, above n 86.

369 The groundwork for the Conference had been laid by an Intergovernmental Preparatory Committee, including a nuclear group of countries. Preparatory works had been divided in three parts: two Sessions of the Preparatory Committee, at London (from 15 October to 26 November I946) and Geneva (from 10 April 1947 through 30 October 1947); and the meeting of a technical Drafting Committee in New York, between the two sessions. The outcome of the First Session of the Preparatory Committee (London session) was a draft Charter for an ITO ('London draft'), embodied in a report which also included a narrative account of the treatment of the various agenda items (published as *Report of the First Session of the London Preparatory Committee of the United Nations Conference on Trade and Employment*, UN Document E/PCT/33, October 1946). The technical Drafting Committee was appointed by the Preparatory Committee at the end of the First Session for the purpose of editing the draft Charter produced in London. The Drafting Committee met in New York from 20 January to 25 February I947 and prepared a further draft of the Charter and a full draft of a multilateral trade agreement embodying tariff concessions (the GATT) (*Report of the Drafting Committee of the Preparatory Committee of the United Nations Conference on Trade and Employment*, UN Document E/PCT/34, 5 March 1947). The Second Session of the Preparatory Committee (New York) concluded with the submission of a

adoption of the Final Act of the Conference, by 53 of the 56 Governments represented at the Conference.[370] This included the text of the Havana Charter for an International Trade Organization.[371]

Among other outcomes,[372] the Charter established a set of substantive principles for commodity control agreements, as well as a procedural framework for inter-governmental action on commodity problems (Chapter 6 of the Charter). The framework enshrined principles of multilateralism, transparency and consumer-producer cooperation, as detailed in Section 3.2. A co-ordinated and systematic approach to commodity issues was finally in sight.

The Havana Charter, subject to ratification or rejection by the legislative or other appropriate body in the signatory countries, never came into legal force.[373] However, the principles laid down in Chapter 6 of the Charter (the 'Havana principles') were officially endorsed by the ECOSOC as "a general guide in inter-governmental consultation or action with respect to commodity problems".[374] Sanctioned by the ECOSOC, the commodity policy provisions of

---

revised draft Charter as a basis for discussion at the Havana Conference (the 'Geneva draft', above n 49).

370 Fifty-six countries sent representatives to the Conference. Fifty-three signed the Final Act at the closing of the Conference; one (Turkey) signed after its closing; and two (Argentina and Poland) did not sign.

371 On the Havana Charter, see generally William Adams Brown, *The United States and the Restoration of World Trade: An Analysis and Appraisal of the ITO Charter and the General Agreement on Tariffs and Trade* (Washington, D.C.: Brookings Institution, 1950) and Clair Wilcox, *A Charter for World Trade* (New York: Macmillan Co., 1949).

372 The Charter included chapters on Employment and Economic Activity, Economic Development and Reconstruction, Commercial Policy, Restrictive Business Practices, and Intergovernmental Commodity Agreements, in addition to institutional provisions.

373 In the US, the Charter was subject to ratification or rejection by the legislative (the Congress). Eventually, it was not ratified. To the contrary, Congressional approval was not required for the GATT, which was adopted by executive agreement under delegated authority to the President, pursuant to the Trade Agreement Act of 1934. See Brown, above n 371, at 16–22.

374 In Council Resolution 30 (iv) of 28 March 1947 (U.N. Doc. No. E/403), the ECOSOC recommended "[...] that, pending the establishment of the International Trade Organization, members of the United Nations adopt as a general guide in intergovernmental consultation or action with respect to commodity problems the principles laid down in Chapter VII as a whole, i.e. the chapter on intergovernmental arrangements". What was Chapter VII in the London draft (the draft Charter text provisionally agreed at the end of the First Session of the Preparatory Committee) became in due course Chapter VI (Geneva draft, above n 49). In the same Resolution the ECOSOC requested the Secretary-General

the Charter were then endorsed by the GATT 1947. The original text of GATT Article XX(h), as in force until 1957, recognised ICAs conforming with the Havana Charter principles as an exception to GATT disciplines.[375] The exception set out the basis for a special regime for commodities, comprehensively carved out from general trade disciplines. A set of substantive principles to which commodity control agreements were to conform, as well as an interim machinery for the co-ordination of inter-governmental action on commodity problems were created in this, rather convoluted, way.[376] As remarked by Rowe, "a new era in the development of commodity control had begun".[377]

The approach of the Havana Charter soon bore its fruits. International study groups were appointed for tin, rubber and wool. Three existing bodies, the International Cotton Advisory Committee, the International Sugar Council and the International Wheat Council were 'grafted in'.[378] Later on, international UN study groups would be established for lead, zinc, cocoa and coffee. The Food and Agriculture Organization of the United Nations (FAO) had also its own study groups, such as those for jute, kenaf and allied fibres. Efforts were made to relate actions being taken on various commodities under a single umbrella. More importantly, in 1947, an Interim Co-ordinating Committee for International Commodity Arrangement (ICCICA) was appointed by the UN Secretary-General to co-ordinate inter-governmental consultation and action with respect to commodity problems. It was followed in 1954 by a Commission on International Trade. The FAO had also created its own

---

to appoint an Interim Co-ordinating Committee for International Commodity Arrangements. Council Resolution 30 (iv) of 28 March 1947 was reaffirmed in Resolution 373 (XIII) of 13 September 1951.

375 Article XX:I(h) of the General Agreement, as concluded on 30 October 1947, excepted measures "undertaken in pursuance of obligations under intergovernmental commodity agreements, conforming to the principles approved by the Economic and Social Council of the United Nations in its Resolution of 28 March 1947, establishing an Interim Co-ordinating Committee for International Commodity Arrangements." The 'principles' referred to in the Resolution were those laid down in the commodity chapter of the Havana Charter. See WTO Secretariat, *GATT Analytical Index*, above n 46, at 589.

376 An Interim Co-ordinating Committee for International Commodity Arrangements (ICCICA) was set up to convene commodity study groups, make recommendations regarding calling conferences to negotiate commodity agreements, and co-coordinate the activities of study groups and councils administering commodity agreements. Council Resolution 30 (iv) of 28 March 1974, above n 374.

377 Rowe, above n 55, at 159.

378 Ibid, at 161.

committee on commodity problems in agriculture. Within this articulated framework, inter-governmental commodity control agreements were concluded for five commodities by the early 1960s: wheat, sugar, tin, coffee and tea. As reported in Rowe, their operation was fraught with considerable difficulties; none of them successfully stabilised prices for more than relatively short periods.[379]

A few contextual aspects deserve some consideration before turning to consider subsequent multilateral discussions within the GATT framework.

First, at the time of the Havana negotiations, price intervention in commodity markets was not new. Commodity price intervention had been the rule, rather than the exception, through the 1930s and 1940s (Section 2.2). The Havana Charter negotiations were held in the aftermath of the Second World War, during 1946–48. Two major shocks stood vividly in the background: the Great Depression economic turndown in the 1930s, and major disruptions associated with the war. Both occurrences had stimulated State intervention on commodity prices, at both the domestic and international levels: during the 1930s, to relieve existing critical conditions among primary producers;[380] during the Second World War, to ensure critical supplies of foodstuffs and minerals, by means of domestic price controls, combined boards,[381] purchase

379 Rowe, above n 55, at 209. ICA's control over sugar was limited, as the sugar agreements only covered the 'free market' segment. The sugar control scheme was eventually suspended in December 1961. The tin buffer stock lost control twice: in 1958 it went out of cash, in the attempt to counter the price decline; and in 1961, when it sold all its stocks trying to counter the price spike. The wheat agreements performed relatively better. This was essentially thanks to the two largest exporters, the United States and Canada, who supported the working of the control scheme by means of stockpiling and other forms of supply management. See, Rowe, above n 55.

380 During the Great Depression in the 1930s, Governments in the Western economies stepped-in vigorously to relieve existing critical conditions for primary commodity producers. Governments were faced with strong pressure from rural constituencies to support farmers; and from industry and workers to keep staple prices low. Rowe, above n 55, at 89–90 and 130; Johan F.M. Swinnen, *Agricultural Protection Growth in Europe, 1870–1969*, The World Bank, Agricultural Distortions Working Paper 80 (Washington, D.C., 2009), at 150.

381 Combined boards were wartime commodity control agencies. Examples include the Combined Raw Materials Board and the Combined Production and Resources Board and Combined Food Board, set up by the United States and Great Britain for the combined use of their resources. Relevant texts are reproduced in International Labour Office, above n 44, at 158–77.

and reserve stock agreements;[382] and, in the post-war period, through the orderly liquidation of surplus stocks[383] (Section 2.2).

Second, care has to be taken not to frame the early debate around commodity price stabilisation in terms of a divide between North and South. At the time of the Havana Conference, the South still largely consisted of colonies, dependencies and other territories whose interests were complexly mingled with those of their 'mother countries'. Nor was development economics a recognised science in 1948.[384] Yet, some divergence of interest between industrial (developed) and developing economies had already commenced to surface. For example, there was substantial disagreement as to whether the commodity policy provisions of the Charter should also provide a framework for encouraging industrialisation in commodity-dependent developing counties. Likewise, though development economics was not at that time an established science, discussion at Havana already anticipated some central tenets of UNCTAD's IPC. This included the claim that developing countries' terms of trade tended to deteriorate, and the quest for some fair relationship between the price of exported commodities and imported manufactures.[385]

### 3.1.2 *GATT Discussions (1954–1955 Review Session)*

Efforts to set multilaterally agreed principles for action on commodity prices continued in the GATT context. These developments are to be assessed against

382 Wartime and post-war commodity purchase and stocking agreements. See, for example: Agreement between the Governments of the United States of America and of the United Kingdom for the Exchange of Cotton and Rubber, signed at London, 23 June 1939; Exchange of Notes between the Secretary of State for Foreign Affairs of the United Kingdom and the United States Chargé d'Affaires regarding the Establishment of a Reserve of Australian Wool in the United States of America, London, 9 December 1940; Agreement between the Government of the United Kingdom and the Belgian Government Relating to the Purchase of Commodities from the Belgian Congo, London, 21 January 1941; Memorandum of Agreement Annexed to Exchange of Letters between the Secretary of State for Foreign Affairs of the United Kingdom and General de Gaulle concerning Commercial and Economic Relations between the United Kingdom and the Cameroons under French Mandate, 21 January 1941. Texts reproduced in International Labour Office, above n 44, at 178–206.

383 For example, schemes for the orderly marketing of the accumulated wool stocks owned by the British government. These and other minor schemes are discussed in detail in Davis, above n 86, at 201–19.

384 Rowe, above n 55, at 311.

385 On these issues, as developed within UNCTAD, see Section 3.1.3 in this Chapter.

the background of the Havana Charter negotiations[386] and in interplay with later developments at UNCTAD.

The question of GATT's involvement in commodity matters, and specific proposals for an internationally agreed code of conduct for ICAs were examined in some detail during the Review Session of 1945–1955.[387] Three issues were extensively discussed: the relationship between general commercial policy (the GATT) and commodity policy; specific proposals for principles and objectives to govern inter-governmental commodity arrangements; and possible amendments to the original GATT Article XX(h).[388]

#### 3.1.2.1 Commodity Policy and General Commercial Policy

With regard to the first issue, the majority of the GATT contracting parties considered that the commodity field should be brought within the purview of the GATT, since commodity problems were closely related to other trade matters.[389] Yet, there were diverging views as to whether the contracting parties ought to be given the power to decide on the merits of a particular commodity

386 It is important to recall, in this respect, that the GATT negotiations were initially 'entangled' with the wider UN ITO negotiations. For details, *GATT Analytical Index*, above n 46, at 3–6.

387 As mentioned, the Havana Charter never entered into force. The GATT parties then convened a review session (Review Session of 28 October 1954 to 8 March 1955) to examine whether the GATT ought to be "amended, supplemented or maintained" (GATT Article XXIX(3)). See also *GATT Analytical Index*, above n 46, at 998. The Review Session of 1954–1955 resulted in agreement on a few amendments to the original text of the GATT, as well as on an Agreement on the Organization for Trade Cooperation (OTC). These amendments were incorporated in three instruments. Only one (the Protocol Amending the Preamble and Parts II and III) eventually entered into force. For details, *GATT Analytical Index*, above n 46, at 7.

388 Commodity issues were debated in the context of the Review Working Party on Organizational and Functional Arrangements. In December 1954, the contracting parties established a separate Working Party on Commodity Problems (Document L/301; SR.9/27). The Working Party was established to consider specific proposals for principles and objectives to govern inter-governmental commodity arrangements, and their relationship with the GATT (Document L/301; SR.9/27).

389 See, for example, statements by Valladao (Brazil) (SR 9/19, at 4); Johnsen (New Zealand), (SR. 9/27, at 6); Cohen (United Kingdom) (SR 9/19, at 4). Eventually, the GATT parties ruled that they were competent, pursuant to Article XXV:1, to deal with commodity problems. See specifically *CONTRACTING PARTIES – Tenth Session – [27 October–3 December 1955] – Summary Record of the Nineteenth Meeting – Held at the Palais des Nations, Geneva, on Thursday 1 December 1955, at 2.30 p.m* (SR.10/19), at. 218.

agreement.[390] Likewise, there were a wide range of views as to the relationship between the GATT and the draft framework agreement for international commodity arrangements, under consideration by the GATT parties, as discussed hereafter. Some favoured a close link with the GATT;[391] some felt that instead the framework agreement should be tied directly to the United Nations.[392]

This debate discloses a rather sharp cleavage of opinion. Some viewed international commodity control arrangements as a normal device for conducting international trade in commodities and tended to delink commodity policy from general commercial policy. Others perceived commodity control as a narrowly defined exception to the general rules of commercial policy, to be framed within the GATT context.

Overall, some reluctance to openly admit commodity matters under the GATT ambit reflects some separation, in practice and theory, of commodity-related arrangements from general commercial policy. It should be stressed that even within the wider ITO negotiations commodity matters were disentangled from wider commercial policy issues, and considered separately.[393] Disjoined from general merchandise, commodities would then be 'segregated' under special

---

390 Cf., for example, the positions of the United Kingdom (SR 9/34, at 8; SR 10/13, at 14) and of Brazil (SR10/13, p. 143).

391 The United Kingdom, for example, maintained that "[...] any framework for international commodity arrangements should be related to that of commercial policy as a whole, and that effective action was most likely to be achieved through a new agreement closely related to the GATT" (SR 10/13, at 141). Among other, "[...] it would thus be possible to fill the gap which had existed for so long as a result of the absence of any body empowered to administer the basic principles of Chapter VI of the Havana Charter, or to bring these principles into line with experience since 1947" (SR 9/34, at 8).

392 Czechoslovakia, for example, was of the opinion that commodity problems should be dealt with within the scope of the UN ECOSOC, whose work should not be interfered with by the GATT parties (see *Final Report of the Working Party on Commodity Problems*, October 1955 (L/416), at 2, para. 20).

393 At the First Session of the Preparatory Committee, the detailed examination of commercial policy issues (including GATT issues) was entrusted to Committee II, while inter-governmental commodity arrangements fell within the purview of Committee IV (see London Report, above n 49, at 3). Through the Second Session, Commission A prepared texts for consideration by the Preparatory Committee relating to the chapters on Employment and Economic Activity, Economic Development and General Commercial Policy, while Commission B dealt with the other pending issues, including commodity agreements (see Geneva draft, above n 49, at 6, footnote 7). Finally, at the Havana Conference, the Third Committee was responsible for the examination of commercial policy (the Geneva draft text of Chapter IV), while the Fifth Committee was charged with the examination of commodity policy (Chapter VI of the Geneva draft).

rules and arrangements, a sort of *lex specialis*, and comprehensively carved out from general GATT disciplines.

#### 3.1.2.2 A Framework Agreement for ICAs

Turning to the formulation of principles and objectives to govern ICAs, the GATT parties established a separate Working Party on Commodity Problems to this purpose. In February 1955, the Working Party submitted an interim report to the GATT parties, containing a text of a draft Special Agreement on Commodity Arrangements (SACA). The SACA was meant to govern international action in the field of commodity problems, along the lines of Chapter 6 of the Havana Charter.[394] The draft SACA set substantive and procedural disciplines for ICAs, with only minor deviations from the commodity chapter of the Charter. As conceived by the Working Party, the SACA had to become "the main centralizing and co-ordinated organization for all Commodity arrangements".[395]

Discussions on the draft SACA did not result in consensus,[396] and the issue was deferred to the Tenth Session of the Contracting Parties to the GATT (Geneva, 27 Oct.–3 Dec. 1955). In that context, the Working Party on Commodity Problems submitted a revised draft agreement to the contracting parties, with the recommendation that "it be accepted by them as embodying the criteria to which intergovernmental commodity arrangements should conform in order to benefit from the exception provided in the first part of paragraph (h) of Article XX of the General Agreement, as revised at the Ninth Session".[397]

Yet, due to divergence on key issues, the Working Party Report and the draft Agreement were not adopted, and the issue was deferred to the Eleventh Session (Geneva, 11 Oct.–17 Nov. 1956).

Eventually, in the fall of 1956, the Working Party finally acknowledged that "it was unlikely that agreement could be reached along the lines of SACA and that therefore an alternative approach should be explored".[398] The

394 See Annex A appended to the Interim Report of the Working Party on Commodity Problems (L/320, 11 February 1955).

395 L/320, at 3. As to the legal relationship between the SACA and the GATT, there was on this subject a wide range of views: at one extreme were proposals to incorporate the SACA provisions into the text of the GATT; at the other extreme was a suggestion that the link between the SACA and the GATT should be established by a suitable amendment to the then Article XX:1(h) (for an assessment of the different positions, L/320, at 2).

396 See discussions at the nineteenth, twenty-third, twenty-seventh, thirty-fourth and thirty-eight meetings of the Ninth Session of the Contracting Parties (SR 9/19, SR 9/23, SR 9/27, SR 9/34, SR 9/38).

397 L/416, at 2, para. 4.

398 L/592/Rev.1, at 1, para. 1.

new approach, outlined in the Resolution annexed to the Working Party report, which was this time adopted, was to focus on "[…] general multilateral review, problem-specific consultations and the possible convening of an intergovernmental meeting on a case-by-case basis".[399]

### 3.1.2.3 Amendment of GATT Article XX(h)

Pending resolution of outstanding differences on the SACA, it was agreed to amend GATT Article XX, subparagraph (h). As discussed, the GATT 1947, in the original paragraph (h) of Article XX, had exempted ICAs compliant with the Havana Charter from key GATT disciplines. This reflected the formal pledge, by the 23 GATT parties, to observe, to the fullest possible extent, the general principles laid down in the Havana Charter, pending its ratification.[400] During the Review Session, that sub-paragraph of the Article was deleted and new text was inserted, "in view of the steps being taken to develop new principles relating to the conclusion of commodity agreements", a reference to the SACA negotiations.[401] The amended paragraph (h) exempted measures "[…] undertaken in pursuance of obligations under any intergovernmental commodity agreement which conforms to criteria submitted to the CONTRACTING PARTIES and not disapproved by them or which is itself so submitted and not so disapproved".[402]

The exception provided in the first part of paragraph (h) was intended to cover arrangements negotiated within the terms of the proposed SACA; exception under the last phrase would allow flexibility to exempt arrangements negotiated outside the terms of the proposed SACA framework.[403] An interpretative note was added to the amended Article, in order that the exception provided for in the original Article XX, subparagraph (h) might continue to apply "to commodity agreements concluded or which may be concluded, in accordance with the principles approved by the Economic and Social Council in its Resolution of 28 March 1947 [i.e. the 'Havana principles'] ".[404]

### 3.1.2.4 Subsequent Developments within the GATT Framework

Failure to agree on the SACA can be viewed as a setback in the effort to set a coherent normative framework for action on commodity prices. Yet, as made

399 GATT *Analytical Index*, above n 46, at 590.

400 GATT Article XXIX.

401 L/327, para 20.

402 GATT Article XX (h).

403 L/416, at 2, para. 4.

404 L/327, para 22.

explicit by the Working Party on Commodity Problems, this should not prevent the GATT parties from determining, in the future, general objectives and principles on ICAs.[405] Nor did it prevent consideration of principles and objectives elsewhere, outside of the GATT framework, under the aegis of UNCTAD.

Through the 1960s, the GATT did not remain impervious to ideas and influences from outside. Discussions at UNCTAD filtered into the Kennedy Round of multilateral trade negotiations (1963–1967).[406] In that context, many developing countries pressed for unilateral, non-reciprocal, concessions by developed countries in terms of tariff and non-tariff liberalisation, in the GATT context. Eventually, a new set of provisions, Part IV (Articles XXXVI to XXXVIII), was inserted into the GATT.[407] Articles XXXVI:4 and Article XXXVIII:2(a), added to the GATT by the 1965 Part IV Protocol, reaffirmed the permissibility, and desirability, wherever appropriate, of "measures designed to attain stable, equitable and remunerative prices" to commodity producers. This language was intended to accommodate developing countries' quest for a new commodity trade order, as articulated in the framework of UNCTAD.

Finally, concerns about price stability underlined two Tokyo Round 'codes' (plurilateral agreements) established within the GATT framework: the Arrangement Regarding Bovine Meat[408] and the International Dairy Arrangement.[409] Both included economic stabilisation clauses, though their primary objective was the expansion and liberalisation of trade. Specifically, the two treaties laid down procedures for the adoption of GATT-consistent stabilisation measures, to prevent and deal with serious supply and demand imbalances. In addition, under the Dairy Arrangement, participants committed to enforce minimum export prices. In force since January 1980, the two Agreements were terminated in 1997. Their stabilisation clauses remained largely inoperative.

### 3.1.3 *UNCTAD's IPC (1964–1989)*

Through the 1960s and 1970s, UNCTAD emerged as the principal negotiating forum where the developing countries framed their new collective stance on commodity matters. Other major fora for discussion included the Non-Aligned

405 L/592/Rev.1, at 3, para. 8.

406 Subsequent developments – the *Enabling Clause* – would restate the non-reciprocity idea embedded in Article XXXVI. Douglas Irwin et al., *The Genesis of the GATT* (Cambridge: Cambridge University Press, 2008), at 132–33.

407 Done in 1965, the Protocol Amending the General Agreement on Tariffs and Trade to Introduce a Part IV on Trade and Development entered into force on 27 June 1966 (*GATT Analytical Index*, above n 46, at 7).

408 26S/84, 1186 UNTS 344.

409 26S/91, 1186 UNTS 54.

Movement and the Group of 77;[410] Special Sessions of the United Nations General Assembly;[411] and, as mentioned, multilateral trade negotiations within the GATT framework.

Convened by the General Assembly to address the "urgent trade and development problems of the developing countries",[412] the first United Nations Conference on Trade and Development was held in Geneva from 23 March to 15 June of 1964.[413] As an inter-governmental forum, UNCTAD was soon to become "the major caucusing forum for the developing countries and a major vehicle for the expression of their economic concerns".[414] As a 'think-tank', it provided the fundamental tenets and conceptual underpinnings of developing countries' quest for a new trade regime in commodities.

#### 3.1.3.1 UNCTAD's Quest for a New Trade Policy

When UNCTAD was first convened in the early 1960s, the context had changed considerably from that of Havana. As stated by Rowe, with the independence movement had come "the consciousness of underdevelopment"; and with the Marshall Plan "the notion of planned development" became more mature.[415] This was the background against which a change of ideas as to the nature and function of commodity policy took place since the early 1960s.

---

410 The Group of 77 (G-77) was established in 1964 by seventy-seven developing countries signatories of the *Joint Declaration of the Seventy-Seven Countries*, issued at the conclusion of the first session of UNCTAD in Geneva. Although China is not a member of the Group of 77, it has associated itself with the group's policy declarations and statements (hence the term 'Group of 77 and China'). An offspring of the first session of UNCTAD, the Group of 77 developing nations evolved into a permanent institutional structure, the largest coalition of developing countries in the United Nations. UNCTAD's major constituency, the Group of 77 entertained with UNCTAD a close but complex relationship, as summarised by Rothstein (Robert L. Rothstein, *Global Bargaining: UNCTAD and the Quest for a New International Economic Order* (Princeton, New Jersey: Princeton University Press, 1979), at 104 and 111–23).

411 Since 1974, the developing countries had also vigorously asserted their position in the UN General Assembly (for a review, Remarks by Charles R Johnston, Jr., above n 86, at 131–32; Vastine, above n 284). This was the framework where the developing countries articulated their quest for a 'New International Economic Order'.

412 Final Act adopted by the United Nations Conference on Trade and Development (Geneva, 23 March – 13 June 1964), at 4, paragraph 8 (contained in *Proceedings of the United Nations Conference on Trade and Development* (New York: United Nations, 1964), vol. I).

413 All States member of the United Nations and members of the specialised agencies and of the International Atomic Energy Agency were invited to take part in the Conference, which would then be established as a permanent organ of the General Assembly.

414 Vastine, above n 284, at 405.

415 Rowe, above n 55, at 311.

As detailed in Section 3.2.1.1 below, the basic contention by the UNCTAD secretariat was that the prices of commodity exports tended to fall relative to the prices of more sophisticated manufactured products.[416] According to this theory, developing countries, exporters of primary commodities and importers of manufactured goods, were locked in a structurally disadvantageous pattern of export specialisation. This structural pattern, which resulted in a structural current account imbalance for the developing countries, ought to be redressed by means of purposive policy intervention.

In this direction, the Secretary General's report suggested an "integrated programme of measures" as part of a comprehensive "trade policy for development".[417] In particular, two converging measures were envisaged to "guarantee the purchasing power of exports of primary commodities": direct action on prices through international commodity agreements, and compensatory financing.[418] Commodity agreements, which could involve "whatever system of export quotas may be necessary",[419] were to "establish minimum prices or improve prices, as the case may be, by maintaining their parity with those of manufactures".[420] Compensatory financing, a complement to commodity agreements, should be made available to developing countries to compensate, in Prebisch's conception, for the deteriorating terms of trade. Other measures to redress imbalances included what would be termed South-South regional integration; and trade preferences in the form of unilateral, non-reciprocal, preferential access granted by the developed countries for the manufactures and semi-manufactures of the less developed countries. In the view of UNCTAD's secretariat, these policies altogether would redress developing countries' trade imbalances.

#### 3.1.3.2 A Complex Bargaining

These views were soon reflected in developing countries' mainstream position on commodities. They expressed a radical agenda for change and endorsed principles that the US and other developed countries had generally opposed. Efforts to translate these proposals into concrete actions continued at the

416 The slow growth of primary exports was considered an inevitable result of technological progress in the industrial countries, leading to the increasing substitution of synthetics for natural products and to smaller raw material content of finished goods; to which must be added the effects of the propagation of modern agricultural techniques in the advanced countries.

417 *Towards a New Trade Policy for Development*, above n 32, at 4.

418 Ibid, at 61.

419 Ibid.

420 Ibid.

second (New Delhi, 1968) and third (Santiago, 1972) sessions of UNCTAD, but with limited results, in a climate of open confrontation between the North and the South.[421]

As discussed in Rothstein, the debate was only outwardly polarised. It certainly created opposition between the Group of 77 and the so-called 'Group B', the negotiating bloc representing the OECD industrial market economies within UNCTAD. However, it also reflected other complex bargaining processes: between the UNCTAD's secretariat and the Group of 77; within the Group of 77; within Group B; and within individual countries.[422] Developing countries were not as united as it may appear. UNCTAD had to secure support from developing countries that would not directly benefit from the programme, as the IPC did not provide equitable benefits to all.[423] Similarly, the spectrum of views within the Group B countries varied significantly: from strong ideological opposition and downright rejection by the so-called 'hard-liners', such as the USA and West Germany, initially Japan and, to some extent, the United Kingdom; to outwardly more sympathetic by the 'progressives', in particular, the Netherlands and the Scandinavian countries, and to some extent France; with the rest keeping a lower profile.[424] Conflicting views existed not only between countries, but also within countries. It has been observed in this respect that

421 Vastine, above n 284, at 409; [William D. Rogers], "Comments by William D. Rogers," *American Society of International Law Proceedings* 71 (1977): 142.

422 Rothstein, above n 410, at 103–66.

423 As noted by Rothstein, the relationship between UNCTAD and the Group of 77 was overall "close and supportive" (Rothstein, above n 410, at 122). Yet, UNCTAD had to secure support from developing countries that would not directly benefit from the programme. Indeed, the IPC did not provide equitable benefits to all: a few developing countries, including the major oil exporters, were net importers of the 10 core commodities for which prices ought to be stabilised; others (e.g. India, South Korea, Singapore, Taiwan and Yugoslavia) were exporters of manufacturers, heavily reliant on cheap raw material imports. Eventually, shared values prevailed over conflicting interests. This convergence was facilitated by the fact that potential losers from UNCTAD's stabilisation proposal mainly included high-income developing countries that could be compensated from oil proceeds or from proceeds from manufactures/services (e.g. Saudi Arabia, Iran, Iraq, Algeria, Libya – some major oil exporters; Morocco and Jordan – compensated by high phosphate proceeds; and the Bahamas, South Korea, Singapore and Yugoslavia – proceeds from services and manufactures). See Rothstein, above n 410, at 111–23.

424 Geoffrey Goodwin, "The OECD Industrialised Countries' Response," in *A New International Commodity Regime*, ed. Geoffrey Goodwin and James Mayall (London: Croom Helm, 1979), at 111; Rothstein, above n 410, at 123–24. Some commentators (Rothstein, at 122–23) note that these views did not necessarily parallel the breakdown between potential winners and losers: the US, for example, was among the likely beneficiaries of the IPC, yet

in Western industrial countries left-wing parties tended to believe that the new commodity trade regime was justified; while pro-liberalisation groups thought that it was "bad politics, worse economics".[425]

Divergences, it is important to acknowledge, were not only ideologically inspired, but also proceeded on technical grounds. Indeed, the theoretical and empirical underpinnings of UNCTAD's arguments were hotly disputed by external experts.[426] The very assumption of UNCTAD's quest for a new commodity trade regime, the alleged deterioration of developing countries' terms of trade, was a matter of academic controversy.[427] The modalities and opportunity costs of commodity price stabilisation were similarly contested. There was serious disagreement among outside experts about commodities amenable to buffer stock stabilisation;[428] much discussion about the relative costs of price stabilisation *versus* compensatory financing; and questions as to whether expansion of trade opportunities and direct aid would not be more effective than price manipulation in order to transfer resources from rich to poor countries.[429] Furthermore, there was confusion about who would reap the benefits of increased commodity prices. It was argued that UNCTAD's IPC did not provide equitable benefits to all the developing countries, and that

---

it vigorously opposed it. Others remark some correlation between the stance taken and the vested interest on commodities (Congressional Budget Office, above n 80, at 18–19).

425 Rothstein, above n 410, at 33. Internal political developments played a role in shifting external policy posture. In the US, for example, the departure of the Ford administration (republican) and the arrival of the Carter administration (democratic) is accounted to have contributed to ease some "psychological obstacles" to constructively engaging in the debate on the IPC. For a detailed assessment, Vastine, above n 284; see also Klein, above n 86.

426 On this aspect, Hager, above n 269, at 310–11; Gerald M. Meier, "UNCTAD Proposals for International Economic Reform," *Stanford Law Review* 19, no. 6 (1967): 1185.

427 On the declining terms of trade, cf. *Towards a New Trade Policy for Development*, above n 32, at 15 and Johnson, above n 41, at 249–50.

428 Cf. John A. Pincus, "What Policy for Commodities?" in *Readings in International Economic Relations*, ed. Finn B. Jensen and Ingo Walter (New York: Ronald Press, 1966), 459–60 with Gerda Blau, "International Commodity Arrangements and Policies," in *Proceedings of the United Nations Conference on Trade and Development*, vol. III (New York: United Nations, 1964), at 150.

429 The World Bank had estimated that, if trade barriers were eliminated in the multilateral trade negotiations, foreign exchange earnings by 1985 would improve for Latin America by 29 billion constant 1977 dollars; by contrast, the integrated commodity program by 1985 would increase earnings by two to four billion dollars, if the ten core commodities doubled in price as a result of the integrated commodity program. As reported by Rogers, above n 421, at 141–42.

some middle-income developing countries would benefit comparatively more than the poorest ones.[430] Requests by some members to elaborate further on these technical issues, including on the asymmetric pattern of benefits from the IPC, were largely deflected by UNCTAD.[431]

#### 3.1.3.3 The Integrated Programme for Commodities (IPC) (Resolution 93 (IV))

The final outcome of UNCTAD IV reflected these complex dynamics.[432] Eventually, all parties came to terms. In the wake of OPEC's success,[433] the 'hardliners' were brought to the negotiating table, in spite of strong ideological reservations. In parallel, the UNCTAD proposal for an IPC, at least on paper, had become progressively more moderate. Emphasis had shifted more explicitly towards price stabilisation, rather than price support. The controversial issue of indexation was ambiguously left aside. More concern was expressed for relatively uncontroversial long-term issues, such as economic diversification and market access.[434]

---

430 It was found, for example, that for 1970 and 1973, middle-income developing countries had been more dependent on the commodities of special export interest to developing countries identified by UNCTAD, for which the prices ought to be sustained/stabilised, than the poorest or high-income developing countries; and that the economies of Latin America and Africa would benefit more than those of Asia or Oceania. See Congressional Budget Office, above n 80, at 15–18.

431 According to some commentators, UNCTAD had an interest not to expose the technical weakness of the IPC: more rigorous discussions at the technical level would have exposed the conflicting interests among developing countries, and possibly undermined their collective support for the Programme. Christopher P. Brown, *The Political and Social Economy of Commodity Control* (London: Macmillan, 1980). See also Rothstein, above n 410.

432 For insights on UNCTAD IV and more generally on the commodity negotiations in UNCTAD, see in particular: Alfred Maizels, *Commodities in Crisis. The Commodity Crisis of the 1980s and the Political Economy of International Commodity Policies* (Oxford: Clarendon Press, 1992); Gamani Corea, *Taming Commodity Markets: The Integrated Programme and the Common Fund in UNCTAD* (Manchester; New York: Manchester University Press, 1992); Dragoslav Avramovic, "Commodities in Nairobi," *Development and Change* 8 (1977).

433 By the mid-1970s, it is important to stress, the political environment had changed considerably from what it had been a few years earlier. In particular, the success of the OPEC cartel in 1973 contributed significantly to change perceptions as to the possibility that developing countries could 'go alone'. See Klein, above n 86, at 284–86; Vastine, above n 284, at 426–54.

434 Cf. the 1964 Report by the Secretary General of UNCTAD, above n 417, and the language of Resolution 94 (IV), agreed upon at the final plenary of UNCTAD IV on 31 May 1976. Rothstein, above n 32, at 122.

The IPC, agreed upon at the final plenary of UNCTAD IV on 31 May 1976 under Resolution 93 (IV), represented a major confluence of these political and economic developments; and "the latest stage in the evolution of the intergovernmental primary commodity trade regime".[435] The Conference adopted the Resolution without dissent. However, a number of Western governments, i.e. the US, Great Britain and the Federal Republic of Germany, made explanatory statements in which they qualified their approval of the IPC with a number of reservations.[436]

Two major decisions were agreed upon at the final plenary of UNCTAD IV on 31 May 1976.

First, Resolution 93 (IV) launched a parallel process of negotiations for 18 commodities of export interest to developing countries, including 10 core commodities identified by the UNCTAD secretariat as suitable for buffer stock stabilisation.[437] The Resolution set out the procedure and timetable for this purpose, with a target completion date at the end of 1978.[438] The outcome of these commodity-specific negotiations would be a series of concurrent commodity agreements on commodities of export interest to developing countries.

Second, the Resolution envisaged a single financial mechanism, a Common Fund for Commodities (CFC), for the financing of buffer stock operations. The proposed new international financial institution was to be "the first non-aid financial institution not firmly under the control of the major Western countries".[439] The Resolution set a tight framework. It was agreed that a negotiating conference on the CFC would be held within the framework of UNCTAD no later than March 1977. Yet, there were profound differences regarding the objectives and modalities of the CFC. Some envisaged the Fund as an assured

435 Remarks by Charles R Johnston, Jr., above n 86, at 132.

436 In its statement of clarification, in particular, the US specified that it had only committed to participating in preparatory meetings to examine whether further agreements were desirable. *Proceedings of the United Nations Conference on Trade and Development, Fourth Session, Nairobi, 5–31 May 1976* (New York: United Nations, 1977), vol I (TD/218 (Vol. I)), at 52.

437 Res. 93 (IV) of 30 May 1976, *sub.* Objectives, par. 2(a).

438 Preparatory meetings were to be convened by UNCTAD on individual commodities from 1 September 1976 to February 1978, with a view to negotiating a series of international commodity agreements. The preparatory stage was to lead to negotiating conferences by the end of 1978. An 'Ad hoc Inter-Governmental Committee' was to be established in UNCTAD to oversee the process and ensure coherence. The timetable, tight and ambitious, "reflected the mood at Nairobi that a real breakthrough had occurred and that the international community was now genuinely ready to fashion a new deal on commodities". Corea, above n 432, at 136.

439 Maizels, above n 432, at 119.

'source' of finance for the stock operations of existing and new ICAs, endowed with substantial capital of its own.[440] A few, particularly within the Group B, viewed the Fund as a 'pool' of finance provided by ICAs. Others expressed reservations on the very idea of a Common Fund.

Eventually, results proved modest.

Only one new commodity control agreement was negotiated within the context of the IPC in UNCTAD. This was the 1979 International Natural Rubber Agreement (INRA), which provided for rubber price stabilisation exclusively through stocking operations.[441] Two additional agreements, the 1982 International Agreement on Jute and Jute Products and the 1983 Agreement on Tropical Timber, were successfully negotiated in the IPC context, but neither of them contained economic provisions for price stabilisation. All of the other ICAs essentially continued arrangements set up prior to the establishment of UNCTAD (such as the ISA, ITA, ICoA, and IWA), or negotiated later, but outside the IPC framework, as is the case of the International Cocoa Agreement.[442]

The CFC was established only in 1989, almost a decade after the negotiation of its Articles of Agreement.[443] Endowed with modest capital resources, the CFC was to act as a 'pool' of finance provided by ICAs, instead of a 'source' of finance. This significantly hindered its catalytic role. The financing requirements originally proposed for the CFC amounted in total to $6 billion.[444] Eventually, the 1980 Articles of Agreement of the Common Fund provided for only some $400 million of direct government contributions, for working

440 The financing requirements originally proposed amounted to $6 billion, of which 2 billion would consist of direct capital subscriptions from members, while the remainder would be raised from borrowing. Maizels, above n 432, at 121.

441 See above n 121.

442 Other arrangements were negotiated outside the UNCTAD framework. These included the Arrangement Regarding Bovine Meat (26S/84) and the International Dairy Arrangement (26S/9), which were negotiated during the Tokyo Round of multilateral trade negotiations.

443 These Articles stipulated that the Agreement would enter into force when no less than 90 countries had ratified the Agreement, accounting for at least two-thirds of the Fund's directly contributed capital. The delayed establishment of the Fund was due to non-ratification by both the United States and the Soviet Union: without either country the capital contribution threshold could not be attained.

444 Of this, one-third (or $2 billion) was to be raised by direct contributions from governments; the remainder by borrowing, as and when necessary (Maizels, above n 432, at 121). According to some commentators, this requirement was low: effective buffer stocks for the ten core commodities would have required considerably more than $10 billion. [Joseph M. Finger], "Comments by Joseph M. Finger," *American Society of International Law Proceedings* 71 (1977): 136.

capital and administrative expenses.[445] As for voting, the Group B countries, the market-based developed economies, retained power to block all substantive decisions.[446]

Was the IPC proposal ($6 billion) excessively costly for the international community? To put things in perspective, the Common Agricultural Policy (CAP) in 1977 reportedly cost taxpayers $8.6 billion.[447] The $6 billion IPC requirement was comparatively not high, especially considering that this was a one shot contribution. What was lacking was a common political resolve to carry out the objectives of the IPC; which in turn reflected fundamental disagreement as to the rationales for and objectives of commodity price regulation.

## 3.2 Objectives and Principles of Multilateral Action on Commodity Prices

Important inferences can be drawn for today from past efforts to set multilateral agreed criteria for action on commodity prices. Results in practice have been modest. Yet, the normative objectives and principles evolved at Havana and Nairobi had weight, and are still momentous. It is thus useful to examine them in detail. This is what this Chapter seeks to do.

The following analysis tries to extricate the objectives and principles of multilateral action on prices, as framed by the drafters of the Havana Charter and of UNCTAD's IPC and in light of relevant GATT discussions. It addresses the following questions. What can be inferred, from a textual and contextual reading of Chapter 6 of the Havana Charter and of UNCTAD's Resolution 93 (IV),

---

445 A second window, with a target of $280 million, was to be established by voluntary contributions from member governments, with provision for the transfer of at least $70 million to the first window for market stabilisation. Additional funds required for the financing of stock operations of ICAs ought to be borrowed from private capital markets. The ICAs would make cash deposits with the Fund and provide the Fund with stock warrants as collateral, while the Fund would also have government guarantees in the form of callable capital (Maizels, above n 432, at 121).

446 The Group of 77 obtained 47 percent of the total votes; Group B 42 percent; Group D (socialist countries of Eastern Europe) 8 percent; and China 3 percent (Maizels, above n 432, 122). The Group B countries retained power to block all substantive decisions, which required a qualified majority. This included decisions with 'significant financial implications' (such as increases in the Fund's capital), which required a three-fourths majority; as well as 'other important' decisions (such as projects to be financed by the second window), approved at a two-thirds majority (Maizels, above n 432, at 123).

447 "The EEC's Farm Policy," *The Economist*, 1 April 1978, 60–62.

about the rationales for institutional price intervention in commodity markets? What were the broad normative objectives sought? What ordering principles were applied? Which common intent, if any, can be disentangled from the views and positions of the key negotiating parties as to the specific price objectives to be sought?

The analysis defines the extent of agreement, while also pointing to divergence and disagreements that existed in the background. It first reviews the objectives and principles of concerted price intervention in international commodity markets, as enshrined in the Havana Charter and UNCTAD's IPC (3.2.1). The analysis then assesses the extent to which these objectives and principles were accepted in practice as general guide in intergovernmental action on commodity prices, and closes with some summary observations (3.2.2).

### 3.2.1 *A Textual and Contextual Reading*

There are important contextual differences, in terms of underlying normative values, between the Havana Charter and UNCTAD's IPC. The normative objectives of Chapter 6 of the Havana Charter as a whole were deeply rooted in those that lay beneath the whole Charter: post-war concerns for reconstruction and development. The normative underpinnings of UNCTAD's IPC are to be found in the quest for a NIEO, a highly politicised endeavour, geared to establish more equitable relationships between developing and developed countries. Economic theory had also evolved: from the Keynesian economics underlying the Havana Charter, to the 'structuralist' perspectives underlying UNCTAD's IPC.

Yet, the two endeavours have common traits. In particular, they both involved a purposive, 'substantive' legal rationale, which infused some political orientation to international trade regulation. This 'substantive' rationale, as stated in Teubner, " [...] is to be found in the perceived need for the collective regulation of economic and social activities to compensate for inadequacies of the market".[448] Instead of providing an enabling framework for private action, 'substantive' law directly regulates social behaviour by setting substantive prescriptions.[449] In doing so, law "becomes increasingly oriented to social roles and statuses".[450] Under both the Havana principles and UNCTAD's IPC, commodity market outcomes were not accepted as 'natural'. They were critically assessed against some normative benchmarks: social and political stability, in the case of Havana; and developmental gains, within the UNCTAD's framework.

---

448 Teubner, above n 42, at 253–54.

449 Ibid.

450 Ibid, at 254.

These normative benchmarks invited principled decisions rooted in value systems. As such, they were inherently subjective, discretionary and thus political.

This normative attitude challenged some basic tenets of international economic law as conceived in the aftermath of the Second World War in some important respects.[451] The UNCTAD's approach, in particular, by introducing the economic factor into legal analysis, challenged the postulate of abstract legal equality of States, a basic principle of international law. It also stood contrary to principles of non-discrimination and reciprocity, the basic tenets of the international trade system, as conceived in the aftermath of the Second World War.[452]

With all this in mind, it is worth considering the economic rationale, objectives and principles of multilateral price intervention in international commodity markets, as inferred from relevant instruments and material. Considerations of principles, objectives and economic rationale are, in practice, intermingled. For ease of description, they are here presented separately.

#### 3.2.1.1 Economic Rationale for Price Regulation

##### a) *The Havana Charter*

Chapter 6 of the Havana Charter, "a code within a code",[453] segregated commodities under a special regime, comprehensively carved out from general commercial disciplines. Indeed, the Chapter as a whole deviated substantially from the general principles of commercial policy laid down in the Charter.[454] The central commercial policy objective of the Havana Charter was the re-establishment of a multilateral, non-discriminatory world trading system. This was to be based on "the reduction of trade barriers, the elimination of discrimination, and the conduct of trade on commercial principles".[455] Against

---

451 Christine M. Chinkin, "The Challenge of Soft Law: Development and Change in International Law," *International and Comparative Law Quarterly* 38, no. 4 (1989): 853, with reference to the changes in legal thought and practice brought about by the NIEO.

452 Ibid, at 853. Instead of a single set of rules with exceptions, the NIEO substituted "a dual system that makes a distinction between, on the one hand, the rules applicable as between developed countries that follow the traditional rules of international economic law and, on the other, the rules applicable as between developed and developing countries, which purport to redress the inequalities of development by introducing a compensatory inequality in favour of the countries of the South" (Ahmed Mahiou, *Declaration on the Establishment of a New International Economic Order*, United Nations Audiovisual Library of International Law, at 2. http://legal.un.org/avl/pdf/ha/ga_3201/ga_3201_e.pdf).

453 Brown, above n 371, at 217.

454 Ibid, at 217–22.

455 Ibid, at 167.

the basic tenets of this regime, the commodity policy provisions of the Charter sanctioned the legitimacy of institutionalised restrictive practices in international commodity markets.

The rationale for this special commodity regime was found in the special characteristics of commodity trade. It was generally felt that international trade in commodities was subject to special difficulties, not associated with other merchandise goods. In particular, commodities exhibited a "tendency towards persistent disequilibrium between production and consumption", which involved "the accumulation of burdensome stocks and pronounced fluctuations in prices".[456] These special difficulties "may, at times, necessitate special treatment of the international trade in such commodities through inter-governmental agreement".[457] It was on these grounds that the possibility of establishing intergovernmental commodity agreements was envisaged by the Charter.

Yet, Chapter 6 still reflected a free market orientation. Commodity control arrangements were regarded as a 'necessary evil', a remedy when things could not be redressed by market forces alone. Agreements of a restrictive nature, involving regulation of production, trade or prices (commodity 'control' agreements, in the Charter jargon) should be used only in two specific circumstances: first, when a burdensome surplus, actual or impending, would cause serious hardship to small producers; second, where special difficulties may give rise to widespread unemployment or under-employment.[458] The first circumstance concerned smallholder production; the second covered the case of more capital-intensive industries employing wage workers, i.e. estate production and the extractive sector. Resort to restrictive agreements was allowed only when these circumstances "could not be corrected by normal market forces" in time to prevent hardship.[459] Being an exceptional device, to be resorted to only in abnormal circumstances, control agreements ought to be transitional in nature. They shall be concluded by a period of not more than five year, and renewal shall be for a period not exceeding five years.[460]

### b) *UNCTAD's IPC*

In certain important respects, the IPC marked a departure from the Havana Charter approach. Most prominently, regulation of commodity markets was

456 Havana Charter, Article 55.
457 Havana Charter, Article 55.
458 Havana Charter, Article 62.
459 Havana Charter, Article 62 (a) and (b).
460 Havana Charter, Article 65:1.

viewed as a norm rather than an exception to be resorted to in emergencies. This reflected the perception that the problems of commodity markets were structural and chronic, rather than occasional and contingent. It further reflected the conviction that the spontaneous course of economic forces would only reinforce and magnify existing disparities and imbalances.

The main tenet of UNCTAD's commodity policy was the alleged deterioration in the terms of trade of commodity-exporting developing countries.[461] A country's terms of trade indicate the price of a country's exports in terms of its imports, that is, the ratio of export prices to import prices.[462] It was argued that for commodity-exporting economies, mainly developing countries, the terms of trade tended to deteriorate. The contention was that primary commodity exports, with certain exceptions, developed fairly slowly, while demand for industrial imports tended to accelerate more quickly.[463] Accordingly, the prices of commodity exports tended to fall relative to the prices of more sophisticated manufactured products imported from developed countries, thus the deteriorating terms of trade.[464] Developing countries, as exporters of primary commodities and importers of manufactures, were locked in a structurally disadvantageous pattern of export specialisation.

Purposive action was needed, which, by "rationally influencing and modifying the course of events",[465] would lead to "a more just and rational international economic order".[466] Underlying this was a 'positive conception' of economic policy, in the sense of a "rational and deliberate design for influencing economic forces so as to change their spontaneous course of evolution and attain clear objectives".[467]

This, with some oversimplification, was the thesis posited by Raúl Prebisch, Secretary-General of UNCTAD, one heavily debated in the academic community.

---

461 UNCTAD's approach to commodity prices was officially expounded in the report *Towards a New Trade Policy*, above n 32.

462 A country's terms of trade reveal "the purchasing power of exports over imports". *Towards a New Trade Policy for Development*, above n 32, at 9.

463 *Towards a New Trade Policy for Development*, above n 32, at 9. The slow growth of primary exports was considered an inevitable result of technological progress in the industrial countries, leading to the increasing substitution of synthetics for natural products and to smaller raw material content of finished goods. To this must be added the effects of the propagation of modern agricultural techniques in the advanced countries.

464 Ibid.

465 Ibid, at 7.

466 Ibid, Foreword.

467 Ibid, at 7.

#### 3.2.1.2 Normative Underpinnings and Objectives

##### a) *The Havana Charter*

The special regime for commodities enshrined in the Charter was purposively framed by the overall objectives that underlie the whole Charter, those being: "[to realise] the aims set forth in the Charter of the United Nations, particularly the attainment of the higher standards of living, full employment and conditions of economic and social progress and development, envisaged in Article 55 of that Charter".[468]

Security of employment, and more broadly the well-being of people, ought thus to be the cornerstone of the multilateral trading system, the 'critical benchmark' against which to assess the desirability of specific commercial policies.[469] Behind this framing were post-war concerns for reconstruction and development: the need to "create conditions of stability and well-being which are necessary for peaceful and friendly relations among nations".[470] This is the background against which to assess the normative objectives and principles of the commodity policy provisions of the Charter.

On commodity matters, the objectives pursued were multiple. As stated in Article 57, inter-governmental commodity agreements were justified as a means to: ease imbalances of supply and demand, when production and consumption could not be balanced by normal market forces alone "as rapidly as the circumstances require"; encourage local processing in commodity-dependent countries, and expansion of consumption; "prevent or moderate pronounced fluctuations in the price of a primary commodity"; further the conservation of exhaustible natural resources; expand supply, if advantageous to both producers and consumers; and "assure the equitable distribution of a primary commodity in short supply".[471] These stated objectives variously reflected producers' and consumers' concerns and most frequently concealed competing interests and unresolved divergences, as discussed in Section 3.2.1.3.

##### b) *UNCTAD's IPC*

As discussed, the context at Nairobi had changed considerably from that at Havana. Commodity problems had by then become inextricably interlocked

468 Havana Charter, Chapter I (Purpose and Objective), Article 1.

469 Daniel Drache, *The Short but Significant Life of the International Trade Organization: Lessons for Our Time*, University of Warwick, Centre for the Study of Globalisation and Regionalisation, CSGR Working Paper 62/00 (Warwick, 2000), at 8–12. See also Brown, above n 371, at 165.

470 Havana Charter, Chapter I (Purpose and Objective), Article 1. See also: London Report, above n 49, narrative account of the treatment of Chapter I, at p. 4.

471 Havana Charter, Article 57.

with the development needs of newly independent states; and the commodity debate was reassessed in terms of North–South divide.

The normative underpinnings of UNCTAD's IPC are to be found in the quest for a NIEO, as spelled out in the Declaration and the Programme of Action on the Establishment of a New International Economic Order,[472] as well as the Charter of Economic Rights and Duties of States.[473]

Ultimately, the NIEO was a highly politicised endeavour, geared to establish more equitable relationships between developing and developed countries, based on considerations of equity and fairness in international economic relations. It entailed also classical issues of enhanced market access for developing countries in agricultural products, in line with the GATT. Overall, it rested on the assumption that the existing economic regime had disproportionally benefited the developed world. It advocated a redistribution of benefits from the North to the South. Its claims were deeply imbued with considerations of equity and fairness; and tended to translate economic and ethical arguments, primarily, the notion of redistributive justice, into legal concepts.

The NIEO's ultimate objective was to "correct inequalities and redress existing injustices" and eventually "eliminate the widening gap between the developed and the developing countries".[474] To this purpose, a number of actions were envisaged, premised on three interlocking sets of principles: sovereign equality, self-determination and the related principle of permanent sovereignty over natural resources; considerations of fairness and equity, and particularly of re-distributive justice; and the idea of a common interest, and a duty of co-operation among all states.[475]

---

472 UN GA Res. 3201 (S-VI) and 302 (S-VI) of 1 May 1974.

473 UN GA Res. 3281 (XXIX) of 12 December 1974.

474 UN GA Res. 3201 (S-VI), para. 1.

475 Based on these principles, UN GA Res. 3201 (S-VI) called, among other for: the restoration of effective control over a State's natural resources, including by means of nationalisation; the transfer of technology and the regulation of multinational enterprises; preferential and non-reciprocal treatment of developing countries, in commercial policy and other areas; financial and technical assistance to developing countries, untied and unconditional; restitution and full compensation for colonial and alien domination. Three specific objectives concerned directly commodity policy: the establishment of "just and equitable relationship" of prices between "raw materials, primary commodities, manufactured and semi-manufactured goods"; the positive endorsement of the role which producers' association may play "within the framework of inter-national cooperation"; and a commitment to improve the competitiveness of natural materials relative to synthetics.

Three tenets of the NIEO directly concerned commodity policy:[476] the quest for a "just and equitable relationship" of prices between "raw materials, primary commodities, manufactured and semi-manufactured goods"; the positive endorsement of the role which producers' association may play "within the framework of inter-national cooperation"; and a commitment to improve the competitiveness of natural materials relative to synthetics. These objectives touched upon extremely controversial issues such as indexation, unilateral producer action, and the competitiveness of natural products relative to synthetics; and endorsed rules and principles that the industrial economies had generally opposed. As noted by Vastine, by pressing into the Declaration some of the most controversial concepts being dealt with in the context of UNCTAD, the developing countries employed the "not uncommon technique of using a more politicised forum to press for concessions they were not able to obtain from more technically oriented negotiations".[477] It is important to acknowledge, however, that the NIEO was not merely interventionist. It contained an important component of liberalising agricultural trade and improving market access for developing countries. The industrialised countries had failed to honour their liberalisation commitments due to protectionist agricultural policies, despite the neoliberal rhetoric at the time.

UNCTAD's IPC represented the first major effort to give 'substantive meaning' to the NIEO.[478] In line with the NIEO precepts, the purpose of the IPC was, in the Resolution language, "to eliminate the economic imbalance between developed and developing countries".[479] In the area of commodity trade, this required purposive action to improve the terms of trade for developing countries.

Towards this end, UNCTAD members agreed, with some important qualifications and reservations, to promote seven specific objectives. Some were relatively undisputed such as improved market access for developing countries (Resolution 93 (IV), Section I, objective 3), diversification and value addition in commodity-dependent producing countries (objective 4), improved market structures (objective 6) and trade logistics (objective 7). These objectives had already filtered into the Kennedy Round of multilateral trade negotiations (1963–1967).[480] In that context, many developing countries had pressed for institutional amendments that would allow for unilateral, non-reciprocal, concessions by developed countries in terms of tariff and non-tariff liberalisation,

476 Points j, m and t, UN GA Res. 3201 (S-VI).

477 Vastine, above n 284, at 417.

478 Rothstein, above n 410, at 3.

479 Res. 93 (IV), Sec. I (Objectives), at 7.

480 See above, Section 3.1.2.4.

eventually leading to the Enabling Clause. Other objectives were highly controversial, and far from settled: the price stabilisation and income support objectives, as ambiguously phrased in the Resolution (objectives 1 and 2); and commitments to improve the competitiveness of natural products relative to synthetics (objective 5). As discussed below, sharp distrust and basic disagreements remained on these price objectives. Yet, little effort was made to dispel doubts and clarify fundamental ambiguities.

#### 3.2.1.3 Ordering Principles

Multilateral action on prices, as sanctioned in Chapter 6 of the Havana Charter, was firmly committed to the principle of multilateralism and transparency, in line with the Charter's overall principles. It is worthwhile to consider these principles in some detail, as they are incorporated, by indirect reference, into the GATT.

First, ICAs were to be open, multilateral treaties. The general procedure for initiating ICAs envisaged: the calling of a study group;[481] the convening of an inter-governmental commodity conference, open to all interested countries, for the establishment of the agreements;[482] and the establishment of an international organisation, a Commodity Body, to administer the arrangement which had been agreed upon.[483] ICAs should be open to participation by any ITO member who considered that it had a substantial interest in the commodity concerned, as well as to invited non-members.[484] It should take into consideration the interests of non-participating members and of any non-member invited to participate. Countries would decide for themselves whether their interest in a commodity was sufficient to warrant their attendance at a study group or at a conference.[485] Full publicity ought to be given to their terms.

---

481 Havana Charter, Article 58. The study group would be established upon request of "any Member which considers itself substantially interested in the production or consumption of, or trade in, a particular primary commodity" (Article 58:1). Each member could appoint representatives, and non-members may be invited (Article 58:2). The study group would report its findings and recommendations to the ITO.

482 Havana Charter, Article 59. The Conference would be convened by the ITO on the basis of the recommendations of the study group, or at the request of members whose interests represent a significant part of world production or consumption of that commodity, or on its own initiative (Article 59:1). The Conference was opened to interested members; non-members may also be invited to participate (Article 59:2).

483 Havana Charter, Article 64.

484 Havana Charter, Article 59:2, Article 60:1.

485 United Nations Interim Co-ordinating Committee for International Commodity Arrangements, above n 86. Wide participation in arrangements was sought, by various means.

Second, the general principle was adopted in the Charter stating that there had to be adequate participation of importing and consuming countries, as well as exporting and producing countries;[486] and that the interests of countries that did not have a substantial interest in the trade should also be adequately represented. In control arrangements, countries engaged on the consumption or import side and on the production or export side should together have parity of vote.[487] Other safeguards were introduced to further protect the interests of consumers and to limit the long-term distortive effects of control arrangements.[488]

The Charter was restrictive. All inter-governmental commodity agreements ought to conform to the internationally agreed 'code of conduct' enshrined in the Charter.[489] Signatories would then be prohibited from negotiating or concluding commodity agreements except in accordance with the principles laid down in the Charter. This meant that existing commodity agreements, or agreements being negotiated at the time when the Charter would come into force, would have to be either harmonised with the Charter provisions

For example, the International Coffee Agreement 1962 would enter into force when ratified/accepted by at least twenty exporting countries having at least 80 percent of total exports in the year 1961, and at least ten importing countries having at least 80 percent of world imports in the same year (ICA 1961, Article 64(1)).

486 Havana Charter, Article 60:1 (d).

487 Havana Charter, Article 63 (b); Article 64:2. First, the principle required equal voting rights of exporters and importers on the governing body of the control agreement (the Council). Typically, the exporting members shall together hold 1,000 votes and the importing members shall together hold 1,000 votes. Within each category of members, each member shall have a specific amount of basic votes; the remaining votes be divided among members in proportion to their average trade volumes in specified reference periods. There shall be no fractional votes. Second, substantive decisions were to be taken by a 'distributed' – simple or two thirds – majority, i.e. a majority of the votes cast by producing countries and a majority of the votes cast by consuming countries, counted separately. Annual financial contributions from members were assessed in proportion to their votes, which in turn were proportioned to their trade volumes.

488 In particular, it was provided that: control agreements would assure adequate supplies to meet world demand at prices "fair to consumers" (a safeguard against cartel-type arrangements) (Havana Charter, Article 63 (a) and Article 57 (c)); they would be conducive to a satisfaction of demand from efficient sources, due regard however to the position of less efficient producers (a compromise language that attempted to reconcile the interests of low-cost and high-cost producers) (Article 63 (c)); and would be accompanied by programmes of internal economic adjustment, typically designed to diversify the economy of commodity-dependent producing countries (Article 63 (d) and 57 (b)).

489 Brown, above n 371, at 217. Havana Charter, Article 61:4 (a) and (b); Article 65:3.

or abandoned.[490] Unilateral or regional action was proscribed. Members shall enter into any new commodity agreement only through a commodity conference, open to all interested countries.[491] An escape clause was introduced, allowing for direct negotiation between concerned members in exceptional cases, subject to safeguards.[492]

In terms of operative principles and procedures, the UNCTAD framework did not depart substantially from the Havana Charter approach. Resolution 93 (IV) did not expressly disavow the Havana principles; and ICAs under the aegis of UNCTAD confirmed them.[493] In this respect, as pointed out by a distinguished commentator, the IPC approach remained a 'conformist' and moderate one, in spite of the very progressive nature of its claims.[494]

#### 3.2.1.4 Specific Price Objectives

Zooming on the specific price objectives sought, both the Havana Charter (Chapter 6) and UNCTAD' IPC aimed to stabilise prices at levels variously qualified as "fair" or "equitable" to consumers and as providing "a reasonable return to", or "remunerative and just" to producers. The price objective, as stated in the Havana Charter, was:

> To prevent or moderate pronounced fluctuations in the price of a primary commodity with a view to achieving a reasonable degree of stability on a basis of such prices as are fair to consumers and provide a reasonable return to producers, having regard to the desirability of securing long-term equilibrium between the forces of supply and demand.[495]

490 Brown, above n 371, at 217.

491 Havana Charter, Article 61:6 and Article 59. For commodity control agreements, only after an appropriate finding had been made, through the conference or by general agreement, as to the conditions justifying the use of this restrictive type of agreements (Article 61:6 and Article 62).

492 This was possible where there had been "unreasonable delay in the convening or in the proceedings of the study group or the conference", only in cases of actual or impending "burdensome surplus", causing or likely to cause hardship to small producers, or "widespread unemployment", and provided that the agreement conformed to the other provisions of the Charter. See Havana Charter, Article 61:6 and Article 62.

493 See Res. 93 (IV), Sec. IV (Procedures and time-table), paras. 4 and 5. In particular, it continued to be premised on the principles of multilateralism, consumer/producer cooperation and transparency.

494 Corea, above n 432, at 30.

495 Havana Charter, Article 57 (c).

The avowed price objective in UNCTAD's Resolution 93 (IV) was

> To achieve stable conditions in commodity trade, including avoidance of excessive price fluctuations, at levels which would: (a) be remunerative and just to producers and equitable to consumers; (b) take account of world inflation and changes in the world economic and monetary situations; (c) promote equilibrium between supply and demand within expanding world commodity trade.[496]

In both cases, concerns about price stability and price levels were in practice intermingled. Much ambiguity remained as to the genuine price objectives that were to be pursued, whether to moderate short-term price fluctuations around the market trend, or to influence the price trend itself. Questions also arise as to the level at which prices ought to be stabilised, a divisive issue, not only between exporting and importing countries, but also among exporters themselves. Ambiguous phrasing concealed major divergences as to the specifics of price stabilisation arrangements. As discussed in the following Section, the negotiating record points to major divergences on this issue; and testifies of difficulties in translating broadly shared, though not universal, concerns and convictions into workable terms.

### 3.2.2 *State Practice and Attitudes*

Questions arise as to whether the objectives and principles discussed above have ever been genuinely accepted as general guide in intergovernmental action on commodity prices. As discussed, Chapter 6 of the Havana Charter had received only endorsement in principle by the ECOSOC, and the Charter never entered into force. The IPC was declaratory and transformative in its endeavour to restructure the status quo. State practice and *opinion juris* may help ascertain whether any agreement has ever been reached on this matter. The following analysis defines the extent of agreement and convergence, while also pointing to divergence and disagreements that continued to exist in the background.

#### 3.2.2.1 State Practice

As discussed, the Havana principles, predicated on the ideals of multilateralism, cooperation between consumers and producers, and transparency, informed State practice, to a significant extent. Yet, they were far from reflecting consistent and uniform state practice.

---

496 Res. 93 (IV), I.1.

Inter-governmental arrangements in tin, sugar and wheat broadly conformed to the substantive and procedural principles laid down in the Havana Charter.[497] Arrangements in tea (the International Tea Agreement, 1950–1955) and coffee (the Mexico City Agreement of 1957–1958, the Latin America Coffee Agreement of 1958–1959, and the International Coffee Agreement of 1959–1962) did not conform to the UN procedures and principles.[498] Yet, no consumer countries challenged their legality.[499]

Other significant deviations were the cartel-type arrangements set up by producing countries alone in the early 1970s. As discussed (Section 2.2.1.1), the early 1970s witnessed a proliferation of formal cartel organisations, sparked by the success of OPEC.[500] These arrangements, of which only commodity-dependent producing countries were parties, were in essence 'restrictionist', directed to curb supply and sustain prices above market levels. As a matter of fact, none of the cartel arrangements was contested in the GATT; nor has OPEC, the sole lasting formal cartel, ever been challenged under WTO rules. Practical political considerations clearly overshadowed legalistic concerns.

The principles embodied in UNCTAD's Resolution 93 (IV) did not reflect uniform state practice, either. The IPC was declaratory and transformative; it longed for an order that eventually failed to crystalise.

#### 3.2.2.2 Attitudes

The negotiating record of discussions at Havana, Geneva and Nairobi reveals some general assent to the conclusion that a greater degree of stability was desirable in commodity markets, but much less as to what ought to be done to achieve this objective.

---

497 In form, the inter-governmental agreements on tin, sugar and wheat were open, multilateral treaties, with broad membership. All agreements were dual-interest arrangements, with equal representation of producers and consumers. Finally, their stated objective essentially referred to price stability, with an emphasis on assurance of supplies in wheat.

498 These arrangements were by large 'price defence' cartel-type schemes very similar to their pre-war predecessors.

499 As discussed in Rowe (above n 55), the tea arrangement did not restrict supplies drastically; the coffee control arrangement was backed by the major coffee consumer, the United States, willing to bolster up export revenues of Latin American coffee producers. The International Tea Agreement was not renewed on its expiration in 1955. The 1959 International Coffee Agreement eventually evolved into a dual-interest agreement involving both producers and consumers (starting from the International Coffee Agreement, 1962), though it was not until 1976 that price stability replaced 'price defence' in the operation of the Coffee Agreement.

500 See above n 145.

### a) *Havana*

At Havana, sharp differences arose as to the specific price objectives to be pursued: whether to moderate short-term price fluctuations around the market trend, or influence the price trend itself. In a related vein, there were wide divergences as to the level at which prices ought to be stabilised, a divisive issue not only between developed and developing countries, but also within the developing ones.

'Indexation' was a particularly intractable issue. A number of delegations from developing countries were in favour of some mechanism to relate the prices of primary commodities to those of manufactured goods. The proposals of El Salvador[501] and Cuba,[502] strongly backed by delegates from countries in their early stages of development or industrialisation moved in this direction. Others, notably several industrialised countries, categorically opposed such an endeavour.[503] Eventually, it was agreed not to openly disagree. The tactics chosen were to leave the wordings 'fair' and 'reasonable return' unqualified; and to postpone the complete elaboration of this wording to a later stage, when negotiating individual commodity agreements.

Another thorny issue was whether prices should be stabilised at levels remunerative to 'efficient' producers or to producers in general. The former option was favoured by the industrialised countries and by a few low-cost producers among the developing ones. The latter was advocated by comparatively high-cost producers among the developing countries. Eventually, in consideration of the proposals submitted by Ceylon, El Salvador, the Philippines, Uruguay and Venezuela, the use of the term 'efficient' producers was deleted in the final

---

501 Jimenez (El Salvador) suggested that the term "remunerative prices" should be understood to mean "prices which, while enabling the maintenance of fair labour standards, maintain an equitable relation with the prices which the producers of primary commodities have to pay for manufactured production goods and general consumption goods". *Draft Charter – El-Salvador: Proposed Amendment* (E/CONF.2/C.5/3/Add.8 dated 6 December 1947). See also *Summary Report of the 10th Meeting* (E/CONF.2/C.5/SR.10 dated 31 December 1947), at page 5.

502 Document C.5/3/Add.3. According to the Cuban proposal, the selling price of commodities should "afford countries capable of efficient production a reasonable return adequate to maintain the purchasing power of their inhabitants, as importers and consumers". *Draft Charter – Cuba: Proposed Amendment* (E/CONF.2/C.5/3/Add.3 dated 5 December 1947).

503 Among the developed countries, some delegations (the United States) were strongly opposed to the Salvadorian amendment; others (Belgium and Switzerland) opposed it in milder terms; whereas others (France and Canada) sympathised with the principle, while opposing the incorporation of the amendment in the Charter (*Summary Report of the 11th Meeting* (E/CONF.2/C.5/SR.11 dated 2 January 1948)).

text of the Charter.[504] Yet, much ambiguity remained in practice as to the level at which prices should be stabilised; and as to the genuine price objectives sought, whether price stabilisation or price support.

Finally, in terms of the objectives to be pursued through price intervention, there was substantial disagreement as to whether Chapter 6 should provide a framework for encouraging value-addition in commodity-dependent developing countries. In this direction, Uruguay proposed an amendment that would include processing equipment in the definition of 'commodities'.[505] Mexico favoured specific reference, in the stated objectives of ICAs, to the promotion of processing in producing countries.[506] Eventually, the industrialised countries conceded to the Mexican proposal, but reformulate in 'best-endeavour' terms, deprived of binding language.[507]

### b) *Geneva*

In terms of 'attitudes', did the GATT contracting parties regard themselves "morally bound not to go back on the principles evolved at Havana"?[508] On commodity matters, the historic record points in the opposite direction.

Overall, discussions during the Review Session of the GATT testify to major divergences regarding international action on commodity prices. The majority of the contracting parties agreed that they should seek a solution to the problems that excessive commodity price instability posed, and that collective international action was warranted. Yet, this was "the limit of the area of agreement",[509] on account of important differences on almost every aspect of

504 *Havana Reports*, above n 49, at 129.

505 *Draft Charter – Uruguay: Proposed Amendment* (Document E/CONF.2/C.5/3/Add.12 dated 7 December 1947).

506 *Draft Charter – Mexico: Proposed Amendment* (E/CONF.2/C.5/3/Add.9 dated 6 December 1947).

507 The members recognised that inter-governmental commodity agreements were appropriate "[…] to provide, during the period which may be necessary, a framework for the consideration and development of measures which have as their purpose economic adjustments designed to promote the expansion of consumption or a shift of resources and man-power out of over-expanded industries into new and productive occupations, including as far as possible in appropriate cases, the development of secondary industries based upon domestic production of primary commodities" (Havana Charter, Article 57 (d)).

508 *CONTRACTING PARTIES – Second Session – Summary Record of the Eighteenth Meeting* (GATT/CP.2/SR.18 dated 3 September 1948), p. 2.

509 Chairmen's statement on points of differences (*CONTRACTING PARTIES – Tenth Session – [27 October–3 December 1955] – Summary Record of the Fourteenth Meeting* (SR10/14 dated 23 November 1955), p. 158).

the problem. For most of these divergences, "it was difficult to foresee a compromise solution".[510] Most importantly, serious differences remained not only as to the specific terms to be agreed upon, but also on the need to agree on a set of goals and principles.

With regard to the terms to be agreed upon, some saw the approach of Chapter 6 of the Havana Charter, properly adjusted, to be the right basis for commodity arrangements, and would not view any other approach sympathetically.[511] Yet, others expressed views critical of certain aspects of the Havana Charter provisions.[512]

The restrictive nature of the Havana Charter, as of the SACA also came into question. In particular, some delegations stressed the need for caution in assuming obligations more restrictive than those imposed by the GATT. This latter, it is important to note, did not limit the freedom of contracting parties to regulate prices or to restrict production. It only prohibited the use of border restrictions, unless a waiver was granted.[513]

Multilateralism and equality of votes between importers and exporters, two basic tenets of the Charter approach, were equally called into question. Few major producers, such as Australia, questioned the inability of countries with a major interest in the trade to negotiate a commodity agreement among themselves – without the possibility that all countries, including some without a real interest, would be present at the negotiations.[514] It was also argued that the distribution of votes as between consumers and producers should be left for determination on the merits of the case when a commodity agreement was being negotiated.[515] In particular, arrangements that involved disproportionate financial commitments might not lend themselves to equal voting.[516]

---

510 Ibid.

511 Statement by Mr. Sanders (United Kingdom) (*CONTRACTING PARTIES – Ninth Session – Summary Record of the Thirty-fourth Meeting* (SR 9/34 dated 22 February 1955), p. 8).

512 See in particular, Australia. Statement by Mr. Crawford (Australia) (*CONTRACTING PARTIES – Ninth Session – Summary Record of the Ninetenth Meeting* (SR 9/19 dated 23 November 1954), p. 2; *Ninth Session – Summary Record of the Twenty-seventh Meeting* (SR 9/27 dated 29 December 1954), p. 7).

513 SR 9/34, above n 511, p. 5.

514 As stated by Australia (*Final Report of the Working Party on Commodity Problems* (L/416, 3 October 1955), para 4, p. 2).

515 Ibid.

516 Statement by Australia (*CONTRACTING PARTIES – Tenth Session – [27 October–3 December 1955] – Summary Record of the Thirteenth Meeting* (SR10/13 dated 22 November 1955), pp. 143–44).

Crucially, there were different views concerning the need to agree on normative objectives and principles to govern international action on commodity prices. For some, a general set of principles and an overall machinery was essential.[517] Others expressed the view that an agreement on a broad set of principles was neither desirable nor necessary, and reserved the right to judge each particular commodity arrangement on its merits.[518] As discussed, it was eventually recognised that it was unlikely that agreement on principles could be achieved and an alternative, case-by-case approach was adopted.

### c) *Nairobi*

UNCTAD's Resolution 93(IV) similarly reflects a fundamental difference of views as regards the objectives and modalities of price intervention in commodity markets. Eventually, the text of the Resolution was carefully drafted to accommodate irreconcilable views, which resulted in deliberately general language, when not in textual inconsistencies.

Thus, for example the expression 'indexation of prices', which was anathema to many Group B countries, is absent in the Resolution. Yet, preambular language to Section I (Objectives) keeps reference to the need to improve the 'terms of trade' of developing countries, with implicit reference to the import purchasing power of commodity exports. Discussions at the plenary reveal irreconcilable interpretations. The representative of Algeria, for example, insisted "on the necessity for the indexation of commodity prices", a position shared by the Group of 77, as "clearly reflected in various sections of the resolution".[519] On the other hand, the United Kingdom, the Federal Republic of Germany and the US restated their reservations on the concept of indexation.

Beyond the controversial issue of indexation, a fundamental difference of thought and attitude emerges concerning the ultimate price objective of

---

517 Ceylon (Corea): SR10/14, p. 154.

518 Mr. Wilson (Canada) said that the attitude of his Government to commodity arrangement was to judge each particular one on its merits (SR10/13, above n 516, p. 147); Sweden was not convinced that prevailing conditions made necessary or practicable international measures within an elaborate framework, as proposed in the draft Agreement; Mr. Leddy (United States) recalled that at the Ninth Session his delegation had expressed the view that an agreement on commodity problems was neither desirable nor necessary, and that the United States Government would not be able to participate in such an agreement (SR10/14, above n 510, p. 157). See also the position of Australia (SR10/13, above n 516), pp. 143–44.

519 *Proceedings of the United Nations Conference on Trade and Development, Fourth Session, Nairobi, 5–31 May 1976* (New York: United Nations, 1977), vol. I, Part 2 (*Summary of Proceedings*), paras. 34–35.

commodity control. The Group of 77 advocated price defence and support, and a real transfer of resources from the North to the South.[520] The Group B countries advocated price stabilisation at levels consistent with long-term equilibrium.[521] For the members of the Group of 77, the Resolution would operationalise the tenets of the NIEO; the 'hardliners' made it clear that, in joining the consensus, they would continue to reject the NIEO.

There was also a fundamental difference of views on the 'practical content' of Resolution 93(IV): the decision to convene a negotiating conference on a common fund, and preparatory meetings prior to the conference;[522] and to hold preparatory meetings for the negotiation of individual commodity agreements and convene, "as and when required", commodity negotiating conferences[523] (Section IV). The Group of 77 upheld the view that, according to the Resolution, there should be established a common fund as the sole means of financing buffer stocks;[524] and commodity negotiating conferences were to be convened. A number of Group B countries, in qualifying their endorsement of the Resolution, interpreted Section IV differently: the outcome of the preparatory meetings would determine whether the establishment of a common fund was warranted and which commodity agreements could be established.[525]

Ultimately, the ambiguous phrasing and generalities of the language agreed upon at UNCTAD IV reflect, in the words of Robert L. Rothstein, the "tactics of non-settlement" and show "how to disguise disagreement to permit the game to go on".[526] A consensus was reached on a resolution that, as qualified by limitations and reservations, did not possess sufficient determinacy to provide direction and policy. Eventually, contradictions and incoherence would come to the surface when trying to implement the Resolution terms.

---

520 Ibid, paras. 14–17 and *Manila Declaration and Programme of Action*, above n 284.

521 See the Group B position paper on commodities, subparagraph 1.(b) (reproduced in *Proceedings of the United Nations Conference on Trade and Development, Fourth Session, Nairobi, 5–31 May 1976* (New York: United Nations, 1977), vol. I, annex VII, Section A, 1).

522 Res. 93 (IV), Sec. IV, paras. 1 and 2.

523 Res. 93 (IV), Sec. IV, paras. 4 and 5.

524 *Proceedings of the United Nations Conference on Trade and Development, Fourth Session, Nairobi, 5–31 May 1976* (New York: United Nations, 1977), vol. I, Part 1 (*Summary of Proceedings*), para. 16.

525 This was the position of the Federal Republic of Germany and the United States. *Proceedings of the United Nations Conference on Trade and Development, Fourth Session, Nairobi, 5–31 May 1976* (New York: United Nations, 1977), vol. I, Part 2 (*Summary of Proceedings*), paras. 21 (Federal Republic of Germany) and 38–39 (United States).

526 Rothstein, above n 410, at p. 39.

### 3.2.3 *Assessment*

To conclude, it is open to question whether any genuine agreement has ever been reached on a coherent set of objectives and principles to govern international action on commodity prices.

In practice, the approaches of the Havana Charter and UNCTAD concealed a variety of opinions and attitudes, concerning commodity control. As discussed in the following analysis, this divergence has continued to be in evidence, right to the present.

On the one hand were those who regarded commodity control as an exceptional remedy when things could not be redressed by market forces alone. Price regulation was called upon to remedy market imperfections and failures, but not to radically recast or corner market dynamics. This position still reflected a free market orientation, advocating reformed, but not transformed, international market structures.

The other school of thought held that the economic system, as it had hitherto functioned, had structurally failed to realise equitable outcomes. The spontaneous course of economic forces would only reinforce and magnify existing disparities and imbalances. Purposive action was needed to restructure market dynamics. This policy stance envisaged a radical restructuring of the commodity economy towards some form of "deliberately planned international control".[527]

By some accounts, the Havana Charter essentially endorsed the 'free-market' approach; UNCTAD's IPC endorsed the interventionist stance. As a matter of fact, as discussed, the two contending views were not successive, but co-existed. Most importantly, they co-existed within single approaches. Both the Havana Charter and UNCTAD's IPC tried to adjust or settle these conflicting claims, which ultimately resulted in inherent contradictions and a substantial indeterminacy as to the objectives and modalities of price control.

Yet, the normative objectives and principles evolved at Havana and Nairobi had weight, and are still momentous. The broad normative objectives of multilateral price intervention in commodity markets, as laid down in the Havana Charter and UNCTAD's IPC, are still analytically relevant. So are the ordering principles of multilateralism, transparency and cooperation that were to apply.

As discussed, the Havana Charter 'grafted' into trade regulation the broad aspirational goals envisaged in Article 55 of the UN Charter: "... the attainment of the higher standards of living, full employment and conditions of economic

527 Ibid, at 157–58.

and social progress and development".[528] Security of employment, and more broadly the well-being of people, ought thus to be the cornerstone of the multilateral trading system, the 'critical benchmark'[529] against which to assess the desirability of specific commercial policies. This idea continues to have echoes down to the present. It resonates into the 2030 Agenda for Sustainable Development, and has gained momentum again in the economic debate on trade and employment.[530]

Important deductions and implications for present times can also be drawn from UNCTAD's IPC. What is certainly still relevant about the UNCTAD's IPC approach is the idea of 'redistributive justice'. The NIEO had tried to translate redistributive concerns into legally binding obligations. Under UNCTAD's IPC, redistributive justice aspired to become the basic tenet of commodity trade regulation. Today, redistributive ideals continue to inform the debate about a fair allocation of value along commodity chains. As discussed in Chapter 5, they can certainly provide a useful analytical framework for rethinking market price intervention in commodities.

On a more general level, what is still pertinent is the 'substantive' rationale underlying the commodity trade regime set forth in Havana and Nairobi: the idea that commodity market outcomes shall not be apprehended as naturally justified, but benchmarked against normative values, grounded in ethical foundations. The legacy left is in the end one of thought and spirit, more than one of concrete operative mechanisms.

---

528 Havana Charter, Article 1, Preamble; Geneva draft, above n 49, Article 1; London Report, above n 49, narrative account of the treatment of Chapter I, at 4.

529 Drache, above n 469, at 8–12.

530 The existing neoliberal orthodoxy is quite discredited; alternative conceptual frameworks are emerging. These alternatives call for a reorientation of the macroeconomic strategy of both developed and developing countries. In particular, it has been argued, domestic and regional demand should be given greater role in economic growth. This calls for strengthened domestic purchasing power through a combination of better paying jobs in formal sector and income redistribution. See UNCTAD, *Trade and Development Report, 2013: Adjusting to the Changing Dynamics of the World Economy* (New York and Geneva: United Nations, 2013).

CHAPTER 4

# From Market Intervention to Free Trade and Back to Managed Trade? (1989–2011)

Developments in the late 1980s and 1990s spearheaded major changes of attitude towards agricultural price control. At the international level, restrictive ICAs were abandoned. At the domestic level, policy emphasis shifted from price to income stabilisation and from trade policy to social protection policies.

A new paradigm shift, which is still unfolding, then occurred in the aftermath of the 2007–08 and 2010–11 commodity crises. Two major price shocks in a three year span spurred much discussion on the adequacy of the market as a stabilising device. Two contrasting tendencies then arose, representing two fundamental creeds towards agricultural stabilisation arrangements. There was a call for a further deepening of the free trade regime, and a revival of interventionist policies.

This Chapter elaborates on these paradigm shifts, and assesses their implications for trade law and policy. It first considers relevant trade policy developments in the late 1980s and 1990s. It then explores the scholarly and policy debate on trade rules and agricultural stabilisation policies in the aftermath of the 2007–08 and 2010–11 commodity crises.

## 4.1 The Market-based Interlude (1989–2007)

Through the late 1980s and into the 1990s, commodity policy realigned. Attitudes changed towards intergovernmental commodity control. In a context of global recession, combined with the ascendancy of neoliberal economic theory, international action on commodity prices was no longer warranted. Instead, the free play of market forces was perceived as the most cost-efficient and operationally effective way to stabilise international commodity prices. The shift in policy paradigm could not be more pronounced, moving from 'structuralist' perspectives,[531] which used trade policy to redistribute income, to 'neoliberal' insights.[532]

531 See, in particular, UNCTAD's quest for a new trade policy for development, discussed in Chapter 3.

532 These insights are associated with neo-classical strands of thought in economics that rejected market intervention as inefficient (above n 35).

 | DOI 10.1163/9789004350540_005

What were, in commodities, the major trade policy developments associated with this paradigm shift? This Chapter attempts to address this question. It first discusses changes of attitudes towards price control in the scholarly and political debate. It then takes a cursory look at major trade policy developments associated, in commodities, with this paradigm shift. Finally, it elaborates on the extent to which multilateral trade rules in agriculture follow neoliberal precepts of economic efficiency. For ease of convenience, an indicative time frame is set. The narrative starts in 1989, when the term 'Washington Consensus' was first coined,[533] and when a 'down-sized' Common Fund for Commodities was eventually established. It ends with the commodity crisis of which revived the debate on the normative underpinnings of the multilateral commodity trade regime.

### 4.1.1 *The 'Neoliberal' Agenda: Trade Policy Implications*

Through the 1980s, under the 'neoliberal' agenda,[534] the 'rule of the market' became the accepted framework for thinking about and acting upon the global commodity economy. If we take regulation broadly, as synonymous with a systematic ordering of activities,[535] we can even argue that markets emerged as a 'regulatory device'; that the shift was from 'control regulation' by the State to 'regulation by the market', or market-based regulation. At the international level, 'just' prices were again equated with market prices,[536] and the market became the device through which distributive outcomes were increasingly apprehended as 'naturally' justified.[537]

It is worth to briefly recall the basic tenets of this approach, by reference to its key policy prescriptions, the values and assumptions behind, and related modes of legal thought and practice.

533 On the original and subsequent uses of the term 'Washington Consensus', see John Williamson, "What Should the World Bank Think about the Washington Consensus?" *World Bank Research Observer* 15, no. 2 (2000).

534 Reference is to neo-classical strands of thought in economics (above n 35). Politically, the neoliberal wave is famously associated with the liberalisation policies of Margaret Thatcher in the United Kingdom and Ronald Reagan in the US. At the international level, it found institutional expression in the World Bank's analytical work and structural adjustment programmes.

535 Terence Daintith, "Regulation," in *International Encyclopedia of Comparative Law*, ed. David et al., vol. 17, Part 10 (Mohr Siebeck, 1997).

536 On the notion of 'just' prices, Oscar Schachter, "Just Prices in World Markets: Proposals De Lege Ferenda," *The American Journal of International Law* 69, no. 1 (1975).

537 On the role played by the market as a device which legitimises and 'naturalises' distributive outcomes, see Teubner, above n 42, at 268.

#### 4.1.1.1 Key Policy Prescriptions

In the 1980s, mainstream economists vigorously questioned the desirability of price intervention, whether direct or indirect, as a means to stabilise agricultural prices.[538] The orthodox view was that price intervention was neither efficient nor effective. The optimal approach to stabilise prices, it was argued, was to leverage market dynamics.

With special reference to commodity price stabilisation, this shift entailed two dimensions.

First, the policy prescription was that the market, rather than the State, should be relied upon to the maximum extent possible as a device to stabilise commodity prices. In the assumption of well-functioning, competitive markets, traders are the ones responsible for storage and assumption of price risks, in return of which they earn a profit. Free trade acts as a stabilising device, by transferring supplies from years of high production to years of low production, and from surplus to deficit areas.

Second, some degree of price volatility was increasingly acknowledged as an inherent attribute of well-functioning commodity markets. This acknowledgement prompted a shift in emphasis from price stabilisation policies to 'risk management' and 'coping' strategies, from efforts to manage prices to measures aimed at managing or mitigating the impacts of price changes.

#### 4.1.1.2 Conceptual Underpinnings

What were the conceptual underpinnings of the market-based commodity trading system? The 'philosophical foundations' of this new commodity trade stance were laid on one or both of two grounds: promotion of economic efficiency ('economistic' rationale); and / or individual liberty (libertarian approach). The analysis will briefly consider each in turn.

##### a) *'Economistic' Rationale: Efficiency*

At the root of the market-oriented move was the promotion of 'economic efficiency'. The dismantlement of commodity control arrangements (and broadly the elimination of trade distortions and restrictions) was predicated upon efficiency gains; and efficiency became the normative objective, the goal to be sought by means of commodity policy reform. Trade liberalisation, in particular, was deemed to be efficiency enhancing. The theoretical underpinnings were (and are) furnished by the law of comparative advantage. Based upon the division of labour and the gains from specialisation, this orthodox, and increasingly disputed, theory posits that "[...] each and every country is best off

538 See above, n 35.

eschewing trade protection and adopting free trade regardless of the policies of others".[539]

What do we mean by economic efficiency, and how does efficiency translate in a legal concern?[540] Economists employ a variety of efficiency notions.[541] For our purposes, what matters is the idea of some effective allocation of scarce resources, as a means to maximise economic welfare. Economic efficiency thus becomes a proxy for economic welfare maximisation. It reflects "[...] the general citizen interests in trade liberalisation as a means for obtaining more, better and a larger variety of goods and services at lower prices".[542] Ultimately rooted in utilitarian or contractarian and consent driven arguments, [543] trade liberalisation, and the efficiency gains thereof, become the final aim of trade regulation. This approach assumes wealth maximisation as the prime mover and goal of human action; and has at its core the ontological construct of the individualistic, rational, and utility-maximising, *homo economicus*.[544]

This normative approach employs the conceptual paradigms developed by economic theory, starting with the assumption that human beings are rational and will seek to maximise their gains and minimise their losses.[545] As discussed in the following analysis, when this approach is pushed too far, much is lost. What is eventually lost is a specific contribution of legal reasoning and legal contents *vis-à-vis* economics. This specificity lies in the ability to weigh and balance considerations of efficiency and equity, and to bring ethical values into the logical working of economics.

539 Introduction to *The International Political Economy of Trade*, vol. I, ed. David A. Lake (Aldershot Hants; Brookfield Vt: Edward Elgar, 1993), at xiii.

540 These questions are raised and comprehensively addressed, from a law and economics perspective, in Jules L. Coleman, "Efficiency, Utility, and Wealth Maximization," *Hofstra Law Review* 8, no. 3 (1980): 512–13.

541 'Productive efficiency', or the ability to produce more cheaply; Pareto notions of efficiency; Kaldor-Hicks efficiency criteria; wealth maximisation, etc. For a review, Coleman, above n 540.

542 Ernst-Ulrich Petersmann, "Human Rights and International Trade Law: Defining and Connecting the Two Fields," in *Human Rights and International Trade*, eds. Thomas Cottier, Joost Pauwelyn, and Elisabeth Bürgi (Oxford; New York: Oxford University Press, 2005), 87.

543 See Coleman, above n 540, at 516–17.

544 Anup Dash, "Towards and Epistemological Foundation for Social and Solidarity Economy" (paper prepared for the UNRISD Conference Potential and Limits of Social and Solidarity Economy, 6–8 March 2013, Geneva, Switzerland).

545 See "Symposium on Efficiency as a Legal Concern: Introduction," *Hofstra Law Review* 8, no. 3 (1980): 485–86.

### b) *Libertarian Defence: Individual Freedom*

A separate strand of thought brings into focus the "moral foundations of market freedom".[546] As summarised in Petersmann, "[…] market economies and economic welfare are only instruments for enabling and promoting individual freedom as the ultimate goal of economic life and the most efficient means of realizing general welfare".[547] These freedoms are conceptualised in terms of "individual decisional autonomy", individual "immunity from encroachment", and "substantive opportunity to achieve".[548]

Free trade is here not merely an instrument for the promotion of efficiency and economic welfare. It is justified, on libertarian grounds, as an "enabling device for individual autonomy".[549] Its historical foundations trace back as far as the early XIII century, with the inclusion of freedom of trade in the guarantees of the Magna Carta (1215). As discussed in Cottier, this "libertarian trait" is shared with the classical body of civil rights.[550] Both trade regulation and civil and political rights are ultimately "emanations of the rule of law", and "share a common libertarian aspiration".[551] They both set boundaries to how far states may go in regulating private conduct.[552]

Statutory marketing and other commodity control arrangements were challenged on libertarian grounds. From a libertarian perspective, commodity control encroached with individual farmers' freedom 'to achieve'. This critique has some weight: particularly in tropical Africa, state marketing boards had frequently set farmgate prices at below market levels; and bureaucracies, rather than the peasant farmer, often reaped the benefits of high prices. With

---

546 Petersmann, above n 542, at 48–49. This strand of thought reflects "a long tradition in economic thought – from Adam Smith via Friedrich Hayek up to Nobel Prize laureate Amartya Sen" (ibid). See also Thomas Cottier, "Trade and Human Rights: A Relationship to Discover," *Journal of International Economic Law* 5, no. 1 (2002).

547 Petersmann, above n 542, at 40. Professor Petersmann argues for the normative priority of human rights over other interests, and for a human rights view of economic liberties, whereby the right to produce and exchange goods and services is acknowledged as a human right.

548 Amartya Sen, *Rationality and Freedom* (Belknap Press, 2003); Petersmann, above n 542, at 40, note 29.

549 John Gray, *The Moral Foundations of Market Institutions* (London: Institute of Economic Affairs, Health and Welfare Unit, 1992); Petersmann, above n 542, at 48–49.

550 Cottier, above n 546.

551 Ibid, at 116.

552 Ibid, at 115–16, discussing shared foundations between trade liberalisation under the GATT and human rights.

liberal reform, some commentators argue, commodity producers were set free from this type of abusive encroachment.

#### 4.1.1.3 Modes of Regulation Involved

This shift in policy paradigm, from 'structuralist' to market-based, was paralleled by a profound change in the rationale of regulation: from 'substantive' to 'formal'; from the regulation of market outcomes to the regulation of market processes.[553]

As discussed (Section 3.2), commodity 'control' regulation had involved a purposive, substantive orientation of the law. State power was deployed to pursue social objectives that countered market dynamics. The normative objectives sought invited principled decisions rooted in value systems, which ultimately questioned the separation of law and politics.

The role of international trade law under the neoliberal paradigm became increasingly formal and procedural. It was to remove impediments and distortions to trade, so as to provide a competitive 'level playing field' within which substantive decisions are made by commercial actors. In this setting, the law was essentially called upon by policy makers to 'enable', or 'underpin' market dynamics. The market, the economy, furnished the content, by framing the distributive outcomes.

In a related vein, the law evolved towards primarily 'formal attributes'.[554] 'Formal law' has been defined as internally structured according to standards of "analytical conceptuality, deductive stringency and rule-oriented reasoning."[555] Commodity trade regulation, to some extent, evolved in this direction. Legal reasoning about commodity trade, and about trade in general, became internally structured according to formal standards of rule-oriented reasoning. Trade regulation was eventually set as a highly specialised, complexly technical discipline, in relatively insulation from public international law.

It is open to question whether this formal orientation can bring forth equitable results in commodities. Note, in this respect, that the trade rules interpreted and applied formally are, in essence, negotiated disciplines. They reflect the relative negotiating capabilities and leverage of the various parties, and codify specific power dynamics. As discussed in Chapter 5, a fundamental reorientation may be needed, in terms of modes of legal thought and practice, from a formalist, positivist approach towards a more substantive, principle-based approach.

553 For a discussion of formal *versus* substantive modes of regulation, Teubner, above n 42.

554 Ibid.

555 Ibid., at 256.

### 4.1.2 *The Extent of Policy Reform in Commodities*

Two major trade policy developments were associated with the conceptual shift towards a market-based paradigm in commodities. First, there was a move towards liberalisation and deregulation, with some important exemptions and qualifications. Key moves in this direction included: the dismantling of intergovernmental commodity price-stabilising arrangements; the abolition of State commodities trading monopolies in a few developing countries; and the shift from price stabilisation to income stabilisation in major developed economies. Second, the retreat of the State from direct commodity price intervention was paralleled by a shift in emphasis from price stabilisation policies to 'risk management' and 'coping' strategies; and from market intervention tools to social protection policies and market-based instruments.

Overall, it seemed that the era of commodity control had come to an abrupt end. At closer scrutiny, however, the picture is more nuanced than it may at first appear. At the international level, there was certainly a retreat of the State from the commodity economy. Countries in practice relinquished the possibility to take joint multilateral action through ICAs for the stabilisation of prices of agricultural commodities. Yet, efforts at manipulating global prices continued, at the unilateral and plurilateral level, including through private cartels. At the country level, the picture is even more articulated. A few developing countries, notably, sub-Saharan African countries, liberalised and deregulated the agriculture sector. Yet, other developing countries, particularly in Asia, continued to rely extensively on direct market intervention. As for the advanced economies, as mentioned, what was at stake was a change in the form of intervention, from price support to income support.

These developments are outlined below. The analysis concludes on a note of caution: the dismantlement of ICAs and marketing boards did not set the market free, but opened the way for more subtle and complex forms of intervention.

#### 4.1.2.1 Deregulation and Liberalisation

Through the late 1980s and the 1990s, all restrictive ICAs lapsed or collapsed. Statutory marketing was abandoned in tropical Africa, in some contexts almost overnight. Major liberal reforms were implemented in the highly subsidising high-income economies. Taken together, developments at the multilateral and national level seemed to show that the era of commodity control had come to an end.

All of the price-stabilising agricultural ICAs either collapsed or lapsed between 1985 and 1999. The Council of the International Coffee Organization decided to suspend export quotas from 4 July 1989. This was in part related to changed attitudes towards the scheme by the largest consuming country, the US, and producing country, Brazil. The fourth ISA terminated in 1984 and was replaced by an agreement which did not contain intervention clauses. In cocoa, economic clauses have been abandoned since the fifth ICCA (1993). The INRA was formally terminated in 1999 after Malaysia and Thailand withdrew from the scheme, following the 1997 Asian financial crisis. As mentioned, the flexibilities towards ICAs enshrined in the GATT continued to exist, though only on paper. In practice, they fell into disuse.

The demise of the inter-governmental commodity 'control' agreements occurred in parallel with the abandonment of state-controlled marketing, internal and external, in several commodity producing countries. This is notably the case of the West African countries, where state marketing institutions had played a dominant role in commodity trade. As reviewed by Irfan ul Haque,[556] Nigeria dismantled its marketing boards virtually overnight in 1986. Cameroon abolished its public marketing body in 1990. The liberalisation process in Côte d'Ivoire was initiated in the mid-1990s, though its stabilisation fund was abolished only in 1999. Ghana was the only state in West Africa where the state continued to play a dominant role in export commodity trade, though internal marketing had been liberalised since the early 1990s.

Market liberalisation and deregulation also occurred in the industrial countries.[557] Yet, differently from what had occurred in tropical Africa, for example, here the 'liberal' wave did not involve a retreat of the State from the farm sector. What occurred, as discussed *infra*, was a change in the form of intervention: from price support to income support; and from managing prices to managing the effects of price instability. In terms of policy tools deployed, the shift was from price intervention (through administered prices, intervention purchases and border measures) to income stabilisation (for example, by means of direct

556 Irfan ul Haque, *Commodities under Neoliberalism: The Case of Cocoa*, G-24 Discussion Paper Series, no. 25 (United Nations, 2007), 8. See also Akiyama et al., above n. 241. As discussed by Irfan ul Hauqe, reforms were mainly triggered by external pressure: major forces behind these moves were the structural adjustment programme by the IMF and World Bank and conditional lending by the European Union. However, external factors are to be assesses in interplay with, and against the background of internal political pressures: after independence, state marketing institutions had become "large bureaucracies, influenced by politics, and increasingly inefficient in their designated functions" (ibid, at 8).

557 Agricultural stabilisation and support polices underwent substantial liberal reforms in the United States and in the European Union between 1990 and 1996. For a review, Robert Paarlberg, "Agricultural Policy Reform and the Uruguay Round: Synergistic Linkage in a Two-Level Game?" *International Organization* 51, no. 3 (1997): 434–39.

payments to producers, or publicly-backed insurance schemes). Some of these income stabilisation measures were unrelated to prices and outputs, and were deemed to have minimal trade-distorting effects. Others were triggered by price and output thresholds, and had sizeable trade distortive impacts.

Questions arise as to the reasons why price-stabilising ICAs failed. The shift in policy paradigm certainly played a role: under the neoliberal paradigm, international action on prices was no longer warranted, but dismissed as ineffective and inefficient. Yet, the demise of multilateral price controls was not only ideologically inspired. It essentially moved from practical considerations. In practice, the operation of ICAs had been fraught with considerable difficulties; none of them successfully stabilised prices for more than relatively short periods.[558] What were then the reasons why price-stabilising ICAs were so difficult to negotiate, performed poorly, and were eventually dismissed?[559]

According to a few commentators, technical and economic difficulties were paramount. Technical problems reflected the difficulty to counter long-term or cyclical factors by means of policy intervention.[560] On account of long frequencies of price cycles in agriculture, buffer stocks sometimes need to buy or sell continuously for long periods and easily go out of cash or stocks.[561] There are also technical difficulties in the determination of the long-term price trend around which to stabilise prices. Available options – moving averages, base-period average prices, or prices set on the cost of production of efficient producers – all raise complex methodological issues.[562]

Another line of arguments is mainly political. It yields three sets of reasons why ICAs failed.

558 Christopher Gilbert, "International Agreements for Commodity Price Stabilisation: An Assessment," OECD *Food, Agriculture and Fisheries Papers*, no. 53 (OECD Publishing 2011), 21–23; Rowe, above n 55, at 209.

559 For an overview see UNCTAD, *Policy Actions to Mitigate the Impact of Highly Volatile Prices and Incomes on Commodity Dependent Countries, and to Facilitate Value Addition and Greater Participation in Commodity Value Chains by Commodity-Producing Countries*, Document TD/B/C.I/MEM.2/14, 2 February 2011. See also Niek Koning, Muriel Calo, Roel Jongeneel, "Fair Trade in Tropical Crops is Possible," North South Centre, North-South Discussion Paper 3 (Wageningen, The Netherlands, 2004).

560 Cannen M. Reinhart and Peter Wickham, *Commodity Prices: Cyclical Weakness or Secular Decline?* IMF Staff Papers, vol. 41, no. 2 (1994).

561 For a few tropical commodities, price lows tend to last longer than booms. Inter-annual price stabilisation is difficult in this context: even large stabilisation (buffer) funds tend to go bankrupt. See Varangis and McIntire, above n 205, at 3.

562 See Christopher Gilbert, "International Commodity Agreements: An Obituary Notice," above n 86 and Wight and Prakash, above n 220, at 239–40.

First, there were problems in coordinating the conflicting interests of the parties to the stabilisation agreement, and strong incentives to renege.[563] This reading underscores the political difficulty to agree on a price range, as well as disagreement between countries over the allocation of quotas. The debate over these issues was only outwardly polarised, between producers and consumers. Divergences and frictions also arose within the block of producing countries, between high-cost and low-cost producers. Incentives to renege and free riding were other major issues.

Second, multilateral stabilisation efforts were undermined by farm support policies in the developed countries. This holds certainly true for some temperate commodities of export interest to both developed and developing countries, such as sugar. It has been observed, in this respect, that the 1977 ISA collapsed mainly because of the sugar policies of the European Community.[564] The Community refused to participate in the sugar agreement and to restrict its exports accordingly. It continued its sugar subsidy system, which resulted in surplus sugar 'dumped' on export markets. This in turn contributed to depress global sugar prices and defeated efforts by the ISA to defend a floor price. As recognised by a GATT panel ruling on a case brought by Brazil,

> [...] increased Community exports of sugar through the use of subsidies in the particular market situation in 1978 and 1979, and where developing contracting parties had taken steps within the framework of the ISA to improve the conditions in the world sugar market, inevitably reduced the effects of the efforts made by these countries.[565]

Third, the 'political' strand of thought points to lack of adequate funding as one of the main reasons why ICAs failed. There are views that buffers stocks can be effective in stabilising prices, but only if large enough.[566] This is on account of long frequencies of price cycles in certain agricultural commodity markets. Further, small buffer stocks may cause speculation, with destabilising effect.[567] Questions arise as to whether buffer stocks under the IPC were large enough

563 Paul Cashin, C John McDermott and Alasdair Scott, "Booms and Slumps in World Commodity Prices," *Journal of Development Economics* 69, no. 1 (2002); Gilbert, "International Agreements for Commodity Price Stabilisation," above n 144.

564 In this direction, Koning et al., above n 559, at 10–12.

565 GATT Panel Report, *European Communities – Refunds on Exports of Sugar*, above n 267, Conclusion at p 21.

566 See "Comments by Joseph M. Finger," above n 444, at 138.

567 Ibid, at 139.

to perform their economic function. The financing requirements originally proposed for the CFC amounted in total to $6 billion.[568] According to a commentator, effective buffer stocks for the ten IPC core commodities would have required significantly more than $10 billion.[569] Eventually, the 1980 Articles of Agreement of the Common Fund provided for only some $400 million of direct government contributions, for working capital and administrative expenses.[570] As discussed (3.1.3.3), the $6 billion IPC requirement was comparatively not high, especially considering the cost of domestic stabilisation arrangements in Europe. What eventually lacked was a common political resolve to carry out the objectives of the IPC, which in turn reflected fundamental disagreement as to the rationales for and objectives of multilateral action on prices.

To sum up, it seems that technical problems were certainly relevant in the past, but they were essentially entangled with financial, and ultimately political, difficulties. The majority of ICAs collapsed or were demised either because they were poorly financed, or due to political disagreement between countries as to the allocation of quotas or the levels at which prices ought to be stabilised, or due to non-participation of major producing and consuming countries. In some instances, farm policies in the developed countries frustrated multilateral efforts to stabilise prices. It is open to question as to whether experiments in commodity control would be viable, given adequate financial resources and a strong political commitment by governments.[571]

568 Of this, one-third (or $2 billion) was to be raised by direct contributions from governments; the remainder by borrowing, as and when necessary (Maizels, above n 432, at 121).

569 "Comments by Joseph M. Finger," above n 444, at 139.

570 A second window, with a target of $280 million, was to be established by voluntary contributions from member governments, with provision for the transfer of at least $70 million to the first window for market stabilisation. Additional funds required for the financing of stock operations of ICAs ought to be borrowed from private capital markets. The ICAs would make cash deposits with the Fund and provide the Fund with stock warrants as collateral, while the Fund would also have government guarantees in the form of callable capital (Maizels, above n 432, at 121).

571 In this direction, LN Rangarajan, "Commodity Conflict Revisited: from Nairobi to Belgrade," *Third World Quarterly* 5, no. 1 (1983). Indeed, technical obstacles had not been intractable in other contexts, if we only consider agricultural price support schemes in the industrial countries, or price intervention by private concerns in diamonds, copper, and lead. Nor where technical obstacles undefeatable where northern interests were engaged as producers (the cases of rubber, tin and tea in the 1930s), or when domestic stocking policies where used to support, rather than hinder, international commodity arrangements (as in the case of wheat).

#### 4.1.2.2 From Managing Prices to Managing Price Changes

A second, related, policy development was a shift in emphasis from price stabilisation to risk management and coping strategies, from efforts to manage prices to measures aimed at cushioning the social effects of adverse price changes. The new policy prescription was that countries should avoid trade intervention for purposes of commodity price stabilisation. Instead, they should turn to non-trade instruments to cope with or mitigate the effects of commodity price volatility, or attain other social objectives, such as ensuring minimum standards of livelihood to producers. At the domestic level, emphasis in particular shifted towards social protection policies and market-based risk-management instruments.

Social protection instruments include both contributory 'social security' schemes and non-contributory interventions, typically called 'social assistance programmes' or 'safety nets'.[572] The latter encompass a wide variety of schemes, such as cash and food transfers, school feeding programmes, guaranteed employment schemes, and other programmes such as food-for work or food-for-training.[573] They all share a focus on coping with risk, rather than mitigating it, and tackle poverty and vulnerability directly, without interfering with market dynamics. To be effective, social protection interventions need to be specifically targeted and strictly followed-up. This entails institutional sophistication, good governance, and extremely high transaction costs. These requirements raise issues of workability and implementation in contexts of limited institutional and financial resources.

Market-based price risk management instruments refer to a variety of financial instruments, collectively known as 'derivatives',[574] aimed at reducing

---

572 As pointed out by the High Level Panel of Experts on Food Security and Nutrition, social protection became prominent in the 1990s (HLPE, *Social Protection for Food Security: A Report by the High Level Panel of Experts on Food Security and Nutrition of the Committee on World Food Security* (Rome, 2012), at 25). As summarised in the report, in the early 2000s, the "social risk management" framework provided a more coherent way of assessing risks and articulating suitable "reduction", "mitigation", or "coping" responses. This approach established "an implicit hierarchy: reducing risk (e.g. raising incomes or assets) is preferred to mitigating risk (e.g. insurance), which is preferable to helping people 'cope' with risk (e.g. emergency food aid, which is a last resort)" (HLPE, above, at 25). More recent thinking on "social protection for social justice" argues that social protection should be provided on an "entitlement" or "claims-based" rather than a discretionary basis, and that it should be "underpinned by enforceable legislation that transforms a benevolent gesture into a justiciable right" (ibid, at 25).

573 For a detailed review, HLPE, *Social Protection*, above n 572.

574 In that their value is 'derived' from that of the underlying asset.

exposure to price variability. Commodity derivatives may be traded through the interposing of a commodity exchange (exchange-traded derivatives),[575] or directly between two contracting parties (off-exchange, or over-the-counter (OTC) trade).[576] The major commodity derivatives include forward and futures contracts, options and swaps.[577] To put it simply, by locking-in the price for future delivery, these contracts allow market participants (commercial hedgers, with an interest in the underlying asset) to 'hedge' against unfavourable price movements that may occur in the underlying physical market before the delivery date.[578] A futures contract locks-in the selling and buying prices. Options set a price floor in the case of put options or a price ceiling for call options, without giving away any potential upside or downside. The price risk is not reduced, but shifted to other market participants (commercials with inverse risk, or speculators). In this respect, market-based hedging instruments simply allow producers and consumers to mitigate their exposure to price volatility. They do not reduce price volatility or earning instability, nor do they influence long-term price trends.

Market-based instruments arose prominently in the 1990s among the options available for mitigating exposure to commodity price volatility without disrupting market dynamics. Even within UNCTAD, the work of the secretariat became increasingly focused on risk management and other modern financial instruments. Overall, emphasis shifted from market price intervention to

---

575 A commodity exchange is "a market in which multiple buyers and sellers trade commodity-linked contracts on the basis of rules and procedures laid down by the exchange derivatives markets" (UNCTAD, *Overview of the World's Commodity Exchanges*, UNCTAD/DITC/COM/2005/8, 2006, at 5). In developed countries, such exchanges typically act as a platform for trade in commodity-linked 'derivatives' instruments. In the developing world, commodity exchanges essentially focus on physical trade, though several exchanges are evolving towards trade in commodity-linked financial instruments.

576 OTC derivative markets are characterised by privately negotiated transactions directly entered into by two counterparties. The OTC derivatives market permits customisation of contractual terms, in contrast to exchange-traded contracts, which are standardised. Further, in OTC markets each party assumes the default risk of the other, while exchange-traded derivatives are centrally cleared (i.e. clearinghouses act as middlemen between two transacting parties and take on the default risk).

577 For a detailed description of these instruments, UNCTAD, *A Survey of Commodity Risk Management Instruments*, UNCTAD/COM/15/REV.2, 1998.

578 This is done by taking offsetting positions in the cash (physical) and futures market. Beyond this hedging function, derivatives are also used for speculation and arbitrage. Speculators do not hedge, but seek to profit from the successful anticipation of price movements. Arbitrage refers to the exploitation of price differentials between markets.

non-intervention tools, and from managing prices to dealing with the effects of price instability.

#### 4.1.2.3 A Critical Assessment

The liberal reforms outline above showed a marked change in governmental policy from largely interventionist approach to a more market-oriented one in agricultural commodities. Yet, the demise of 'control' strategies in commodities, i.e. the dismantlement of ICAs and of statutory marketing, has not set the market 'free'. In particular, commodity policy reform overlooked the complex, multi-layered coexistence of 'rules' of diverse origin and form in commodity regulation. The outer layer of ICAs was removed, but inner layers of regulation, notably unilateral governmental action and the 'orderly marketing' of merchants, were left relatively untouched. It follows that today's commodity trade regime is not a liberal one, but one framed by unilateral State intervention and the merchant order, with a substantial lack of global governance and responsibility.[579] Two instances of 'governance failure' are briefly discussed below.

##### a) *Governmental Intervention*

Was there, with the demise of ICAs, a genuine retreat of the State from the farm economy? Or have agricultural commodity markets continued to be 'managed', though by different means? It appears that subtle forms of distortion have continued to operate. The shift has essentially been in the level and means of regulation: from concerted multilateral action to un-coordinated unilateral intervention by individual states; and, in the OECD economies, from direct price controls to more indirect forms of intervention. Indeed, when it comes to agricultural commodities, institutionalised restrictive practices, trade barriers and other forms of market intervention are commonplace rather than the exception, and increasingly so. Some details are briefly discussed below.

Farm support policies are still as strong as they were forty years ago. In the most advanced economies, domestic farm support policies underwent substantial liberal reforms through the late 1990s and 2000s. Yet, what was at stake was more a difference in intervention tools and strategies, than a substantial reduction in overall support. The bulk of support has shifted from the Amber Box category of trade-distorting, non-exempt policies, to the Green Box category, which is exempt (so-called 'box shifting').[580] Green Box, or Annex 2,

---

579 In that sense, see also Thomas Cottier, "Multilayered Governance, Pluralism, and Moral Conflict," *Indiana Journal of Global Legal Studies* 16, no. 2 (2009), at 651.

580 For a review, Irene Musselli, *Farm Support and Trade Rules: Towards a New Paradigm under the 2030 Agenda*, UNCTAD, Policy Issues in International Trade and Commodities,

support is permissible under the terms of the AoA. Yet, there is growing consensus that, by providing incentives for resource use that may be inconsistent with market signals, Green Box subsidies tend to have effects on production decisions.[581] Turning to the emerging economies, support technically qualified as 'trade-distorting' has there increased dramatically over the past years.[582]

Tariff protection remains high for agricultural products across developed and developing countries alike. For example, in the EU, MFN applied tariffs on agricultural products average 13.2 percent, over three times more than duties on non-agricultural products. Sensitive items, such as dairy products, livestock, sugar and some cereals, are hit by prohibitively high tariffs.

The level of export subsidisation continued to be high through the 1990s and early 2000s, including on items of special export interest to low-income countries. This was notably the case for cotton. US domestic and export support subsidies to upland cotton exceeded $4 billion in 2001, greater than the value of total US cotton production.[583] It was only at the 10th Ministerial Conference in Nairobi that WTO members eliminated export subsidies, except for some products.[584]

Other competition-distorting instruments remain largely unregulated, or under-regulated. These include: export taxes and other export restrictions; international food aid as a means of surplus disposal; export credits and export credit guarantees; and state trading in exports. As stated in Häberli, "[t]hese

---

Study Series, no. 74 (Geneva, 2016). In the EU, for example, Green Box support rose from an average 19.7 billion euros per year during 1995–97 (then 22 percent of overall farm support) to an annual average of about 63 billion euros over 2007–09 (80 percent of support); direct payments, the most controversial form of Green Box support, accounted for about 88 percent of all Green Box subsides during 2007–09. Overall, the rise in Green Box support more than offset the decline in trade-distorting support, as measured by Amber Box notifications (Data source: WTO, Datasets of Notified Information, Table DS:1 (notification of domestic support measures). Downloaded from http://www.wto.org/english/tratop_e/agric_e/transparency_toolkit_e.htm on 24 July 2013).

581 See above n 266.

582 Market price support has increased appreciably in key emerging economies, including China, Turkey and Russia (OECD data, Emerging Economies: Producer Support Estimate by country, Dataset 2011 E).

583 *Statement of Available Evidence with regard to the Existence and Nature of the Subsidies in Question and the Serious Prejudice Caused to the Interest of Brazil*, WT/DS267/R/Add.3 dated 3 October 2002, ANNEX N-1, Page N-6. The United States Agricultural Act 2014 introduced major changes in cotton farm support policies in the US.

584 World Trade Organization, Ministerial Decision on Export Competition of 19 December 2015, WT/MIN(15)/45, WT/L/980.

policy instruments have an obvious bearing on the famous 'level-playing field' by which an optimal level of global food security could be achieved."[585]

To sum up, the playing field is far from level. The Nairobi Package on agriculture, agreed at the 10th Ministerial Conference of the World Trade Organization (WTO) in December 2015, eliminated agricultural export subsidies.[586] But important distortions and imbalances in the area of domestic support stay. Market intervention remains a structural, systemic issue in agricultural trade, across developed and developing countries. This discloses a pervasive discrepancy between claim and reality. It also points to a widening cleft between international commitments and domestic action. When it comes to agriculture, governments continue to be involved in the management of the economy, while attempting to uphold an international commercial system based on non-interventionist market principles.

The WTO AoA has created leeway in this state of affairs. This reflects a complexity of factors, mainly political in nature. Indeed, the AoA rules were not derived by a process of syllogistic logic and deductive stringency. They were negotiated disciplines, and reflect the relative negotiating capabilities and leverage of the various parties. Eventually, the OECD countries showed remarkable pragmatism in protecting their interests in agriculture. As discussed in Häberli and Paarlberg, their concessions were flawed, in some important respects.[587] In particular, the Amber Box of trade-distorting support was "carefully written" to exclude key internal policy support instruments in the EU and the US. [588] Notably, this included most forms of direct cash payments to producers, exempted under the Blue and Green Boxes.[589] Furthermore, the

585 Christian Häberli, "Food Security and WTO Rules," in *Food Crises and the* WTO, ed. Baris Karapinar and Christian Häberli (Cambridge: Cambridge University Press, 2010); Christian Häberli, "Do WTO Rules Improve or Impair the Right to Food?" in *Research Handbook on International Agricultural Trade*, ed. Melaku Desta and Joe McMahon (Cheltenham, UK: Edward Elgar, 2012); Christian Häberli, "The WTO and Food Security: What's Wrong with the Rules?" in *The Challenge of Food Security: International Policy and Regulatory Frameworks*, ed. Rosemary Rayfuse and Nicole Weisfelt (Cheltenham, UK: Edward Elgar, 2012); Häberli, "God, the WTO and Hunger," in *Poverty and the International Economic Legal System: Duties to the World's Poor*, ed. Krista Nadakavukaren Schefer (Cambridge: Cambridge University Press, 2013), at 94.

586 The WTO's 10th Ministerial Conference was held in Nairobi, Kenya, from 15 to 19 December 2015. Its most important outcome in agriculture was the elimination of agricultural export subsidies.

587 Paarlberg, above n 557; Häberli, above n 585.

588 Robert Paarlberg, above n 557, at 428.

589 Paarlberg, above n 557, at 428. Direct payments to farmers were excluded from counting towards the AMS if made under production limiting programmes, based on historical/

AoA disciplines on market access and domestic support were structured so as to allow massive "product support focusing".[590] Commitments were often 'sector-wide', or underweighted, which allowed continued protection for sensitive items. Finally, data periods and base points were carefully selected to inflate the base levels of protection from which the EU and USA would calculate reduction commitments.[591] All together, these expedients significantly undermined the meaningfulness of liberalisation commitments under the AoA, and introduced a number of loopholes in regulation.

### b) *The 'Orderly Marketing' of Merchants*

The multilateral commodity trade regime is flawed, in a second respect: it acknowledges and tries to redress, with limited success, institutionalised distortions, but not those that stem from the 'merchant order'. There have been attempts by private actors to manipulate market prices for most of the major internationally traded commodities. It is thus important to look beyond market intervention in its governmental form, and venture, if not only incidentally,

---

fixed areas/yields, and made on 85 percent or less of base production (Blue Box). In practice, this exempted from internal-reduction commitments two major instruments of farm support in the US and the EU: the US deficiency payments to producers; and the EU compensation payments, under the terms of the 1992 MacSharry reform plan for the CAP, a major instrument of farm support in the EU (Paarleberg, at 428).

590 Paarlberg, above n 557, at 429–30. Under the Uruguay Round AoA, the tariff cut was sector-wide (though minimum 15 percent cuts were required for each line), and 'unweighted'; which allowed continued protection for sensitive items. As regards current and minimum access opportunities, sensitive products could be aggregated with less sensitive items (rather than measuring tariff access line by line, at a very disaggregated level); and special trading relationships were allowed to be counted. Regulatory holes and loopholes in WTO rules are discussed at length by Häberli (see above n 585).

591 As detailed in Paarlberg (above n 557), reduction commitments in domestic support and export subsidies were from historically high levels (1986–88 baseline). In particular, the outdated 1986–88 base period did not count reductions in internal support and export subsidisation that had already been implemented unilaterally in the United States and EU, outside the WTO, in the late 1980s and early 1990s. Thus, the EU could count towards its domestic-support reduction commitments internal-support reductions that were already underway unilaterally, outside the WTO framework, under the 1988 'stabiliser' reform (Paarlberg, above n 557, at 428). Similarly, the 1986–88 base period generated bound tariffs so high that they would exceed more recent levels of effective protection from non-tariff measures even after the 36 percent reduction called for by the AoA (ibid, at 430). Finally, little real liberalisation was achieved on export subsidies, as the 1986–88 base levels did not count reductions that had already been implemented unilaterally in the following years. For a detailed assessment of these issues, see also Häberli, above n 585.

into the secretive area of private cartels. A historical survey of private commodity cartels is well beyond the reach of this study. Suffice here to mention a few aspects that deserve some consideration.

In a few developing countries, particularly the least developed, the dismantlement of commodity control arrangements resulted in a vacuum. It had been somewhat assumed that the retreat of the State would liberate genuine market dynamics. Little attention was paid to the fact that the most basic market infrastructures were not in place.[592] The reforms accomplished the *pars destruens*: they effectively dismantled intergovernmental commodity price-stabilising arrangements and domestic statutory marketing. Yet, they failed on the *pars construens*: the 'market-creating' function of establishing the underpinnings of the market economy.

The vacuum was filled by the logistics strength of international traders and processors. Statutory marketing was replaced, in many instances, by private oligopsony, and private rents replaced public rents. Today, a few firms dominate international trade and processing in key tropical commodities, and a few are dominant across a large number of commodities.[593] For the peasant farmers, the problem is further compounded by concentration in the input markets. The process there is threefold: growing horizontal concentration in the seed industry; increasing vertical concentration between seed producers and agrochemical companies, with a trend towards larger and more integrated operations, the so-called 'life science' companies; and strategic alliances between the life science companies and major trading and processing complexes such as Cargill or ADM.[594] These patterns of concentration may give rise to 'market power', [595] and abuse thereof.[596]

592 Hard infrastructure, such as storage facilities, and feeder roads; and soft infrastructure, such as competition law, and transparency.

593 For a review, World Bank, *World Development Report 2008: Agriculture for Development* (Washington, D.C.: The World Bank, 2007), 136.

594 Jelle Bruinsma, ed., *World Agriculture: Towards 2015/2030: An FAO Perspective* (London: Earthscan, 2003); World Bank, above n 593, at 323; UNCTAD, *Tracking the Trend towards Market Concentration: The Case of the Agricultural Input Industry*, UNCTAD/DITC/COM/2005/16, April 2006.

595 Market power is here understood as "[...] the ability of a firm, or a group of firms acting jointly, to raise (or decrease) and profitably maintain prices above (or below) the level that would prevail under competition for a significant period of time." UNCTAD, *Cocoa Study: Industry Structures and Competition* (New York and Geneva: United Nations, 2008), at vi.

596 Market concentration is not be straightforwardly equated with 'market power'. Yet, at least for certain tropical commodities, there is enough evidence to claim that the global

In the present 'liberalised' environment, market power asymmetries in input and output commodity markets would deserve more global attention than is presently the case. Interestingly, under the Havana Charter, movements towards greater trade openness under Chapter IV were to be accompanied by tightened multilateral regulation of restrictive business practices under Chapter V. This significant link was severed in the GATT and then the WTO. Critical issues of private abuse of market power are left unaddressed, which leads to question how 'just' market-prices are in the present setting.

A further examination of these matters goes well beyond the reach of this Chapter. They have been recalled here to question the efficiency argument; to challenge the idea that free (unregulated) commodity markets lead to efficiency, as if guided by unseen forces. They are instances of market and governance failures that should warn us against equating officially 'undistorted' commodity markets with efficient markets. They should also caution against 'the danger of abstract reasoning' when discussing efficiency gains from liberal reforms. None of the assumptions of neoclassical economic thinking (the efficient market hypothesis, the assumption of the 'economic' as separate from the 'social', the instrumentally rational, utility maximising agent) have much analytical significance in a context of peasant farmers trapped in the vicious cycle of subsistence.[597]

### 4.1.3 *Which Orientation for the WTO Agreement on Agriculture?*

The commodity policy developments outlined above are to be assessed in interplay with the negotiation and adoption of the WTO AoA. The terms of the AoA required varying degrees of liberalisation in three related policy areas, called the 'pillars' of the AoA:[598] internal support;[599] border protection

---

deregulation of commodity markets has re-distributed value along the global commodity chain away from the peasant farmers in producing countries. See World Bank, above n 593, at 136; Bruinsma, above n 594, at 277; John M. Talbot, "Where Does Your Coffee Dollar Go? The Division of Income and Surplus along the Coffee Commodity Chain," *Studies in Comparative International Development* 32, no. 1 (1997).

597 For an overall critique of the real world significance of the assumptions of the neoliberal orthodoxy, Dash, above n 544.

598 For concise but in-depth assessments, Paarlberg, above n 557.

599 As regards domestic support, it was agreed that support measures with a price distortive effect would be reduced by 20 percent from a 1986–88 baseline over the six-year implementation period of the Agreement (1995–2000).

(market access);[600] and export subsidisation.[601] In all these areas, the AoA represented a breakthrough towards a rule-framed regime in agriculture. This ended the so-called 'agricultural exception' in trade law, under which agricultural commodities had been effectively shielded from key GATT disciplines.[602]

To what extent does the AoA follow neoliberal precepts of economic efficiency? Two strands of thought have, in recent years, dominated the debate over the normative objectives of the AoA and of WTO law in general: the 'liberal model' theory of the WTO, and 'constitutional' perspectives on trade law. It is worth to recall the main tenets of these doctrines, and assess their relevance with regard to the flexibility for stabilisation policies under the AoA.

#### 4.1.3.1 'Liberal' Model

Under the 'liberal model' theory, trade law pursues a liberal trade agenda. The approach derives its normative rationale from economics: greater efficiency through liberalised market access (see above, Section 4.1.1.2 a). Its focus is on the commercial aspects of trade. The 'liberal' approach interprets WTO law "as an instrument to substantially restrain the grasp of domestic politics on the

600 On the issue of border protection, it was agreed that all non-tariff border measures should be converted to tariffs, and bound ('tariffication'). These newly bound tariffs, as well as those bound earlier, had to be reduced by 36 percent on average over the six year implementation period (for developed countries), with a minimum 15 percent cut in all lines. Since the 'tariffication' process could result in prohibitively high tariffs, the Agreement provided for 'current' and 'minimum access opportunities', by means of tariff-rate quotas. Members should ensure access for no less than the average annual import quantities during 1986–88 (current access); if this average was less than 5 percent of domestic consumption, minimum access opportunities should be provided by low or minimal duties for imports equal to 3 to 5 percent of domestic consumption (minimum access). Developing countries benefited from gentler cuts and longer implementation periods. *Modalities for the Establishment of Specific Binding Commitments under the Reform Programme* (MTN.GNG/MA/W/24, 20 December 1993).

601 As regards export subsidies, historic volumes and value of directly subsidised exports were to be reduces by 21 and 36 respectively over the six year implementation period (from the 1986–88 base period); countries were not allowed to introduce new subsidies. *Modalities for the Establishment of Specific Binding Commitments under the Reform Programme* (MTN.GNG/MA/W/24, 20 December 1993).

602 For a detailed assessment, GATT, Consultative Group of Eighteen, *Agriculture in the GATT – Note by the Secretariat* (CG.18/W/59/Rev.1, 20 January 1982).

economy and – in different variants – to increase international competition and to some extent deregulation".[603] Under this approach, as described by Professor Krista Nadakavukaren Schefer, "the tools of choice within the system are mainly economic, with some legal instruments added where necessary to ensure adherence to the economic instruments".[604]

There are exceptions to the liberal commitments, built into the text of the various WTO agreements. Market access restrictions are permitted, for example, on the basis of security concerns, or development needs. Yet, according to the 'liberal' strand of thought, liberalised market access remains the paramount goal, and exceptions are narrowly framed. In more nuanced terms, "[…] there remains an implicit hierarchy of values in the system which places trade liberalization above other governmental interests".[605] The possibility of a better balance between economic and social objectives in trade law is not excluded, but "it will not happen on its own": purposive action is needed to align trade and social trajectories, in a perspective *de lege ferenda*.[606]

This approach is reflected in a few 'stabilisation cases',[607] where the object and purpose of the WTO AoA has been interpreted narrowly. For example, according to the Panel in *Canada – Dairy*, as upheld by the Panel in *Chile – DSB*, the object and purpose of this Agreement is,

> […] to 'establish a basis for initiating a process of reform of trade in agriculture' in line with, inter alia, the long-term objective of establishing 'a fair and market-oriented agricultural trading system'. This objective is pursued in order 'to provide for substantial progressive reductions in agricultural support and protection sustained over an agreed period of

---

603 Armin von Bogdandy, "Legitimacy of International Economic Governance: Interpretative Approaches to WTO law and the Prospects of its Proceduralization," in *International Economic Governance and Non-Economic Concerns: New Challenges for the International Legal Order*, ed. Stefan Griller (Vienna: Springer Verlag, 2003), 114.

604 Krista Nadakavukaren Schefer, *Social Regulation in the WTO* (Cheltenham, UK: Edward Elgar, 2010).

605 Ibid, at 274, for a discussion on the standard of non-discrimination set out in WTO law and exceptions to the non-discrimination principle.

606 Nadakavukaren Schefer, above n 604, at 11. Professor Nadakavukaren outlines a number of paths to achieve social regulation through trade law, considering both intra-WTO and WTO-external solutions.

607 Cases that dealt explicitly with price stabilisation issues in agriculture. See, in particular, *Chile – Price Band System*, above n 210; *Peru – Agricultural Products*, above n 211; *Canada – Dairy*, above n 330.

time, resulting in correcting and preventing restrictions and distortions in world agricultural markets'.[608]

#### 4.1.3.2 'Constitutional' Perspectives

'Constitutional' perspectives argue for a different reading of trade law.[609] The 'constitutionalisation' doctrine expounds the view that trade is not an end in itself, but a means to an end. The ultimate objective, as enshrined in the preamble of the WTO Agreement, is global welfare. As discussed, the Havana Charter 'grafted' into trade regulation the broad aspirational goals envisaged in Article 55 of the UN Charter: "[...] the attainment of the higher standards of living, full employment and conditions of economic and social progress and development".[610] These welfare objectives are enshrined in the preamble of the GATT and of the WTO Agreement and purposively frame their interpretation. It is also recalled that considerations of social and political stability were central to the very fabric of the GATT. Indeed, the original purpose of the GATT was not to maximise efficiency, but to maintain peace through avoidance of beggar-thy-neighbour policies.

In setting the framework for the conduct of trade relations, the WTO strives for a reasonable balance between different policy goals. WTO law in general acknowledges the political and social need for a 'just balance' between liberal trading principles and 'social justice'.[611] As stated in Petersmann, "WTO objectives extend far beyond economics".[612] The Preamble of the WTO Agreement only pledges WTO members "[...] to preserve the basic principles and to further the objectives underlying this multilateral trading system", without specifying what these 'basic principles' are.[613] These objectives and guiding principles, as embodied in many articles, include 'liberal' trading principles of freedom of trade, non-discrimination, reciprocity, private property rights, transparency

608 Panel Report on *Canada – Dairy*, above n 330, paras. 7.25–7.26. See also Panel Report, *Chile – Price Band System*, above n 210, para. 7.57.

609 On constitutionalism, Thomas Cottier, "Limits to International Trade: the Constitutional Challenge," in *International Law in Ferment: A New Vision for Theory and Practice*, Proceedings of the 94th Annual Meeting, 5–8 April 2000, Washington, D.C., S. 220–22.

610 Havana Charter, Article 1, Preamble; Geneva draft, above n 49, Article 1; London Report, above n 49, narrative account of the treatment of Chapter I, at 4.

611 In Petersmann's words, "[t]he political and social need for a 'just balance' between the aspirations for individual freedom and the demands of organized society for 'social justice' is reflected in numerous 'exceptions' and 'public interest' provisions in WTO law". Petersmann, above n 542, at 69–70

612 Ibid.

613 Petersmann, above n 542, at 68.

and the rule of law.[614] These 'liberal' principles complexly coexist with other goals and principles, enshrined in the system. These are a host of non-trade concerns, broadly defined 'public goods',[615] and equity, this latter central to the very notion of S&DT.

How is the balance attained? Not necessarily through a set of liberal norms and narrowly framed exceptions, as generally perceived. The 'constitutional' strand questions the prioritisation of liberal trade interests over competing claims. It rejects a hierarchy of values which places liberalisation over competing claims. In WTO law, it is held, exceptions are just as normatively important as general obligations. Trade law is capable of taking into account and balancing a broad range of issues beyond liberalised trade, including environmental protection, health concerns, moral or cultural values, and development.[616] In some cases, the system accords preference to non-trade values over liberal trade interests. For example, under GATT Article XX, non-trade concerns override liberal trade obligations. Eventually, "[…] the words of the agreements leave open the possibility of 'coordinating' the laws of the trade agreements with the social interests protected by general international law".[617] This is a matter of strengthening the constitutional features of WTO law, through a framework capable of "balancing and weighing different, equally legitimate, democratically defined basic values and goals".[618]

#### 4.1.3.3 Which Model for the AoA?

The 'liberal' model holds more in theory than in practice. As discussed in Section 4.1.2.3, today's agricultural trade regime is not a liberal one, but one resulting in managed trade under extensive domestic and international regulation. On the issue of stabilisation, the system provides significant flexibilities for policies geared to stabilise agricultural prices or farm income, as discussed in Section 2.3. Multilateral efforts to stabilise prices are excluded from the scope of the AoA market access disciplines, if covered under GATT Article XX (h). Domestic stabilisation policies are not proscribed as such under the AoA, but they are regulated in their trade-distortive components.

614 See Petersmann, above n 542, at 85; James Cameron and Kevin R. Gray, "Principles of International Law in the WTO Dispute Settlement Body," *International and Comparative Law Quarterly* 50, no. 2 (2001); Meinhard Hilf, "Power, Rules and Principles: Which Orientation for WTO/GATT Law?" *Journal of International Economic Law* 4, no. 1 (2001).

615 For example, GATT Articles XVIII–XXI, GATS Articles XIV, XIVbis, Articles 6–8, 30–31, 40 of the TRIPS Agreement (Petersmann, above n 542, at 85).

616 Cottier, above n 609.

617 Nadakavukaren Schefer, above n 604, at 267.

618 Cottier, above n 609, S 221.

Overall, the AoA acknowledges both trade and on-trade values, and this complexity of motives and drivers is reflected in the way prescriptive provisions are formulated and how they operate. In essence, the trade regulation of agriculture proceeds through a complex set of liberal commitments and 'policy space' escapes. The final balance between 'liberal' and protectionist interests ultimately depends on the extent of the escapes provided. This latter is a matter of technical details whose practical ramifications are often difficult to anticipate. Take the example of domestic support disciplines under the AoA. In this, as in other areas of regulation, negotiators faced what Häberli calls "a dilemma" between the benefits of more liberal trade disciplines and the reduction in "policy space" these same disciplines entail.[619] This dilemma, in Häberli's words, explains the "softeners" by which countries are still entitled to "shield their producers from competition".[620] These 'softeners' include: the Green Box exemption under Annex 2 of the Agreement on Agriculture; the exemption for Blue Box production-limiting programmes, notified under Article 6.5 of the AoA; "Development Programmes" notified by developing countries under Article 6.2 of the Agreement on Agriculture; and *de minimis* levels of support,[621] exempted from the AMS calculations.[622] Eventually, the reach and impact of the 'liberal' reform programme on domestic support was significantly impaired by the escapes provided. These escapes, opened to introduce flexibility, eventually turned into systemic flaws.[623]

As is clear from the above analysis, 'constitutional' strands of thought resonate in the AoA. Yet again there is a gap between theory and reality.

In theory, the AoA aspires to balance trade and social values. Its normative objectives are not purely 'economistic', but extend far beyond economics with a view to achieve certain public policy goals. The AoA endorses trade liberalisation (and efficiency) as a relevant normative goal, while qualifying it with reference to competing and complementary sets of interests. Thus, in the preamble of the WTO AoA, the long-term objective to establish a "market-oriented agricultural trading system" is not unqualified. It is tied to competing policy

619 Häberli, "Food Security and WTO Rules," above n 585, at 321.

620 Ibid, at 321.

621 The threshold is generally set at 5 percent (10 for developing countries) of a product's value of production (VOP) for product-specific support and of total agricultural production for non-product specific support. Specific *de minimis* provisions have been negotiated for some newly acceding countries.

622 If support (product-specific or non-product-specific) exceeds the *de minimis* threshold, it is fully accounted in the AMS calculation, not only for the fraction above the threshold.

623 Musselli, above n 580.

objectives and principles: due account for "non-trade concerns, including food security and the need to protect the environment", and consideration of the "particular needs and conditions of developing country Members".[624] The AoA 'built-in' reform agenda (Article 20) also refers to a complex set of interests and objectives,[625] as does the Doha mandate.[626] Overall, the specificity of agricultural trade regulation lies in the intertwining of 'liberal' trade objectives and competing interests. In a strenuous effort to resolve this duality, trade law is informed by internal tensions and contradictions and the movement towards unity, or compromise.

In practice, questions arise as to whether the Agreement has provided a suitable framework capable of reasonably balancing different equally legitimate interests, such as 'liberal' trade interests and stabilisation concerns. This is doubtfully the case, in this author's view. The problem is not necessarily with the prioritisation of trade over non-trade interests, but with disciplines that lack coherence and direction. As mentioned above (Section 4.1.2.3), the disciplines of the AoA are quite defective. As further discussed *infra* (Section 5.1.2.2), they are riddled with double standards and imperfections.[627] With specific reference to farm support and stabilisation policies, there are asymmetries in the treatment of different stabilisation approaches and tools, irrespective of considerations of actual trade impacts. For example, price bands are proscribed, even if transparently administered and predictable. Yet direct transfers to producers are unrestrained if 'decoupled', in spite of growing theoretical and empirical evidence of their commercial impacts. In practice, stabilisation

---

624 WTO AoA, Preamble.

625 Including "non-trade concerns, special and differential treatment to developing country members, and the objective to establish a fair and market-oriented agricultural trading system, and the other objectives and concerns mentioned in the preamble to this Agreement" (WTO AoA, Article 20 (c)).

626 At Doha, WTO members reconfirmed "the long-term objective [...] to establish a fair and market-oriented trading system". In parallel, they restated the need to "take into account" non-trade concerns and meaningfully operationalise special and development treatment (SDT) for developing countries (WT/MIN(01)/DEC/1, para. 13).

627 Interpreted as a first step towards a more equitable order, the AoA eventually froze up imbalances. This is mainly on account of the fact that only those countries that subsidised their farm sector in a base period (for the most part, developed countries) now have scheduled domestic support commitments under the AoA. These commitments provide a legal basis to maintain subsidies above the *de minimis* threshold, even if at reduced level from historically high base levels. The other members, mostly developing countries, should keep domestic support within the *de minimis* upper limit. For a more detailed assessment, Musselli, above n 580, 3–5.

tools that better match developing countries' set-up, such as variable import levies and price controls, are in principle proscribed; while more sophisticated instruments, suitable to the developed economies, such as 'decoupled' direct payments, are unrestrained.

### 4.1.4 *Assessment*

Through the 1980s, economic policy-making and designs were strongly influenced by the neoliberal paradigm while in reality protectionist paradigms continued to prevail in the field of agriculture. Predicated upon efficiency grounds, the liberal stance emphasized distortions associated with governmental intervention in the economy. On the issue of stabilisation, the policy prescription was that the market, rather than the State, should be relied upon to the maximum extent possible as a device to stabilise commodity prices. Some degree of price volatility was eventually acknowledged as an inherent attribute of well-functioning commodity markets. This prompted a shift in emphasis, from efforts to manage prices to measures aimed at managing or mitigating the impacts of price changes.

Three major trade policy developments were associated with this paradigm shift in commodities: the dismantlement of intergovernmental commodity price-stabilising arrangements; the abolition of State trading monopolies in a few developing countries; and the shift from price stabilisation to income stabilisation in major developed economies. Taken together, these developments seemed to show that the era of commodity control had come to an abrupt end. At closer scrutiny, however, the picture is more complex. At the international level, there was certainly a retreat of the State from the commodity economy. All restrictive ICAs lapsed or collapsed and countries abandoned joint action through ICAs for the stabilisation of prices of agricultural commodities. At the country level, however, the picture is mixed. A few developing countries, notably, sub-Saharan African countries, liberalised and deregulated the agriculture sector. In many of them, statutory marketing was replaced by private oligopsony, and private rents replaced public rents. Other developing countries, particularly in Asia, continued to rely extensively on market intervention. As for the advanced economies, what was at stake was a change in the form of intervention, from price support to income support. It follows that today's agricultural trade regime is not a liberal one, but one framed by unilateral State intervention and the merchant order, with a substantial lack of multilateral governance.[628]

628 Cottier, above n 579, at 651.

Turning to multilateral trade rules, the AoA conceptually represented a major breakthrough towards a rule-based trade regime in agriculture. In terms of underlying motives, the AoA moves beyond a purely economic rationale, by weighing and balancing competing policy objectives. In theory, the AoA aspires to balance trade and social values. Its normative objectives are not purely 'economistic', but extend far beyond economics with a view to achieve certain public policy goals. In practice, its disciplines often lack coherence and direction. With specific reference to farm support and stabilisation policies, there are asymmetries in the treatment of different stabilisation approaches and tools, irrespective of considerations of actual trade impacts.

In the end, the reality is much less market-based than theory suggests. The current trade regime in agriculture is certainly market-oriented, but in a spurious way. Beyond the surface, trade restrictions and distortions continue to be pervasive and there is room for inequality and discrimination.

## 4.2 Towards Re-Regulation? The 2007–08 and 2010–11 Commodity Crises

The market-oriented commodity trade system came under severe strain by the late 2000s. Two major commodity price shocks in a three-year span (2007/08 – 2010/11) spurred much discussion on the adequacy of the market as a stabilising device. Major challenges ahead, from climate change to the threat of depletion, cast further doubt on the adequacy of the current market-based regime. Policy consensus grew, in academic and political circles, that the commodity trading system, as it had hitherto functioned, had fallen short of achieving acceptable outcomes; and that a new approach was needed to curb excessive commodity price volatility.[629] Yet, as to what ought to be done to achieve this objective, there was far from any consent.

629 The Group of Twenty (G20) first examined the issue at the 2009 Pittsburgh Summit, where policy leaders committed to "improve the regulation, functioning, and transparency of financial and commodity markets to address excessive commodity price volatility". See *The G20 Pittsburgh Summit Commitments*, issued in Pittsburgh on 25 September 2009, para. 41, available at http://www.g20.utoronto.ca/analysis/commitments-09-pittsburgh.html (visited on 18 April 2013). The G20 reiterated its strong commitment to increase transparency on physical and financial commodity markets at the Cannes Summit in 2011. See, in particular, para. 32 of the G-20 Cannes Summit *Final Declaration – Building Our Common Future: Renewed Collective Action for the Benefit of All*, Cannes, 4 November 2011, available at http://www.g20.utoronto.ca/summits/2011cannes.html (visited on 18 April 2013).

Policy discussions in the aftermath of the crisis reveal some strong and polarised views as to the way ahead. Two contrasting tendencies arose, opposing two fundamentally different creeds, or attitudes, towards commodity control. There were those who advocated a 'deepening' of the market-based order, by means of correcting restrictions and distortions; and those who endorsed the notion that the market mechanism alone could not suffice to assure stability in commodity markets, and that State intervention was needed. In the background, the economic debate was, and still is, extremely polarised and divisive. Economists fundamentally disagree among themselves on the causes of the price shocks, as well as on the medium to long-term commodity price outlook.

This Chapter briefly reviews these developments. It first takes a cursory look at major price developments in international commodity markets; and at how they challenge the efficacy and legitimacy of existing multilateral trade disciplines. The analysis then explores the two major trade-related approaches that have emerged to deal with commodity price volatility; and the normative values and assumptions behind them. It then briefly considers the extent to which these trade policy stances reflect in WTO law, and concludes with a few summary observations.

### 4.2.1 *Recent Price Developments in Commodity Markets*

It is worth to briefly recall major recent price developments in commodity markets; and outline key challenges ahead. The analysis will only review some basic economic facts, to set the stage for the legal analysis.

#### 4.2.1.1 Looking Backward: The 2007–08 and 2010–11 Commodity Crises

Since the mid-2000s there has been a trend of rising and increasingly volatile commodity prices, with two major price shocks in 2007–08 and 2010–11. In June 2008, the prices of major food commodities on international markets reached their highest levels in 30 years,[630] triggering food riots across countries. After a steep fall, international food commodity prices resumed their upward trend in 2010, before spiking again in February 2011.[631] The new price spike triggered outbreaks of civil unrest across North Africa and the Middle East, and stoked inflationary pressure in the euro zone.

630 Food and Agriculture Organization of the United Nations, *Food Price Index* (monthly, 2002–2004 = 100) [hereafter, FAO *Food Price Index*], available at http://www.fao.org/worldfoodsituation/foodpricesindex/en/ (downloaded on 28 March 2014).

631 Ibid.

**Box 8: Recent price developments in agricultural markets**

In June 2008, cereal prices on international markets reached their highest levels in 30 years.[632] After falling sharply, prices resumed their upward trend and hit a new record high in May 2011.[633] Medium-run to short-run boom and bust episodes were recorded across many agricultural food and non-food commodities beyond cereals.

Significant controversy exists on the socio-economic ramifications of booming commodity prices, particularly for staple foods. In 2009, the FAO estimated that an additional 115 million people had been forced into chronic hunger in 2007–08, mainly due to high food prices.[634] About 1.2 billion people were reported undernourished in 2009 – more than at any time since 1970.[635] The FAO then revised its series in 2012, and reversed its findings. More accurate figures set the number of hungry people at approximately 870 million. There has been a steady decline in the number of hungry people over the past two decades, though progress has slowed down since the 2007–08 food crisis.[636]

There was, and still is, substantial disagreement as to the interpretation of these price dynamics. It was generally agreed that multiple factors had contributed to what appeared to be higher and more volatile food commodity prices:[637] the increased incidence of weather-induced supply shocks; subsidised production

632 Food and Agriculture Organization of the United Nations (FAO), *Cereals Price Index* (monthly, 2002–2004 = 100) [hereafter, FAO *Cereals Price Index*], available at http://www.fao.org/worldfoodsituation/foodpricesindex/en/ (downloaded on 7 May 2015).

633 Ibid.

634 FAO, *The State of Agricultural Commodity Markets 2009: High Food Prices and the Food Crisis – Experiences and Lessons Learned* (Rome: FAO, 2009), 6.

635 FAO, *The State of Food Insecurity in the World 2009: Economic Crises – Impacts and Lessons Learnt* (Rome: FAO, 2009).

636 FAO, WFP and IFAD, *The State of Food Insecurity in the World 2012: Economic Growth Is Necessary but not Sufficient to Accelerate Reduction of Hunger and Malnutrition* (Rome: FAO, 2012), 8.

637 For a review, FAO, *The State of Agriculture Commodity Markets 2009*, above n 634; Brian D. Wright, *International Grain Reserves and Other Instruments to Address Volatility in Grain Markets*, the World Bank, Policy Research Working Papers, no. 5028 (Washington, D.C., 2009); European Commission, *Historical Price Volatility*, Directorate-General for Agriculture and Rural Development, 2009; *Inter-agency Report on Price Volatility*, above n 68; World Bank and FAO, above n 21; World Bank et al., *Improving Food Security in Arab Countries* (Washington, D.C.: World Bank, 2009); World Bank, *Responding to Global Food Price Volatility and Its Impact on Food Security* (Washington, D.C.: World Bank, 2011).

of biofuels; high and volatile petroleum prices; the relative depreciation of the US dollar; and increased commodity speculation.[638] Yet, there was, and still is substantial disagreement as to the relative weight of these factors in framing the new price pattern.

Economists were divided, particularly on the issue of financial speculation. Some analysts argued that activities of financial participants had driven commodity prices away from fundamentals, or at least amplified movements related to fundamental factors.[639] Excessive buying by some categories of financial investors, in particular, was alleged to have contributed to rapid run-up in prices, beyond what justified by underlying supply and demand factors. Others pointed to the lack of conclusive evidence for any systemic influence of speculation by financial investors, and related the violent price swings to market fundamentals.[640]

Likewise, there is significant controversy over the nature of these price developments, and scholarly debate as to the medium- to long-term price outlook. Some analysts argue that the new price situation reflects a breakthrough in the way market behaves: the pattern ahead is one of high and increasingly volatile commodity prices.[641] For others, there is no novelty in these price

638 Biofuel subsidies reduce supply of land dedicated to food production, putting upward pressure on prices; high and volatile prices of petroleum, via the price of fuel and fertilizer (petroleum-based), are passed on to output prices in agriculture; the depreciation of the US dollar increases nominal prices for commodities priced in dollars; financial speculation may also contribute to higher and more volatile prices as investors shift to real assets, including commodities, during periods of uncertainty. The World Bank and FAO, above n 21, at 2–4.

639 See, in this direction, UNCTAD, *Price Formation in Financialized Commodity Markets*, above n 19; Jörg Mayer, *The Growing Interdependence between Financial and Commodity Markets*, UNCTAD Discussion Paper Series, no. 195 (Geneva, 2009); UNCTAD, *Trade and Development Report 2009* (New York; Geneva: United Nations, 2009); UNCTAD, *The Global Economic Crisis: Systemic Failures and Multilateral Remedies* (New York; Geneva: United Nations, 2009). See also Bargawi, above n 27.

640 In this direction, Scott Irwin and Dwight R. Sanders, "Index Funds, Financialization, and Commodity Futures Markets," *Applied Economic Perspectives and Policy* 33, no. 1 (2011); Scott Irwin and Dwight R. Sanders, "Testing the Masters Hypothesis in Commodity Futures Markets," *Energy Economics* 34, no. 1 (2012); Thomas Glauben, Ingo Pies, Sören Prehn, and Matthias Georg Will, "Alarm or Rather False Alarm? A Literature Review of Empirical Research Studies into Financial Speculation with Agricultural Commodities," Leibniz-Institut für Agrarentwicklung in Mittel- und Osteuropa, IAMO Policy Brief 9e (2012). See also IOSCO Technical Committee, Task Force on Commodity Futures Markets, *Final Report* (2009).

641 In this direction, Otaviano Canuto, *The Commodity Super Cycle: Is This Time Different?* The World Bank, Economic Premise note series, no. 150 ([Washington, D.C.], 2014).

dynamics, which reflect a consistent pattern of commodity price cycles.[642] There are on-going conflicting views on this issue with respect to both price levels and price volatility.

As regards price levels, it is open to question whether the long-term trend in commodity prices will remain lifted, or if it will reverse. Certainly, a few commodities appear to have been transformed from low-priced commodities in chronic oversupply to high-priced commodity in relative scarcity. Yet, for some commodities the trend is already reversing, in line with changing macroeconomic conditions in key consuming markets. [643]

Turning to price volatility, it is difficult to say whether price volatility has increased or not compared to the past. One's conclusions depend very much on the statistical method used, on the coverage of countries and commodities, and on the time period examined.[644] It has been observed, in this respect, that price volatility appears to have increased over the past 20 year period; but if we go backward in time, and bring in the 1970s, we might be less convinced that overall agricultural price volatility is increasing.[645]

Overall, the time series of agricultural commodity prices is historically characterised by long depressed flat periods punctuated by periodic bouts of volatility. It is very difficult to discern whether the situation now is just a continuation of that type of trend or if it does represent some new development, like a breakthrough in the way markets behave.

#### 4.2.1.2 Looking Forward: Climate Change and the Threat of Depletion

The economic debate is thus unsettled. Yet, as pointed out by many analysts, there are a number of reasons to believe that things have changed permanently: that the long-term trend, at least in food prices, will remain lifted; and that

642 See David S. Jacks, 'From Boom to Bust: A Typology of Real Commodity Prices in the Long Run', National Bureau of Economic Research, NBER Working Papers, no. 18874 (2013). For a discussion on the end of the super-cycle in commodities, UNCTAD, Global Commodities Forum 2015, above n 88.

643 Even in the past, commodities that used to be in chronic oversupply, e.g. sugar, turned for some periods into relatively scarce commodities, with an inversion of price trends. See Vincent A. Mahler, "The Political Economy of North-South Commodity Bargaining: The Case of the International Sugar Agreement," *International Organization* 38, no. 4 (1984): 717–18.

644 See Meier, above n 426, at 1185.

645 Hallam, above n 69. See also Marilyne Huchet-Bourdon, *Agricultural Commodity Price Volatility*, OECD Food, Agriculture and Fisheries Papers, no. 52 (Paris: OECD Publishing, 2011): price volatility during the 2006–10 period was higher than in the 1990s, but in general, not higher than that experienced in the 1970s, except for some commodities.

commodity prices will remain highly volatile around an upward trend in the near future.[646] This is on account of two main structural, systemic developments: climate change and the threat of resource depletion.

Most analysts agree that climate change will likely exacerbate the inherently volatile nature of commodity markets.[647] In the short-term, the increase in the frequency of weather-induced supply shocks is likely to translate into frequent and pronounced price spikes. In the medium and long term, temperatures on the rise may disrupt cropping patterns and ecosystems, which are highly dependent on specific climate conditions: some regions, principally arid and semi-arid zones, will come under increasing pressure; others, such as humid forest or sub-humid zones, will become more productive.[648]

Resource scarcity, or the risk of depletion, is a concurrent issue. Essential inputs to commercial agriculture (water, phosphorus and fossil fuels) are becoming scarce. Water for food production is currently physically scarce in densely populated arid areas of Central and West Asia, and North Africa, with projected availabilities of less than 1000m3/capita/year.[649] Demand for phosphorus, a key fertilizer ingredient, may outpace supply as early as 2035, with strong upward pressure on prices.[650] Depletion of oil 'proved', or recoverable reserves is projected for 2055. Under resource pressure, production costs are projected to rise, and productivity growth to slow down.[651] In parallel, demand is expected

646 International Food & Agricultural Trade Policy Council and OECD-FAO, above n 87; World Bank and FAO, above n 21, at 1.

647 Global warming is being accompanied by an apparent increase in extreme weather events: according to the UN, the number of recorded natural disasters has doubled from roughly 200 to over 400 a year in the past two decades; nine out of ten of these events are linked to climate change (UN High Commissioner for Refugees (UNHCR), *Climate Change, Natural Disasters and Human Displacement: A UNHCR Perspective*, 23 October 2008, available at: http://www.refworld.org/docid/492bb6b92.html [accessed 28 March 2014]). See T.F. Stocker et al., eds., *Climate Change 2013: The Physical Science Basis. Working Group I Contribution to the Fifth Assessment Report of the Intergovernmental Panel on Climate Change* (Cambridge: Cambridge University Press, 2013), 1–27; OECD/FAO, above n 87; World Bank and FAO, above n 21.

648 S. Niggol Seo et al., "A Ricardian Analysis of the Distribution of Climate Change Impacts on Agriculture across Agro-Ecological Zones in Africa," *Environmental and Resource Economics* 43, no. 3 (2009).

649 Frank R. Rijsberman, "Water Scarcity: Fact or Fiction?" *Agricultural Water Management* 80, no. 1–3 (2006).

650 Dana Cordell, 'The Story of Phosphorus: Sustainability Implications of Global Phosphorus Scarcity for Food Security', Linköping University, Studies in Arts and Science, no. 509 (Linköping, 2010).

651 OECD/FAO, above n 87.

to expand. Population estimates suggest that by 2050 the planet will be home to 9.1 billion persons, up from the current population of 6.8 billion.[652]

These concurrent developments, it is widely held, are likely to exert upward pressure on commodity prices, and translate in increased short-term volatility.

These views command wide, though not general, support. Some, in particular, argue that climate change is a naturally recurring process, rather than a man-induced one; and one that is cyclical in nature, and not permanent. Others stress that mankind will cope with the shrinking resource base thanks to technology breakthroughs and changes in consumption patterns. Waste can be reduced. 'Probable' fossil fuel reserves can become recoverable as new technology, such as shale oil and gas, becomes available, etc. Certainly, the spectre of impending raw materials shortage is not new. For example, a study undertaken for the Club of Rome in 1971–72 had concluded that if the existent exponential rates of economic and population growth would continue, there would be a critical land shortage and exorbitant food prices before the year 2000, and mineral resources would become insufficient within the next 100 years.[653] Since then, mankind has showed remarkable pragmatism and creativity in reacting and adjusting to major external constraints.

A few considerations arise from this cursory treatment of major commodity price developments since the mid-2000s.

First, it is important to acknowledge that the underlying economic facts are still unsettled. There is lack of certainty as to the medium to long-term price outlook, though many point to a pattern of high and increasingly volatile commodity prices. Furthermore, there is substantial disagreement as to the causes of price volatility, whether market fundamentals, or distortive speculation, or a combination of both. Evidence for and against price regulation is thus contradictory and view-dependent. This means that policy options, whether in the direction of 'deepening' the market-based orientation of commodity trade, or bring the State back, are bound to be inherently biased.[654] Indeed, when law needs economics to regulate and economics is inconclusive, lawmakers are essentially 'regulating in the dark', under inevitable pressure from a variety of sectional interests. This raises questions as to the genuine nature of the

652 *Inter-agency Report on Price Volatility*, above n 68, at 15; [FAO], *How to Feed the World in 2050*, High level Expert Forum on How to Feed the World, Rome, 12–13 October 2009.

653 Donella H. Meadows et al., *The Limits to Growth: Report for the Club of Rome's Project on the Predicament of Mankind* (New York: Universe Books, 1972). See also C. Fred Bergsten, "The Threat from the Third World," *Foreign Policy* 11 (1973).

654 In this direction, Bruce Tozer, "Outcomes of the Public-Private Initiative on Commodity Market Volatility" (presentation given at UNCTAD's Global Commodities Forum 2013, Geneva, 18–19 March 2013).

interaction between law, economics and politics in commodity policy, one of the fascinating intricacies of this area of inquiry.

Second, recent price developments have called into question the very rationale for price intervention. Emphasis in the past was on raising commodity prices from unsustainably low levels, in addition to smoothing price volatility around the downward trend.[655] Emphasis is now on levelling price spikes, while continuing to address the need to raise prices from unsustainably low levels for those agricultural commodities where the issue remains important. This change in fundamentals challenges the relevance, in the present context, of past intervention mechanisms; and questions the adequacy of existent multilateral trade disciplines. It is widely felt that past international price stabilisation tools, from output restraints to international buffer stocks, may not be effective to moderate price spikes.[656] Likewise, the adequacy of WTO provisions to protect the interests of net food importers has come under scrutiny. Some argue that existing WTO disciplines were established at a time of relative commodity abundance and low prices, and that they reflect "a bias towards protecting the interests of exporting countries".[657] In a context of commodity shortage and price spikes, it is argued, multilateral disciplines, particularly those on export restrictions, must adjust to also address importers' concerns.[658]

With these considerations in mind, the analysis shall now turn to consider two major trade-related approaches that have profiled, as to the way forward.

### 4.2.2 *Trade Rules and Commodity Prices: Trade Policy Trajectories*

The trade policy debate as to the way ahead is extremely polarised and divisive. Suffice here to recall the exchange, which was distinctly polemical, between

---

655 Until the early 2000s, over the past 60 years, real prices for agricultural commodities, i.e. prices adjusted for inflation, had experienced a marked decline; for products where longer time series are available this downward trend can often be extended back for more than 100 years. Such briefly was the economic background against which regulatory experiments in commodity markets took place.

656 The point is frequently made that quotas and other output restraints are better suited to sustain prices than to calm price spikes. Likewise, buffer stocks work better to smooth moderate price fluctuations than price spikes.

657 Panos Konandreas, "Global Governance: International Policy Considerations," in *Safeguarding Food Security in Volatile Global Markets*, ed. Adam Prakash (Rome: FAO, 2011); Ramesh Sharma and Panos Konandreas, 'WTO Provisions in the Context of Responding to Soaring Food Prices', FAO Commodity and Trade Policy Research Working Papers, no. 25 (Rome: FAO, 2008); Anania, above n 223.

658 Konandreas, "Global Governance," above n 657; Sharma and Konandreas, "WTO Provisions in the Context of Responding to Soaring Food Prices," above n 657.

Olivier de Schutter, UN Human Rights Council's Special Rapporteur on the Right to Food, and Pascal Lamy, then WTO Director General.[659] Underlying the debate are two conflicting attitudes, or postures, towards commodity 'control'. To stabilise commodity markets, some argue for a 'deepening' of the liberal trade regime, and point to regulatory holes and loopholes that need to be closed. For others, commodity markets are structurally incapable of attaining socially desirable price outcomes, and market intervention is needed to redress imbalances. These diverging trade policy trajectories are discussed below.

#### 4.2.2.1 'Deepening' the Free Trade Regime

##### a) *The Approach Outlined*

To correct price distortions and stem price spikes, the first strand of thought advocates a 'deepening' of the free trade regime through further liberalisation of trade, and increased market-orientation of production. This is the prevailing trend of opinion in the WTO, also upheld in key programmatic documents by the UN. It resonates in the 2010 Updated Comprehensive Framework for Action of the UN High Level Task Force on the Global Food Security Crisis,[660] and in the Inter-agency Report on Price Volatility prepared for the G-20 by various UN and UN-affiliated agencies.[661]

This 'liberal' approach is based on a set of premises. It moves from a 'constat': the acknowledgement of the pervasiveness of restrictions and distortions in world commodity trade. Export restraints, in particular, are singled out as one of the key drivers of recent price spikes in commodities. It also moves from the assumption that markets of internationally traded agricultural commodities are 'thin'. Trading volumes, measured in terms of exports as

---

659 Cf. Special Rapporteur on the Right to Food (Olivier de Schutter), *The World Trade Organization and the Post-Global Food Crisis Agenda: Putting Food Security First in the International Trade System*, Activity Report (November 2011) and Pascal Lamy, letter to Dr de Schutter and attached comments, available at http://www.wto.org/english/news_e/news11_e/agcom_14dec11_e.htm#letter; http://www.wto.org/english/news_e/news11_e/agcom_14dec11_e.htm#comments.

660 The Updated Comprehensive Framework for Action, in its relevant part, reads: "[...] more liberalised international markets would contribute to global food and nutrition security through increased trade volumes and access to diverse sources of food imports." See United Nations High Level Task Force on Global Food Security Crisis, *Updated Comprehensive Framework for Action*, September 2010, para. 76.

661 See *Inter-agency Report on Price Volatility*, above n 68. The Report states "[...] trade is an essential component of any food security strategy [...] Policies that distort production and trade in agricultural commodities potentially impede the achievement of long run food security" (at 23).

a share of production, are judged as being low; which is deemed to cause more pronounced price swings than would be the case in more 'liquid' or 'deeper' markets.[662] 'Deeper', and undistorted international markets, it is argued, will stimulate more efficient production, and expand supply. Furthermore, they will efficiently move supplies from surplus to deficit areas, and transfer stocks from years of high production to years of low production. Overall, trade integration and liberalisation will help smooth price volatility.[663]

The policy prescription that follows is thus to correct and prevent restrictions and distortions in world commodity markets, in accordance with the long-term objective of establishing a genuinely market-oriented commodity trading system.[664] This involves closing regulatory holes and loopholes that allow for trade-distorting practices.

#### b) *Unpacking the Approach*

A few areas are singled out as issues to be addressed, and a few proposals are on offer. Suffice here to recap the main terms of the advocated reforms.

Multilateral disciplines on export restraints are identified as major instances of 'under-regulation' or 'regulatory deficiency' that exacerbate price volatility.[665] It is widely felt that existing WTO rules on export restrictions are weak, and 'imbalanced' relative to the regulation of import restraints.[666] Export taxes are substantially undisciplined, even if set at prohibitive levels.[667]

662 For a critical assessment, Pete Liapis, *Structural Change in Commodity Markets: Have Agricultural Markets Become Thinner?* OECD Food, Agriculture and Fisheries Papers, no. 54 (Paris: Organisation for Economic Co-operation and Development, 2012).

663 On agriculture, see, for example, the speech delivered by Harsha Singh, then WTO Deputy Director-General: Harsha Singh, "We Need an Open and Predictable Trading System to Address Price Volatility" (speech delivered on 26 May 2010, transcript available at http://www.wto.org/english/news_e/news10_e/agri_26may10_e.htm).

664 With reference to agriculture: US Proposal G/AG/NG/W/15.

665 Häberli, "Food Security and WTO Rules," above n 585; Konandreas, "Global Governance," above n 657; Sharma and Konandreas, above n 657.

666 Häberli, above n 585; Konandreas, "Global Governance," above n 657. Current WTO disciplines on export restraints are relatively liberal, though WTO jurisprudence points towards a narrow interpretation of these rules. See Robert Howse and Tim Josling, *Agricultural Export Restrictions and International Trade Law: A Way Forward*, IPC Position Paper, International Food & Agricultural Trade Policy Council, September 2012.

667 Article XI does not cover export taxes/charges: WTO members enjoy full policy space in their use. However, countries cannot discriminate in levying export taxes, pursuant to the MFN obligation in Article I of the GATT 1994. It is also possible to bind export tariffs in GATT Schedules (WTO Secretariat, *Export Restrictions and Charges*, Doc. MTN.GNG/NG2/W/40, at 4 and 6).

Disciplines on other export restrictions, such as bans, quotas, minimum export prices, or restrictive export licenses, are deemed too vague to be effective.[668] Hence, there was a call for a clarification and tightening of existing procedural requirements; or for more stringent substantive disciplines, well beyond what actually exists. These issues are discussed in some detail in Section 5.2.

Beyond export restrictions, the scope of reform is broad, covering all measures that distort commodity prices and trade.[669] In agriculture, further reform is being pushed under the three 'pillars' of the AoA, with the commitment to attain: "substantial improvements in market access; reductions of, with a view to phasing out, all forms of export subsidies; and substantial reductions in trade-distorting domestic support".[670] By encouraging more efficient production and trade, the removal of restrictions and distortions is deemed to act as an 'insurance policy' against price volatility.[671]

In terms of 'market access', the objective is to lower tariffs, to reduce policy-induced distortions. The Doha Round, if concluded, would result in major advances in this direction. The December 2008 revised draft modalities envisage a tiered formula of substantial reduction of all final bound tariffs, with steeper cuts for higher tariffs. Tariff cuts for developed countries would range from 50 percent for lower tier tariffs, to 70 percent for tariff peaks, subject to a 54 percent minimum average.[672] Developing countries and other 'special' countries are offered more lenient terms. For developing country members, the reduction shall be 2/3 of these cuts.[673] SVEs and 'recently-acceded members' (RAMs) are entitled to further moderate the cuts,[674] while LDCs are exempted entirely.

With regard to domestic support, the focus is on the destabilising impact of subsidies and other policies in rich countries which distort agricultural trade markets. The call is to cut support that stimulates over-production, artificially lowers international prices, and distorts trade. In this direction, the December 2008 proposals envisage a 'three-pronged approach':

---

668 A listing of GATT provisions relating to export restrictions and charges can be found in WTO Doc. MTN.GNG/NG2/W/40 and in the Annex to the Tokyo Round Understanding regarding Export Restrictions and Charges (Statement of Existing GATT Provisions Relating to Export Restrictions and Charges).

669 For a more detailed assessment, Häberli, "Food Security and WTO Rules," above n 585, at 308–22.

670 World Trade Organization, Ministerial Declaration of 14 November 2001, WT/MIN(01)/DEC/1, para. 13.

671 See Häberli, "Food Security and WTO Rules," above n 585. See also Singh, above n 663.

672 December 2008 revised draft modalities, above n 65, paras. 61 and 62.

673 Ibid, para. 63.

674 Ibid, paras. 65 and 66–69.

(i) Each category of support (Amber, Blue Box and *de minimis*) is to be cut or limited. Amber Box subsidies are cut by a tiered formula, with steeper cuts for higher level of support.[675] Blue Box and *de minimis* are cut through limits and caps;[676]

(ii) Within each category, product-specific caps and limits are set;[677]

(iii) The overall amount of trade-distorting support (OTDS) from Amber Box, Blue Box, and *de minimis* is cut by a tiered formula.[678]

Disciplines on export subsidies are meant to tackle the aggressive disposal of surplus production on foreign markets. This is a practice which much contributed in the past to artificially depress agricultural prices, divert trade from potentially efficient sources, and displace domestic production in non-subsidising countries. It was envisaged that developed countries would eliminate their remaining scheduled export subsidy entitlements by the end of 2013; developing countries would do so by 2016.[679] This only occurred at the 10th WTO Ministerial in Nairobi.[680] Under the Doha Round, WTO disciplines should be tightened for 'hidden' export subsidies. Some areas have been singled out as issues to be addressed: 'non-genuine' food aid, used as a means of surplus disposal; trade-distorting export financing support through export credits, export credit guarantees and insurance programmes; and the trade-distorting practices of agricultural state trading enterprises.

Finally, attention is called on other practices such as strategic releases of public stocks, and two-tier pricing structures, not meaningfully addressed by the Doha proposals.

### c) *Assessment*

In terms of underlying values and assumptions, the policy stance outlined above does not depart significantly from the 'market-based' approach discussed in Section 4.1. The law is again called upon to play a fundamental 'enabling' or 'underpinning' role *vis-à-vis* market dynamics. Furthermore,

675 Ibid, para. 13.

676 December 2008 revised draft modalities, above n 65, paras. 32, 33, 38 and 48.

677 See in detail December 2008 revised draft modalities, above n 65, paras. 21–29 (product-specific AMS limits) and paras. 40–47 (product specific limits on Blue Box entitlements).

678 December 2008 revised draft modalities, above n 65, para. 7.

679 Ibid, paras. 162–63.

680 World Trade Organization, Ministerial Decision on Export Competition of 19 December 2015, WT/MIN(15)/45, WT/L/980.

regulatory reform is widely felt as technically-oriented and politically neutral. Its objective is to unleash genuine market dynamics; the market will then frame the price outcomes.

Yet, at closer scrutiny, this policy stance is possibly less neutral and impartial than it may at first appear. In particular, its assumptions are inherently subjective and discretionary, in at least two important respects.

First, its fundamental tenet, the price-stabilising effects of international trade, is controversial.[681] International trade can effectively smooth out domestic price shocks. Yet, it can also channel international price volatility. As discussed in the following analysis, trade liberalisation, by enhancing border-to-domestic price transmission, may well make countries more vulnerable to external price shocks. Against a background of increasingly volatile *international* prices, countries may wish to retain the flexibility to 'decouple' domestic from international prices, and cushion the effects upon domestic producers and consumers of external price fluctuations. Furthermore, in certain contexts, it may be useful to safeguard a minimum level of domestic production as part of a risk mitigating strategy that combines trade, domestic production and stocks.

Second, the 'market-only approach' assumes that markets work efficiently. Yet questions remain as to the efficiency of agricultural markets. As mentioned, for most tropical commodities, markets are highly imperfect, with evidence of abuse of market power. Market failures are further exposed when sustainability concerns are brought into the analysis. In agriculture, externalities and public goods are largely not 'factored' into market prices. Market prices for agricultural commodities do not fully internalise the various costs of industrial agriculture, or the ecological efficiencies of small-scale conservative agriculture. In this setting, with limited room for full-cost accounting, industrial agriculture outcompetes alternative farming systems. A deepening of this market-based order, flawed by imperfections and failures, will likely enhance the competitive edge of industrial agriculture, and further marginalise alternative farming systems. Under its apparent technical neutrality, the market-based system thus conceals its advocacy for a set of values associated with industrial agriculture.

---

681 In particular, there is mixed evidence on the impact of trade liberalisation on food security in developing countries. See Steve McCorriston et al., *What is the Evidence of the Impact of Agricultural Trade Liberalisation on Food Security in Developing Countries? A Systematic Review* (London: EPPI-Centre, Social Science Research Unit, Institute of Education, University of London, 2013).

#### 4.2.2.2 'Insulating' from International Markets

##### a) *The Approach Outlined*

The second strand of thought claims that market mechanisms alone cannot adequately tackle commodity price volatility and calls for government intervention to manage commodity price dynamics. With a focus on staple food commodities, it posits to replace import dependence through domestic production, or at least to 'decouple' domestic prices from international price movements and to revive coordinated efforts to manage prices.

This stance moves from a set of assumptions that shall be set forth explicitly.

First, it is premised on the idea that international trade channels price volatility rather than mitigating it. This is true to the extent that commodity price shocks are exogenous;[682] and that exogenous price shocks are transmitted, through trade, to domestic prices.[683] This appears to have been the case for several import-dependent countries during the 2007–08 and 2010–11 commodity crises. Major price shocks, whether policy-induced or 'natural', then originated on world markets; and where transmitted, through the trading system, across countries.[684] It has been observed, in this respect, that there are only a few major grain suppliers to the world market, while demand is dispersed.[685] This supply concentration suggests that unfavourable weather episodes or other shocks in major exporting countries are likely to transmit, through trade, to virtually all countries. Hence the call to 'relocalise' production, in order to reduce exposure to both supply and price risks; or at least to 'decouple' domestic prices from price movements in international markets, in a bid to mitigate price risks.

In a related vein, it is posited that "[...] markets are not just making new supply available – they are also introducing new forms of competition for scarce resources in the form of new demand."[686] For example, biofuel feedstock

682 Exogenous shocks originate from outside, on world markets.

683 When domestic price volatility arises from outside, the transmission of international price developments to domestic prices is not linear: the extent of the pass-through depends, among other, on a country's trade openness, as well as on its domestic policies to decouple domestic from international prices. HLPE, above n 185, at 44–47. See also Nicholas Minot, *Transmission of World Food Price Changes to Markets in Sub-Saharan Africa*, International Food Policy Research Institute, IFPRI Discussion Paper 01059 (Washington, D.C., 2011).

684 Lines, above n 3.

685 This holds for the two major internationally traded staples, wheat and maize; to a lesser extent for rice. FAO, *FAO Statistical Yearbook 2013: World Food and Agriculture* (Rome: FAO, 2013), at 132.

686 HLPE, above n 185, at 40.

demand by large biofuel companies in high- and medium-income countries is acknowledged to have exerted significant upward pressure on international grain prices, with price increases passed on to the urban poor in import-reliant low-income countries.[687] Overall, as stated in a report by the High Level Panel of Experts on Food Security and Nutrition (HLPE), "[o]pen markets imply competition between rich and poor consumers for access to food. It is a world where the behaviour of rich consumers [relatively insensitive to food price increases] creates problems for poor consumers [more price sensitive]".[688]

Again, the policy prescription is to 'isolate', or 'decouple' domestic prices in poor countries (price-takers) from price dynamics in large, rich countries (price-makers). This is deemed to be "[…] a more effective solution than the insistence on a single world market flanked by international safety nets, as promoted during the last 20 years".[689]

This approach, it should be observed at the outset, is not the prevailing trend of opinion, including in UN environments. It has been endorsed by the UN Special Rapporteur on the Right to Food, Olivier de Schutter; [690] and upheld, in some of its tenets, by the HLPE.[691] Yet, it is far from mainstream. The prevailing sentiment, as discussed, is still that 'deepened' international markets would contribute towards commodity price stabilisation.

### b) *The Approach Unpacked*

The 'insulationist' approach, as expounded by the Special Rapporteur on the Right to Food, Olivier de Schutter, is quite generic. It interlaces domestic and international price perspective; mingles price support and stabilisation concerns; and cuts across peasant foodstuff and cash crop production in developing countries. For analytical convenience, it is useful to extricate domestic action from international action on commodity prices, and distinguish between staple foods and cash crops, when needed.

---

687 Murphy, above n 301.

688 HLPE, above n 185, at 37.

689 Ibid, at 39.

690 Special Rapporteur on the Right to Food (Olivier de Schutter), *Putting Food Security First,* above n 659. See also the video debate between Pascal Lamy, Director-General of the WTO, and Olivier De Schutter: "Trade liberalization and the right to food" (May 2009) (http://www.wto.org/english/forums_e/debates_e/debate14_e.htm (accessed on 13 may 2014); WTO News Item – http://www.wto.org/english/news_e/news09_e/ag_02jul09_e.htm (accessed on 13 may 2014)); and Special Rapporteur on the Right to Food (Olivier de Schutter), *Mission to the World Trade Organization*, A/HRC/10/5/Add.2 (4 February 2009).

691 HLPE, above n 185.

i) Domestic Level: 'Relocalise' and 'Insulate'

At the domestic level, the basic tenet is that developing countries shall be allowed, or encouraged, to "insulate domestic markets from the volatility of prices on international markets".[692] In essence, the policy prescription is to reduce 'excessive' reliance on imports, by stepping-up domestic production; and to 'decouple' domestic prices from price movements in international markets by means of domestic price stabilisation schemes. Reference is here specifically to staple food commodities, and particularly to rice, maize and wheat, the major internationally traded cereals.

Hence, the need is to retain and expand policy flexibility across various areas of multilateral and plurilateral trade disciplines, rather than 'lock-in' policy space. Indeed, domestic price stabilisation and support is effected through a mixture of trade policy instruments, which are complexly interlocked. Administered price schemes, statutory marketing, stockpiles and variable levies and taxes are routinely used and combined, in many developing countries, to mitigate price volatility, or the effects thereof. These stabilisation techniques vary widely, and intertwine with one another.[693]

This complex policy matrix points to the need to retain flexibility across a variety of multilateral and plurilateral disciplines. As discussed (Section 2.3.3), while domestic price stabilisation schemes are not regulated as such in WTO law, they are regulated in their trade-distorting aspects under multiple headings. For example, physical food stockpiles for emergency or stabilisation purposes are not disallowed, per se. Yet, their discrete components are scrutinised under the dissecting scope of various WTO disciplines. These include:

i. Domestic support disciplines. The problematic aspect is when procurement prices are set at above market levels, and the amount of price support granted exceeds a threshold (the members' bound AMS or the *de minimis* level);
ii. Plurilateral disciplines on public procurement, if applicable, when the produce is procured from small-scale farmers out of formal tender procedures, if a member signs the Agreement on Government Procurement;
iii. Proposed tightened disciplines on agricultural exporting STEs. Here, two aspects may come under scrutiny: export monopoly powers granted to STEs to improve marketing and prices of small-scale farmers' products; and government underwriting of STEs losses; and

692 Olivier de Schutter, above n 690.

693 See above, Section 2.2.

iv. Tariff disciplines under the GATT and the AoA, when variable import tariffs are used to offset the domestic-border price gap or when the national stockpile is funded through import levies not foreseen in a country's tariff concession list.

The trade policy issues involved thus straddle across distinct sets of plurilateral and multilateral disciplines: domestic support, tariffs, and state trading. In all these areas, the prescription is to retain or enhance policy space.

ii) International Level: 'Manage' International Price Volatility

At the international level, the call is for countries to take joint action, through suitable measures, to stabilise international prices. In de Schutter's proposal, there is some ambiguity as to the measures envisaged. In particular, while reference is mainly to food reserves, there are *ad passim* allusions to international supply management schemes (output ad export restraints).[694] Furthermore, reference to food reserves seems to encompass both emergency reserves, to be used as a safety net in shortage situations, and international buffer stocks, used to stabilise prices. To bring more conceptual clarity, it is useful to distinguish between staple food commodities, on the one hand; and cash crops, and non-crop commodities on the other.

a) *Staple Food Commodities*

With regard to staple food commodities, emphasis at the international level is on measures to prevent or mitigate the effects of price spikes on global markets. Reference is mainly to international food reserves.

Food reserves are a complex taxonomy. They may be buffer stocks, established to stabilise prices; or they may be emergency reserves, a safety net to be used in emergency situations. The former, price-stabilising reserves or buffer stocks, buy and release stocks according to the way prices are moving. Their price objective may be stabilisation and/or support, depending on the level at which the intervention price is set relative to the market price. Emergency reserves act as a supplier of last resort, to face critical shortages or ease price spikes. They include both general security stocks and strategic reserves; and humanitarian stocks, targeted specifically at vulnerable groups.[695] In practice, the line between buffer stocks and emergency reserves, as between price support and price stabilisation arrangements, is not easy to draw. Note also that

694 Olivier de Schuter, above n 690, at 8–10.

695 Gilbert, "International Commodity Agreements and Their Current Relevance for Grains Price Stabilization," above n 86.

food reserves, whether buffer stocks or emergency reserves, can be set at different levels. There are global, regional, national, local and community level reserves. They may be structured as 'virtual reserves' (call options); or as physical reserves.

There has been a revival in political interest in staple food rcserves.[696] From a trade policy perspective, a key issue is the compatibility of existing trade rules, and of those under negotiation, with international and national reserves. Reserves are not disallowed per se. Yet, they are regulated in their distorting aspects, if any, under multiple sets of disciplines. The extent of the encroachment depends on how reserves are designed and operated, in terms of objectives and administrative modalities.[697] From an economic perspective, a critical aspect is the efficiency and effectiveness of food reserves, particularly in comparison with market-based alternatives such as private storage.

b) *Cash Crops*

With respect to tropical cash crops and other non-crop agricultural exports from developing countries, emphasis is still on ensuring 'remunerative' producer prices, in addition to smoothing price volatility around the trend. This implies a 'revival' of the 'managed economy' provisions enshrined in the GATT: Article XX(h), as well as the provisions of Article XXXVIII, which, inter alia, stipulate that the WTO members could take "joint action" through "international arrangements" for ensuring "stable equitable and remunerative prices" for exports of primary agricultural commodities. The viability and desirability of coordinated efforts to manage commodity prices have raised much reservation among commentators. Many view ICAs as extremely distortive and costly; ineffective, on account of intractable technical difficulties; and politically difficult, when not impossible, to negotiate.[698] On the other hand, it has been argued, technical, political and administrative difficulties would not

696 G8 Summit held in L'Aquila, Italy, July 2009 (L'Aquila Joint Statement on Global Food Security); World Summit on Food Security, FAO, Rome, November 2009; G20 Summit, Cannes, France, November 2011. See also the UN-framed Updated Comprehensive Framework for Action, above n 660.

697 Murphy, above n 301.

698 The mainstays of this approach are that past efforts to stabilise prices have been extremely costly, in terms of direct costs (budgetary outlays) and indirect costs (economic inefficiencies generated). Furthermore, they have resulted in some perverse distributive outcomes, often to the detriment of the most vulnerable. It is widely felt that the costs associated with price intervention outweigh the benefits of price stability; and that less distortive options (income support, or measures to mitigate / cope with price instability) are more cost-effective and efficient. See above, n 35.

be insurmountable, if sufficient political will, backed by adequate financial resources, were there.[699]

c) *Assessment*

In essence, the trade policy stance outlined above does not depart substantially from the 'interventionist' commodity trade stance of the 1960s and 1970s. Essentially, it involves a shift to some form of 'managed economy'. The underlying idea is that markets do not always deliver politically acceptable outcomes. In some instances, this is due to market imperfections or failures. In other instances, it is on account of the fact that well-functioning markets do not 'factor in' equity concerns. Market-based outcomes and dynamics are 'benchmarked' against normative goals; normative parameters are set within which commodity market dynamics are to be contained and managed. This approach marks a significant departure from orthodox laissez-faire liberalism (the 'market-only' approach); and a shift in what has been called "the balance between 'authority' and 'market'".[700] In terms of the type of 'rationality' involved, it reintroduces 'substantive' modes of legal thought and practice.

This approach has been challenged on grounds of efficiency, effectiveness, and workability.

In terms of efficiency, a revival of price stabilisation is held to be a very costly policy. In particular, domestic price stabilisation arrangements are deemed to be "a very costly policy, with little success and high production and trade distortion effects".[701] The Thai rice mortgage scheme is often brought as an example. Total losses under the program stood at around 120 billion baht (about $4 billion) per year.[702] Exports of Thai rice dropped significantly under the scheme. Eventually, the country was "knocked off its perch" as the top-ranking rice exporter by India and Vietnam.[703] Emergency food reserves are likewise costly and distortive, though less controversial. In terms of costs, they

699 In this direction, Rangarajan, above n 571.

700 John Gerard Ruggie, "International Regimes, Transactions, and Changes: Embedded Liberalism in the Postwar Economic Order," *International Organization* 36, no. 2 (1982), at 386, with reference to the shift to nineteenth century 'orthodox liberalism'.

701 Lamy, above n 659; *Inter-agency Report on Price Volatility*, above n 68.

702 As relayed by the market intelligence service Oryza: "Thailand Rice Mortgage Program Could Continue Indefinitely, Says Commerce Minister," at: http://oryza.com/news/rice-news/thailand-rice-mortgage-program-could-continue-indefinitely-says-commerce-minister#sthash.4pZZzjYo.2HUcNnO7.dpuf.

703 "Less Paddy Power: Populist Politics Mess up Thailand's Biggest Crop," *The Economist*, 14 July 2012.

entail fixed capital costs, costs incurred when building up and replenishing stocks, and extra-costs of stock-holding.[704] As for distortions, if large, reserves may crowd out private storage by hindering arbitrage and storage incentives; and may depress prices when released.[705]

Yet, if equity considerations are 'factored in', the cost-benefit assessment becomes more complex. The same is true if precautionary considerations are fully accounted for. Turning again to the Thai rice mortgage system, for example, the scheme was relatively successful in sustaining farm income and fostering rural development. It reportedly helped improve living standards of about 4.5 million farmer households in Thailand.[706] As regards food reserves, they are certainly more costly than reliance on free trade to transfer supplies to deficit areas. Yet, in the language of a commentator, they are "a relatively cheap public insurance policy in the face of tremendous uncertainty, when the risk of failure includes starvation".[707]

In terms of effectiveness in stabilising prices, it is open to question whether 'insulation' will reduce exposure to supply and price risks. Some contend, in particular, that staple food production in 'unfavourable' agro-ecological zones (such as semi-arid or arid and dry or moist savannah zones, which are particularly vulnerable to climate change)[708] is unviable. Accordingly, many countries, particularly in sub-Saharan Africa and the Middle East, have no alternative but to rely upon international markets to meet their staple food requirements. It is also argued that domestic price fluctuations often arise from domestic sources of instability. In these instances, trade helps smooth out domestic price shocks, while 'insulation' from international markets may exacerbate price shocks.[709] Eventually, it is maintained, the problem is not too much trade, but too little trade.[710] More trade with 'deeper' and less distorted international markets is needed to effectively mitigate price volatility.

---

704 World Bank and FAO, above n 21.

705 For a detailed discussion, Shahidur Rashid and Solomon Lemma, *Strategic Grain Reserves in Ethiopia: Institutional Design and Operational Performance*, International Food Policy Research Institute, IFPRI Discussion Paper 01054 (Washington, D.C., 2011).

706 Oryza.com, above n 702.

707 Sophia Murhpy, *Grain Reserves: A Smart Climate Adaptation Policy* (Institute for Agriculture and Trade Policy, 2010), at 2.

708 Niggol, above n 648.

709 For a review, HLPE, above n 185, at 44–47.

710 See the video debate between Pascal Lamy, Director-General of the WTO, and Olivier De Schutter: "Trade liberalization and the right to food" (May 2009) http://www.wto.org/english/forums_e/debates_e/debate14_e.htm (accessed on 13 may 2014).

Finally, in terms of workability, the contention is that there is no novelty in government market intervention to stabilise commodity prices. It was attempted and it failed. But has commodity price stabilisation failed? Is it inherently bound to fail? None of these questions is to be taken for granted. Price stabilisation efforts, at the domestic or international level, have yielded mixed results. At the international level, ICAs were certainly highly distortive, and suffered from various pathologies, notably rent-seeking behaviours. Yet, several attempts were relatively successful in sustaining prices. The same holds for domestic price stabilisation schemes. Stabilisation policies in the OECD and Asia have been successful in cushioning domestic consumers and/or producers from the vagaries of international markets. In a world of second best options, there may be a place for joint action on commodity prices through international control arrangements.[711] The question is how these arrangements can be made more effective; and where to set safeguards, so as to avoid abuse.

### 4.2.3 *Assessment*

To sum up, the debate as to the way ahead is extremely polarised and divisive. Two antagonistic views, or postures, emerge. Some argue that commodity price stabilisation is best served by open markets. For others, the market mechanism alone can hardly suffice to stabilise prices. Government intervention is needed. The first approach advocates further substantial liberalisation; the latter advocates a new form of market intervention.

This variety of opinion stems from a fundamental difference of creeds, a divergence as regards basic assumptions that cannot be easily recomposed. On the one hand are those who argue that the public good is best served by open markets, and point to holes and loopholes in the current liberal trade regime that need to be closed. For others, commodity markets are structurally incapable of attaining equitable outcomes, and market intervention is needed to redress imbalances. What is at stake is a fundamental divergence of views as to the balance between 'market' and 'authority' in commodity trade regulation. This divergence has always been in the background, at Havana, Geneva and Nairobi, and continues right to the present.

Both the 'market' and 'authority' strands of thought resonate in WTO law. It is often assumed that multilateral trade disciplines, existing and under negotiations, endorse the 'market-only' approach, while disallowing the interventionist stance. As a matter of fact, both the interests of trade liberalisation and of non-trade goals and thus policy space are addressed. Thus, multilateral efforts to stabilise prices are covered under GATT Article XX (h). Domestic

711 Hager, above n 269, at 313.

stabilisation policies are not proscribed as such, but they are regulated in their trade-distortive components. Overall, the trade regulation of agriculture proceeds through a complex set of commitments and escapes, and rules and exemptions.

This complex coexistence of conflicting policy postures within the same body of law is key to understanding the outlook and possible reach of the 'market-only' and the 'interventionist' stances. Both are bound to fail, when pushed too far. Indeed, there is a limit to how far the elimination of trade restrictions and distortions can be pushed in agriculture. Agricultural commodities carry too much political sensitivity. If the liberal reform is stretched too far, it will bounce back, with a retrenchment behind unilateral and protectionist policies. Likewise, there is a limit to how far the 'interventionist' stance can be furthered. It can be tolerated as an exception, not as a rule, since it counters the basic tenets and objectives of multilateral trade rules. If pushed too far, it will unravel the fabric of multilateral trade rules, as they exist. To move beyond the impasse, it is necessary to move beyond the dichotomy between 'market' and 'authority' which has tended to dominate earlier discussions. The way ahead is discussed in the following Chapter.

CHAPTER 5

# Beyond the Impasse: Towards a New Normative Approach

Drawing and combining insights from the previous analyses focusing on different policy approaches and tools, this Chapter proposes a way out of the impasse. It takes a step back in accordance with the adage: *Reculer pour mieux sauter*. Specifically, it draws the contours of a new normative framework that may offer guidance in assessing the interface between trade rules and agricultural stabilisation policies. The approach outlined is hybrid and eclectic. It draws upon the two antagonist policy postures that have been discussed in Chapter 4, and steers a middle course between them. The analysis is threefold. It first outlines the framework: a set of 'normative benchmark' objectives and principles against which to assess agricultural stabilisation policies from a trade law angle. It then tests the framework with reference to the issue areas of stockpile food purchases, price bands, state-trading, and export restraints, considered in their domestic price stabilisation dimension. It also considers the framework's potential and challenges with reference to concerted price action. It concludes by considering possible avenues of litigation and decision-making to implement this framework through trade law.

## 5.1 The Framework Outlined

What should be the overarching objectives of international trade policy and law with regard to stabilisation arrangements in agriculture? In this field, it is argued, the thrust of multilateral trade rules should not be trade liberalisation, but trade regulation. Such regulation is to be polycentric, that is to say, with several legitimate normative 'poles': rural livelihood, food security, environmental sustainability, in interplay and against the background of considerations of trade 'fairness'. Questions arise as to the balance of competing interests, in the regulation of stabilisation arrangements. When conflicts arise, how can a 'line of equilibrium' be drawn between liberal trade interests and stabilisation concerns, or between peasant interests at home and abroad? The expedient suggested is to make equity a standard incorporated into trade law. This, in turn, is to be attained by various means which imply various degrees of modulation of the rules and in the application of the rules, to take into account factual

 DOI 10.1163/9789004350540_006

differences. This approach will be discussed in due course (Sections 5.1.2 and 5.1.3). Attention is first drawn to the conceptual underpinnings and legal bases of this approach.

### 5.1.1 *Conceptual Underpinnings and Legal Bases*

The approach here outlined moves from constitutionalist strands of thought in legal doctrine.[712] In a quest for policy coherence, it embeds WTO law in an overall international system consistently informed by 'sustainability' concerns. The call is for a coherent normative order where international trade regulation contributes to protect and further fundamental 'constitutional' values.[713] These values should purposively frame international law as a whole, beyond its fragmented landscape.

This normative stance is in line with the concept of 'multifunctionality' of agriculture. It reflects the idea that agriculture is a "multi-output activity producing not only commodities (food, fodder, fibers, biofuel and recently pharmaceuticals) but also non commodity outputs such as environmental benefits, landscape amenities and cultural heritages that are not traded in organized markets".[714] These non-commodity outputs may exhibit the characteristics of externalities, largely not 'factored' in market prices, or public goods, for which markets function poorly.[715]

In regulatory terms, this approach entails a shift in the nature of commodity trade regulation from narrowly defined and functional to broadly encompassing and aspirational.[716] As discussed in the following Chapter, such a move involves a purposive reinterpretation of WTO law informed by non-trade concerns.

The legal bases upon which this regulatory shift is advocated involve elements of soft and hard law.

In terms of soft law and in a perspective *de lege ferenda*, attention is drawn to the transformative dynamics that are reshaping the trade policy discourse. WTO law is embedded in an international normative environment that is

712 For a comprehensive review, Introduction to Cottier and Panagiotis, above n 54.

713 Ibid.

714 Beverly D. MCIntyre, Hans R. Herren, Judi Wakhungu, and Robert T. Watson, eds., *Agriculture at a Crossroads: International Assessment of Agricultural Knowledge, Science, and Technology for Development – Global Report*, 2d ed. (Washington, D.C.: Island Press, 2009), 61.

715 OECD, *Multifunctionality: Towards an Analytical Framework* (Paris: OECD, 2001).

716 Cottier, above n 546, at 121; Tomer Broude, "The Rule(s) of Trade and the Rhetos of Development: Reflections on the Functional and Aspirational Legitimacy of the WTO," *Columbia Journal of Transnational Law* 45 (2006–2007).

evolving. Reference is here to the 2030 Agenda for Sustainable Development and the Sustainable Development Goals (SDGs),[717] the third International Conference on Financing for Development (FFD),[718] and the twenty-first session of the Conference of the Parties to the United Nations Framework Convention on Climate Change.[719] This process has outlined "a new pathway to human well-being".[720] Its central tenets are social inclusiveness, the eradication of poverty and sustainability. The quest is for a world that is "just, equitable and inclusive".[721] This, still evolving, framework sets an inescapable normative reference. All technical cooperation activities and intergovernmental programmatic documents refer to its tenets.

If WTO law is to remain relevant, it should align and reorient itself to this evolving framework. Trade law is to become an 'enabler' of social inclusiveness and poverty alleviation. This change is more profound than it may appear. It leads to assess the legitimacy of trade rules in the light of the fairness of their distributional outcomes. The call is to bridge the rift between legitimacy and fairness, between law and justice.[722] This invites a move beyond a formalist, technically-oriented conception of the law, and towards a more 'substantive' legal rationality. Aspirations of social justice are imported into trade law. Ultimately, this process will likely expand the prescriptive significance of purposive WTO language about the relevance of non-trade concerns. It is important to stress, in this respect, that the political commitments enshrined in the 2030

717 United Nations Sustainable Development Summit, New York, 25–27 September 2015, *Transforming Our World: The 2030 Agenda for Sustainable Development*, UN GA Res. 70/1 (*adopted* on 25 September 2015), downloadable at http://www.un.org/ga/search/view_doc.asp?symbol=A/RES/70/1.

718 Third International Conference on Financing for Development, Monterrey, N.L., Mexico, 8–22 March 2002, *Addis Ababa Action Agenda*, UN GA Res. 69/313 (*adopted* on 27 July 2015), downloadable at http://www.un.org/ga/search/view_doc.asp?symbol=A/RES/69/313&Lang=E.

719 Twenty-first session of the Conference of the Parties to the United Nations Framework Convention on Climate Change, Paris, 30 November to 13 December 2015, *Paris Agreement*, 54113 UNTS 1, downloadable at https://treaties.un.org/doc/Publication/UNTS/No%20Volume/54113/Part/I-54113-0800000280458f37.pdf.

720 United Nations, *The Road to Dignity by 2030: Ending Poverty, Transforming All Lives and Protecting the Planet*, Synthesis Report of the Secretary-General on the Post-2015 Agenda, New York (December 2014), para. 9.

721 United Nations, *The Future We Want*, outcome document of the United Nations Conference on Sustainable Development, annexed to UN GA Res. 66/288 of 27 July 2012.

722 On the distinction between legitimacy and fairness, Thomas M. Franck, "Fairness in the International Legal and Institutional System: General Course on Public International Law," *Collected Courses* 240 (1993): 42–44.

Sustainable Agenda and other soft law texts are normatively significant. They assist in interpreting existing rules and contribute to the gradual formation of new rules through the political law-making process (Sections 1.1 and 5.3).

From a hard law perspective, a purposive reading of WTO law informed by non trade concerns imports into trade law legal claims, such as the right to food, which are rooted in bodies of law outside the WTO. As distinctly articulated in human rights law and environmental law, these norms set on states obligations to respect, to protect and to fulfil. They engage legal obligations that states have undertaken in non-WTO fora, and the need to avoid breaching them. Yet, as normative objectives, they are also acknowledged and 'written' into the WTO Treaty (see below, Section 5.1.2). As such, they are an integral part of WTO law. It is argued here that they should be rediscovered in their prescriptive content. This is not only a matter of assessing and reconciling two different bodies of law (WTO law *versus* non-WTO law). What is at stake here is to give full operational meaning to the non-trade concerns enshrined in WTO law; and use them to argue for a different interpretation or an amendment of liberal trade rules, when needed (Section 5.3). The underlying principle is that obligations across and within bodies of law should be interpreted in a harmonious manner. This is eventually built under the general principle of good faith, which posits that states do not intentionally undertake conflicting commitments.[723]

The normative objectives and principles discussed in the following analysis are rooted in either hard or soft law, or both. Food security, sustainable rural livelihood and environmental sustainability (Section 5.1.2) are distinctly articulated as hard law obligations in bodies of law outside the WTO such as human rights law and environmental law, as discussed in the following sections. Yet, they are also 'written' into the WTO Treaty. The legal bases of the principles discussed in Section 5.1.3 are more heterogeneous in character. Though unwritten in international trade regulation, the principle of multilateralism (Section 5.1.3.1) is the cornerstone of the WTO system and informs the whole WTO Treaty. The quest for modulation (Section 5.1.3.3) rests on equitable constructs. It involves standard of reasonableness, fairness and proportionality. Whatever their customary status, these equitable principles hold specific legal significance. As pointed out by Oscar Schachter, they can be characterised "[…] as general principles of law or as basic factors in legal reasoning applicable to all systems".[724] Finally, the principle of redistributive

---

723 For a discussion, Cottier and Panagiotis, above n 54, at 25.

724 Oscar Schachter, "International Law in Theory and in Practice: General Course in Public International Law," *Collected Courses* 178 (1982): 85.

justice (Section 5.1.3.2) is basically rooted in 'soft law'. Principles of distributive justice informed the call for a NIEO in the past. They continue to have normative relevance today, enshrined in SDG 10. In hard law terms, they are expressed in the S&DT provisions for developing countries of the WTO Treaty, among other instruments.

With these considerations in mind, we shall now turn to the normative objectives and principles that are to subtend and inform the interface of trade rules and price stabilisation in agriculture. These normative values represent the connecting glue, or integrating framework, of an approach that, otherwise, would lack internal coherence. As discussed in Section 5.2, the approach envisaged to frame the interface between trade rules and agricultural stabilisation policies is heavily contextual, differentiated, specific. It ultimately results in a 'rainbow' of targeted solutions, with costly implications in terms of fragmentation. To avoid disintegration, some coherence is needed, in terms of underlying principles and objectives.

The analysis first discusses overarching objectives of international trade policy and regulation with regard to stabilisation arrangements. It then turns to the ordering principles to be applied to avoid or solve conflicts, in the face of competing normative claims. This will set the stage for the following discussion (Section 5.2) on how to rethink areas of tension between international trade rules and commodity price stabilisation policies.

### 5.1.2 *Normative Goals*

When dealing with agricultural commodities, three overarching objectives of international trade policy and regulation are identified: 'food security'; 'sustainable rural livelihood'; and 'environmental sustainability'. These 'non- or supra-trade interests' represent the intrinsic finality, the ultimate objective of trade liberalisation commitments in agriculture. In interplay with and against the background of considerations of trade 'fairness', they should purposively frame the regulation of agricultural price stabilisation policies.

As normative objectives, these 'supra-trade' concerns are rooted and distinctly articulated in bodies of law outside the WTO such as human rights law and environmental law. Yet, they are also acknowledged and 'written' into the WTO Treaty. As such, they are an integral part of WTO law. As discussed later (Section 5.3), they could be invoked to argue for a different interpretation of WTO rules, so as to allow leeway for otherwise WTO-inconsistent stabilisation arrangements.

The following analysis briefly considers the prescriptive content of these supra-trade interests, as articulated in bodies of law outside the WTO, and as enshrined in WTO law. It concludes with some remarks on their complex interplay with liberal trade rules.

#### 5.1.2.1 Food Security

In principle, WTO law acknowledges the right of countries to pursue agricultural policies supportive of food security and livelihood concerns. This right was enshrined in the Preamble of the AoA, in the 'built-in' negotiating mandate under AoA Article 20, and in a few substantive provisions.[725] It was later reaffirmed in the negotiating mandate on agriculture, as set out in the Doha Ministerial Declaration[726] and articulated in the 2004 July Framework.[727] Lastly, it was operationalised in the Bali Ministerial Decision on Public Stockholding for Food Security Purposes,[728] as reaffirmed in Nairobi.[729]

Outside the WTO, the notion of food security has been distinctly articulated in human rights law. Within this framework, food security translates into a legal entitlement, with human beings as the right holders, and states and private companies as the duty bearers. The right to food as a human right is defined as "the right of every individual, alone or in community with others, to have physical and economic access at all times to sufficient, adequate and culturally acceptable food that is produced and consumed sustainably, preserving access to food for future generations".[730]

---

725 The acknowledgment of food security concerns is contained in the preamble of the AoA and in Article 20 of the AoA (as a non-trade concern). It is articulated in several substantive provisions, including: AoA Article 12 (disciplines on export prohibitions and restrictions) 1 (a); AoA Annex 2, para. 3 (public stockholding for food security purposes); AoA Article 4, para. 2 (special treatment provisions with respect to market access reflecting factors of non-trade concerns, such as food security and environmental protection). See also World Trade Organization, Decision on Measures Concerning the Possible Negative Effects of the Reform Programme on Least-Developed and Net Food-Importing Developing Countries, adopted as part of the outcome of the Uruguay Round negotiations on agriculture.

726 World Trade Organization, Ministerial Declaration of 14 November 2001, WT/MIN(01)/DEC/1, para. 13.

727 World Trade Organization, Doha Work Programme, Decision Adopted by the General Council on 1 August 2004, WT/L/579, 2 August 2004, Annex A, *Framework for Establishing Modalities in Agriculture* [hereafter, *July Framework*], para. 2.

728 World Trade Organization, Ministerial Decision of 7 December 2013, WT/MIN(13)/38, WT/L/913.

729 World Trade Organization, Ministerial Decision of 19 December 2015, WT/MIN(15)/44, WT/L/979.

730 Special Rapporteur on the Right to Food, *Final Report: The Transformative Potential of the Right to Food*, A/HRC/25/57 (24 January 2014) (Olivier De Schutter), at 3. The normative bases are found in Committee on Economic, Social and Cultural Rights, General Comment 12, Right to Adequate Food, UN Doc. E/C.12/1999/5 (1999), reprinted in Compilation of General Comments and General Recommendations Adopted by Human Rights Treaty Bodies, UN Doc. HRI/GEN/1/Rev.6 at 62 (2003), paras. 6 and 7.

Recognised and reaffirmed in a range of international and regional instruments,[731] the right to food has been given concrete and operational content in various instruments, including General Comment 12 on the right to adequate food,[732] the FAO Right to Food Guidelines,[733] and various Reports of the Special Rapporteur on the right to food.[734] The core content of the right to food implies the availability and accessibility of food, the latter encompassing both economic and physical accessibility.[735] Access can be ensured through three channels: self-, or own production, also referred to as 'subsistence staple food production'; access to income-generating activities, allowing for the purchase of food on the market; and social protection.[736] In terms of prescriptive

731 For a listing of all relevant instruments, Special Rapporteur on the Right to Food, *Interim Report*, A/68/288 (7 August 2013) (Olivier de Schutter), at 3–4, paras. 1–3. The right to food was enshrined in article 25 of the Universal Declaration of Human Rights, reaffirmed in the International Covenant on Economic, Social and Cultural Rights (Article 11), and in the International Covenant on Civil and Political Rights (Article 6) (through the right to life). It was also recognised in the Convention on the Rights of the Child (Articles 24 (2) (c) and 27 (3)), the Convention on the Elimination of All Forms of Discrimination against Women (Article 12 (2)), and the Convention on the Rights of Persons with Disabilities (Articles 25 (f) and 28 (1)). The right to food is enshrined in regional instruments, including the Additional Protocol to the American Convention on Human Rights in the Area of Economic, Social and Cultural Rights (Protocol of San Salvador) (1988) (article 12), the African Charter on the Rights and Welfare of the Child (1990) (Article 14 (2) (c)) and the Protocol to the African Charter on Human and Peoples' Rights on the Rights of Women in Africa (2003) (Article 15). It has received renewed attention in recent years, since its restatement at the 1996 World Food Summit in the Rome Declaration on World Food Security.

732 Committee on Economic, Social and Cultural Rights, General Comment 12, above n 730.

733 Voluntary Guidelines to Support the Progressive Realization of the Right to Adequate Food in the Context of National Food Security [hereafter, *Right to Food Guidelines*], adopted by member states of the Food and Agriculture Organization of the United Nations (FAO) on 23 November 2004, available at http://www.fao.org/3/a-y7937e.pdf.

734 Official reports of the Special Rapporteur on the right to food are available at: http://www.ohchr.org/EN/Issues/Food/Pages/Annual.aspx (accessed 16 June 2015).

735 General Comment 12, above n 730, paras. 12 and 13.

736 Special Rapporteur on the Right to Food (Olivier de Schutter), *Interim Report*, above n 731, at 4, para. 6. See also, Special Rapporteur on the Right to Food (Olivier de Schutter), *From Charity to Entitlement: Implementing the Right to Food in Southern and Eastern Africa*, Briefing Note 05 (26 June 2012); and Special Rapporteur on the Right to Food (Olivier de Schutter), *Countries Tackling Hunger with a Right to Food Approach*, Briefing Note 1 (14 May 2010), at 8.

content, the right to food sets on states obligations to respect, to protect, and to fulfil.[737] The first requires that states "refrain from interfering with the existing levels of enjoyment of the right to food".[738] The obligation to protect "requires that the State protect individuals' enjoyment of the right to food against violations by third parties", including private companies.[739] Under the obligation to fulfil, states must proactively pursue agricultural and social security policies that are supportive of the right to food ('progressive realisation'). They must also provide that right directly, in emergency situations ('fulfil').[740] Once incorporated in the domestic legal order, and possibly enshrined in domestic law as a constitutional right, the right to food is to be construed as a justiciable right. Victims "should have access to effective judicial or other appropriate remedies at both national and international levels", and "are entitled to adequate reparation".[741]

#### 5.1.2.2 Sustainable Rural Livelihood

A second objective sought is to safeguard sustainable rural livelihood. In economic terms, emphasis is here on living standards and purchasing power. For the peasant farmer, it means 'fair and remunerative' prices which cover the actual expenses incurred by the farmer, whether in cash or in kind,[742] plus a 'reasonable' profit margin.[743] For agricultural labourers, it means receiving a 'decent' salary, or 'fair wages'. The former is a matter of price dynamics; the latter relates to labour standards and corporate responsibility. Both involve socially 'sustainable' commodity supply chains.

As for food security, livelihood security and rural development are enshrined in WTO law. The need to safeguard rural livelihood and employment is recognised in the Preamble of the AoA and reaffirmed in the negotiating mandate on agriculture, as articulated in paragraph 13 of the Doha Ministerial

---

737 General Comment 12, above n 730, para. 15.

738 Special Rapporteur on the Right to Food, *Interim Report*, above n 731, at 6

739 Ibid, at 7.

740 Ibid, at 7 and 8.

741 General Comment 12, above n 730, para. 32.

742 The expenses incurred by the farmer shall include "[...] rent paid for leased land and imputed value of wages of family labour, rent for owned land and interest on fixed capital", as specified in the definition of MSPs for major agricultural commodities in India. WTO Secretariat, *Trade Policy Review: India*, above n 187, at 134.

743 A criterion taken into account when setting Fair and Remunerative Prices (FRP) for sugarcane in India, for example (WTO Secretariat, *Trade Policy Review: India*, above n 187, at 103).

Declaration[744] and paragraph 2, Annex A of the 2004 July Framework.[745] It also resonates in the first recital of the Preamble to the WTO Agreement, where reference is to "raising standards of living" and "ensuring full employment".

Outside of the WTO framework, livelihood and development concerns are historically rooted in the pledge of states to promote "higher standards of living, full employment and conditions of economic and social progress and development", as expressed in Article 55 and 56 of the Charter of the United Nations.[746] The right to an adequate standard of living was recognised in Articles 22 and 28 of the Universal Declaration of Human Rights.[747] It was later reaffirmed in the International Covenant on Economic, Social and Cultural Rights.[748] Article 11(1), in particular, recognises "the right of everyone to an adequate standard of living for himself and his family, including adequate food, clothing and housing, and to the continuous improvement of living conditions".[749] Articulated in terms of a 'human right to development', it was then restated in various resolutions, recommendations and other instruments of the United Nations.[750] At the core of this principle stands the inherent "dignity and worth of the human person", and ideals of 'social justice'[751] rooted in 'natural justice' precepts.[752]

#### 5.1.2.3 Environmental Sustainability

Environmental sustainability, as a normative objective, finds expression in the first paragraph of the Preamble to the WTO Agreement.[753] The principle has

744 World Trade Organization, Ministerial Declaration of 14 November 2001, WT/MIN(01)/DEC/1, para. 13.

745 *July Framework*, above n 727, para. 2.

746 United Nations, Charter of the United Nations, 1 UNTS XVI, 24 October 1945.

747 Universal Declaration of Human Rights, GA Res. 217 (III) A, UN Doc. A/RES/217(III) (10 December 1948).

748 International Covenant on Economic, Social and Cultural Rights, GA Res. 2200A (XXI), 21 UN GAOR Supp. (No. 16) at 49, UN Doc. A/6316 (1966), 993 UNTS. 3, entered into force 3 January 1976.

749 Ibid, Article 11 (1).

750 See, in particular, the Declaration on Social Progress and Development, GA Res. 2542 (XXIV) of 11 December 1969 and the Declaration on the Right to Development, GA Res. 41/128 of 4 December 1986.

751 Declaration on Social Progress and Development, above n 750.

752 Franck, above n 722; Schachter, above n 724.

753 On the concept of 'sustainable development' in international trade law, Elisabeth Bürgi Bonanomi, *Sustainable Development in International Law Making: International Food Governance and Trade in Agriculture* (Cheltenham: Edward Elgar, 2015). See also Elisabeth Bürgi Bonanomi, "Right to Food, Sustainable Development and Trade: All Faces of the

also been acknowledged by the Appellate Body: the objective of sustainable development shall add "colour, texture and shading" when interpreting the WTO Agreements.[754] In the WTO AoA, it is referred to in the Preamble, which specifically refers to "the need to protect the environment"; and provides the rationale for the Green Box exemption.

Outside the WTO, the sustainability principle has been acknowledged by the international community in a number of instruments.[755] In the 2030 Agenda,[756] sustainability is set as the most pressing concern and the unifying aspirational goal. The SDGs integrate economic, social and environmental aspects and recognise their interlinkages in achieving development in all its dimensions.[757] The Human Rights discourse is moving in the same direction: Olivier de Schutter, discussing the right to food, advocates a "shift to agro-ecological modes of production" and "sustainable consumption".[758] Overall, sustainability has emerged as the most pressing public issue of our time and as the integrating framework for policy action worldwide.

---

Same Cube?" in *The Challenge of Food Security: International Policy and Regulatory Frameworks,* ed. Rosemary Rayfuse and Nicole Weisfelt (Cheltenham: Edward Elgar, 2012), 70–91.

754 Appellate Body Report, *United States – Import Prohibition of Certain Shrimp and Shrimp Products*, WT/DS58/AB/R, adopted 6 November 1998, DSR 1998: VII, p. 2755, Section VI C 1 para. 155. Cameron, above n 614, at 267.

755 United Nations Conference on Environment and Development, Rio de Janeiro, 3–14 June 1992, *Rio Declaration on Environment and Development*, UN Doc. A/CONF.151/26 (Vol. I), Annex I (12 August 1992); United Nations Conference on Environment and Development, Rio de Janeiro, 3–14 June 1992, *Agenda 21*, UN Doc. A/CONF.151/26 (Vol. II), Annex II (12 August 1992); UN GA Res. S/19-2 (19 September 1997), *Programme for the Further Implementation of Agenda 21*; World Summit on Sustainable Development, Johannesburg, South Africa, 26 August–4 September 2002, *Johannesburg Declaration on Sustainable Development*, UN Doc. A/CONF.199/20, Resolution 1, Annex (4 September 2002) and *Plan of Implementation of the World Summit on Sustainable Development*, UN Doc. A/CONF.199/20, Resolution 2; The Future We Want, outcome document of the United Nations Conference on Sustainable Development (above n 721); and UN GA Res. 65/1 (19 October 2010), *Keeping the Promise: United to Achieve the Millennium Development Goals*, outcome document of the high-level plenary meeting of the General Assembly on the Millennium Development Goals.

756 Transforming Our World: The 2030 Agenda for Sustainable Development, above n 717.

757 The Future We Want, above n 721, para 3.

758 Report of the Special Rapporteur on the right to food, Olivier De Schutter, above n 730, at 8–9.

### 5.1.2.4 Interplay with Trade Fairness

Questions arise as to the balance between stabilisation policies supportive of food security and rural livelihood security, on the one hand, and liberal trade commitments, on the other. As briefly discussed in Section 2.3, agricultural stabilisation policies may well clash with liberal trade rules. For example, administratively set prices trigger the AoA domestic support provisions if the *de minimis* or AMS threshold is exceeded.[759] Likewise, price band systems can be easily challenged under the AoA market access disciplines.[760] How far should the notion of domestic 'policy space' be expanded, beyond existing flexibilities, to provide lee-way for trade-distortive agricultural stabilisation policies? Where can a 'line of equilibrium' be marked out between the right of a country to support its peasant producers and legitimate interests elsewhere?

Some argue that, when dealing with stabilisation arrangements in developing countries, the balance of rights and obligations is to be construed in favour of supra-trade interests. Multilateral trade rules should thus allow unqualified leeway for trade-distortive agricultural stabilisation policies, if genuinely supportive of food security, sustainability and livelihood concerns. This is the trade policy stance upheld by the human rights community.[761]

Yet, this account fails to appreciate the complex interconnections of global markets, and particularly the reality of South-South export-competition and import-dependence. In the current setting, stabilisation measures intended to serve peasant interests in a developing country can well hit the interests of small farmers in another developing country. The debate here is not to be framed in terms of trade *versus* non-trade concerns. The trade-off is between critical livelihood concerns of equally vulnerable constituencies across countries. This can be appreciated in a number of respects, as discussed in Section 5.1.3.3.

It follows that agricultural stabilisation policies supportive of food and rural livelihood security are to be multilaterally regulated. They are to be regulated in their extra-territorial effects, i.e. the potential to generate surplus production 'dumped' on international markets, or to restrict vital supplies, when prejudicial to poor constituencies elsewhere. Trade fairness and market-based export competition, qualified by equity, as discussed below, thus remain relevant normative values that set limits to how far states can go with their domestic stabilisation policies. The operational principles outlined below provide further guidance on how to arbitrate trade-offs.

---

759 See above, Section 2.3.3.1.

760 See above, Section 2.3.3.3.

761 Special Rapporteur on the Right to Food, Olivier de Schutter, above n 690.

### 5.1.3 *Operational Principles*

What are the limits to the domestic pursuit of stabilisation policies supportive of food security, rural development and sustainability? When conflicts arise with legitimate interests elsewhere, how can a 'line of equilibrium' be marked out between competing interests? The analysis turns to consider some operational principles that may provide guidance on how to arbitrate trade-offs and transcend frictions. Specifically, attention is drawn to three ordering principles, all rooted in equitable considerations. The first is termed, after David Held, 'cosmopolitan multilateralism'.[762] The second involves substantive notions of equity. The third refers to the operational principles of modularity and graduation, also grounded in equitable constructs. These principles are, for the most part, unwritten in international trade regulation. Yet, they underlie specific rules and disciplines (the case for equitable constructs), or even run through the whole WTO Treaty (like multilateralism). In this author's view, such principles represent the fundamental legal concepts and values that are to inform the trade and price stabilisation policy interface. The remainder of this analysis briefly reviews these operational principles. They are considered broadly, and in their bearing on agricultural price dynamics.

#### 5.1.3.1 'Cosmopolitan' Multilateralism

Multilateralism is the cornerstone of the WTO system.[763] The historical roots of the trading system are grounded in post-war concerns. It was widely felt, in the aftermath of the Second World War, that never again should governments be allowed to resort to the beggar-thy-neighbour trade and monetary policies of the interwar period; and that "[…] governments owe a responsibility not only to their own citizens but also to the citizens of other countries".[764] Infused with universal and cosmopolitan values, multilateralism was to become the ordering principle of the world trading system, at least until recently.

Since the Second World War, the world has become more complexly interconnected, and multilateral perspectives have evolved, enriched with insights from cosmopolitan theories. A specific kind of multilateralism, what David Held has termed "cosmopolitan multilateralism", has emerged.[765] This form of

762 David Held, "From Executive to Cosmopolitan Multilateralism," in *Taming Globalization: Frontiers of Governance*, ed. David Held and Mathias Koenig-Archibugi (Oxford: Polity Press, 2003), 160–86.

763 As argued by Hilf, "[…] the very essence of the WTO consists of overcoming the unilateral or bilateral conduct in international economic relations." Hilf, above n 614, at 119.

764 London Report, above n 49, Part II, Chapter I, Section B.

765 Held, above n 762.

multilateralism acknowledges the intricate and dense network of global interdependence and calls for more effective and accountable decisions at transnational levels. In substantive terms, it acknowledges cosmopolitan duties of states to citizens and aliens globally, including those beyond their borders, expanding the ambit of state responsibility. In institutional terms, it advocates a shift from the current hierarchical inter-state system of intergovernmental multilateralism[766] to multi-layered and transnational governance networks; and from the secrecy of diplomatic exchange to standards of transparency and accountability.[767] This type of multilateralism draws some of its tenets from the cosmopolitan constructs of a just world order.[768]

With regard to commodity price stabilisation, why is multilateral action warrantable? Shouldn't price stabilisation policies be regarded as a matter for domestic jurisdiction? There are at least two sets of reasons to be sceptical about the desirability of uncoordinated domestic policy responses. Both rest on considerations of equity and fairness. Both point to the need for cosmopolitan models of multilateral governance.

First, the effects of domestic price stabilisation may well extend beyond domestic borders, which raises issues of accountability and inclusion. This was notably the case for farm support and stabilisation policies in the EU and US. In the past, these policies stimulated overproduction in the subsidising countries, and resulted in large exportable surplus, including in agricultural commodities of export interest to developing countries such as cotton and sugar. Disposed

766 "Executive multilateralism", as termed by Held, above n 762.

767 See Held, above n 762, at 181.

768 Moving from the idea that all human beings are owed equal respect as moral persons, cosmopolitans conceive "[...] the world at large as a unified polis, a cosmopolis" (Laura Valentini, *Justice in a Globalized World: A Normative Framework* (Oxford; New York: Oxford University Press, 2011), 23). As summarised in Valentini, (non-relational) cosmopolitanism is based on the following tenets: all human beings are owed equal respect as moral persons; there are universal moral values / goods that all human beings value (civil and political liberties, opportunities, income and wealth); all and any person is entitled to equal rights, opportunities and wealth, irrespective of morally arbitrary factors, such as a person's place of birth; equal respect requires that liberties, opportunities, income and wealth should be roughly distributed across the world's population (ibid, at 46–47). Domestic principles and constructs of what is just and fair are applied to citizens and aliens globally, "beyond borders" (Simon Caney, *Justice Beyond Borders: A Global Political Theory* (Oxford; New York: Oxford University Press, 2006)). At the institutional level, states should be progressively superseded or supplemented by global political institutions. These include multi-stakeholder partnerships that involve private and public constituencies across boundaries. These ideals are largely aspirational. Yet, they do possess guidance implications.

of, 'dumped', on foreign markets, this surplus production exerted significant downward pressure on world prices, causing serious prejudice to the trade interests of developing exporting countries.[769] Similar risks may be incurred with public stockholding for food security schemes. Guaranteed prices and purchases high above the market prices may result in higher production, lower domestic consumption and a large exportable surplus. In large producers, intervention stocks have been building up; and need to be sold out as exports to make room for new procurements. The impacts on the global market will depend on how the government handles the surplus of the product concerned. The extra-territorial effects of domestic price stabilisation policies have been even more conspicuous, and distinctly visible in the case of export restrictions to calm inflating domestic food prices.[770]

Overall, price-related policies in countries whose supply and demand are large will tend to have global repercussions. For these so-called 'price-makers', it is very difficult to disentangle domestic and international perspectives. Unilateral action on domestic prices almost inevitably entails important repercussions beyond the border. Accordingly, these countries have to "move slowly in making policy changes",[771] and take into account the complex global ramifications of what may appear at first as genuinely domestic policy choices. This can better occur in a multilateral setting, whereby unilateral decisions are 'multilateralised'.

There is another side of the coin, a second, related aspect, which ought to be considered. The vast majority of low-income countries, and of countries in general, are 'price-takers'. They need to adjust to policy decisions elsewhere that have a bearing on global prices. This adjustment places a heavy financial burden on the government. For example, it is widely acknowledged that biofuel policies in a few large countries have exerted upward pressure on global cereal prices; and that these increases have been passed on to vulnerable consumers in import-dependent developing countries. Questions arise as to why resource-poor countries should pay the costs of price developments that originate elsewhere. The problem is particularly acute as the costs incurred into

769 See above n 267 and 268.

770 In 2007–08 and 2010–11, surging food prices put pressure on governments in food exporting countries to restrict exports, in a bid to keep domestic prices low. Vietnam and India, two of the world's largest rice exporters, restricted rice exports in March 2008, contributing to a price shock in the international rice market. More recently, the 2010 Russian export ban put upward pressure on prices. By restricting supply to the international market, these export restrictions caused further price increases, contributing to the price peaks in 2008 and 2010. For a detailed assessment, Slayton, above n 20.

771 Murphy, above n 301, at 6.

by the poorest countries are frequently not monetised in financial terms: they are human costs, paid in terms of human livelihood. Indeed, the magnitude of international price fluctuations is such that many countries, particularly the poorest, are unable to cushion the impacts upon their domestic producers or consumers of such price variability by means of domestic stabilisation policies.

Drawing from political science, it may be argued that in all the above cases the market amounts to a form of "systemic coercion".[772] Market dynamics indeed place significant constraints on some agents' basic entitlements, compared to what would have occurred in their absence.[773] This coercion, as with any form of coercion, stands in need of justification. There is a pressing need to assign legal significance to systemic interdependence, particularly if its costs are borne by the weakest. Causal responsibility must bear consequences. This flows from basic 'natural justice' considerations of fairness. It proceeds from a cosmopolitan conception of a just world order.

On matters of commodity prices, 'cosmopolitan' multilateralism thus has two implications.

First, it sets limits to the policy discretion countries enjoy in their pursuit of farm support and stabilisation policies. These policies should not jeopardise equally legitimate interests in other countries. Where to locate a line of equilibrium between competing interests, when conflicts arise, is a highly contextual exercise, informed by equitable considerations, as discussed in Section 5.2.

Second, and in a related vein, it points to the need to 'multilateralise' policy decisions that are still perceived as a matter of domestic discretion such as decisions on biofuel policies, or on commodity de-stocking. In large producers, whether developed countries, like the US, or developing, like China or Brazil, these decisions have global impacts, well beyond the national borders. Hence there is a need to restore symmetry between the jurisdiction where the decision is taken and the jurisdiction where that decision's effects occur, as a matter of 'equity'. As discussed in Section 5.2.5, this requires setting up suitable institutional frameworks where all those who are affected can have a say, at least formally, in the decisions that affect them. The object is to reduce the scope for beggar-thy-neighbour policies, by locking-in the parties into co-operative behaviour.

Multilateralism, qualified by considerations of solidarity and equitable differentiation (below), should be central to the trade regulation of agricultural stabilisation policies.

772 Valentini, above n 768, at 137–41 and 186–87.

773 Ibid.

#### 5.1.3.2 Equity as Fairness: Good Faith and the Quest for Distributive Justice

Equity[774] can and should have a prominent part in the regulation of agricultural stabilisation policies. Two relevant concepts of equity have distinctive guidance and prescriptive implications for framing the interface between trade law and agricultural stabilisation policies: equity as 'individualised justice' and equity as 'fairness'. The former essentially involves a legal methodology. The latter engages with substantive contents. These equitable constructs and principles need to be re-examined in their distinctive guidance implications for the regulation of commodity price policies.

The role of equity "as a basis for 'individualised' justice tempering the rigours of strict law"[775] is considered in Section 5.1.3.3. In the current analysis, instead, we shall consider the role of equity as a source of law in the assertion of rights and obligations. Equity here amounts to a standard of reasonableness, fairness and good faith. Whatever their customary status, these equitable principles hold specific legal significance. As pointed out by Oscar Schachter, they can be characterised "[...] as general principles of law or as basic factors in legal reasoning applicable to all systems".[776]

Equity, as fairness, has distinctive guidance and prescriptive implications for trade law and agricultural stabilisation policies. Specifically, it leads to assess the legitimacy of trade rules in the light of the fairness of their distributional outcomes. By doing so, equity sets the basis for a fundamental revision

774 Equity is a rather elusive term. Oscar Schachter distinguishes, for example, five uses of equity: as a basis to temper the rigid application of rules; as a standard of fairness, reasonableness and good faith; as general principles in legal reasoning (estoppel, abuse of rights, unjust enrichment etc.); as a mode of scarce resource allocation; and as redistributive justice (Schachter, above n 724, at 82. See also Franck, above n 722, at 63–97). Likewise, the use of equitable constructs in legal reasoning is manifold: *infra legem* (as a method of interpretation of the law), *praeter legem* (to fill regulatory gaps) and *contra legem* (as a corrective to the rule of law) (Schachter, above n 724, at 84; Pellet, above n 7, at 726). A line is also drawn between equitable constructs and a decision *ex aequo et bono*: while equity is part of the law, a decision *ex aequo et bono* seeks an appropriate settlement outside the realm of law, in light of extra-legal considerations (Franck, above n 722, 69–71). This latter distinction is analytically convenient, yet somewhat arbitrary. Ultimately, equitable constructs give legal significance to moral sentiments. Grounded in moral and philosophical conceptions, equity (as law) transmutes extra-legal considerations into law. For a comprehensive most recent review on history and functions of equity, Thomas Cottier, *Equitable Principles of Maritime Boundary Delimitation: The Quest for Distributive Justice in International Law* (Cambridge: Cambridge University Press, 2015).

775 Schachter, above n 724, at 82.

776 Ibid, at 85.

of relevant WTO provisions. Its ultimate goal is to bring about a more 'just' legal order that narrows the rift between law and justice.[777] Issues of fairness here complexly intertwine with standards of proportionality and good faith, and with the quest for redistributive justice.

### a) *Good Faith, Proportionality and Reasonableness*

Equitable constructs and principles challenge the legitimacy of existing trade rules in agriculture, in light of the unfairness of their distributional outcomes. As widely discussed elsewhere,[778] existing WTO disciplines on agriculture are riddled with asymmetries and double standards. They are informed by political expediency.

The inequity in the rules is evident in the current subsidy set-up. Huge subsidies are allowed for the high income and advanced economies; while, for most small developing countries, subsidies are capped at comparatively lower *de minimis* levels. For example, the EU with 2.5 million poor, mainly urban poor, can spend up to €62.2 billion per year in farm price support.[779] A country like India with 397 million poor, mainly rural, cannot exceeds its *de minimis* threshold, a roughly estimated $46.2 billion,[780] plus unlimited spending on Article 6.2 input and investment subsidies.[781]

The inequality in the rules is further compounded by the fact that, in practice, trade policy tools that better match developing countries' set-up (such as variable import levies and price controls) are proscribed; while more sophisticated instruments, suitable to the developed economies (publicly backed insurance schemes, 'decoupled' direct payments to producers, etc.) are in principle permissible. In some extreme cases, permissibility was artificially crafted to accommodate the needs of some. In particular, the Amber Box of

777 As stated in Franck, "[...] law's legitimacy is not determined by the fairness of its distributional outcomes" (Franck, above n 722, at 42). The author illustrates this proposition by reference to the legal principle of *uti possidetis*, whereby newly independent states were entitled to the territory attributed to them as colonies – which often cut across tribal lines and unequally allocated resources.

778 For a review, Musselli, above n 580. See also Paarlberg, above n 557 and Häberli, above n 585.

779 EU Final Bound Total AMS, 2009 (Consolidated Domestic Support Profiles) (Cut-off date: 28 February 2013).

780 Given a total agricultural production of 230.8 billion $ in 2012 (FAOSTAT, Value of agricultural production), a roughly estimated $46.2 billion for product- and non-product-specific support combined (10 percent of 230.8 billion $ x 2 (PS + NPS *de minimis* AMS)).

781 A notified 31.6 billion $ in 2010/11. See India's Notification to the WTO Committee on Agriculture, G/AG/N/IND/10 (10 September 2014).

trade-distorting support was carefully designed to exclude key support instruments in the EU and the US (notably, most forms of direct cash payments to producers, exempted under the Blue and Green Boxes).[782]

From an equity perspective, there is a need to redress imbalances in the current subsidy set-up. If a fair outcome cannot be assured, mitigation or remedial action is needed. This may entail, among other actions, the re-opening of locked-in flexibilities, including leeway for countercyclical trade policies in the most vulnerable economies, to cushion the domestic effects of external price fluctuations.

The principle of equity can also be invoked in a second respect. As an implied principle of 'good faith', it should discourage the highly subsidising states from contesting stabilisation schemes in poor countries. A country like the US, for example, has intervened massively in its farm economy, with notable trade impacts. For example, about 45 percent of the farm value of cotton was received in the US in the form of subsidies during the 2000s.[783] As the US is by far the largest cotton exporters, these subsidies clearly distorted production and trade, to the detriment of peasant farmers in countries like Benin, Burkina Faso, Mali and Chad, among others. Equitable constructs should impose on the US and on other traditionally high-subsidising countries at least some degree of self-restraint in challenging policies of which they set an example, currently or in the past.

### b) *Distributive Justice*

The equitable constructs outlined above essentially involve standards of good faith, proportionality and reasonableness, short of redistributive justice. Distributive justice deserves separate attention as a comprehensive framework for thinking about the interface between trade law and price stabilisation arrangements. It is useful to briefly recall the historic roots and legal significance of redistributive ideals, and then turn to their guidance implications for a legal assessment of agricultural stabilisation policies.

Ideals of solidarity and distributive justice trace back to ancient times, and are deeply rooted in human consciousness. As pointed out in Häberli, the notion of distributive justice is the common element in the largest monotheistic religions – Judaism, Christianism, and Islam. It runs through these theologies "[n]ot in a simple sense of charity but as an inherent obligation for all members

782 Paarlberg, above n 557, at 428.

783 Terry Townsend (Cotton Analytics), "The 2014 US Farm Bill and Its Implications for Cotton Producers in Low-income Developing Countries" (presentation delivered at UNCTAD's Global Commodities Forum 2015, Geneva, 13–14 April 2015).

of the compact, of the ecclesia, or of the Dar al Islam".[784] Moving to contemporary moral theory, distributive justice stands at the core of cosmopolitan principles of global justice. These principles posit that all beings should have equal rights *pro* moral persons; inequalities should be condemned as unjust.[785]

From an international economic law perspective, redistributive concerns were to take the place of legal concepts under what has been referred to as 'international development law'.[786] The quest for a NIEO, in particular, tried to translate redistributive concerns into legally binding obligations. Under UNCTAD's IPC, distributive justice aspired to become the normative framework for thinking about and acting upon the global commodity economy. Beyond the IPC, principles of distributive justice translated in other major initiatives in the past: the cancellation of Third World debt; UNCTAD's code of conduct for the transfer of technology; and the common regime for the commercial exploitation of manganese nodes in the deep sea. Redistributive ideals continue to have echoes down to the present. As discussed in Simon Caney, they have informed: principles of fair trade; the proposed taxes on financial transactions, to be spent on alleviating poverty (known as 'the Tobin tax'); and a number of proposals mooted by the Commission on Global Governance.[787] Finally, in the WTO, the principle of distributive justice is expressed in terms of S&DT for developing countries.[788] As reaffirmed in the Doha mandate on agriculture, the principle of S&DT "shall be an integral part of all elements of the negotiations and shall be embodied [...] in the rules and disciplines to be negotiated, so as to be operationally effective".[789]

Today, redistributive ideals continue to inform the debate about a fair allocation of value along commodity chains. They can certainly provide a useful

784 Christian Häberli, "Right to Food and Right to Water," above n 585, See also Häberli, "God, the WTO and Hunger," above n 585.

785 For an assessment of cosmopolitan perspectives, Valentini, above n 768.

786 The term refers to the network of international instruments, mainly 'soft law' instruments, pertaining to development. Among the most influential: United Nations Declaration on the Establishment of a New International Economic Order, GA Res. 3201 (S-VI), 1 May 1974; the Charter of Economic Rights and Duties of States, GA Res. 3281 (XXIX), 12 Dec. 1974; and the Declaration on the Right to Development, GA Res. 41/128, 4 Dec. 1986. For a definition of the contours of an international law of development, Oscar Schachter, "The Evolving International Law of Development," *Columbia Journal of Transnational Law* 15, no. 1 (1976).

787 Caney, above n 768.

788 Hilf, above n 614, at 119.

789 Doha Work Programme, para. 13 (World Trade Organization, Ministerial Declaration of 14 November 2001, WT/MIN(01)/DEC/1).

analytical framework for rethinking market price intervention in commodities. This with one notable difference with respect to the past: a shift from state-centred to individualist perspectives. UNCTAD's IPC was indeed predicated on 'statist' assumptions. It implied some antagonism between rich and poor countries; and a transfer of resources, via high prices, from the rich countries to the poor ones. This overlooked two aspects: the variety of interests between the developing countries; and distributional concerns about who, within a country, would reap the benefit of higher commodity prices. Redistributive concerns should today move towards individualist assumptions. Redistribution is owed to individuals and not states; and especially to individuals in need. This holds important implications. In particular, redistribution is to be coupled with transparency and accountability to monitor how states use the transferred resources.

So qualified, ideals of distributive justice can provide a useful analytical framework for thinking about trade rules and commodity price stabilisation policies.[790] As discussed (Section 2.1.2), domestic price stabilisation schemes tend to have discrete welfare effects across groups within the same society; international price stabilisation schemes tend to transfer resources across countries. In both cases, the transfer can be redistributive, pro-poor, when resources, via high prices, flow from the relatively affluent to the poorer; or it may carry an anti-poor bias, against redistributive ideals, when the transfer is from the neediest to the better-off. These distributive dynamics and outcomes are to be taken into account when devising new multilateral trade disciplines on domestic and international price stabilisation policies.

Ideals of distributive justice should lead policymakers to weigh different interests differently. Sustained cocoa prices are expected to make Easter eggs more costly? From a distributive justice perspective, society shall bear these costs. The interests of poor cocoa farmers in low-income countries deserve more consideration than those of relatively affluent chocolate consumers in high income countries. Indeed, the bare livelihood concerns of cocoa farmers matter more than the minimal loss suffered by comparatively wealthy

790 Trade in agricultural commodities raise distinctive issues of distributive justice. In particular, there is enough evidence to substantiate the claim that existing patterns of pricing and value allocation in agricultural commodity chains are distorted and unfair: the share of value retained at source by producers – and producing countries – has progressively declined. World Bank, above n 593, at 136; Bruinsma, above n 594, at 277; John M. Talbot, "Where Does Your Coffee Dollar Go? The Division of Income and Surplus along the Coffee Commodity Chain," *Studies in Comparative International Development* 32, no. 1 (1997).

consumers. This is understood in the light of ethical issues of social justice, as well as economic considerations of marginal utility.

It follows that trade rules should provide leeway for pro-poor price stabilisation arrangements, while disciplining more tightly arrangements that carry an anti-poor bias.

#### 5.1.3.3 Equity as 'Individualised Justice': Modulation and Graduation

The third operational principle is termed 'modulation'. It calls for a fine-tuning of trade regulation in accordance with varying factual differences. WTO regulation of agricultural stabilisation policies, it is argued, is to be particular and circumstantial. It should acknowledge the distinct factual circumstances that exist across countries and modulate regulatory response accordingly. This can be attained through a modulation of the rules themselves (modulation) or in the application of the rules (graduation). Both approaches involve some paradigm shift, beyond traditional notions of S&DT for developing countries.

Modulation is itself ultimately grounded in equitable constructs. Equity calls for 'particularisation' in the application of law,[791] allowing for exceptions to be made when individual circumstances appear to call for them. As articulated in maritime boundary delimitation, it essentially results in a methodology whereby decisions are shaped and adjusted to the facts of the case.[792] By attributing weight to the specifics of each case, equity particularises and contextualises the law in order to bring about an appropriate settlement. This approach ultimately involves the weighing and balancing of competing interests and perspective, in the light of the relevant "factual matrix".[793] As pointed out by Thomas Cottier,[794] this methodology has the potential to be applied to other areas of regulation, beyond maritime boundary delimitation. This also includes the issue at stake, the trade regulation of agricultural stabilisation policies.

The rule of equity as a methodology provides a means to bring about more equitable results in the issue area of trade rules and stabilisation policies. It can serve as a methodology for adjudication, to temper the rigid application of the law, but only to an extent, as discussed in Section 5.3. In a more unconstrained

---

791 Schachter, above n 724, at 74. See also George Schwarzenberger, "The Principles and Standards of International Economic Law," *Collected Courses* 117 (1966): 79.

792 See Cottier, *Equitable Principles of Maritime Boundary Delimitation*, above n 774.

793 As stated by Judge Jiménez de Aréchanga, "[…] the judicial application of equitable principles means that a court should render justice in the concrete case, by means of a decision shaped by and adjusted to the relevant 'factual matrix' of that case". *Tunisia /Libya* case, *ICJ Reports 1982*, individual opinion, at p. 100, para. 24.

794 Cottier, above n 774.

fashion, it can provide distinctive guidance to the WTO legislator in negotiations. Equity here calls for modularity and graduation in trade law, beyond the existing WTO fabric of relatively rigid rules and exceptions.

Against this background, the following analysis first challenges traditional perceptions of S&DT in agricultural trade law. It then sketches alternative modulated frameworks that can offer more pertinent guidance on how to move further in the regulation of agricultural stabilisation policies.

### a) *S&DT Perceptions: Drawbacks*

On matters of agricultural stabilisation policies, there is a need to move beyond traditional notions of S&DT for developing countries. This need stems from at least two sets of reasons. First, traditional S&DT constructs conceal the great variety of interests that the developing countries have in agriculture. Second, it fails to capture the complex ramifications of South-South interdependence. It is worth considering each aspect in turn.

#### i) Diversity among Developing Countries

Developing countries have different agricultural profiles, different vulnerabilities to external price shocks in agriculture, and different needs for price stabilisation and support policies. Without entering into the particulars, suffice here to map out some major sub-groups, drawing on relevant distinctions in a submission by Mauritius.[795]

Some developing countries are major exporters of agricultural commodities. Their importance in a given commodity is such that they act as 'price fixer'.[796] This is the case of Brazil, for sugar and soybeans; Argentina for soybeans; and Thailand for rice, just to name some. As discussed, these countries need to move with caution in their domestic price policies, as their unilateral action would likely entail repercussions beyond the border.

A partially overlapping group includes other large, diversified economies, still largely agrarian in employment structure, such as India and China. As a distinctive feature, these countries face pressing equity and food security concerns, notably in terms of gaps in rural and urban incomes.[797] The trade regulation of domestic price stabilisation policies here raises particularly intractable issues, mainly for staple food commodities and notably rice. On the

795 World Trade Organization, *Note on non-Trade Concerns*, G/AG/NG/W/36/Rev.1 (9 November 2000), Attachment 5, *Developing Countries and non-Trade Concerns* (prepared by Mauritius).

796 Ibid, at 47.

797 Ibid.

one hand, trade rules should provide significant lee-way for domestic price stabilisation in these countries, including at support levels. Indeed, farm stabilisation and support is here critical for social and political stability. It not only serves domestic policy concerns; it also serves global consumer interests. As a matter of fact, if China or India abandoned their farm support and reserve policies, and increased reliance on the world market, there would be significant demand shocks in cereal markets, which would be transmitted on to consumers elsewhere. On the other hand, constraints on policy space are to be multilaterally set, to avoid abuse. In fact, these countries have huge budgetary outlays for domestic farm stabilisation and support policies. Furthermore, though their export orientation is low, their exports are high in absolute terms. Note in this respect that India outranked Thailand in 2011/12 to become the world's top rice exporter, with total shipments at about 10 million tonnes per year since 2011/12.[798] The potential to cause serious prejudice to peasant producers elsewhere is high, if subsidisation policies lead to increased output and surplus disposal on foreign markets.

Another category includes the large and medium net food-importing developing countries (NFIDCs).[799] These are relatively large and differentiated developing economies, mainly in the lower middle-income group.[800] They are heavily dependent on staple food imports, and generally exporters of cash crops. Among these countries are Senegal and Côte d'Ivoire, heavily reliant on Asian rice imports, as well as a few North African countries (including Egypt, Morocco and Tunisia). In all these countries, urban consumers are politically influential constituencies, and price inflation in basic commodities, whether staple foods or fuels, carries acute political sensitivities.

Another group of countries with discrete characteristics is a sub-set of developing countries particularly vulnerable to external price movements in agricultural commodities: small developing economies dependent on single commodity exports. These are relatively small states in the middle- and low-income groups. They are generally net food-importers, and dependent on one, or at best two, cash crops, for the bulk of their export proceeds. A few examples include the small island developing states in the Caribbean, which are heavily reliant on sugar and or banana exports, along a few sub-Saharan African states.

798 "India Basmati Rice Exports to Hit Record 4mn Tonnes," accessed 30 September 2014 (http://www.dawn.com/news/1078968).

799 WTO Doc. G/AG/NG/W/36/Rev.1, at 47.

800 Defined as those with a GNI per capita, calculated using the World Bank Atlas method, of more than $1,045 but less than $12,746 (http://data.worldbank.org/about/country-and-lending-groups).

Being 'price-takers' for both imports and exports, these countries are extremely vulnerable to exogenous price shocks in agricultural commodities. In some respects, they are hostage of the policy decisions of the large price setters.

The last category includes the LDCs, as recognised by the Economic and Social Council of the United Nations.[801] These are low-income countries suffering from severe structural impediments to sustainable development. Market infrastructures are poorly functioning, and acute supply side constraints persist. Still largely agrarian societies, in agriculture LDCs tend to exhibit a dual-structure, with a commercially-oriented export sector in cash crops and subsistence-oriented staple food production. Trade rules shall provide complete leeway for these countries to pursue agricultural stabilisation policies supportive of rural livelihood and food security.

Equitable principles call for a 'particularisation' of trade rules, accounting for these differences.

### ii) South-South Trade-offs in Agriculture

Second, traditional perceptions of S&DT for developing countries fail to acknowledge the reality of South-South interdependence. This complex interdependence can be grasped in terms of South-South export competition, import dependence, and import competition in the domestic market.

First, the right and duty of a developing country to support its peasant farmers can encroach on the right of small producers in other developing countries to compete on fair terms in third markets or at home. Take the example of long-grain, aromatic basmati. Indian export dynamism, backed by vigorous support policies, is eroding the market share of other developing countries. Indian basmati exports to the EU reportedly increased by over 30 percent in 2012–13, while exports from Pakistan to the EU dropped by about 9 percent in the same period.[802] Similar concerns have been raised in relation to India's sugar export subsidies. As producers and exporters of sugar, Colombia, El Salvador and Paraguay shared concern that subsidised exports from India could depress world prices; Pakistan and Thailand also registered concern.[803]

---

801 At the time of writing, there are 48 least-developed countries on the UN list; 34 have become WTO members. See the official list at: http://www.un.org/en/development/desa/policy/cdp/ldc/ldc_list.pdf

802 "India Surges Ahead of Pakistan in 2012–13 Basmati Rice Exports to the EU," Oryza.com, 21 May 2012 (http://www.oryza.com/content/india-surges-ahead-pakistan-2012-13-basmati-rice-exports-eu).

803 Refer to WTO Doc. G/AG/W/126 at 14–17.

On the import side, trade-offs have emerged between a developing country's right to restrict its food exports to calm domestic inflation and the legitimate expectation of poor, net food-importing countries to satisfy their vital food requirements through trade. For example, export restrictions on rice by Vietnam and India in 2007–08, coupled with aggressive buying by the Philippines, were held liable for the disastrous price spike in rice of May 2008.[804] These policies hit the interests of poor urban consumers in countries, for example, Senegal, Côte d'Ivoire, Liberia and Cameroon, which are heavily reliant on Asian rice shipments.

Finally, tensions might arise between agricultural price stabilisation policies in a developing country and the WTO-enshrined market access rights of other developing countries. Most remarkably, the two WTO disputes on variable import levies in agriculture have involved developing countries: Chile's price band scheme on wheat, wheat flour, sugar and edible vegetable oils was challenged by Argentina;[805] Peru's additional duties on certain agricultural products, such as milk, maize, rice and sugar, was disputed by Guatemala.[806]

This complex pattern of interaction can no longer be eschewed if the trade and development discourse is to regain its practical significance.

### b) *Towards Modulation and Graduation*

In light of the above, there is a need to redesign, or move beyond, the traditional notion of S&DT for developing countries. When dealing with agricultural price policies, trade rules should not only acknowledge the special situation of developing countries. They should also give legal meaning to differences that exist among developing countries. The call is for a fine-tuning of regulatory response based on distinct factual settings.

How can rights and obligations be tuned, or modulated in accordance to varying factual differences? A number of avenues for targeted solutions are available, as discussed in Cottier.[807] They involve three alternative or complementary pathways: a refining of country groups, to better reflect varying factual circumstances; variable geometry, or plurilateral approaches; and the use of thresholds for modulation and graduation.

---

804 For a detailed assessment, Slayton, above n 20.

805 *Chile – Price Band System*, above n 210.

806 *Peru – Agricultural Products*, above n 211.

807 Thomas Cottier, "From Progressive Liberalization to Progressive Regulation in WTO Law," *Journal of International Economic Law* 9, no. 4 (2006).

Under the first approach, exceptions and safety valves should be targeted and modulated through the refining of country groups, to take into account factual differences. The move is towards more country-specific S&DT provisions. This could reasonably take place when discussing a revision of the AoA disciplines on domestic support, for example.

The notion of 'variable geometry' can also serve to modulate regulatory response. It would allow certain countries to proceed at a faster pace in the liberalisation and integration process, without undermining the multilateral fabric. This approach is particularly relevant when debating more stringent disciplines on export restraints.

Finally, as suggested by Stevens[808] and articulated in Cottier,[809] the application of rules can be made dependent on specific thresholds and triggers, based on socio-economic factors. Below a threshold a member would not be bound by the pertinent rule, while reaching the threshold would trigger it. Eventually, this approach sets uniform rules for all WTO members, but "graduate them in application".[810] As pointed out by Cottier, it essentially involves the differential and progressive application of norms, the phasing in of obligations, rather than opting out and exceptions.[811] This practice is well established in trade law. Recourse to factual triggers is to become even more prominent under the Doha Development Agenda. The difficulty is which trigger or threshold to set, on the basis of which factual parameter, given the multitude of relevant facts in the circumstances of each case. These issues are explored in some detail in Section 5.2. It suffices to highlight that triggers are to be norm-specific, suitable for the purposes of a specific rule. They are to be, to the fullest possible extent, industry or product-specific, so as to give normative meaning to the varying factual matrixes of discrete agricultural commodity sectors.

All the avenues outlined above are viable pathways which can lead to more equitable outcomes. To varying extent, they all involve some degree of modulation and graduation. To be tested, they need to be worked out more explicitly in the analysis. This is what the ensuing analysis seeks to do.

---

808 Christopher Stevens, *The Future of Special and Differential Treatment (SDT) for Developing Countries in the WTO*, Institute for Development Studies, IDS Working Paper 163 (Brighton, Sussex, 2002). See also Alexander Keck and Patrick Low, *Special and Differential Treatment in the WTO: Why, When and How?* WTO Economic Research and Statistics Division, Staff Working Paper ERSD-2004-03 ([Geneva], 2004).

809 Cottier, above n 807.

810 Ibid, at 17.

811 Ibid, at 16.

## 5.2 Testing the Framework: A Reassessment of Key Trade Policy Issues in the Stabilisation Debate

The previous analysis has outlined the normative framework to be applied. It is time now to test the framework, with reference to specific issue areas. This Chapter seeks to reappraise some areas of tension between 'liberal' trade rules and commodity price stabilisation policies, in the light of the normative objectives and principles outlined in Section 5.1. The analysis reassesses, in the light of this approach, key trade policy issues at the centre of the commodity price stabilisation debate: public stockholding for food security purposes; price bands; state trading; and export restraints. Finally, it briefly considers ambiguities and gaps in trade rules applicable to ICAs, and how to bridge these gaps in the light of the principles outlined in the previous Chapter. The objective is not to exhaust these topics in their relevant dimensions. Any of them would require clinical dissection to draw off all pertinent legal issues. And certainly each would deserve separate monographic treatment, far beyond the reach of this cursory analysis. Here the objective is simply to review these topics in the light of the principles expounded in the previous Section. This will help to assess the potential and the limits of a principled approach to multilateral trade rules, in the area of commodity price policies.

### 5.2.1 *Public Food Purchases at Administered Prices*

#### 5.2.1.1 Background

In India (270 million poor, mainly rural),[812] the 2013 National Food Security Act (NFSA) has incorporated the right to food in the domestic legal order, making it a justiciable right.[813] The NFSA envisages large-scale procurement and distribution operations.[814] Eligible beneficiaries account for about 75 percent of India's rural population and 50 percent of the urban population, or two-thirds

---

812 Government of India, Planning Commission, "Press Note on Poverty Estimates, 2011–12," July 2013. The percentage of persons below the national poverty line in 2011–12 was estimated at 25.7 percent in rural areas, 13.7 percent in urban areas and 21.9 percent for the country as a whole.

813 The National Food Security Act 2013, Registered No. DL-(N)04/0007/2003-13, http://indiacode.nic.in/acts-in-pdf/202013.pdf. The act entitles every person belonging to priority households (about two-thirds of India's population) to 5 kilograms of foodgrains per person per month at specified subsidised prices from the State Government under the Targeted Public Distribution System (TPDS).

814 Possibly in tension with the second sub-paragraph of paragraph 3 of Annex 2 to the AoA, which requires that stocked volumes correspond to "determined targets related solely to food security".

of India's total population of 1.25 billion.[815] Food stocks are set up and replenished through purchases from farmers at minimum support prices (MSPs). The Food Corporation of India buys nearly one-third of all rice and wheat produced in the country at the MSP.[816] Procured quantities will be likely scaled up under the NFSA.[817]

As a result of large-scale public food purchases at support prices, India is at risk at exceeding, or has already exceeded, its product-specific *de minimis* threshold (2.6 billion $ for rice in 2013/14).[818] Other countries such as China, Pakistan, Egypt, Turkey, and the Philippines, may face similar compliance problems, particularly if they scale up their food-grain procurement and distribution systems.[819] It seems that, at least for a few large developing economies, the current flexibilities enshrined in multilateral disciplines are under strain.[820]

---

815 USDA Foreign Agricultural Service, *Indian Cabinet Approves National Food Security Bill 2013*, GAIN Report IN3037 (11 April 2013).

816 Konandreas and Mermigkas, above n 299, at 17; Avinash Kishore et al., "India's Right to Food Act: A Novel Approach to Food Security," *2013 Global Food Policy Report*, ed. in Andrew Marble and Heidi Fritschel (Washington, D.C.: International Food Policy Research Institute, 2014), 3.

817 In this direction, Kishore et al., above n 816, at 31. See also Rashmi Banga, 'Greening of Subsidies and Food Security' (presentation delivered at UNCTAD's Global Commodities Forum 2015, Geneva, 13–14 April 2015). Cf. Narayanan, above n 299, for whom current procurement levels would suffice to satisfy the NFSA requirements.

818 DTB Associates (2011), above n 299, at 33. India has notified that its support does not exceed the *de minimis* level. See India's domestic support notification for the marketing years 2004–2005 to 2010–2011, WTO document G/AG/N/IND/10 dated 10 September 2014. Some commentators have observed that the method followed by India for its notifications does not comply with the requirements of the AoA, as laid down in Annex 3, para. 9 and Article 1(h)(ii). Specifically, India uses $ denominated rupees in calculating the current AMS, while its base notification (as reported in WTO document G/AG/AGST/IND) was denominated in Indian rupees. Furthermore, the price gap is multiplied by the actually procured quantity, rather than total production. The practice used by other WTO members, as endorsed in a WTO ruling, is to use total production (see Appellate Body Report, *Korea – Various Measures on Beef*, para. 120). India would be in breach of its rice-specific *de minimis* threshold if the notification conformed to the requirements of the AoA. Cf. Narayanan, above n 299, at 7–8; DTB Associates, *Agricultural Subsidies in Key Developing Countries: November 2014 Update*, at 33; Konandreas and Mermigkas, above n 299, at 12–13.

819 DTB Associates (2011) and Konandreas and Mermigkas, above n 299.

820 A few developing countries thus call for expanded policy space in this area. They argue that public food purchases is the most suitable policy instrument at their disposal to address food security concerns, given their current level of economic development. Other countries raise concerns about the "potential distortiveness" of public stockholding schemes and about the "systemic impact" of loosening the

Should existing disciplines on domestic support be relaxed to allow more leeway for price stabilisation arrangements allegedly supportive of food and rural livelihood security, such as India's scheme? If so, where should limits be set, and how to arbitrate trade-offs?

#### 5.2.1.2 The G33 Proposal for a Comprehensive Carve-out

There are different venues to ease WTO strictures on food stockholding programmes. The first option is to comprehensively exempt developing countries' public stockholding for food security purposes from WTO domestic support disciplines. In November 2012, the G-33 coalition tabled a proposal in this direction (Box 9).[821] Under the proposal, reiterated in July 2014,[822] stockpile food purchases from peasant farmers at support prices shall not be counted as trade-distorting support. The proposal intended to 'fast-track agreement' on language already 'stabilised' in the draft Doha accord.[823] It has been noted, in this respect, that the Bali decision on stockholding for food security[824] marked a step backward from the negotiating *acquis* under the December 2008 revised draft modalities.[825] Also note, however, that the 2008 draft negotiating text on public stockholding had been tentatively agreed upon as part of a broader package of subsidy and market-access reforms. It became contentious only once taken out of this context.[826]

**Box 9: G33 proposals on public stockholding for food security**

In November 2012, the G33 tabled an informal proposal to seek flexibility for public stockholding for food security (JOB/AG/22, 13 November 2012).

---

AoA domestic support disciplines. For a review, WTO Secretariat, *Public Stockholding for Food Security purposes. Note by the Secretariat*, TN/AG/W/8 (21 January 2015).

821 Submission by the G-33, *G-33 Proposal on Some Elements of TN/AG/W/4/Rev.4 for Early Agreement to Address Food Security Issues*, JOB/AG/22 (13 November 2012).

822 Submission by the G-33, *G-33 Proposed Permanent Solution on Public Stockholding for Food Security Purposes*, JOB/AG/27 (17 July 2014).

823 December 2008 revised draft modalities, above n 65, Annex B; JOB/AG/22, above n 821, paras. 1–6.

824 WT/MIN(13)/38-WT/L/913, 11 December 2013.

825 Martin Khor, "WTO Food Fight Before and at the Bali Ministerial," *South Bulletin* 78 (2014): 5–9.

826 Christophe Bellmann, "The Bali Agreement: Implications for Development and the WTO," *International Development Policy | Revue internationale de politique de développement*, 5.2 [Online] (2014), accessed on 20 June 2015. URL: http://poldev.revues.org/1744 ; DOI: 10.4000/poldev.1744.

The proposal envisaged that "[…] acquisition of stocks of foodstuffs by developing country Members with the objective of supporting low-income or resource-poor producers shall not be required to be accounted for in the AMS" (JOB/AG/22, at 4). The proposal was intended to fast-track formal adoption of text already 'stabilised' in the December 2008 revised draft modalities (TN/AG/W/4/Rev.4). It would involve amendment to Annex 2 of the AoA (Annex 2, para. 3 and footnote 5 to para. 3).

In the run-up to Bali, the G33 circulated an unofficial 'non-paper' to further advance discussion, without prejudice to the G-33's November proposal (JOB/AG/25, 3 October 2013). The paper outlined three options to ease structures on public stockholding programmes in developing countries, for consideration by the Bali Ministerial Conference. The first option involved a redefinition of the 'external reference price' in the context of footnote 5 of Annex 2. For food security purposes, the 'external reference price' should be one of two options: a three-year average (f.o.b. or c.i.f.) based on the preceding five-year period, excluding the highest or the lowest entry; or the previous year's average producer or farmgate price in the 1 to 3 largest suppliers of a foodstuff in the country (JOB/AG/25, at 11). This proposal would involve an amendment of the AoA. The second option (adjustment for inflation) envisaged to compare the actual rate of inflation in a country with a "comparator normal rate of inflation" and adjust administrative prices based on the gap between actual and normal levels of inflation. The normative ground for inflation-adjusted figures was found in Article 18.4 of the AoA which requires WTO members to "[…] give due consideration to the influence of excessive rates of inflation on the ability of any Member to abide by its domestic support commitments" (JOB/AG/25, at 11–13). Administered prices would be reduced to the extent of 'excessive rates of inflation'. This option would likely not involve a formal amendment of the AoA, but an authoritative interpretation of the Agreement. The final option envisaged a peace clause. This would temporarily shield from legal challenge the acquisition and release at administered prices of food stocks by developing country members, provided they are undertaken with the objective of meeting food requirements of urban and rural poor in developing countries.

Eventually, an interim solution was found in Bali in the form of a peace clause, temporarily shielding certain stockpile programmes from legal action under the WTO AoA (WT/MIN(13)/38-WT/L/913, 11 December 2013).[827]

827 See above, n 305.

The Bali 'peace clause' was reaffirmed in Nairobi (WT/MIN(15)/44-WT/L/979, 19 December 2015), in the absence of consensus on a permanent solution on public stockholding for food security purposes.

Source: JOB/AG/22, 13 November 2012; JOB/AG/25, 3 October 2013; WT/MIN(13)/38-WT/L/913, 11 December 2013; WT/MIN(15)/44-WT/L/979, 19 December 2015. For a detailed narrative account: Christophe Bellmann, Jonathan Hepburn, Ekaterina Krivonos and Jamie Morrison, *G-33 Proposal: Early Agreement on Elements of the Draft Doha Accord to Address Food Security*, ICTSD Programme on Agricultural Trade and Sustainable Development, Information Note, September 2013; Konandreas and Mermigkas, above n 299.

The focus is hereafter on public stockholding for food security purposes in the context of footnote 5 to Annex 2. Yet, the broader issue involved is a mitigation of disciplines on price support, as laid down in Annex 3 to the AoA. As a matter of fact, stocking programmes for food security in developing countries are complexly interlaced with farm price stabilisation and support objectives. For example, India's procurement of food grains serves three objectives under the NFSA: setting up and replenishing strategic stocks; farm price support; and maintaining supplies under the public distribution system.[828] In practice, these objectives are complexly entangled.

Should existing disciplines on domestic support be relaxed, as advocated by the G33, to allow more leeway for price stabilisation arrangements allegedly supportive of food and rural livelihood security? Whatever the normative focus (footnote 5 to Annex 2, relating to public stockholding for food security purposes, or the AMS calculation methodology under Annex 3), there is a trade-off between two legitimate concerns: expanding policy space for farm support policies in a developing country; and minimising the risk of adverse impacts on peasant interests in another developing economy.

#### 5.2.1.3 A Reassessment in the Light of a 'Principled' Approach

Under a principled approach, arrangements to ensure stable and remunerative prices to poor farmers should in principle find legal cover and support under WTO rules.[829] In contexts of extreme rural poverty, public purchases of farm produce at set prices are an effective, though often inefficient, way to stabilise

828 Narayanan, above n 299, at 5.

829 This may involve expanded *de minimis* thresholds to meet specific needs, or exemption of defined public market intervention from AMS calculations, as envisaged in the original G33 proposal.

and support farmgate prices.[830] Equitable considerations should also play a role. As discussed, considerations of fairness, justice and reasonableness point to the need to "correct imbalances in the treatment of subsidies".[831] A relaxation of WTO strictures on public stockholding for food security would contribute to redressing imbalances. Developing countries would have broader flexibility to pursue the same price-stabilisation objectives that developed countries pursue, but through policy instruments that suit their stage of development.

However, flexibility towards rural price support and stabilisation schemes in developing countries should not be unqualified. A line of equilibrium is to be marked out between the competing rights of equally vulnerable constituencies *within* and *across* countries. This holds two corollaries.

First, to justify a departure from WTO strictures, the scheme should be genuinely pro-poor in terms of its domestic effects. In terms of producer support, public purchases from farmers should effectively target poor producers, rather than large, commercially-oriented producers. Further, interstate or inter-regional imbalance in procurement should be dealt with. Moving to the consumer end, the stocking scheme should not result in high food price inflation, to the detriment of the urban poor. The performance of the scheme should also be closely monitored to spot and correct the most frequent pathologies associated with large-scale food safety nets. Those pathologies being: poor targeting due to exclusion and inclusion errors in providing food assistance; high leakage by the diversion of procured grains to the open market; and administrative inefficiency, including corruption.[832]

Second, farm support in a developing country should not, as a side-effect, adversely affect vulnerable constituencies in other developing countries. A key

830 Certainly, in abstract terms, the same objective may be more efficiently served by less distortive alternatives such as hedging instruments, price insurance schemes, and direct payments to producers. Yet, these market-based options are comparatively costly for the peasant producer, and institutionally complex. They may not offer viable alternatives to market intervention in contexts of budgetary constraints, low human capabilities, and weak local governance. In particular, they are logistically infeasible and financially unsuitable in contexts were the targeted poor represent the vast majority of the population. In the short term, relatively more distortive but simpler schemes, such as direct public purchases from farmers at a set price, may eventually yield better results, in terms of rural livelihood improvement.

831 South Center, "The WTO's Bali Ministerial and Food Security for Developing Countries: Need for Equity and Justice in the Rules on Agricultural Subsidies" (report drawn upon discussions in two Expert Group Meetings held in 2013 on the Multilateral Trading System organised by the South Centre in the preparation of the WTO's 9th Ministerial Conference in Bali in December 2013).

832 Kishore et al., above n 816.

lesson from the CAP is that internal efforts to stabilise domestic producer prices at relatively high levels, if not coupled with output restrictions, may stimulate oversupply and result in large exportable surplus. Large-scale procurement of cereals to set up and replenish food stocks in developing economies that are also major players in the cereal trade (e.g. India and Thailand) can well result in large exportable surplus. Two pathologies are involved in this situation: overstocking and leakages. Regarding the former, in both Thailand and India, buffer stocks of rice and wheat have risen to extremely high levels under procurement and intervention schemes. If aggressively disposed of on export markets, these stocks can severely depress world market prices; displace other developing countries' exports; and, in a vicious circle, exert downward pressure on domestic farmgate prices elsewhere. Note in this respect that the end of intervention buying in Thailand in February 2014, saw an acceleration of exports, especially to Africa.[833] Leakage and corruption is a second pathology. It is estimated that, in India, 40 percent of grain channelled through the food safety net system is diverted to the open market.[834] If bought by traders and sold for export, leaked stocks end up 'dumped' on foreign markets. Any relaxation of existing disciplines on domestic support should regulate these instances of abuse. The loosening of WTO strictures on stocking programmes, and price support in general, should not give way to a 'race to the bottom' in the form of government-funded export competition between developing countries. This would be to the detriment of vulnerable communities, notably sub-Saharan countries that are trying to 'relocalise' domestic cereal production.

#### 5.2.1.4 A Balanced Trade-off

In light of the above discussion, a comprehensive carve-out of public stockholding for food security, without inbuilt policy constraints, is probably not desirable. Possible disposal of stocks in the open market via exports invites scrutiny, as it can harm farmers in other poor countries. Safeguards need to be set against abuse. The difficulty remains: how to provide leeway for domestic support, while minimising the threat of prejudice against vital interests elsewhere. Deciding where to set a line of equilibrium between competing claims is not simply a matter of weighing and balancing trade and non-trade

833 Thai exporters aggressively priced exports in order to gain market share from competitors, triggering heavy selling of white and parboiled rice to customers in Africa. Amy Reynolds (International Grains Council, London), "Recent Developments and New Challenges in Commodity Markets, and Policy Options for Commodity-based Inclusive Growth and Sustainable Development" (presentation delivered at UNCTAD's Multi-year Expert Meeting on Commodities and Development, Geneva, 15–16 April 2015).

834 Kishore et al., above n 816.

concerns. Nor are equitable constructs of distributive justice of any help. The distributional struggle is not between the poor and the relatively affluent, but between equally poor constituencies in developing countries. Thus, an alternative approach is warranted.

The approach here outlined involves a fine-tuning, or modulation of the public stockholding exemption, to make the exception coherent with the normative objectives and principles outlined in Section 5.1. What is foreseeable is a modulated approach, based on threshold criteria that reflect varying degrees of socio-economic vulnerability and trade distorting potential.[835] The approach entails various sets of disciplines, triggered by the attainment of specified thresholds, as exemplified in the diagram below (Figure 3). Rights and obligations would be tuned, or modulated in accordance with a country's factual conditions in the sector concerned. The assessment is to be sectoral, on a product by product (or product category) basis; and dynamic, to capture changes over time. Eventually, no country would be permanently locked into static boxes or categories.

In a nutshell, stockpile food purchases from peasant producers should not be counted as trade-distortive support upon two conditions. The first is that they benefit low-income and resource-poor farmers, with pro-poor effects, based on multilaterally agreed criteria of food security, livelihood security and rural development. The second is that they do not cause injury to peasant producers in equally if not more vulnerable economies, based on multilaterally agreed indicators of trade impact. The problem is to spot the relevant factual parameters on the basis of which to trigger the application of relevant rules (Box 10). The specifics of these indicators, it is suggested, should not be defined in the WTO context. They should be worked out elsewhere, in more suitable, sector-specific and development-oriented fora.[836] These include the

835 For a comprehensive review of approaches to modulate trade rules based on factual parameters, Cottier, above n 807. Recourse to factual parameters to modulate trade rules is not new in agriculture. A notable example is the *de minimis* threshold of trade-distorting domestic support, set at 10 percent of the value of agriculture for most developing countries. Beyond this threshold, domestic support disciplines do not apply. The threshold is used to modulate the application of the law. Another example is the illustrative list of indicators for the designation of special products, subject to gentler tariff cuts as being negotiated under the Doha Round (Annex F of December 2008 revised draft modalities, above n 65). Criteria of food security, livelihood security and rural development are there used to mitigate trade liberalisation commitments, by means of modulations in the rules, rather than in their application.

836 For a detailed discussion of, in Foltea's words, the various "linking techniques" available ("deference", "incorporation", "co-operation and observership", and "the right to seek information"), see Foltea, above n 54, Chapter 2.

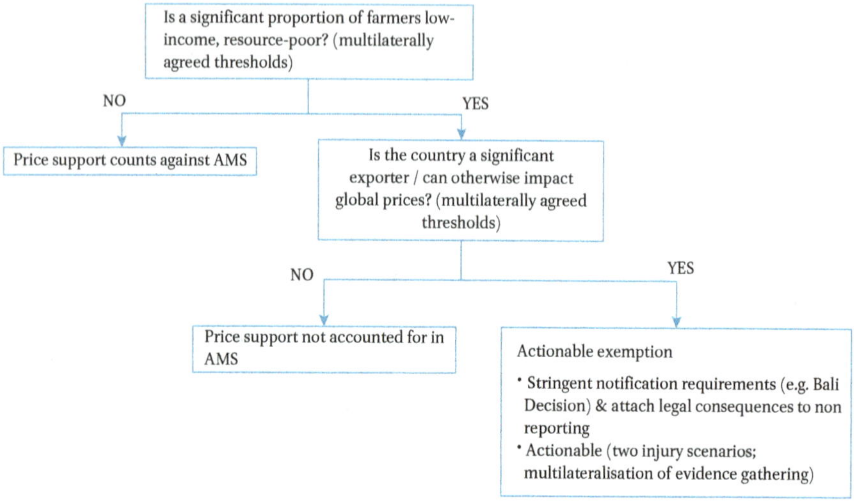


FIGURE 3 *A modulated approach to the public stockholding for food security exception*
SOURCE: ELABORATED BY THE AUTHOR.

intergovernmental development bodies, for product-specific thresholds, as well as UNCTAD, the FAO and the ILO. This would be a way to move the political confrontation on agricultural commodities out of the WTO, while preserving its role as the key negotiating forum.

### Box 10: Thresholds and triggers to modulate the AoA domestic support disciplines

For agriculture as a whole, Stevens identifies a combination of three criteria to modulate the application of the AoA domestic support disciplines, under a revised AoA: daily per capita calorie intake of less than 2,500 calories; agriculture accounting for over 20 percent of GDP; and agricultural exports not exceeding 0.25 percent of world exports.[837] Beyond these thresholds, countries will have lee-way to support their farm sector. Exceeding the threshold will trigger the application of domestic support disciplines. Other criteria and indicators can be used to trigger the application of domestic support provisions. For example, relevant indicators of agricultural dependence may be specified in terms of employment shares in agriculture, as a percentage of total employment. This will serve to include countries where agriculture

837 Stevens, above n 808, at 20 and Cottier, above n 807.

is largely subsistence oriented and still absorbs the bulk of the labour force, while accounting for a small share of GDP. For product-specific thresholds, a requirement may be that a specified proportion of the rural labour force is employed in the sub-sector, either in a particular region or at the national level. Indicators of vulnerability may include reference to farming structures as being subsistence-oriented, and income levels showing incidence of poverty in the sector or sub-sector. Indicators which assess the potential to disrupt trade or cause injury to peasant producers elsewhere could include competitiveness indexes and/or trade share, whether sector-wide or for specific products. More stringent export share thresholds may be adopted for staple foods than for export cash crops, as cereals raise more serious concerns about surplus disposal on foreign markets than, say, cocoa. In all cases, it is important to combine two sets of indicators, i.e. domestic socio-economic vulnerability and threat of injury.

Three sets of disciplines would be triggered by the attainment of specified thresholds.

When food is procured from competitive, commercial oriented producers, based on multilaterally agreed thresholds, the price support component, if any, should be required to be accounted for in the AMS.

When the sector exhibits high socio-economic vulnerability and there is limited threat of injury to peasant interests elsewhere, based on established threshold criteria, purchases at support prices from small farmers should not be counted as trade-distorting support (AMS).

When the criteria that indicate socio-economic vulnerability are met, but the country is a significant exporter of the product concerned or can otherwise influence global prices, the exemption would need to be made 'actionable'. The following disciplines would apply.

To benefit from the exemption, a country should establish a twofold rebuttable presumption. First, the public stockholding programme effectively target poor farmers without hindering the interests of poor consumers. Second, the programme must not stimulate overproduction, disposed of in the open market, in a way prejudicial to peasant interests in other poor countries.[838]

838 The Bali decision on public stockholding for food security has moved in the above direction, by introducing the obligation for the benefiting country not to "distort trade or adversely affect the food security of other Members" (World Trade Organization, Ministerial Decision of 7 December 2013, WT/MIN(13)/38, WT/L/913, para. 4). The reach of this

The exempted public stockholding scheme should thus be subject to stringent notification and transparency requirements on the benefiting member. These requirements should be very much in line with those specified in the Bali decision on public stockholding for food security (Annex and Statistical Appendix).[839] Given poor compliance with notification obligations to the WTO Committee on Agriculture, some legal consequence must be attached to lack of notification. Failure to notify could trigger a presumption of WTO-inconsistency of the scheme. Otherwise, the WTO judiciary could be instructed to "draw adverse inferences from instances of non- cooperation" in a subsequent injury case.[840] Lack of cooperation would then trigger a relaxation of the applicant's burden of proof in a subsequent injury investigation,[841] and some reversal of the *in dubio pro reo* principle.

If 'injury' is claimed, the burden of proof would then move to the claiming party, which would need to counter or refute the claimed consistency. This would imply that the public stockholding scheme is assessed simultaneously under the AoA and the ASCM. Yet, only some of the ASCM disciplines would apply. In particular, the only relevant injury considered should be to peasant farmers in other poor countries or disadvantaged regions. The poverty assessment should be based on objective criteria of food and rural livelihood security spelt

anti-circumvention safeguard is, however, unclear. On the export side, it means no surplus dumping on foreign markets. The focus is here on the disposal on foreign markets of exportable surpluses generated by the stocking programme. On the import side, it could mean that domestic food stockpile programmes in one country cannot jeopardise the WTO-enshrined market access rights of countries trying to compete in the subsidising country's domestic market. In this author's view, the anticircumvention provision should be more narrowly framed, in two respects. First, the focus should be on the export side of the trade equation. The scheme should be tolerated, if it only causes displacement of imports to the market of the subsidiser, thus raising market access, rather than export competition issues. Second, it should be 'actionable' by other developing countries only. The obligation for the 'stabiliser' is not to hinder the rural livelihood and food security of other poor countries. If the stocking schemes causes prejudice to commercial interests in the advanced economies, it should however be permissible, on equitable grounds.

839 World Trade Organization, Ministerial Decision of 7 December 2013 on Public Stockholding for Food Security Purposes, WT/MIN(13)/38, WT/L/913.

840 As provided for under para. 7 of Annex V of the ASCM.

841 Under the ASCM, the burden of proof on the applicant is rather cumbersome. In particular, to initiate a countervailing duty investigation (unilateral track), the applicant shall provide "sufficient evidence of the existence of (a) a subsidy and, if possible, its amount, (b) injury within the meaning of Article VI of GATT 1994 as interpreted by this Agreement, and (c) a causal link between the subsidised imports and the alleged injury. Simple assertion, unsubstantiated by relevant evidence, cannot be considered sufficient to meet the requirements of this paragraph" (ASCM, Article 11.2).

out in multilaterally agreed guidelines. Furthermore, only two injury scenarios should be foreseeable: a displacement of peasant exports from the affected country to a third country;[842] or enhanced competition at home, in the domestic market of the claiming party.[843] The examination of trade diversion (first injury scenario) would typically include evidence about a change in relative market shares to the detriment of the non-subsidizer.[844] A determination of the second case (injury at home, to import-competing small producers) should be based on such factual parameters as increase in imports, in absolute terms or relative to production and consumption, or price undercutting in the domestic economy.[845] Injury in terms of displaced imports to the subsidising member should not qualify for remedial action, if the scheme is genuinely targeted at relieving rural poverty. It is somewhat assumed here that, in context of rural deprivation, poor peasant producers have a prior claim on the domestic market, and deserve protection.

To ease the burden of proof on small developing countries, the information-gathering process should be facilitated and multilateralised, to the fullest possible extent. A number of avenues to this effect are provided for under the ASCM Annex V procedure.[846] In particular, “where information is unavailable due to non-cooperation by the subsidising and/or third-country Member, the panel may complete the record as necessary relying on best information otherwise available”.[847] The DSB could designate a representative “to serve the function of facilitating the information-gathering process”.[848] Finally, a Group of Experts composed of highly qualified, independent experts could be established to assist the panel.[849] This Group of Experts would perform the market and price analysis and provide advisory opinion as to the existence of injury.

842 This is one of the instances where “serious prejudice” may arise under the ASCM (Article 6.3(b)). To deal with this type of injury, the ASCM establishes a multilateral remedy track (Article 7 of the ASCM).

843 Under the ASCM, “material injury” to the domestic industry (Article 5(a)) – which may trigger remedial action under the unilateral, countervailing duty track (Arts. 10–23 of the ASCM).

844 Patterned after Article 6.4 ASCM.

845 Drawing on Article 15.2 ASCM.

846 ASCM Annex V: Procedures for Developing Information Concerning Serious Prejudice. The issue of appointing a DSB representative to facilitate the information-gathering process, pursuant to the Annex V procedures under the ASCM, had been invoked by Brazil in its panel request in the *United States – Subsidies on Upland Cotton* case.

847 Annex V, para. 6.

848 Annex V, para. 4.

849 ASCM Article 24.3.

The approach outlined in this Section may provide inroad for price stabilisation arrangements in large emerging economies that face pressing rural poverty and food security concerns, such as India. At the same time, it would set safeguards to guard against abuse. The negative elements are the complexities and the burdensome nature of injury investigations, which place a heavy burden of proof on small and vulnerable economies. As mentioned, this burden could be eased if the information-gathering process were facilitated and multilateralised. Questions, however, would remain as to the political viability of this approach, which could antagonise developing countries that have different political leverage – small, vulnerable economies and large emerging ones.

### 5.2.2 *Price Band Systems (PBS)*

#### 5.2.2.1 Background

Tariffs have been extensively used to cushion the domestic effects of external price variations; and remain an attractive tool to manage price volatility in developing countries.[850] They are relatively easy to administer, and do not involve budgetary outlay commitments, unlike direct transfers and other social protection policies. Note also that most poor countries have *de jure* flexibility to manage tariffs without renegotiating tariff bindings. Applied tariff rates in many developing countries tend to be significantly below bound levels, which allows leeway to counter import price variations via managed tariffs.[851]

Among managed tariffs, PBS are a particularly interesting tool. They share similarities with variable import levies and minimum import prices. Yet, they

850 As briefly outlined in Chapter 2, managed tariffs for price-stabilisation purposes cover different options. Under variable import levies, tariffs are adjusted upward to offset a decrease in import prices, and downward to counter import price increases. Variable import tariffs are triggered by import price movements relative to domestic prices (domestic market prices or administratively set reference prices). Managed tariffs are also at the heart of price band schemes, widely used in the past to establish price floors and ceiling on import prices: when import prices drop below a lower threshold, a surcharge is applied; when they exceed an upper band price, importers receive a rebate. Price bands are typically based on international prices recorded in the most relevant markets and compare historic (a moving average, a base-period price average, or other) and current market prices.

851 In practice, when tariff bindings are set above actual tariff levels, tariffs can be freely adjusted – upward or downward – within bound ceilings. In fact, the spread between applied and bound tariffs ('water', or 'tariff overhang') allows countries to 'manage' their tariffs without renegotiating tariff bindings.

are structurally different. They are set in relation to world prices and do not involve domestic price parameters. Furthermore, their proscription is largely a matter of judicial interpretation (see above, Section 2.3.3.3). They may possibly find legal cover under a different interpretation of WTO rules which is more flexible, and purposive, as discussed in Section 5.3.

Price bands have been found to be WTO-inconsistent in two WTO cases.[852] Questions arise as to the desirability of this comprehensive proscription. Should price bands be banned *per se*, even if transparent and predictable for traders, and relatively effective in containing import price fluctuations within a reasonable margin? In this author's view, the answer is no. There are caveats and qualifications, though, as discussed in the following Section.

#### 5.2.2.2 A Principled Approach

There is here a complex trade-off between liberal trade commitments and legitimate domestic policy concerns. More concretely, what is at stake is the sensitive balancing between WTO-enshrined market access rights, and the right to pursue price stabilisation policies in the importing country. The line of equilibrium is here marked out in favour of the 'stabiliser', that is, the importing country, if the scheme is transparent and genuinely pro-poor (as discussed below). Indeed, if transparent and predictable in their setting and operation, price bands will not nullify market access rights; they will simply make the computation of the import levy more cumbersome. In this authors' view, this is a cost that can be paid, to ensure a reasonable margin of price fluctuations. This is particularly the case when imports are sourced from high income countries. Commodity price stabilisation in vulnerable economies justifies some interference with developed economies' commercial interests. Note also that the 'pathology' involved is that PBS, if not transparent and not predictable, may restrict imports, as exporters are less likely to ship to a market if they cannot reasonably predict the applicable import duties. The key issue is how to ensure that PBS are fully transparent and predictable in their design and operation, not the existence of the PBS *per se*.

Thus, a principled approach to WTO law would encourage a relaxation of the (judicial) prohibition of price bands systems. However, the permissibility of PBS is to be narrowly qualified, to guard against abuse and favour a balanced trade-off. Which mechanisms must then be introduced to guard against abuse? Some lines of approach are outlined below.

852 *Chile – Price Band System*, above n 210 and *Peru – Agricultural Products*, above n 211.

### 5.2.2.3 A Balanced Trade-off

In this author's view, price bands should be permissible if they are:

1. Supportive of food and rural livelihood security in contexts of socio-economic vulnerability;
2. Transparent and predictable, in their setting and operation;
3. Within bound ceilings (*ad valorem*+specific PBS duty);
4. Subject to monitoring and surveillance.

The first requirement involves the pro-poor finality of the price band scheme. Its purpose should be to stabilise sectors designated as 'special' based on multilaterally agreed criteria of food security and rural livelihood. This involves identifying adequate criteria of socio-economic vulnerability and dependence that trigger the applicability of the exemption. Relevant factors should include a country income level and the socio-economic sensitivity of the protected sector. The assessment should be based on multilaterally agreed criteria of food security, livelihood security and rural development, as outlined for staple foods in Annex F of the December 2008 revised draft modalities.[853]

Under the second requirement, the PBS upper and lower thresholds as well as the reference price should be fully transparent and predictable. Traders should be put in the position to calculate for themselves all the price parameters and the duty rebates and surcharges. No margin for administrative discretion should be left to the importing country's customs authority. International agencies may develop model price band schemes, transparent and predictable, to the fullest possible extent minimally trade-distortive. These may serve as an international standard that triggers a rebuttable presumption of conformity with WTO law.[854] Note that the Panel in *Chile – Price Band System* somewhat introduced obligations of transparency and predictability when interpreting Article 4.2 of the AoA and Article II:1(b) of the GATT.[855] Eventually, Chile's

---

853 December 2008 revised draft modalities, above n 65.

854 Patterned after the WTO TBT Agreement. On the use of standards in the TBT Agreement, Erik Wijkström and Devin McDaniels, "International Standards and the WTO TBT Agreement: Improving Governance for Regulatory Alignment," WTO, Economic Research and Statistics Division, Staff Working Paper ERSD-2013-06 (Geneva, 2013).

855 As discussed in Box 5, the operation of the Chilean PBS was characterised by a considerable lack of transparency and predictability. Both the Panel and the Appellate Body placed considerable importance on the "intransparent and unpredictable way in which the Band operated" (Appellate Body Report, *Chile – Price Band System*, above n 210, paras. 266–250; see also Panel Report, *Chile – Price Band System*, above n 210, para. 7.44). As stated by the Appellate Body in *Chile – Price Band System*, "[v]ariable import levies have

price band system was not found to be inconsistent with the AoA as such, but because it exhibited features that frustrated the purpose of Article 4.2.[856]

The third requirement is relatively uncontroversial: the combination of the *ad valorem* and PBS duty should not exceed the tariff rate bound for the product concerned in a member's schedule. As discussed, in most developing countries the spread between applied and bound tariffs, the 'water', or 'tariff overhang', is significant, which allows countries to increase their applied tariffs without renegotiating tariff bindings.

Under the fourth requirement, a member implementing a PBS should: notify the measure to the WTO Committee on Agriculture; provide all technical details about how the applicable PBS values and reference prices are arrived at; provide and continue to provide, on annual basis, statistical information about import flows under the price band. The member concerned should establish a *prima facie* case that the effect of the PBS is not to significantly displace or impede imports into its market. The Committee on Agriculture should monitor and evaluate the information submitted.

### 5.2.3 *Commodity Marketing Boards*

#### 5.2.3.1 Background

State-regulated marketing systems are still common in a number of developing countries. A few have a significant role in the orderly marketing of peasant crops. Ghana's Cocoa Board, for example, plays an important stabiliser role, with respect to intra- and inter-season prices.[857] The same holds true for STEs for the marketing of smallholder crops in India.

As briefly discussed (Section 2.3.3), WTO law recognises a member's right to establish and maintain STEs, including trade monopolies. Yet, STEs are regulated in their potential for circumventing key WTO disciplines. Regulatory holes and loopholes remain, as recalled earlier. More fundamentally, the risk that members evade their liberal trade commitments through STEs is high,

---

additional features that undermine the object and purpose of Article 4, which is to achieve improved market access conditions for imports of agricultural products by permitting only the application of ordinary customs duties. These additional features include a lack of transparency and a lack of predictability in the level of duties that will result from such measures. This lack of transparency and this lack of predictability are liable to restrict the volume of imports" (Appellate Body Report, *Chile – Price Band System*, above n 210, para. 234).

856 Note, however, that in another case on variable levies (*Peru – Agricultural Products*, above n 211) the Panel stated that lack of transparency and predictability is not a separate characteristic that a variable import levy must have.

857 See above, Box 7 and n 251.

whatever the regulatory safeguards set. Some of these holes and loopholes would be closed if the draft Doha disciplines were formally approved.

As outlined in Section 2.3, the discipline being negotiated in the Doha framework, as laid down in the December 2008 revised draft modalities, would set relatively stringent disciplines on agricultural exporting STEs. If approved, the new rules would preclude the granting of trade monopoly powers to STEs, as well as their government financing, direct or indirect. As mentioned, to preserve policy space for development, the draft modalities envisage significant S&DT for developing countries. Most significantly, the draft provisions involve a fine-tuning of the concept of S&DT for developing countries, by setting economic thresholds for the application of specific rules, and by modulating the rules according to specific socio-economic objectives.

**Box 11: Envisaged S&DT for developing countries' STEs under the draft modalities**

> Agro-STEs in developing countries shall be permitted to maintain or use export monopoly powers if: (i) they enjoy special privileges to preserve domestic consumer price stability and to ensure food security; or (ii) the entity's share of world exports of the product or products concerned does not exceed 5 percent in three consecutive years; or (iii) they are based in LDCs or SVEs.[858]

Would the new disciplines provide enough lee-way for price-stabilising STEs in developing countries? Note, in this respect, that a scheme such as the one implemented by Ghana's Cocoa Board (forward cocoa selling through the board's trading arm, Ghana's Cocoa Marketing Company (CMC)),[859] would not easily find legal cover under the envisaged exceptions. Ghana is not an LDC or a SVE. The CMC does not enjoy special trading rights "to preserve domestic consumer price stability and to ensure food security" as cocoa is an export cash crop, not a food staple. Finally, the CMC's share of world cocoa exports well exceeds the 5 percent threshold, as CMC controls the bulk of Ghana's cocoa exports, accounting for about 20 percent of world cocoa exports.

The key issue is how to provide leeway for such schemes as Ghana CMC one, compel adequate targeting, and limit systemic impacts on poor constituencies elsewhere. There is here a complex trade-off between the pursuit of rural livelihood strategies at home, and livelihood concerns elsewhere, beyond the border.

---

858 December 2008 revised draft modalities, above n 65, Annex K, paras. 4–6.

859 For details, see above n 251.

#### 5.2.3.2 A Balanced Trade-off

In this author's view, the envisaged disciplines move in the right direction, by determining the application of S&DT on the basis of relevant socio-economic factors and objectives. Yet, they overlook some relevant factual distinctions that may help to better target exceptions. Relevant facts include the direction of trade flows (South–North *versus* South-South) and patterns of trade specialisation (staple foods *versus* cash crops). A line, in particular, is to be drawn between traditional cash crop exports which are, generally, South–North, and trade in staple food commodities which tend to be South-South and North–South. This distinction is somewhat artificial, as the operations of agro-STEs could well cut across product lines. Relaxed disciplines for one but not the other segment would raise issues of cross-subsidisation. Yet, particularly in developing countries, there are discernible patterns of state trading in agriculture, which reflects high degree of trade specialisation.

##### a) *Non-Staple Export Crops (North–South)*

In the author's view, existing WTO flexibilities should be preserved for agro-STEs that market peasant cash crops. This is with regard to the granting of trade monopoly powers to agro-STEs, their government financing, guarantees, preferential access to capital or other special privileges. The envisaged S&DT provisions under the Doha draft modalities (paras. 4–6 of Annex K)[860] should be expanded accordingly. Yet, this broader exemption is to be made conditional on a number of factual criteria.

First, the product which is exported by such an enterprise is not a predominant staple in the traditional diet of developing countries and has not been designated as 'special' in LDCs or SVEs based on criteria of food security.

Second, the production base for the product in question consists of scattered, small-scale and resource-poor producers (peasant farmers).

Third, the special privileges granted are reasonably necessary and effective to achieve any of the following objectives: counter market asymmetries between peasant farmers and buyers; redress other market imperfections such as serious trade infrastructure deficiencies; or stabilise prices, at least intra-year.[861]

---

860 December 2008 revised draft modalities, above n 65.

861 In a context of scattered peasant farmers and far more concentrated buyers, STE 'pooling' farm produce can serve to counter market asymmetries. Second, where hard (e.g. storage facilities or feeder roads) and soft (e.g. credit and market information) infrastructure are poorly developed, STE can increase operational efficiency (e.g. through economies of scale). STEs are also well positioned to effectively stabilise producer prices through the marketing year (through physical forward selling or financial hedging), and possibly

Fourth, the exemption does not provide room for rent-seeking behaviours by large bureaucracies, with limited pass through of benefits to peasant farmers. In particular, there must be some evidence that a 'fair' share of the f.o.b. price is passed through to producers.

These claims would need to be substantiated with data on marketing structures and trade statistics, alongside time series on f.o.b. prices, STE operating costs, domestic marketing costs, and taxes (all costs to be deducted from the f.o.b. price to work back to the farmgate price). This is to ensure that possibly costly exemptions do not simply provide leeway, as in the past, for inefficient, rent-seeking bureaucracies, at the expense of producers.

When the above factual circumstances exist, agricultural exporting STEs in developing countries which enjoy special privileges shall be permitted to maintain these privileges.

### b) *Agro-STEs in Staple Foods* (*South-South*)

Different issues arise in staple food commodities, particularly in the context of South-South trade. As discussed, many vulnerable economies are seeking to 'relocalise' food production, at least to some extent. The objective is to reduce 'excessive' reliance on imports by stepping-up domestic production. Against this background, it becomes critical to curb all forms of export subsidies that distort trade in food commodities.

Developing countries' STEs are key players in staple food trade, particularly in the rice trade. For example, about half of Viet Nam's rice exports are exported by two state-owned enterprises; one of the two retains exclusive supplier status for government-to-government contracts.[862] In China, two exporting STEs[863] account for the bulk of Chinese maize and rice exports, 98 percent and 80 percent, respectively in 2002. These exports are increasingly destined to developing countries, including the least developed.

Government financing of agricultural exporting STEs, by reducing the STEs operational costs, may act as a 'hidden' export subsidy. This may in turn impact

---

between years (variable export taxes/buffer funds). Trade rules should acknowledge STE potential role to compensate for the greater incidence of market failure in developing countries. In this direction, FAO, *FAO Papers on Selected Issues Relating to the WTO Negotiations on Agriculture* (Rome 2002), at 94; Abbott, above n 243, at 706.

862 Vietnam Northern Food Corporation (Vinafood1) and the Vietnam Southern Food Corporation (Vinafood2). Source: USDA Foreign Agricultural Service, *Vietnam Grain and Feed Annual 2013*, GAIN Report Number VN3016 (3 April 2013).

863 China National Cereals, Oil and Foodstuff Import and Export Co. (Group) and Jilin Grain Group Import and Export Co. See WTO Doc. G/STR/N/9/CHN/Add.1.

the competitive relationship with exporters from other developing countries or with producers in importing countries. Eventually, measures intended to serve peasant interests in one developing country would hit the interests of other peasant farmers in equally vulnerable, if not more vulnerable, economies.

In the light of these considerations, even agricultural exporting STEs in developing countries should be subject to more stringent rules on subsidisation as envisaged in the Draft Modalities. This should be the case if the STE is a significant exporter of agricultural products that are predominant staples in the traditional diet of developing countries; and the exporting STE's share of world exports of the product concerned is significant, that is, above 5 percent.

### 5.2.4 *Export Restrictions*

#### 5.2.4.1 Background

The regulation of export restraints raises particularly intractable trade-offs. As summarised by Baris Karapiner, it is controversial whether export restrictions represent an instance of "under- regulation" or "regulatory deficiency" in WTO law, or whether they provide some "unintended policy space", to correct market failures and promote environmental sustainability and inter-generational equity.[864]

On the one hand, export restrictions have been challenged as a beggar-thy-neighbour policy that 'dumps' on others the costs of domestic policy choices. Export restraints on staple food commodities came to prominence as one of the key drivers of price spikes during 2007–11.[865] There is broad consensus among analysts that export restrictions by large exporters at least magnified, if not triggered, price movements in food commodity markets.[866] They have also

864 Baris Karapinar, *Export Restrictions and the WTO Law: 'Regulatory Deficiency' or 'Unintended Policy Space'*, NCCR Trade Working Papers, no. 2010/11 ([Bern], 2010).

865 Export restrictions on basic commodities had been widely used in the 1970s, in the 1995–2002 period and during the 2003–09 in an effort to 'dampen' domestic price rises at times of inflation (Anania, above n 223). They came to prominence again during the 2007–08 and 2010–11 price crises, when many countries restricted their food exports with quotas or taxes in a bid to calm escalating domestic prices. See also Sharma, above n 1, and Sharma and Konandreas above n 657, at 8. The use of export restrictions is not confined to agricultural markets: export tariffs and quotas have been widely used in key mineral markets for industrial policy, price defence or conservation purposes. A notable example is China's use of restraints on the exportation of various forms of minerals and metals. This policy was challenged twice under the WTO DSU, in 2009 (*China – Raw Materials*) and 2012 (*China – Rare Earths*). See Espa, above n 326.

866 Sharma and Konandreas, above n 657, at 17–20.

been defined as a major source of market distortions and welfare losses, and as neither efficient nor effective in pursuing their alleged policy objectives.[867]

On the other hand, export restrictions can and have been used by resource-rich countries to attain a number of legitimate domestic policy objectives. These include: export prices stabilisation, particularly using variable export taxes and stabilisation funds; supply management via export quotas, minimum export prices, and restrictive export licensing; revenue generation, particularly for countries that rely on indirect taxes rather than the taxation of income for revenue purposes; stimulate local processing and value addition, or offset tariff escalation and restore the exporter's competitiveness; the conservation of exhaustion natural resources; and a number of other purposes.[868] From a public international law perspective, behind their use lies the principle of State permanent sovereignty over natural resources, and particularly,

> [...] the need for developing countries to utilize their resources for their development in the most optimal manner as considered appropriate by them, including processing of their raw materials, setting up industries to diversify their economies and ensuring supplies to domestic industries.[869]

Such policy goals may justify the welfare losses associated with export restraints.

As a stabilisation device, export restrictions[870] are a double-edged sword. They can destabilise global prices, in a bid to calm domestic price rises at

867 In this direction, OECD, *Export Restrictions in Raw Materials Trade: Facts, Fallacies and Better Practices* (OECD, 2014).

868 WTO Secretariat, *Export Restrictions and Charges*, MTN.GNG/NG2/W/40 (8 August 1989), at 1–2.

869 Statement by the Delegation of India, Multilateral Trade Negotiations Group Framework, General Agreement on Tariffs and Trade, MTN/FR/W/23 (6 April 1979).

870 Export restraints encompass a variety of trade policy instruments. For regulatory purposes, a line is drawn between export taxes and non-tax export restraints. Export taxes include a range of tax instruments, including: ordinary export taxes, whether expressed as fixed amount per quantity exported (specific) or charged as percentage of the price (*ad valorem*); variable export taxes, where the applied rate varies with the world market price (i.e. higher the world price, higher the tax); differential export taxes, whereby processed products are taxed at a lower rate than a primary product. "Non-tax export restraints" is a residual category that includes all other restraints on exports, including: minimum export prices, when no export is allowed below the set minimum price; restrictive export licensing; export quotas, indicating the maximum amount of the product that is allowed to be

times of rising inflation or perceived shortages. These trade-offs should be taken into account when designing more stringent disciplines on export restrictions.

#### 5.2.4.2 A Principled Approach

Are stricter disciplines on export restrictions desirable to restrain policies that exacerbate commodity price volatility and hinder vital interests in the most vulnerable countries? The answer is a complex one.

Certainly, more stringent disciplines are welcome to inhibit export restraints that adversely impact the food security position of the most vulnerable countries. The use of these policy instruments is not a matter of domestic discretion. Export restrictions can severely impact other countries, and call for multilateral governance. Multilateral concerns are particularly acute, with regard to food export restraints, as these unilateral measures risk jeopardising the food security interests of other countries.

Yet, tightened disciplines on export restraints should not 'cancel out' the flexibility commodity-dependent developing countries have to leverage their resource base for developmental purposes. Liberal trading principles should not nullify or impair the right to pursue legitimate revenue, industrial and price stabilisation objectives in developing economies.

Eventually, new provisions should inhibit the use of export restraints that adversely impact the food security position of the most vulnerable countries; while leaving leeway for their use as a key policy tool for price stabilisation, revenue generation, and economic diversification in low and middle income countries. The approach endorsed is thus a nuanced one, with gradations in tone. Ultimately, what is at stake is the sensitive balancing of competing rights; and differentiation of solutions, due account being taken for distinct factual differences across countries. The regulatory model involved is differential and progressive, as detailed below.

#### 5.2.4.3 A Balanced Trade-off

Tightened disciplines of export restraints should be highly differentiated and progressive. Beside this is the idea of modulation in the rules and in the application of the rules, using thresholds based on socio-economic criteria.[871] Drawing from other areas of regulation, what is foreseeable is a 'traffic light'

exported; and export ban or prohibition. As reviewed in Sharma, these various instruments are frequently combined, both sequentially and concurrently. Sharma, above n 1.

871 For a discussion, Cottier, above n 807.

approach, entailing three sets of disciplines for different country categories (green, yellow and red), triggered by the attainment of specified thresholds. Threshold criteria should reflect varying degrees of socio-economic vulnerability to domestic food shortages and price inflation, as well as varying impacts on other countries.

a) *Green Category*

Green countries should include poor, food-insecure countries with high socio-economic vulnerability to perceived shortages or rising food price inflation. They should also pose minimal risk to impact global food prices through export restrictions. Relevant indicators may include specified income levels and/or per capita calorie intake. They can be construed based on FAO undernourishment indicators, World-Bank income thresholds, UNDP poverty indexes, or a combination of them. In addition, the country's export share of the restrained product should be below a specified threshold, for example below 5 percent. Countries below the specified thresholds should have unconstrained flexibility to restrain food exports.

b) *Yellow Category*

Yellow countries should include 'significant' exporters of the product concerned (e.g. above the 5 percent threshold) that still show socio-economic vulnerability to domestic food price shocks. Relevant indicators of vulnerability may include a combination of the following: World Bank income thresholds for low and lower-middle income economies, possibly also for upper-middle income economies; poverty thresholds along national lines; and percentages of undernourished population or per capita calorie intake. The inclusion thresholds may take different values, depending on how broad the category is meant to be.

These countries should exercise utmost restraint in restricting shipments, as their unilateral action would almost inevitably entail repercussions beyond the border. This holds particularly true when exports are destined to food-insecure countries in the low or lower-middle income category. Yet, they should be given some degree of flexibility to restrain food exports in a bid to calm escalating domestic prices, or at least to appease political tensions at home about escalating domestic food prices.

For these categories of countries, new disciplines on export restraints ought to be flexibly framed in terms of purpose and product coverage, as well as techniques.

The rationale for tightened regulation should be global food security concerns; not economic concerns about the use of export restraints for competitive advantage or supply management.[872] Accordingly, new, tightened disciplines should only cover export restrictions on staple food commodities that are predominant staples in the traditional diet of developing countries. This leaves out of scope most export cash crops from developing countries, including: agricultural raw materials (e.g. natural rubber, fibres, and tobacco); oilseeds (e.g. palm oil used in the domestic biodiesel industry); as well the tropical beverages (e.g. cocoa, coffee, and tea). As mentioned, in these non-staple product areas all but the most advanced economies should preserve their right to use export taxes, including differential export taxes (DETS), for price support and stabilisation, revenue generation or industrial development purposes.

In terms of procedural requirements, export restrictions on foodstuffs would need to be justified on stringent factual basis (production, stocks and domestic consumption data) to substantiate the 'critical shortage' requirement in GATT Article XI. Some negotiating proposals have moved in this direction,[873] well beyond what is called for in the draft Doha text.[874]

In terms of substantive disciplines, the objective would be to secure a minimum flow of goods and increase policy predictability, while allowing some leeway for export taxes and 'emergency measures'. Some negotiating proposals have moved in this direction. For example, Japan has proposed to: replace export prohibitions and restrictions with export taxes in a sort of 'tariffication' of export restrictions; bind their level; and establish quotas in which

---

872 Accordingly, negotiating proposals should not juggle too many things at once. In particular, they should not equate food security concerns and competitiveness concerns, as in the US reform proposal submitted to the WTO Committee on Agriculture (Submission from the United States, *Proposal for Comprehensive Long-Term Agricultural Trade Reform*, G/AG/NG/W/15 (23 June 2000)).

873 An informal paper was circulated on this subject in April 2008 by Japan and Switzerland. As reviewed in Sharma, new export restrictions would need to be justified on stringent factual basis (based on production, stocks and domestic consumption data). Further, due consideration to importers' food security concerns would include counterfactual analysis of how trade would have flowed absent the restriction. Finally, tightened procedural requirements should include prior notification to the WTO Committee on Agriculture, a standstill requirement pending consultation, and the possibility to defer the proposed export restriction to binding arbitration (see Sharma, above n 1, at 22).

874 The latest draft negotiating text disciplines (2008 December revised draft modalities) do not add much to what already exists. The restricting country would be required to: notify to the WTO (Committee on Agriculture) within 90 days of the coming into force; consult with concerned countries, upon request; apply export restraints temporarily (no longer than a year, unless affected countries consent) (December 2008 revised draft modalities, above n 65, paras. 171–80).

a certain amount of restricted exports will be exempt from the export tax.[875] Temporary and short-term measures to restrict exports under 'emergency measures' would still be allowed; yet, the restricting country would maintain the proportion of exports to domestic production at specified levels.[876] In essence, this amounts to a 'tax-rate quota' (TxRQ) regime, similar to the current tariff-rate quota on imports.[877] As discussed in Sharma, an alternative to TxRQ could be a variable export tax scheme, whereby tariffs vary automatically with the moving averages of world market prices.[878]

Finally, a number of transactions would need to be exempted from the imposition of export restrictions. The international community has moved towards the principle of exemption of 'humanitarian' food shipments, including purchases by the World Food Programme (WFP), from export restrictions.[879]

---

875 Negotiating Proposal by Japan, WTO Doc. G/AG/NG/W/91 (21 December 2000), at 15, para. 32.

876 Ibid, para. 33, at 15–16.

877 Sharma, above n 1, at 23–24. As outlined by Sharma, the quota would be based on past exports, a fixed average for a base period or a moving average, or 75 percent of that if not 100 percent; the in-quota tax could be the average export tax applied in recent years, but no more than 40 percent; the over-quota tax could be set at twice the in-quota rate, or about 80 percent.

878 Patterned after the Indonesian progressive tax regime for palm oil, or Argentinian sliding tax scheme for wheat, maize, soybeans and sunseed. Sharma, above n 1, at 10–11.

879 This commitment was restated at the G8 meeting in Japan in 2008 (Group of 8, *Leaders Statement on Global Food Security*, 8 July 2008, http://www.mofa.go.jp/policy/economy/summit/2008/doc/doc080709_04_en.html, para. 6); at the G8 Summit in L'Aquila, July 2009 (Group of 8, *'L'Aquila' Joint Statement on Global Food Security*, 10 July 2009, http://www.mofa.go.jp/policy/economy/summit/2009/statement3-2.pdf, para. 6); at the World Summit on Food Security (World Summit on Food Security, Rome, 16–18 November 2009, *Declaration of the World Summit on Food Security*, http://www.mofa.go.jp/policy/economy/fishery/wsfs0911-2.pdf, para. 21). Eventually, heads of government at the G20 meeting in Cannes agreed that humanitarian food purchased by WFP will not be subject to export restrictions or extraordinary taxes and committed "[...] to roll back any new protectionist measure that may have risen, including new export restrictions" (Group of 20 Summit, Cannes, 3–4 November 2011, *Communiqué: G20 Leaders Summit*, http://www.g20.utoronto.ca/2011/2011-cannes-communique-111104-en.html, paras. 19 and 22). See also para. 40 of the *Action Plan* agreed by the G-20 agriculture ministers in Paris on 23 June 2011 (Meeting of G20 Agriculture Ministers, Paris, 22 and 23 June 2011, *Ministerial Declaration: Action Plan on Food Price Volatility and Agriculture*, http://www.g20.utoronto.ca/2011/2011-agriculture-plan-en.pdf), reaffirmed at the G-20 Cannes Summit on 3–4 November 2011. In the WTO context, a proposal to exempt 'humanitarian' food shipments from export restraints was tabled by 14 countries (Australia, Canada, Chile, Costa Rica, the EU, the Republic of Korea, Indonesia, Japan,

Another is to exempt shipments to LDCs and NFIDCs from quantitative export restrictions invoked by WTO members that are major exporters of the specific foodstuffs concerned.[880] In practice, however, it may be difficult to implement this type of exemption except for government to government sales, given the reality of export trade to LDCs.[881]

c) *Red Category*

The red category is a residual one, essentially covering high income countries and upper-middle-income economies with reduced socio-economic vulnerability to escalating food prices. For these countries, the use of export restraints on staple foods should be banned. The idea is that these countries can resort to other means such as consumer subsidies and safety nets to mitigate the domestic impacts of price spikes. To provide an escape clause, however, an 'export safeguard mechanism', modelled after import safeguards, could be envisaged, based on price and quantity triggers.[882] As discussed in Espa, thresholds may be diversified based on specific criteria, including the export shares, economic vulnerability, and/or other factors.[883]

The above approach (differential and progressive regulation) is just one possible way to 'modulate' regulatory response in light of varying factual

Mexico, Norway, Saudi Arabia, Singapore, Switzerland and Turkey) for the 2011 Ministerial Conference in Geneva, but did not receive the needed consensus support (WTO Doc. WT/GC/138). The proposed text was drawn from paragraph 40 of the *Action Plan on Food Price Volatility and Agriculture* agreed by the G-20 agriculture ministers in Paris on 23 June 2011, as reaffirmed at the G-20 Cannes Summit on 3–4 November 2011.

880 Within the WTO, a proposal was tabled in this direction by the NFIDCs and African and Arab Groups. The proponents advocated the setting up of a WTO work programme in the Agriculture Committee that would among other "[...] explore the possibility of developing rules to exempt purchases of LDCs and NFIDCs, authorized by their governments under conditions to be defined, from quantitative export restrictions invoked under Article XI.2(a) of the GATT 1994 by other WTO Members, which are major exporters of the specific foodstuffs concerned". See documents WT/GC/140 and WT/GC/140/Rev.1.

881 For example, Asian rice is normally shipped to African countries by international traders on a f.o.b. basis, and the cargo is delivered by large vessels that stop at several ports of different African countries. The exact final destination of rice is often not clearly recorded at the point of export.

882 In that sense, Ilaria Espa, "Designing Coherent and Equitable WTO Disciplines on Export Restrictions" (presentation delivered at UNCTAD's Global Commodities Forum, 13–14 April 2015, downloadable at http://unctad.org/meetings/en/Presentation/SUC%20GCF2015%20Ilaria%20Espa.pdf). For a comprehensive review, Ilaria Espa, *Export Restrictions on Critical Minerals and Metals*, above n 326.

883 Espa, "Designing Coherent and Equitable WTO Disciplines on Export Restrictions," above.

circumstances. There are other avenues available. These include a return to the plurilateral approach and recourse to individual scheduling of commitments.[884]

Under a plurilateral or variable geometry approach, some like-mined countries, straddling existing groups, may go as far as they wish in locking-in their policy space to use export restraints on agricultural products. *Inter-se*, they may even prohibit the use of differential export taxes or other tax instruments for competitive advantage.[885] This is certainly welcomed, and warranted to create a 'fair' trading system, in the sense of a 'level playing field'. The approach taken can be the negotiation of a plurilateral agreement within the WTO framework, as was the case for the Agreement on Government Procurement. Benefits would be extended to all WTO members, while obligations would only bind the participants in the plurilateral arrangement.

Another approach is to hold multilateral negotiations of export duty concessions on a product-by-product basis.[886] As detailed in Espa, this may involve the scheduling and binding of export duty concessions in Part V of GATT schedules, patterned after the Russian model.[887] It could also involve incorporating existing WTO-plus commitments into respective members' GATT schedules, so that GATT-specific adjustment procedures and exceptions would automatically apply.[888] Specific flexibilities may be provided for LDCs or SVEs.

All of these approaches offer viable avenues to fine-tune regulation according to varying socio-economic vulnerabilities and find a balanced trade-off between domestic and international commitments.

### 5.2.5 *Concerted Price Action*

The analysis so far has considered domestic price stabilisation schemes, in their interface with multilateral trade rules. It will now turn to a brief reassessment of concerted action on commodity prices, as framed by multilateral trade rules. The analysis is twofold. It first explores how equitable ideals of distributive justice can be used as a basis to bridge gaps left by WTO rules. It then briefly outlines some lines of approach as to the way forward, beyond the 'old' ICA approach.

884 Cottier, above n 807.

885 In line with the US Submission for Comprehensive Long-Term Agricultural Trade Reform (WTO Doc. G/AG/NG/W/15 of 23 June 2000).

886 Espa, above n 882.

887 Ibid.

888 Ibid.

#### 5.2.5.1 Cartel-type Arrangements

As briefly discussed in Section 2.3, ICAs find legal cover under the GATT, if in the form of open, multilateral treaties. Yet, as mentioned, questions remain as to the legality of producers' arrangements; and as to the complex interplay between permissive GATT disciplines and other Annex 1A Agreements. A principled approach can help to bridge regulatory gaps or ease frictions.

Attention is hereafter directed to one discrete issue: the legitimacy of cartel-type agricultural agreements of which only producing countries are parties. These arrangements have been quite unexpectedly brought back on the trade policy agenda in the aftermath of the 2007–08 commodity crises. Extensive reference to ICAs was included under the Commodities heading in the 2008 December Draft Modalities. Paragraph 95 states that "[p]rovision shall be made to ensure the possibility that Members may take joint action [...] including through adoption of intergovernmental commodity agreements, for stabilisation of prices".[889] The draft text explicitly outlines that relevant action "may be taken either jointly by producing and consuming countries or by commodity-dependent producing countries only";[890] and on "an international or regional basis".[891]

In terms of practice, there have been some recent efforts to reinstate official cartel arrangements. In 2008, Thailand, Vietnam, Burma, Laos, Cambodia envisaged a cartel-type output restraint scheme for rice to sustain prices. The scheme was never implemented, due to international pressure rooted in food security concerns. In the same year, Thailand, Malaysia and Indonesia orchestrated cutbacks in natural rubber to inflate prices through the International Rubber Consortium.[892] The possible end of the 'super-cycle' in commodities is likely to put renewed emphasis on producer coordination and concerted supply-management.[893]

---

889 December 2008 revised draft modalities, above n 65, para. 95.

890 Ibid, paras. 96 and 100.

891 Ibid, para. 98. Unilateral action by producing countries is also contemplated by multilaterally agreed ICAs. The seventh ICCA, for example, envisages that cocoa producers "[...] may undertake to coordinate their national production policies" on the basis of price forecasts to deal with market imbalances in the medium and long term. Seventh ICCA, *supra* n 112, Article 36(4).

892 The scheme was relatively unsuccessful, due to a combination of factors: expanded exports from members (Vietnam, then accounting for about 9 percent of exports); relative pressure from substitutes (synthetic rubber); the financial crisis and falling industrial demand (particularly from the tire industry).

893 The recent retreat in commodity prices may be the start of a long period of low, stagnant prices (commodity 'bust'). This will likely shift the policy debate again to the need for some balance between supply and demand. For a discussion, UNCTAD, Global

Against this background, questions arise as to the legality of producers' arrangements from the standpoint of trade law. As discussed (Section 2.3.2), GATT Article XX does not settle the issue of the permissibility of producers' only and/or plurilateral commodity control arrangements. Little guidance can be drawn from the 'external context', outside the WTO framework.

It is worth exploring whether the normative framework outlined in the previous Chapter can be used as a basis to bridge the gaps left by GATT Article XX. It is argued here that the principles articulated in the previous analysis may provide some guidance, at least in political terms. In particular, they may inform decisions as to the desirability and permissibility of restrictive arrangements by commodity-dependent producing countries only. As detailed below, however, this principle-based assessment is in most cases fraught with difficulty, and often not conclusive.

Equitable ideals of distributive justice can help assessing the desirability and legitimacy of agreements of which only commodity-dependent producing countries are parties. In general, distributive dynamics and outcomes should be taken into account when devising new multilateral trade disciplines on producers' agreements: trade rules shall provide leeway for pro-poor arrangements; while restricting arrangements that carry an anti-poor bias. Likewise, equitable concerns can inform political decisions, short of legal commitments, about permissible non-conforming ICAs. Governments shall consider pro-poor arrangements sympathetically, and exercise utmost restraint in challenging them; while vetoing arrangements that jeopardise the interests of poor countries and poor constituencies.

In practice, this equitable assessment of distributive outcomes is bound to be highly contextual, circumstantial, and complex.

Few cases would be justified on equitable grounds. This is the case of schemes aimed to support peasant producers, when exports are directed from low-income countries to high-income economies. Upon one condition: that these schemes generate benefits for farmers, rather than a windfall for bureaucracies. If effective in sustaining farmgate prices, the transfer is, in these cases, redistributive and pro-poor. Resources, via high prices, flow from relatively affluent consumers in high-income countries (e.g. chocolate consumers in Europe) to poor peasant farmers in low-income countries (e.g. the West African cocoa grower). The problem as briefly discussed below, is the effectiveness of these schemes.

---

Commodities Forum 2015, *End of the Supercycle? Implications for Development and Terms of Trade*, Geneva, Tuesday, 14 April Geneva, 13–14 April 2015 (presentation downloadable at http://unctad.org/en/pages/MeetingDetails.aspx?meetingid=647).

Likewise, some 'cartel' type arrangements are to be rejected on equitable grounds. This is notably the case of concerted action to inflate prices in staple food commodities that are exported to low-income countries, and account for a significant share of total household food expenditure. This is notably the case of rice. Rice output restraint schemes by major Asian producers may possibly benefit small-scale farmers in the restricting countries;[894] yet, the costs would be borne, among other, by the urban poor in Senegal, in Côte d'Ivoire and in other net food-importing developing countries, which are heavily reliant on Asian rice exports.

In other instances the equitable assessment is more complex, and eventually not conclusive. Take the example of recent cartel-type arrangements in natural rubber. Natural rubber cutbacks by major Asian producers[895] were intended to ensure equitable prices for commodity exports from developing countries. Yet, at closer scrutiny, the distributional outcome is varied. Natural rubber involves mixed production patterns (estate and smallholder production); and major rubber importers include developing countries (China in particular), alongside high-income, advanced economies. Thus, sustained rubber prices may benefit smallholders in developing producing countries, and hit large tire manufacturers in advanced economies;[896] but they may also benefit estate owners in developing countries, with limited pass-through to waged labourers, and put under pressure tire manufacturing plants in other developing countries such as China. Eventually, the equity assessment is to be context-specific and circumstantial in terms of farming structures, industry profiles and a country's level of development.

---

894 In 2008, Thailand, Vietnam, Burma, Laos, Cambodia envisaged a cartel-type output restraint scheme in rice to sustain prices. The scheme was never implemented.

895 In 2008, Thailand, Malaysia and Indonesia orchestrated cutbacks in natural rubber to inflate prices (International Rubber Consortium). The scheme was relatively unsuccessful, due to a combination of factors: expanded exports from non-members (Vietnam, then accounting for about 9 percent of exports); relative pressure from substitutes (synthetic rubber); the financial crisis and falling industrial demand.

896 The world tire industry is heavily concentrated, with nine ultimate parent companies with annual sales in excess of $1 billion each accounting for 80 percent of world tire sales. These companies are headquartered in Japan (Bridgestone Corporation, Sumitomo Rubber Industries Ltd., Yokohama Rubber Co. Ltd., and Toyo Tire and Rubber Co. Ltd.), in Europe (Groupe Michelin, Continental A.G., and Pirelli), and the United States (Goodyear and Cooper). Subhrendu K. Pattanayak et al., *Economic Analysis of the Rubber Tire Manufacturing MACT, Final Report*, US Environmental Protection Agency (August 2000).

### 5.2.5.2 From 'Control' ICAs to 'Regulatory' ICAs

The above analysis is somewhat gratuitous. As a matter of fact, obstacles to the successful negotiation and functioning of restrictive ICAs are not legal in nature, but practical. They stem from factual market dynamics such as the high price elasticity of demand, when synthetic substitutes are available; and from political opportunism as with incentives to renege by ICA's participants, or free-riding by non-participants.[897]

Recent attempts to orchestrate output restraint schemes in agricultural commodities testify of difficulties to 'tame' agricultural commodity markets by means of old-style supply management.[898]

In spite of these difficulties, ICBs and ICAs can still be central, in this author's view, to ensuring stable and equitable prices to poor commodity producers in developing countries. In particular, they can provide a framework where potentially adversarial constituencies, notably producers and consumers, but also large producers and 'satellite' producers, can be locked into cooperative behaviours.

Yet, to face new and old challenges, ICAs need to be 'reinvented', in terms of institutional design and stabilisation mechanisms. What is posited here is a move from intergovernmental commodity arrangements to multi-stakeholder initiatives; and from 'control' ICAs to 'regulatory' ICAs.

#### a) *Institutional Design*

In terms of institutional design, what is advocated for is a move from intergovernmental frameworks to some form of transnational, 'networked governance'. The term is here used as to refer to multi-stakeholder partnerships that draw on diverse actors in government and business, across jurisdictions. The shift involved is from traditional forms of intergovernmental cooperation in dual-interest ICAs to what has been termed 'cosmopolitan multilateralism' (Section 5.1.3.1).

This shift is advocated for cogent, practical reasons.

First, price stabilisation is an area where regulation most often lags behind business dynamics. Private sector involvement is essential to favour a richer understanding of price formation and transmission mechanisms in commodities. Further, it may yield insights into key, catalytic interventions that would impact the inner workings of markets, with fairly modest changes in the law, so-called 'smart regulation'.

---

897 Pindyck, above n 146, at 155.

898 See, for example, the difficulties faced by the International Rubber Consortium in coordinating cutbacks in natural rubber to sustain prices.

Second, inclusive, multi-stakeholder frameworks that involve key commercial interests across jurisdictions would be able to bypass the jurisdictional limits of state enforcement. There is a fundamental misalignment, in the commodity sector, between the economic forces at work, which are transnational in nature, and the jurisdictional limits of state response, which are domestic, given the limited permissible scope of extraterritorial measures. Given the global character of transnational business operations, engagement by the private sector would allow coherent and concerted action across jurisdictions, beyond the limited reach of state enforcement. Also, it would contribute to 'hardening' soft law initiatives through inclusion in contractual relationships.

Finally, this is an area where economic interests are heavily entrenched, and states are under inevitable pressure from sectional groups. There is a need to expose these interests, and lock them into cooperative behaviour, within the framework of some public-private implementation network. It should be stressed that extreme price swings are disadvantageous to all but a few commercial actors, and that there may be more interest than expected on the part of business to participate in some form of networked governance regarding commodity markets.

Private sector involvement is thus essential for the design of efficient and effective stabilisation arrangements.

Eventually, the governing bodies of ICAs may evolve towards some form of multi-stakeholder governance. In this direction, a number of ICBs, alongside UNCTAD and the FAO, have already set up inclusive and flexible institutional arrangements for private sector involvement. These include, for example: the World Coffee Conference and the Private Sector Consultative Board, within the framework of the ICO; the Consultative Board on the World Cocoa Economy and the World Cocoa Conference, in the ICCO framework; multi-stakeholder partnerships for sustainable commodity production and trade such as the World Banana Forum within FAO; and multi-stakeholder initiatives like the Global Commodities Forum and UNCTAD's Secretary-General's Multi-stakeholder Consultation on Trade and Development Issues relating to Commodities, at UNCTAD. These venues provide a forum for constructive engagement with the private sector, and may favour the broad uptake of innovative price-stabilising schemes. A further step is to delegate negotiating and regulatory tasks to these consultative bodies.

There is some political sensitivity surrounding this approach, given some discontent among delegates who sit in the Council and Executive Boards of ICBs about the growing substantive role of subsidiary multi-stakeholder bodies that should only function in an advisory capacity to the intergovernmental bodies. A key challenge is how to establish a virtuous circle whereby multi-stakeholder dialogue feeds into decisions at the intergovernmental level, and the other way round.

**Box 12: The 1st World Cocoa Conference and the Abidjan Cocoa Declaration**

The *Abidjan Cocoa Declaration* has outlined a new business model to bring about major changes in the cocoa sector, including more stable and sustainable prices. The new model involves coordinated and concerted producer-consumer intervention through a multi-stakeholder (public-private) approach. The Declaration was adopted by the key players in the value chain at the 1st World Cocoa Conference, held in Abidjan in November 2012. The Conference grouped key stakeholders in the cocoa value-chain, including individual producers, cooperatives, traders, exporters, processors, chocolate manufacturers, wholesalers, producing and consuming countries, governmental and non-governmental organisations, financial institutions as well as donors and international aid and development agencies. It was acknowledged that the cocoa economy could not prosper in the long term without operating in a more sustainable and cooperative manner. Stakeholders recognised that their business operations engaged their responsibility towards the economic, environmental and social sustainability of the cocoa economy. In relation to the strategic management of the sector, stakeholders agreed to develop or assist, as required, "the formulation and implementation of national cocoa development plans, based on transparent and fully participatory local Public-Private-Partnership (PPP) approaches". A 2nd World Cocoa Conference was held in Amsterdam on June 2014, followed by the 3rd World Cocoa Conference in the Dominican Republic in 2016.

Source: World Cocoa Conference 2012, Abidjan, 19–23 November 2012, *Abidjan Cocoa Declaration*, https://www.icco.org/home/world-cocoa-conference-2012.html; Jean-Marc Anga (ICCO), "Latest Developments in the Cocoa Market" (presentation delivered at UNCTAD's Multi-year Expert Meeting on Commodities and Development, Geneva, 15–16 April 2015).

b) *Mechanisms*

In terms of mechanisms, the debate has to move beyond the old market-based or public intervention distinction, towards complex, hybrid solutions. Some lines of approach have been roughly sketched elsewhere.[899] They are recalled hereafter.

899 Irene Musselli, "La régulation des cours et des marchés des produits de base : vers une nouvelle architecture internationale? " *Journal Du Droit International* 3 (2012).

i) Surveillance

Much of the focus should be on market transparency and surveillance. ICAs should favour the establishment of transnational repositories of transaction-level data in physical commodity markets, patterned after the trade repositories that monitor transactions in OTC commodity derivatives. The physical trade repositories, subject to robust regulatory standards and supervision, will stock chain-specific transaction-level information regarding who is buying what, where, when, at what price; and track prices, costs and margins through the chain from farmgate to the point of export, and up to the final retail market.

In developing countries, this information will help domestic authorities detect instances of market abuse in physical commodity markets, and redress price distortions. Eventually, trade repositories may give new impetus to transnational competition law enforcement in physical commodity markets. The evidence generated through these facilities may even favour the integration of consideration of trade impact on developing countries into developed countries' competition law and policy.

Setting up facilities and procedures to collect, process and report strategic market information is a rather complex endeavour, which requires legislative measures and regulatory procedures to: set up trade repositories, subject to robust regulatory standards and supervision; address legal barriers to data collection and dissemination by trade repositories, particularly if the information is covered by commercial secret; and set incentives and requirements for market participants to report to trade repositories. Market Information Systems already exist in most commodity producing countries, but there is clearly room for improvement. There is a need to improve data coverage, in terms of the breadth and depth of the information reported. Data quality issues also arise prominently, in terms of relevance and reliability of the information collected. Finally, further action is needed to consistently apply reporting requirements across jurisdictions, as to avoid competitive disadvantages for producing countries with stringent reporting requirements. It is also critical to operationalise linkages between trade repositories located in different jurisdictions.

ii) Multi-Stakeholder Price Concertation

Another area of empirical investigation is the establishment of mechanisms of multi-stakeholder price concertation, building on the trade repositories. The idea is to cluster and lock-into cooperative behaviour a plurality of key market participants, under guidance and monitoring from the sectoral authority in the producing country. Within these frameworks, reference prices would be set following a process of concertation among the parties, primary producers, traders and manufactures, with due regard to production, processing and marketing costs.[900]

Again, this approach does not start from scratch, but relies on mechanisms that have already been tested through the 'fair trade' model. It is also reminiscent of models of organised supply chains based on the concept of 'total quality management'. In Côte d'Ivoire, for example, a cocoa 'supply-chain management' programme has successfully functioned through groups of participants, each consisting of one exporter, one to three co-operatives and one to three chocolate manufacturers, and with the institutional involvement of the Bourse du Café et du Cacao (BCC).[901]

iii) 'Structured Trade'

Another basic idea is to leverage commodity supply chain dynamics to manage price risk. The model is set by structured finance, where the credit risk is taken by those in the chain who can better manage it. In commodity trade the price risk shall be borne by large traders and processors, actors who can absorb the risk, and act as a stabiliser for peasant farmers. The basic, underlying idea is to move from spot transactions to some form of 'structured' trade, beyond dichotomy of the free market and public intervention. Contract farming and looser schemes framing market ties between plantation factories and satellite small-scale farmers are all avenues to structure trade and stabilise prices. A major challenge is how to bring such embryonic efforts to a scale where they become truly systemic interventions. It is also critical that sectoral authorities step in and 'frame' the interaction between parties with unequal bargaining power. This involves a shift from bilateral contractual relationships (between farmers and off-takers) to triangular public-private partnerships (involving farmers, off-takers and the public sector).

These are just some illustrative examples. Overall, the approach envisaged is procedural, rather than substantive, with a focus on countering market asymmetries than can lead to abuse of market power. It is also a minimalist one, as it remains, by and large, market-based; and individualistic, non-statist, as the focus is on benefits that directly accrue to individual peasant producers, rather than to states.

---

900 See in particular Alistair Smith (Banana Link), "Rethinking Price – The Heart of the Matter" (document tabled at the first meeting of the World Banana Forum, FAO, December 2009, available at http://www.fao.org/fileadmin/templates/banana/documents/Rethinking_price_Nov_09.pdf).

901 For details, ICCO, *Outline of a Cocoa Supply Chain Management Programme*, Doc. EX/130/9, 17 August 2006.

## 5.3 Implementation Avenues

The equitable constructs and principles previously outlined do not simply lay down general and flexible imperatives, deprived of precise prescriptive content. As discussed in Section 5.2, they could be invoked to argue for a different interpretation of WTO rules, so as to allow leeway for otherwise WTO-inconsistent commodity price stabilisation policies. Or they may be drawn upon as a basis to bridge regulatory gaps left by WTO rules. As a source of law, they may be invoked in the assertion of rights and obligations. Short of this legal status, they could serve as criteria to guide discretionary, political deliberations. Two pathways are available for the operationalisation of the normative framework outlined in the previous sections: trade litigation (law-enforcement) and trade negotiations (rule-making). Suffice here to review the main lines of argument, before moving on to some concluding remarks.

### 5.3.1 *Litigation*

The first approach is to ease WTO strictures through the interpretive process. This approach implies a progressive, purposive reading of WTO law in the light of non-trade concerns. It involves 'extrinsic' and 'teleological' interpretative techniques, by which the WTO adjudicator dwells on normative elements external to the WTO treaty, and re-interprets WTO rules in their light.[902] One step further, some commentators argue for the direct application of non-WTO law before a WTO panel to exclude the application of specific WTO provisions.[903] These are not new concepts in the academic discourse. They have been

902 On the use of extrinsic interpretation techniques in the context of the WTO dispute settlement system, see Foltea, above n 54, 93–94.

903 Pauwelyn, "The Role of Public International Law in the WTO: How Far Can We Go?" *American Journal of International Law* 95 (2001): 566. See also Joost Pauwelyn, "How to Win a WTO Dispute Based on Non-WTO Law? Questions of Jurisdiction and Merits," *Journal of World Trade* 37, no. 6 (2003); and Pauwelyn, "Human Rights in WTO Dispute Settlement," in *Human Rights and International Trade*, ed. Thomas Cottier, Joost Pauwelyn, and Elisabeth Bürgi (Oxford; New York: Oxford University Press, 2005). This approach, as articulated by Pauwelyn, builds on the distinction between adjudication and applicable law; and between the use of non-WTO law as a defence or as a claim. Pauwelyn argues that non-WTO law may be invoked before a WTO panel to disapply a specific WTO rule, and permit WTO members to deviate from their trade obligations. This when the following requirements are met: (i) the non-WTO rule is invoked by a party to the dispute as defence against claims of violation of WTO law; (ii) both parties to the dispute are bound by the non-WTO rule; (iii) pursuant to a conflict clause in either treaty or the applicable conflict rules of public international law (*lex posterior* and *lex specialis*), the non-WTO provision prevails over the contradictory WTO rule (Pauwelyn, "Human Rights in WTO

expressed in the literature through a call for greater 'institutional sensitivity' of the WTO adjudicator towards external norms.[904] The concept of 'institutional sensitivity' is here retained in its twofold dimensions: vertical and horizontal.[905] The vertical dimension suggests that there should be some degree of deference by WTO panels to national government decisions.[906] The horizontal dimension refers to the role of other public international law in the WTO interpretation process.[907] As discussed in Foltea, this 'external contribution' can be in the form of law, whether hard or soft law, as well as information and expertise.[908]

As discussed in the literature,[909] there are limits to this approach, along with some openings. The following analysis briefly reviews possible linkage techniques that would allow the WTO adjudicator to flexibly interpret trade rules so as to allow leeway for otherwise WTO inconsistent stabilisation arrangements. It then briefly considers whether customary rules of treaty interpretation allow room for a progressive, purposive reading of WTO law. It concludes with reference to 'internal' constraints,[910] from within the WTO system, to a reading of WTO law informed by non-trade concerns.

#### 5.3.1.1 Possible 'Linkage' Techniques

There are various paths to 'open' WTO law to external norms through the interpretative process. As discussed in Foltea,[911] a number of 'linkage' techniques are already enshrined in the WTO Treaty. These techniques interface WTO law and non-WTO law in a number of issue areas. The most explicit venue involves

---

Dispute Settlement," above n 903, at 208). This approach has been disputed in doctrine. For a critique: Gabrielle Marceau, "WTO Dispute Settlement and Human Rights," *European Journal of International Law* 13, no. 4 (2002); Joel P. Trachtman, "The Domain of WTO Dispute Resolution," *Harvard International Law Journal* 40 (1999): 342; Cameron and Gray, above n 614, at 264.

904 In Foltea's terms, "institutional sensitivity" refers to the extent to which the WTO adjudicator makes use of normative elements that reside outside the WTO system". Foltea, above n 54, at 17.

905 This distinction is drawn from Foltea, above n 54, 28–51.

906 Ibid, at 28.

907 Ibid, 31–44.

908 Ibid, at 17. Foltea distinguishes between horizontal sensitivity "in broad terms", describing the "receptivity of the WTO adjudicator to non-WTO law in the process of interpretation" (Foltea, at 32), and horizontal sensitivity "in narrow terms", with reference to "the role of extra regime soft law in the WTO interpretation process" (at 43).

909 See in particular Foltea, above n 54 and Nadakavukaren Schefer, above n 604.

910 Drawing from Foltea, above n 54, 127–42.

911 Foltea, above n 54, 52–87.

deference to another international regime. As discussed in Foltea, this linkage technique is already entrenched in the WTO Treaty, for example when dealing with problems concerning monetary reserves, balances of payments, or foreign exchange arrangements. Specifically, GATT Article XV(2) requires the WTO to consult with the International Monetary Fund (IMF) and accept the Fund's determination on the consistency of a measure with the IMF's Articles of Agreement.[912] A second type of linkage arises from the incorporation of non-WTO norms in the WTO Treaty. For example, under the WTO Agreement on the Application of Sanitary and Phytosanitary Measures (SPS Agreement), compliance with international standards presumes the WTO-consistency of a measure.[913] The legality of certain trade-restrictive measures is here explicitly linked to external norms that are integrated by reference into the WTO system.[914] Other linkage techniques involve co-operation and observership,[915] and the right of the WTO adjudicator to seek information from other bodies.[916]

These techniques offer a set of methods and practices for interfacing WTO and non-WTO rules. They may provide flexibility in cases where the WTO adjudicator is called upon to consider or deal with problems of price stabilisation in sensitive commodities. Two dimensions – vertical and horizontal – are at stake. The vertical dimension suggests that there should be some degree of deference by WTO panels to national government decisions. The horizontal dimension refers to receptivity of the WTO adjudicator to the standards, guidelines and recommendations established by other international organisations.

This approach can be exemplified by reference to the treatment of price band systems within the WTO. As discussed (Section 2.3.3.3), price band schemes are not textually included in the illustrative list of measures that cannot be maintained under Article 4.2 of the AoA. If considered as "ordinary customs duties", price bands could be maintained, provided that they do not exceed a country's tariff bindings (GATT Article II:1(a)). If held to be border measures "other than ordinary customs duties", they could not be maintained or resorted to under Article 4.2 of the AoA, unless covered by general GATT exceptions. In the past, this interpretative issue was settled by the WTO adjudicator in narrow terms:

---

912 Ibid, 53–60.

913 The international standards to be taken as reference are the standards, guidelines and recommendations established by the Codex Alimentarius Commission, the International Office of Epizootics, and the International Plant Protection Convention (SPS Agreement, Annex A, paragraph 3).

914 For examples of this linkage technique in relation to the WTO TRIPS Agreement, the SPS Agreement, the TBT Agreement, and the SCM Agreement, Foltea, above n 54, 60–71.

915 Foltea, above n 54, 71–79.

916 Ibid, 79–86.

price bands were held to be border measures "other than ordinary customs duties" and proscribed as such under WTO law, irrespective of their trade impacts or administration.

More deferential approaches by the WTO adjudicator would invite to relax this judicial prohibition by reference to the price band stated objective, and its administration. The adjudicator should make a particular consideration of the social (stabilisation) objectives of the measure at stake, and try to protect those interests in a WTO-compatible way. If the measure is intended to moderate the effect of import price fluctuations on the domestic market, some degree of social interest towards its maintenance can be detected. This would warrant a cautious approach in deciding whether the measure is WTO-inconsistent. The fact that price bands are not textually proscribed by AoA Article 4.2 would provide room for purposive, ends-focused interpretations that do not encroach upon treaty language. Eventually, price bands could be held to be ordinary customs duties, if transparently administered and predictable. If intransparent and unpredictable, they should be proscribed as similar to variable import levies. The key issue would be if the price band exhibits features that frustrate the purpose of Article 4.2. Lack of transparency and predictability would thus be a separate characteristic that a price band must have to be WTO-inconsistent. In this way the WTO adjudicator could advance social policy goals (stabilisation), without undermining other equally important systemic goals of the multilateral trading system (transparency and predictability).

The determination of whether a price band is transparent and predictable should not be a matter of domestic discretion. Nor should it be left to the judicial discretion of WTO panels. The assessment should be benchmarked against international standards. UN-sponsored expert groups may develop model price band schemes, transparent and highly predictable, to the fullest possible extent minimally trade-distortive. These may serve as an international standard that triggers a rebuttable presumption of conformity with WTO law.

Overall, the approach involves some measure of deference to national policy determinations, while setting safeguards against abuse.

#### 5.3.1.2 The VCLT Rules of Interpretation

Would the prevailing interpretative rules allow leeway for the interpretative techniques outlined above?[917] As discussed below, there are limits to these interpretative approaches, alongside some openings. The following analysis briefly reviews means of interpretation and interpretive methods applicable

917 For a thorough discussion, Foltea, above n 54, at 88–123.

in the WTO context; existing legal constraints to a progressive, purposive reading of WTO law; and possible inroads for reformist interpretations.

### a) *Interpretative Principles*

Suffice here to review some basic tenets.[918] Pursuant to Article 3.2 of the Understanding on Rules and Procedures Governing the Settlement of Disputes (DSU), WTO rules should be interpreted according to "customary rules of interpretation of public international law".[919] These interpretative rules, as relied upon by the WTO judiciary, are codified in Articles 31 and 32 of the VCLT. The Appellate Body has explicitly recognised these rules as having customary status.[920] Since the *Gasoline* case in 1996, the WTO DSB has strictly adhered to the interpretative canon laid down in the VCLT. As pointed out by Cameron, "[f]ailing to apply this test or using alternative methods of treaty interpretation can result in overturned rulings".[921] The VCLT is thus an inescapable reference text for interpretation. In Sorel and Boré's words, there is, in the WTO jurisprudence, "a type of incantatory reference to this 'sacred text'".[922] This does not necessarily imply, the two commentators note,[923] that the WTO judiciary has always conformed to this reference, which goes beyond strict 'textualism'.

According to VCLT Article 31 (1), "[a] treaty shall be interpreted in good faith in accordance with the ordinary meaning to be given to the terms of the treaty in their context and in the light of its object and purpose". The context, as defined by VCLT Article 31 (2), includes: the treaty preamble and annexes; any agreement made in connection with the conclusion of the treaty; any

918 For a thorough discussion of the rules of interpretation of the VCLT as applied by the WTO adjudicator, see Foltea, above n 54, Chapter 3.

919 Understanding on Rules and Procedures Governing the Settlement of Disputes (DSU), Annex 2 to the Marrakesh Agreement, Article 3.2.

920 In *US – Gasoline*, the Appellate Body acknowledged that the general rule of interpretation, contained in Article 31 of the Vienna Convention had attained the status of "customary or general international law" (Appellate Body Report, *US – Gasoline*, p. 17). In *US – Section 301 Trade Act* stated that Articles 31 and 32 of the VCLT have customary status (Panel Report, *US – Section 301 Trade Act*, para. 7.21). See also WTO Analytical Index: Dispute Settlement Understanding, Principles and Concepts of General International Law Related to Dispute Settlement (https://www.wto.org/english/res_e/booksp_e/analytic_index_e/dsu_e.htm).

921 Cameron and Gray, above n 614, at 255–56. See also Jean-Marc Sorel and Valérie Boré Eveno, "Article 31," in *The Vienna Convention on the Law of Treaties: A Commentary*, ed. Olivier Corten and Pierre Kleins (Oxford; New York: Oxford University Press, 2011), 821.

922 Sorel and Boré Eveno, above n 921, at 821.

923 Ibid, at 821.

instrument made by one or more parties in connexion with the treaty and accepted by the other parties as related to the treaty. Furthermore, Article 31 (3) requires that "account be taken" for subsequent interpretative agreements and practices, as well as for "any relevant rules of international law applicable in the relations between the parties".

The interpretative method articulated in Article 31 (and Article 32) of the VCLT is compounded and hybrid.[924] On balance, Article 31 gives primacy to the textual approach, based on the ordinary meaning of the terms (paragraph 1). Yet, it "leaves many doors opened"[925] to other means of interpretation and interpretive techniques. Thus, paragraph 1 requires that the terms of the treaty be interpreted in their context, and in the light of the object and purpose of the treaty. Reference to the context, as specified in paragraph 2, reintroduces elements of subjective interpretation, based on the parties' real intention (then reintegrated in paragraph 4 and, in a subsidiary way, Article 32). But paragraph 3 allows the interpreter to dwell on extrinsic elements in the interpretative process, including 'subsequent agreements', 'subsequent practice' and 'relevant rules of international law'. This makes space for a dynamic, evolutive interpretation of WTO law, lodged in the problematique of inter-temporal law.[926] It also frames the WTO treaty in the wider context of public international law, including non-WTO law.[927]

Eventually, "Article 31 is no more than a set of scattered principles which make no claim to exhaustiveness".[928] As pointed out by Sorel and Boré, "[t]he absence of hierarchy between the different means of interpretation, their malleability, and the multiple ways of combining them, leaves the door open to countless variations in this complex operation that constitutes treaty interpretation".[929]

To what extent does this complex ensemble of interpretive rules constrain a principle-based interpretation of WTO law? And which openings does it provide for off-track interpretations?

---

924 As pinpointed by Sorel, the text of Article 31 intertwines different interpretative approaches: 'textual interpretation', also known as 'declared intent', or 'objective interpretation'; 'subjective interpretation' based on the parties' real intention; and ends-focused or 'teleological interpretation'. Sorel and Boré Eveno, above n 921, at 808 and 809.

925 Sorel and Boré Eveno, above n 921, at 836.

926 Ibid, at 808.

927 Pauwelyn, "Human Rights in WTO Dispute Settlement," above n 903, at 213.

928 Sorel and Boré Eveno, above n 921, at 836.

929 Ibid.

### b) *Strictures*

The interpretative method outlined above poses several strictures to a reformist, purposive reading of WTO law.[930]

First, as mentioned, the interpretative canon gives priority to the treaty text. Textual interpretation should prevail. If the treaty text is clear, it is difficult to argue for different interpretations. The DSB has strictly complied with this textual approach,[931] often moving from the definition provided by dictionaries for the purpose of establishing the ordinary meaning of the term.[932] WTO jurisprudence does not condone the importation into a treaty of "words that are not there" nor of "concepts that were not intended".[933]

Second, treaty terms are to be ascertained in their context. The context, as specified in VCLT Article 31 (2), includes the text of the treaty, the preamble and possible annexes. A corollary of this interpretive principle, as articulated in the WTO jurisprudence, is that "a treaty should be interpreted as a whole, and, in particular, its sections and parts should be read as a whole".[934] Most prescriptive provisions in the AoA are aimed at removing trade restrictions or distortions. Reference to the 'internal context' makes it difficult to argue for off-track interpretations for specific provisions.

The context also includes supplementary agreements with a bearing on the treaty drawn upon at the time when the treaty was concluded (Article 31(2)

930 For a detailed assessment of internal and external constraints to the "institutional sensitivity" of the WTO adjudicator towards non-WTO law, Foltea, above n 54, at 127–62.

931 As compiled in the WTO Analytical index (DSU): in *Japan – Alcoholic Beverages II*, the Appellate Body highlighted that "Article 31 of the Vienna Convention provides that the words of the treaty form the foundation for the interpretative process" (Appellate Body Report, *Japan – Alcoholic Beverages II*, p. 11); in *EC – Hormones*, the Appellate Body stated that "[t]he fundamental rule of treaty interpretation requires a treaty interpreter to read and interpret the words actually used by the agreement under examination, not words the interpreter may feel should have been used" (Appellate Body Report, *EC – Hormones*, para. 181); in *India – Patents (US)*, the Appellate Body emphasized that the principles of treaty interpretation "neither require nor condone" the importation into a treaty of "words that are not there" nor of "concepts that were not intended" (Appellate Body Report, *India – Patents (US)*, para. 94).

932 Note however that the Appellate Body has cautioned panels against equating the "ordinary meaning" of a term with the definition provided by dictionaries. Under Article 31 of the Vienna Convention, the "ordinary meaning" of treaty terms may be ascertained only in their context and in the light of the object and purpose of the treaty. Appellate Body Report, *China – Publications and Audiovisual Products*, para. 348.

933 Appellate Body Report, *India – Patents (US)*, para. 94.

934 Appellate Body Report, *Korea – Dairy*, para. 81. See also Appellate Body Report, *US – Anti-Dumping and Countervailing Duties (China)*, para. 570.

sub-paragraphs a) and b). This 'internal context' serves to clarify the ordinary meaning of the terms as intended at the time of the treaty's conclusion. It can lead to an analysis of the intention of the parties, as provided for, in a strictly subsidiary manner, in Article 32. The 'state of mind' of the drafters, or the 'real intention' of the parties, will, in many cases confirm a narrow, stringent interpretation of 'liberal' rules. In fact, social inclusiveness and sustainability concerns were, in the mid-1990s, less essential than they are today. In the present post-2015 scenario, we are pressing for contents that were not intended at the time when the Agreement was enacted.

Interpretation in the light of the covered agreement's object and purpose would also likely favour a conservative, functional, narrowly framed interpretation of the AoA provisions. This follows from the fact that the object and purpose is to be assessed for the treaty as a whole, in its entirety; not as the object and purpose of particular provisions.[935] The general aim of the AoA has been narrowly interpreted in a number o 'stabilisation cases', as to achieve greater liberalisation of trade in agriculture, through the removal of distortions and restrictions.[936] WTO panels and the Appellate Body would be inclined to reject interpretations that undermine this object and purpose.[937]

Finally, the principle of effectiveness can be invoked to narrow down a broad, flexible interpretation of WTO rules. Though not explicitly integrated in Article 31, the principle of effectiveness has been applied by the WTO judiciary on several occasions.[938] Pursuant to this principle, "interpretation must give meaning and effect to all the terms of a treaty".[939] A reading cannot render the words of substantive provisions meaningless.[940] The Appellate Body made

935 Appellate Body Report, *EC – Chicken Cuts*, para. 238.

936 See, in particular, *Chile – Price Band System*, above n 210; *Peru – Agricultural Products*, above n 211; *Canada – Dairy*, above n 330, paras. 7.25–7.26. See also the AoA, preambular paragraphs 1, 2 and 3, and the Punta del Este Declaration, Ministerial Declaration on the Uruguay Round, MIN.DEC (20 September 1986), at 6.

937 See, in this direction, Appellate Body Report, *US – Softwood Lumber IV*, para. 64.

938 WTO Analytical Index: In *US – Gasoline*, the Appellate Body considered the principle of effective treaty interpretation as "one of the corollaries of the 'general rule of interpretation' in the Vienna Convention" (Appellate Body Report, *US – Gasoline*, p. 23); in *Japan – Alcoholic Beverages II*, the Appellate Body referred to it as "a fundamental tenet of treaty interpretation flowing from the general rule of interpretation set out in Article 31" (Appellate Body Report, *Japan – Alcoholic Beverages II*, p. 12). See also Panel Reports, *India – Quantitative Restrictions*, footnote 354; *Canada – Patent Term*, paras. 6.48–6.50; *EC – Asbestos*, footnote 22 to para. 8.29.

939 Appellate Body Report, *US – Gasoline*, p. 23.

940 See, in this direction, Appellate Body Report, *Japan – Alcoholic Beverages*, p. 18.

it clear that "[a]n interpreter is not free to adopt a reading that would result in reducing whole clauses or paragraphs of a treaty to redundancy or inutility".[941] This would be the case, if interpretative lee-way is provided for justifying trade-distortive price stabilisation policies.

Note also that, in WTO law, the use of equitable interpretations *praeter legem* (to fill regulatory gaps) and *contra legem* (as a corrective to the rule of law) is explicitly proscribed.[942]

c) *Openings*

Yet, the VCLT interpretative canon also offers some in-roads for progressive interpretations.[943] In particular, VCLT Article 31 (3) leaves many doors open to 'extrinsic' methods and techniques for treaty interpretation. They can serve as a lever towards a principle-based interpretation of WTO law.

VCLT Article 31 (3) brings in the 'external context'.[944] It requires the treaty interpreter to consider subsequent interpretative agreements (sub-paragraph a),[945] subsequent practice (sub-paragraph b)[946] and relevant rules of public international law (sub-paragraph c).[947] These means are not characterised as supplementary. They shall be taken into account "together with the context", in the absence of a clear hierarchy between the different means of interpretation.[948]

Through reference to the external context, paragraph 3 frames the WTO treaty in the wider context of public international law, including non-WTO law.[949] It also makes space for a dynamic, evolutive interpretation of WTO law, through reference to evolving standards. This interpretative method allows some opening for a principled interpretation of WTO law in light of human rights law. It also makes space for a dynamic evolutive interpretation of WTO

941 Appellate Body Report, *US – Gasoline*, at 23.

942 Pursuant to Article 3.2 of the DSU, "[r]ecommendations and rulings of the DSB cannot add to or diminish the rights and obligations provided in the covered agreements".

943 For a thorough discussion, Foltea, above n 54, Chapter 3.

944 Sorel and Boré Eveno, above n 921, at 825–29.

945 VCLT Article 31(3)(a): "any subsequent agreement between the parties regarding the interpretation of the treaty or the application of its provisions".

946 VCLT Article 31(3)(b): "any subsequent practice in the application of the treaty which establishes the agreement of the parties regarding its interpretation".

947 VCLT Article 31(3)(c): "any relevant rules of international law applicable in the relations between the parties".

948 Article 31(3), VCLT.

949 Pauwelyn, "Human Rights in WTO Dispute Settlement," above n 903, at 213. Appellate Body Report, *US – Shrimp*, para. 158 and footnote 157.

law,[950] informed by the transformative dynamics that are reshaping the trade policy discourse.

The WTO panels and Appellate Body have on various occasions drawn from the "international normative environment"[951] to interpret WTO treaty. As stated by the Appellate Body in the *Gasoline* case, WTO law "should not be read in clinical isolation from public international law".[952] Reference to public international law encompasses all generally accepted sources of public international law, that is to say, treaties, customary rules, and recognised general principles of law.[953]

Yet, reference to the 'external context' has been interpreted quite narrowly in WTO jurisprudence.

The reference to 'subsequent interpretative agreements' in VCLT Article 31 (3) sub-paragraph (a) has been interpreted to cover agreements between all the parties specifically bearing upon the interpretation of the WTO treaty. These essentially include multilateral authoritative interpretations pursuant to Article IX:2 of the WTO Agreement,[954] as well as Ministerial Declarations[955] and Decisions. Other interpretative material (unilateral statements and subsequent non interpretative agreements) would likely not be akin to 'subsequent agreements' within the meaning of Article 31 (3) (a) of the Vienna Convention. They would more easily come under the purview of Article 32, as supplementary means of interpretation.

---

950 There are instances were WTO law has been interpreted in an evolutive manner. In *US – Shrimp*, the Appellate Body argued that terms are not static, but evolutionary (para. 130). Drawing from environmental law treaties, the AB interpreted the term "exhaustible natural resources" in an evolutive manner, as also encompassing living resources.

951 Sorel and Boré Eveno, above n 921, at 828.

952 Appellate Body, *US – Gasoline*.

953 Panel Report, *EC – Approval and Marketing of Biotech Products*, para. 7.67. See also (as compiled in WTO Analytical Index): Appellate Body Report, *US – Shrimp*, para. 158 and footnote 157 (the Appellate Body acknowledged that pursuant to Article 31(3)(c) of the VCLT general principles of international law are relevant to the interpretation of WTO provisions); Panel Report, *EC – Approval and Marketing of Biotech Products*, para. 7.67 (the Panel stated that if the precautionary principle were a general principle of international law, it could be considered a "rule of international law" within the meaning of Article 31 (3)(c), and could be taken into account in interpreting WTO law); Panel Report, *China – Raw Materials*, paras. 7.377–7.378 (the Panel referred to Article 31(3)(c) in stating that the provisions of Article XX(g) of the GATT 1994 could be assessed harmoniously with the international law principle of State sovereignty over its natural resources).

954 See, in this direction, Appellate Body Report, *EC – Bananas III (Article 21.5 – Ecuador II) I EC – Bananas III (Article 21.5 – US)*, paras. 390–91.

955 Panel Report, *US – Clove Cigarettes*, para. 7.576.

'Subsequent practice' (VCLT Article 31 (3) (b)) has likewise been interpreted narrowly. As stated in *Japan – Alcoholic Beverages II*, "[a]n isolated act is generally not sufficient to establish subsequent practice; it is a sequence of acts establishing the agreement of the parties that is relevant.".[956] In essence, "[...] (i) there must be a common, consistent, discernible pattern of acts or pronouncements; and (ii) those acts or pronouncements must imply agreement on the interpretation of the relevant provision."[957] Though 'common' and 'concordant' practice does not necessarily require practice by all parties, "it would be difficult to establish a 'concordant, common and discernible pattern' on the basis of acts or pronouncements of one, or very few parties to a multilateral treaty, such as the WTO Agreement".[958] Furthermore, agreement cannot be deduced from a party's "lack of reaction" without further inquiry into associated circumstances.[959] These qualifications exclude subsequent practice broadly intended, including unilateral acts as well as non-interpretative agreements. These acts would not qualify under the general rule of interpretation as provided in Article 31, though they may be included among the subsidiary means of interpretation under Article 32.[960]

Finally, in WTO jurisprudence, Article 31(3)(c), though often referred to, has only been applied "moderately".[961] As discussed in Sorel, "one may notice a certain amount of prudence on the part of the [Dispute Settlement Board] in this domain".[962] In particular, relevant 'external' rules of international law are considered for their informative character, as interpretative material.[963] They are drawn upon to shed light on the meaning and scope of the WTO terms to be interpreted. They are not directly applicable as rules in WTO dispute settlement. As stated by the Panel in *EC – Approval and Marketing of Biotech Products*,

> [...] other relevant rules of international law may in some cases aid a treaty interpreter in establishing, or confirming, the ordinary meaning

956 Appellate Body Report, *Japan – Alcoholic Beverages II*, pp. 12–13.

957 Appellate Body Report, *US – Gambling*, para. 192.

958 Appellate Body in *EC – Chicken Cuts*.

959 Appellate Body Report, *EC – Chicken Cuts*, para. 272.

960 Sorel and Boré Eveno, above n 921, at 861.

961 Ibid, at 829.

962 Ibid, at 827.

963 With reference to 'extra-WTO law soft law regimes', Foltea finds that the WTO adjudicator has 'attributed' acts of other international organisations mostly to supplementary means of interpretation for the clarification of the ordinary meaning of terms, typically for confirmatory purposes. Foltea, above n 54, at 121–22.

of treaty terms in the specific context in which they are used. Such rules would not be considered because they are legal rules, but rather because they may provide evidence of the ordinary meaning of terms in the same way that dictionaries do. They would be considered for their informative character.[964]

#### 5.3.1.3 'Internal' Constraints

To sum up, do current means and method of interpretation allow room for a purposive interpretation of WTO law in light of the principles and objectives outlined in Section 5.1? Only to some extent.

As discussed, there is some opening for a dynamic, evolutive interpretation of the object and purpose of the WTO treaty, drawing from external context. Through reference to the external context, VCLT Article 31 (3) frames the WTO treaty in the wider context of public international law, including non-WTO law. Note also that VCLT Article 31 (1) states that a treaty shall be interpreted in good faith. The general principle of good faith posits that states do not intentionally undertake conflicting commitments.[965] The call is to avoid conflict between WTO law and other public international law.

However, there are limits to how far this ends-focused, progressive interpretation can be stretched. These limits arise from constraints 'internal' to the WTO system, more than from VCLT rules of interpretation. As discussed in Foltea, 'internal' limits emerge form specific treaty language text, from the *de facto* binding force of judicial precedents, and from the political orientation of the WTO.[966]

As regards the former set of constraints, specific WTO provisions may be construed so as to inhibit institutional sensitivity of the WTO adjudicator. Thus, DSU Article 2 (1), which ascribes adjudicating functions to the DSB, may be read as preventing delegation of power to outside bodies. DSU Articles 3 (2) and 19 (2) explicitly state that judicial interpretation may not "add to or diminish the rights and obligations provided in the covered agreements". These provisions can be interpreted to prevent the use of non-WTO law to affect rights and obligations under WTO agreements.[967]

Constraints also arise from WTO restrictive judicial approach in the application of non-WTO rules (see above text accompanying note 962). The *de facto*, though not *de iure*, binding nature of prior judicial reports in the WTO dispute

---

964 Panel Report, *EC – Approval and Marketing of Biotech Products*, para. 7.92.

965 For a discussion, Cottier and Panagiotis, above n 54, at 25.

966 Foltea, above n 54, at 127–42.

967 For a thorough discussion, Foltea, above n 54, at 127–35.

settlement system makes it difficult for the WTO adjudicator to deviate from previous decisions. As pointed out by Foltea, consistency in legal interpretation legitimises the WTO adjudicator.[968] Too many deviations in juridical interpretation would hinder the credibility of the WTO dispute settlement system.

Finally, some limits to a purposive, progressive reading of WTO law in the light of non-trade values arise from 'WTO political choices'.[969] As discussed (Section 4.1.3), the political orientation of the WTO wavers between two paradigms: the neoliberal or trade liberalisation paradigm, which posits trade liberalisation as the final goal; and a regulation paradigm, that attempts at balancing equally legitimate trade and non-trade values. This political indeterminacy affects the receptivity of the WTO adjudicator to other public international law.[970]

Due to these fundamental strictures, WTO adjudication is bound to be inherently conservative, and certainly cannot be instrumental in a subversion of the system from within. The evolution of WTO law is a matter for the WTO 'legislator'. This holds particularly true when dealing with stabilisation issues. As discussed, the analytical framework for assessing the legitimacy of agricultural stabilisation policy most often is not the interface of trade and human rights law. What is genuinely at question is how to achieve a balance between these desirable but sometimes incompatible features: supporting peasant producers at home, while protecting peasant interests elsewhere. On matters of price stabilisation policies in the developing world, tensions and trade-offs often involve equally critical interests: the right (and duty) of a developing country to support its peasant farmers and the right of peasant farmers in other developing countries to compete on fair terms in third markets or at home. Eventually, the distributional struggle is not between the poor and the relatively affluent, but between equally poor constituencies across developing countries. The mediation between these interests involves complex solutions that reflect varying factual circumstances. Setting the normative benchmarks that should frame this highly contextual exercise is not a matter for the judiciary. It is a political endeavour, to be undertaken by the WTO 'legislator'. Possible avenues are discussed hereafter.

### 5.3.2 *Law-Making and Negotiations*

The clarification or amendment of WTO norms in the area of commodity price policies should be a matter of law-making. There are several pathways

968 Foltea, above n 54, at 139.

969 Foltea, above n 54, at 135.

970 As discussed in Foltea, above n 54, at 135–38.

to accommodate a principle-based reading of WTO rules by leveraging the existing procedures. The objective is to provide at least political, when not formal, leeway for otherwise WTO-inconsistent commodity price stabilisation schemes.

The spectrum of options is broad, ranging from formal amendments to political deliberations and 'mainstreaming' practice.[971]

#### 5.3.2.1 Legislative Options

Formal procedures for revising or amending trade rules include: amendments, pursuant to Article X of the WTO Agreement; renegotiation of commitments set out in a member's schedule, as provided for in Article XXVIII of the GATT; waiver procedures, under the terms of Article IX:3 of the WTO Agreement; and authoritative interpretations, pursuant to Article IX:2 of the WTO Agreement.[972] Any of these legislative approaches may be used to further stabilisation objectives through trade law. Authoritative interpretations, in particular, could provide a useful inroad to refine the scope of rules in perspective, in light of the evolving normative framework.[973]

Yet formal procedures are administratively stringent and politically cumbersome. This procedural pathway would likely lead to a deadlock, in the present context of political frictions and sensitivities. The current decision-making system, as captured by Elsig and Cottier, combines three elements.[974] First, it is member-driven. The WTO Secretariat does not have formal agenda-setting power or discretion; a formal Executive Body as existing for example in most ICBs is absent.[975] Second, decision making is consensual. Decisions are taken if no member formally objects. The principle of 'one state, one vote' makes virtually impossible the application of voting in the WTO system.[976] This has

---

971 For a comprehensive review of legislative and non-legislative options for the furtherance of social and political goals through trade law, see Nadakavukaren Schefer, above n 604, at 283–88.

972 For an overview, Claus-Dieter Ehlermann and Lothar Ehring, "Decision-Making in the World Trade Organization: Is the Consensus Practice of the World Trade Organization Adequate for Making, Revising and Implementing Rules on International Trade?" *Journal of International Economic Law* 8, no. 1 (2005). See also Pauwelyn, "The Role of Public International Law in the WTO," above n 903, at 535.

973 Ehlermann and Ehring, above n 972, at 59.

974 Manfred Elsig and Thomas Cottier, "Reforming the WTO: The Decision-Making Triangle Revisited," in *Governing the World Trade Organization: Past, Present and Beyond Doha*, ed. Thomas Cottier and Manfred Elsig (New York: Cambridge University Press, 2011).

975 Ibid, at 291–96.

976 Ibid, at 296–97.

been labelled as a form of "managed hypocrisy", as it generates "a false feeling of equal participation", while decisions in the end reflect strong power imbalances.[977] Finally, the 'single undertaking' approach presses for deals that all parties have to agree in their entirety. It implies the negotiating logic that "nothing is agreed until when everything is agreed".[978] These features combined have led to a deadlock in sensitive areas. This is notably the case with agriculture.

It follows that legislative options offer paths to achieve social objectives through trade law, but their viability is tied to institutional reform of decision-making within the WTO. Potential avenues for reform have been widely discussed in political and academic fora.[979] In agriculture, they would involve a move beyond the logic of consensual decision-making and the single undertaking. The call is also for greater deference to standard setting bodies outside the WTO.

A first reform scenario involves a move towards issue specific and product specific negotiations in agriculture. The Committee on Agriculture could set up product-specific sub-committees/groups charged with major agricultural commodities or groups of commodities. Negotiations would be issue-based and sectoral, or product specific. This would allow for focused, technical discussions that take into account the specifics of each agricultural sub-sector. Though the work of the sub-committees would not be free of interest-based politics, it would likely be more technical and problem-oriented than broad sector-wide discussions.

---

977 Ibid, at 297–98.

978 For a discussion, Elsig and Cottier, above 974, at 299–300.

979 A number of proposals stem from the academic community, NGOs and international organisations. See Thomas Cottier and Manfred Elsig, eds., *Governing the World Trade Organization: Past, Present and Beyond Doha* (New York: Cambridge University Press, 2011); Manfred Elsig, *Functioning of the WTO: Mapping the Challenges and Asking the Hard Questions*, E15 Expert Group on the Functioning of the WTO, Overview Paper (Geneva: International Centre for Trade and Sustainable Development (ICTSD) and World Economic Forum, 2014); Debra Steger, ed., *Redesigning the World Trade Organization for the Twenty-First Century* (Waterloo, ON: Wilfrid Laurier University Press, 2009); Bernard Hoekman, *Proposals for WTO Reform: A Synthesis and Assessment*, The World Bank, Policy Research Working Papers, no. WPS5525 (2011). See also the reform proposals formulated in the Sutherland report (Consultative Board to the Director-General Supachai Panitchpakdi, *The Future of the WTO: Addressing Institutional Challenges in the New Millennium* (Geneva: World Trade Organization, 2004)) and the Warwick Commission report (Warwick Commission, *The Multilateral Trade Regime: Which Way Forward?* (Nottingham, UK: University of Warwick, 2007)).

There is also the need to move beyond consensus towards some sort of qualified majority voting or weighted voting.[980] In product-specific negotiations, the WTO could follow the patterns and allocations chosen in the ICBs. Countries engaged on the consumption or import side and on the production or export side should together have parity of vote. Typically, the exporting members shall together hold 1,000 votes and the importing members shall together hold 1,000 votes. Substantive decisions would need to be taken by a 'distributed' – simple or two thirds – majority, i.e. a majority of the votes cast by producing countries and a majority of the votes cast by consuming countries, counted separately. Within each category of members (producers and consumers), each member shall have a specific amount of basic votes; the remaining votes be divided among members in proportion to their average trade volumes in specified reference periods. Variables for voting weight allocation may also include a combination of vulnerability and dependency indicators. It is important to do justice to small and vulnerable economies that are heavily dependent on the product concerned, even if their trade share is minimal.

Finally, the option of delegating regulatory functions to other bodies outside the WTO system should be further explored. This option is discussed below.

#### 5.3.2.2 More Politically Oriented Solutions

Short of formal rule-making and decision-making procedures, more politically-oriented solutions may yield better results in the current scenario of consensus-based law-making. In this author's view, the way ahead is punctuated by 'peace clauses' and 'due restraint' arrangements, patterned after the Bali Decision on Public Stockholding for Food Security.[981] The pathway is also to be made through interpretative declarations, along the lines of the Doha Declaration on the TRIPS Agreement and Public Health.[982] In essence, members would restate that the AoA should be interpreted and implemented in a manner supportive of WTO members' right to further food and rural livelihood security. They may also spell out specific requirements for stabilisation policies that would

980 For a discussion of models and systems of weighted voting, Thomas Cottier and Satoko Takenoshita, "Decision-Making and the Balance of Powers in WTO Negotiations: Towards Supplementary Weighted Voting," in *At the Crossroads: The World Trading System and the Doha Round*, ed. Stefan Griller (Wien, New York: Springer, 2008).

981 World Trade Organization, Ministerial Decision of 7 December 2013 on Public Stockholding for Food Security Purposes, WT/MIN(13)/38, WT/L/913.

982 WT/MIN(01)/DEC/2 (20 November 2001).

be shielded from legal challenge, as discussed in Section 5.2.[983] For the most part, these statements will result in political commitments, more than in legally binding and enforceable rules, unless formal amendments or authoritative interpretations are involved. However, these arrangements would have legal value. If formally adopted by a political body of the WTO (the Ministerial Conference or the General Council), Declarations are legal acts. Furthermore, irrespective of their hortatory language, they can be legally relevant in a dispute settlement context, though not directly adjudicable. Specifically, a WTO panel could draw guidance from them under Article 31 (3) (subsequent practice or subsequent interpretative agreement) and Article 32 (as a supplementary means of interpretation) of the VCLT.[984]

An even 'softer' approach would engage WTO members in a non-law-making capacity. Reference is here to 'mainstreaming' practices that progressively shape the political orientation of an organisation.[985] There is general assent among WTO members to the conclusion that a greater degree of stability is desirable in agricultural commodity markets. In particular, there is widespread agreement that 'excessive' commodity price volatility is having a detrimental impact on producers and consumers. Through delegates' routine work, stabilisation objectives could be incrementally and progressively mainstreamed in the working of the Committee on Agriculture. This can occur through a number of political venues, including informal submissions, formal notifications, agenda setting, and discussions. This practice would not alone suffice to change substantive rules or make the WTO adjudicator more receptive to external norms. Yet it may contribute to shape the political orientation of the WTO as to which paradigm is to be followed: whether a trade liberalisation paradigm or a more complex trade regulation paradigm that embraces trade and stabilisation concerns. As discussed in Foltea, shifts in political orientation will affect the WTO adjudicator's approach towards the weight it can give to "other societal values than trade".[986] Shifting attitudes and perceptions would also lay the groundwork for formal legislative options (above, Section 5.3.2.1). This approach highlights the potential of Committee work to

983 These policies should be: transparent and predictable; symmetric, in their consideration of the interests of poor urban and rural constituencies; pro-poor, with no diversion of resources from the relatively poor to comparatively more affluent groups; and should not hinder equally critical interests of vulnerable constituencies elsewhere.

984 On the legal standing of Ministerial Declarations, Steve Charnovitz, "The Legal Status of the Doha Declarations," *Journal of International Economic Law* 5, no. 1 (2002).

985 On the integration of social concerns into trade law through mainstreaming, see Nadakavukaren Schefer, above n 604, at 289–91.

986 Foltea, above n 54, at 281.

interpret open-ended norms laid down in the WTO agreements and eventually evolve new norms, through procedural norms and soft law.[987]

WTO members may also agree to exercise due restraint in the WTO context, and move the political confrontation on agricultural stabilisation to more politically-oriented fora, such as UNCTAD, FAO and the ICBs. These are the most suitable fora in which to detail the specifics of 'legitimate' stabilisation arrangements. Eventually, these organisations may develop 'model' agricultural stabilisation arrangements, or standards. These 'model' schemes should lay down criteria for stabilisation schemes that are predictable and transparent, pro-poor, economically rational, financially sound and not prejudiced against the interests of vulnerable constituencies elsewhere. These standards could offer a useful benchmark against which to assess the legality or political legitimacy of price stabilisation arrangements. WTO members and adjudicative bodies would then exert due restraint, and defer to these standards in assessing the WTO conformity of a stabilisation policy. This would possibly preserve the 'functional legitimacy' of the WTO, its core of liberal rules, rooted in the rule of law principle; while allowing circumstantial, contextual and differentiated solutions, informed by principles outside of the WTO framework. Eventually, this approach would allow the WTO to overcome its identity crisis and play a new role, one which reconciles its functional strengths and aspirational goals.

### 5.3.3 *Assessment*

To sum up, the adjudicative process allows some openings for a purposive interpretation of WTO law in light of the outlined normative framework, but only to some extent. It must be in parallel with action at the decision-making level. The process envisaged is incremental and progressive: a process of continuous treaty-making, marked by the enactment of secondary legislation.[988] It also implies operationalisation of the link between the WTO and its 'sister' organisations, UNCTAD *in primis*. What is eventually at stake is the gradual formation of rules through a mix of soft law (interpretative / self- restraint declarations) and progressive jurisprudence (that draws on Declarations and Decisions as interpretive material or facts). This transformative, gradual exercise crossbreeds politics and law and, within law, rule-making and judicial practice. Highly political in nature, it is upstream to the crystallisation of rules through formal rule-making and decision-making. Yet, it results into an evolutive approach

987 In this direction see Andrew Lang and Joanne Scott, "The Hidden World of WTO Governance," *European Journal of International Law* 20, no. 3 (2009).

988 This approach is discussed in Thomas Cottier, *A Two-Tier Approach to WTO Decision Making*, NCCR Trade Working Papers, no. 2009/06 ([Bern], 2009).

towards the crystallisation of rules. This will occur later, typically by means of formal amendments or authoritative interpretations, once a form of *opinion juris* in favour of this evolution has emerged. This incremental approach is possibly the best pathway to integrate 'meta-legal' elements (considerations of social inclusiveness and poverty alleviation) into the working of international trade law.

CHAPTER 6

# Conclusion

A debate is underway as to the appropriate role of trade policy in agricultural price stabilisation. Two contrasting attitudes towards stabilisation have come to dominate the policy discourse in the aftermath of the 2007–08 and 2010–11 commodity crises. The first advocates a 'deepening' of the market-based order through the removal of trade restrictions and distortions. A second approach calls for a reinstatement of efforts to 'tame' commodity markets. This divergence has always been in the background, at Havana, Geneva and Nairobi; and continues right to the present. It reflects ideas and perspectives, 'structuralist' and 'free-market' paradigms, as well as 'substantive' and 'formal' legal rationales, which continue to have echoes down to the present.

In this author's view, there is a need to move beyond these contrasting views, and steer a middle course in between. As pointed out in Rothstein, there is, in commodities, a need to move beyond "the tendency to treat the choice between the market and central regulation in an either/or fashion".[989] What is at stake here is a conceptual shift from the dichotomous classification of free market *versus* intervention to the integrated notion of 'regulated markets'.

In commodities, regulation is called upon to furnish the institutional setting and underpinning of well-functioning markets; and counter market imperfections and failures, in the form of asymmetries and externalities. Moving beyond considerations of market efficiency, agricultural commodities engage interests of rural livelihood, food security and, in general, social stability that invite regulation. Commodity market dynamics, and extreme price swings in particular, should be constrained within some normative perimeters. As stated in the late 1970s by Professor Thomas M. Franck, "[...] the market should operate within boundaries created by a sense of 'just prices'".[990] Towards this objective, the law will have to play a more creative role than it has done this far. Starting from international trade regulation.

Trade law is called upon to play a twofold role in this field.

First, it should set the normative parameters that are to be 'factored' into the working of agricultural markets. Specifically, it should introduce new variables and coefficients linked to social stability in the efficiency equation, grounded in ethical foundations. When dealing with agricultural stabilisation policies, three

989 Rothstein, above n 410.

990 Thomas M. Franck, "Minimum Standards of Public Policy and Order Applicable to Collective International Commodity Negotiations," *Collected Courses* 160 (1978): 412.

 | DOI 10.1163/9789004350540_007

overarching objectives of international trade policy and regulation are identified (Section 5.1.2): food security; sustainable rural livelihood; and environmental sustainability. In interplay with and against the background of considerations of trade 'fairness', these non-trade or supra-trade interests should purposively frame the WTO regulation of agricultural price stabilisation policies. This entails a shift in the nature of commodity trade regulation, from narrowly defined and functional to broadly encompassing and aspirational. It brings back the 'substantive' rationale underlying the commodity trade regime set forth in Havana and Nairobi (Section 3.2): the idea that commodity market outcomes shall not be apprehended as naturally justified, but benchmarked against normative values, grounded in ethical foundations. The legal bases upon which this regulatory shift is advocated involve elements of soft and hard law (Section 5.1.1).

Second, trade law should set principles, techniques and procedures to manage trade-offs. In particular, it should strike a balance between stabilisation policies and liberal trade interests; and between the right of a country to stabilise its farm sector and the right of farmers elsewhere to compete on fair terms at home or abroad. A balanced trade-off, based on considerations of social justice, will define the legal boundaries of 'optimal' stabilisation policies, to be permissible, whatever their current status under existing trade rules. The analysis has brought to light the concept of cosmopolitan multilateralism and equity as conceptual foundations. The first one depicts a dedication to multilateralism, but also entails legal responsibilities on the part of the global community and 'price setters'. Equity is introduced as a foundation for fairness and distributive justice, in line with modern functions the principle assumes in international law. The principle of modulation and graduation also follows from equity. These principles are, for the most part, unwritten in international trade regulation. Yet, they underlie specific rules and disciplines (the case for equitable constructs), or even run through the whole WTO Treaty (like multilateralism). In this author's view, such principles represent the fundamental legal concepts and values that should inform the trade and price stabilisation policy interface.

This 'framing role' of trade law with regard to stabilisation policies can be appreciated at the domestic and international level. Though domestic and international perspectives are complexly intertwined, they also raise separate issues and have been treated separately.

## 6.1 Domestic Stabilisation Policies

With regard to domestic farm stabilisation policies, WTO law should openly follow a paradigm of trade regulation, as distinct from trade liberalisation. The approach outlined (Section 5.2.1) involves a fine-tuning, or modulation of policy space provisions, to align them with the normative objectives and principles outlined in Section 5.1. What is foreseeable is a modulated approach, based on threshold criteria that reflect varying degrees of socio-economic vulnerability and trade distorting potential. The approach entails various sets of disciplines, triggered by the attainment of specified thresholds. Rights and obligations would be tuned, or modulated in accordance with a country's factual conditions in the sector concerned. The assessment is to be sectoral, on a product by product (or product category) basis; and dynamic, to capture changes over time. Eventually, no country would be permanently locked into static boxes or categories.

This legal approach has some potential, in terms of addressing pressing equity concerns and redressing imbalances in multilateral trade rules. It may also serve as a pathway out of the current stalemate in agriculture negotiations. It is interesting to note, in this respect, that WTO law is in fact moving in the direction of complex, graduated solutions. In the December 2008 revised draft modalities, for example, the distinction between developed and developing countries is giving way to a more articulated taxonomy, including SVEs, RAMs, very recently-acceded members, small low-income RAMs with economies in transition, and LDCs. The following step is to make trade regulation even more circumstantial, to reflect, as elsewhere stated by the WTO Appellate Body, "real facts in real cases in the real world".[991] This at least in the sensitive area of agricultural commodities, when balancing competing rights.

Yet, this circumstantial approach has also limits and shortfalls in two important respects. First, as it clearly emerges from the previous analysis, it involves some degree of arbitrariness in setting the line of equilibrium between competing interests. The sense of arbitrariness is particularly acute when competing interests of equally vulnerable constituencies are at stake. Second, this approach leads to some degree of uncertainty and unpredictability. Complexly modulated rules, when not vague standards, take the place of precisely framed, functional legal rules; and much is left to the equitable appreciation of the circumstances of the case. This involves some loss in terms of legal certainty – a basic tenet of the rule-based trading system.

In spite of these limits, the approach outlined in this study may still provide a viable solution. The critics above have valid arguments. Yet, these are not conclusive. Two comments are in order. First, multilateral trade rules in agriculture are negotiated disciplines. They reflect the relative negotiating capabilities and leverage of the various parties, and are highly imperfect, to

---

991 Appellate Body Report, *Japan – Alcoholic Beverages II*, at p. 31, with reference to the interpretive process of WTO rules.

say the least. These disciplines do not lend themselves well to deductive stringency and rule-oriented reasoning, which 'freeze' their imperfections. Highly political in nature, they lend themselves better to a more flexible, equitable reading. A fundamental reorientation may be needed, in terms of modes of legal thought and practice: from a formalist, positivist approach towards a more substantive, principle-based approach. Second, in agriculture, "bright-line" trade rules[992] may not necessarily lead to more certainty and predictability than relatively vague principles. As a matter of fact, agricultural trade rules have led to very unpredictable outcomes, due to the complex balance of commitments and escapes. For example, the outcome of WTO disciplines on domestic support has been a change in intervention tools and strategies ('box shifting'), rather than a substantial reduction in overall support.[993]

Eventually, in a second-best and complex world, the way forward involves complexly textured solutions that reflect distinct factual circumstances. These solutions will need to allow significant leeway for market price intervention. The challenge is where to set safeguards, so as to avoid abuse. As discussed through this study, this is a context-specific, circumstantial exercise, informed by equitable considerations and multilateral concerns.

## 6.2 Intergovernmental Commodity Control Agreements

Turning to international stabilisation arrangements, existing rules provide significant leeway for intergovernmental commodity control arrangements that conform to multilaterally agreed criteria (Section 2.3.2). The proper and underlying role of trade law in this area is to specify the 'normative benchmarks' for assessing the legitimacy of these stabilisation policies, as discussed above.

The broad normative objectives of multilateral price intervention in commodity markets, as laid down in the Havana Charter and UNCTAD's IPC, are still analytically relevant. So are the ordering principles of multilateralism, transparency and cooperation that were to apply. These principles, as discussed in Section 5.1, still represent fundamental legal concepts when assessing the legitimacy of stabilisation policies.

---

992 On aspects of legal certainty associated with rules framed in precise language and vague 'standards' employing terms like 'reasonableness', 'fairness' etc., see Ofer Raban, "The Fallacy of Legal Certainty: Why Vague Legal Standards May Be Better for Capitalism and Liberalism," *Boston University Public Interest Law Journal* 19, no. 2 (2010).

993 See above, Section 4.1.2.3. For a discussion, Musselli, above n 580.

As discussed, the Havana Charter 'grafted' into trade regulation the broad aspirational goals envisaged in Article 55 of the UN Charter.[994] Security of employment, and more broadly the well-being of people, ought thus to be the cornerstone of the multilateral trading system, the 'critical benchmark'[995] against which to assess the desirability of specific commercial policies. This idea continues to have echoes down to the present. It resonates into the 2030 Agenda for Sustainable Development,[996] and has gained momentum again in the economic debate on trade and employment.[997]

The NIEO tried to translate redistributive concerns into legally binding obligations. Under UNCTAD's IPC, redistributive justice aspired to become the basic tenet of commodity trade regulation. Today, redistributive ideals continue to inform the debate about a fair allocation of value along commodity chains. As discussed in Chapter 5, they can certainly provide a useful analytical framework for rethinking market price intervention in commodities.

These normative values are still relevant and inform the framework outlined in Section 5.1. On a more general level, what is still pertinent in the present context is the grounding of international economic law into moral principles, the infusion of ethical imperatives into law. This normative approach, submerged by the neo-classical wave in the 1980s, is surfacing again, in the aftermath of the 2007–08 and 2010–11 economic crises, as if the history of ideas has followed a circular, rather than a linear, path.

Important lessons can also be drawn from the poor implementation record of multilateral post-war efforts to stabilise commodity prices. The knowledge of past failures should inform future endeavours, with a full regard to practical workability and implementation.

As discussed, commodity control agreements under the Havana Charter and UNCTAD's IPC concealed sharp distrust and major divergences about the specific price objectives sought. In the background, there was a fundamental difference of creeds, or attitudes, towards commodity control. Differences, it is important to acknowledge, were not only ideologically inspired. They also

994 Havana Charter, Article 1, Preamble; Geneva draft, above n 49, Article 1; London Report, above n 49, narrative account of the treatment of Chapter I, at 4.

995 Drache, above n 469, at 8–12.

996 Transforming Our World: The 2030 Agenda for Sustainable Development, above n 717.

997 The existing neoliberal orthodoxy is being challenged by alternative conceptual frameworks. These alternatives call for a reorientation of the macroeconomic strategy of both developed and developing countries. The call is for strengthened domestic purchasing power through a combination of better paying jobs in formal sector and income redistribution. See UNCTAD, *Trade and Development Report, 2013: Adjusting to the Changing Dynamics of the World Economy* (New York and Geneva: United Nations, 2013).

proceeded on pragmatic grounds. In particular, there were questions about the opportunity costs of direct price intervention relative, for example, to direct income stabilisation; and doubts about who would reap the benefits of increased commodity prices.

These differences have continued to be in evidence, right to the present. The debate as to the proper way is, again, locked in stalemate, as discussed in Chapter 4. As in the past, the temptation to disguise disagreement so as to break the stalemate is high. And again, contradictions and incoherence would inevitably come to the surface when trying to implement the terms of broadly defined arrangements.

The lesson retained is that a 'grand design' for multilateral action on prices, patterned after the Havana Charter, the SACA, or UNCTAD's IPC is unlikely. A more 'minimalist' approach is desirable.

As discussed in Chapter 5, this minimalist approach will essentially involve action at the domestic level via price stabilisation, but within the framework of multilaterally agreed criteria and frameworks (Section 5.2.1). Taking the example of price bands, international agencies may develop model price band schemes, transparent and predictable, to the fullest possible extent minimally trade-distortive. These may serve as an international standard that triggers a rebuttable presumption of conformity of domestic schemes with WTO law. Likewise, triggers and thresholds used to regulate export restrictions and public stockholding should reflect multilaterally agreed criteria of socio-economic vulnerability and trade distorting potential. In this context, ICAs and UN-sponsored expert groups would play a crucial role as standard-setters. They would not actively engage in stabilising prices, but would set internationally recognised standards for legitimate price intervention at the domestic level.

Beyond this role as standard-setters, ICBs and ICAs can still play a part, in this author's view, in ensuring stable and equitable prices to poor commodity producers in developing countries. In particular, they can provide a framework where potentially adversarial constituencies, notably producers and consumers, but also large producers and 'satellite' producers, can be locked into cooperative behaviours (5.1.3.1). ICBs and ICAs may also effectively catalyse concerted price action, especially if coupled with price monitoring and early warning systems. Stabilisation measures may involve a variety of approaches, from harmonisation of national stocking policies to internationally agreed supply management measures and long-term supply and purchase commitments at agreed prices. Yet, to efficiently perform these roles, ICAs need to be 'reinvented', in terms of institutional design and stabilisation mechanisms. What is posited here is a move from intergovernmental commodity arrangements to multi-stakeholder initiatives; and from 'control' ICAs to 'regulatory' ICAs. As discussed (Section 5.2.2), this involves solutions that are product- or chain-specific, rather than sector-wide; procedural, more than substantive; individualistic and non-statist; and implemented in the context of multi-stakeholder frameworks that leverage supply chain dynamics.

APPENDIX 1

# Product Coverage, Agricultural ICAs

| Product | Coverage (tradable commodities) | Degree of processing |
|---|---|---|
| Coffee (ICA) | Green coffee beans (unroasted) | Primary (relatively) unprocessed |
| | Decaffeinated coffee | Semi-processed |
| | Roasted coffee beans | Semi-processed |
| | Ground coffee | Semi-processed |
| | Liquid and instant (soluble) coffee | Processed (finished products) |
| Rubber (INRA) | Latex concentrates | Primary (relatively) unprocessed |
| | Dry/solid rubber (in sheet, crepe or block forms). | Semi-processed |
| Wheat (IWA) | Wheat grains | Primary (relatively) unprocessed |
| | Wheat-flour | Semi-processed |
| Cocoa (ICCA) | Cocoa beans | Primary (relatively) unprocessed |
| | Cocoa products made exclusively from cocoa beans, such as cocoa paste, cocoa butter, unsweetened cocoa powder, cocoa cake and cocoa nibs | Semi-processed |
| | Other products containing cocoa | May also include processed |
| Sugar (ISA) | Sugar in any of its recognised commercial forms derived from sugar cane or sugar beet, including edible and fancy molasses, syrups, etc. | Semi-processed and processed |

SOURCE: REVIEW OF ICAS ADOPTED WITHIN THE HAVANA CHARTER AND UNCTAD IPC FRAMEWORKS (SEE BIBLIOGRAPHY).

 | DOI 10.1163/9789004350540_008

# Ranking of Economies by Agricultural Export Dependence

| Status | Economy | Total all products | Agr. % | Fuels % | Ores % | Man. % |
|---|---|---|---|---|---|---|
| Developing ex. LDC | Falkland Islands (Malvinas) | 183,333 | 96.57 | 0.03 | 0.01 | 0.74 |
| LDC | Guinea-Bissau | 187,339 | 96.20 | 2.67 | 0.47 | 0.66 |
| Developing ex. LDC | Palau | 7,352 | 94.86 | 0.10 | 1.64 | 2.78 |
| Developing ex. LDC | Micronesia (Federated States of) | 35,000 | 92.36 | 0.15 | 1.57 | 3.43 |
| LDC | Kiribati | 7,304 | 91.57 | 0.01 | 0.18 | 5.80 |
| LDC | Somalia | 533,333 | 89.52 | 0.10 | 4.45 | 4.05 |
| Developed | Faeroe Islands | 1,014,554 | 86.64 | 5.28 | 0.27 | 7.25 |
| Developed | Greenland | 480,219 | 86.38 | 0.00 | 2.32 | 1.75 |
| Developing ex. LDC | Seychelles | 519,288 | 86.09 | 4.23 | 0.77 | 8.89 |
| LDC | Ethiopia | 2,735,413 | 83.47 | 0.00 | 6.84 | 9.67 |
| LDC | Malawi | 1,272,075 | 79.61 | 0.15 | 5.61 | 14.29 |
| Developing ex. LDC | Maldives | 330,606 | 77.13 | 3.35 | 2.23 | 6.29 |
| LDC | Solomon Islands | 449,658 | 76.57 | 0.11 | 12.40 | 0.84 |
| Developing ex. LDC | Uruguay | 8,562,240 | 73.65 | 0.77 | 1.69 | 23.66 |
| LDC | Vanuatu | 50,511 | 73.50 | 0.19 | 0.45 | 24.82 |
| LDC | Tuvalu | 297 | 72.16 | 0.13 | 1.97 | 22.44 |
| Developing ex. LDC | Cabo Verde | 64,631 | 71.31 | 3.08 | 3.78 | 21.42 |
| Developing ex. LDC | Paraguay | 8,155,694 | 70.60 | 18.31 | 1.62 | 9.08 |
| Developing ex. LDC | Tonga | 14,992 | 69.78 | 0.08 | 5.39 | 21.97 |
| Developed | New Zealand | 38,048,065 | 65.62 | 4.52 | 4.71 | 21.57 |
| LDC | Gambia | 94,910 | 65.33 | 1.39 | 13.69 | 19.06 |
| LDC | Uganda | 2,308,102 | 64.13 | 0.71 | 2.04 | 31.01 |
| LDC | Burundi | 118,736 | 62.35 | 0.66 | 17.90 | 18.13 |
| Developing ex. LDC | Belize | 611,261 | 61.12 | 21.08 | 1.00 | 13.77 |
| Developing ex. LDC | Saint Helena | 43,128 | 59.24 | 0.48 | 1.53 | 38.23 |
| Developing ex. LDC | Cook Islands | 5,470 | 57.98 | 0.01 | 1.74 | 36.10 |
| LDC | Sao Tome and Principe | 14,047 | 57.96 | 2.58 | 1.98 | 37.80 |

 | DOI 10.1163/9789004350540_009

| Status | Economy | Total all products | Agr. % | Fuels % | Ores % | Man. % |
|---|---|---|---|---|---|---|
| Developing ex. LDC | Kenya | 5,912,705 | 54.15 | 5.23 | 5.34 | 35.27 |
| Developing ex. LDC | Argentina | 80,537,391 | 53.98 | 5.58 | 6.37 | 31.61 |
| LDC | Afghanistan | 439,909 | 53.12 | 6.97 | 11.34 | 11.82 |
| LDC | Benin | 1,366,926 | 52.93 | 16.22 | 20.94 | 9.91 |
| Developing ex. LDC | Côte d'Ivoire | 11,885,137 | 52.62 | 26.33 | 4.70 | 11.87 |
| Developing ex. LDC | Guatemala | 10,116,975 | 51.18 | 3.95 | 6.48 | 37.71 |
| Developing ex. LDC | Fiji | 1,132,688 | 49.61 | 20.81 | 9.19 | 19.23 |
| Developing ex. LDC | Nicaragua | 2,457,200 | 48.68 | 0.85 | 11.50 | 38.16 |
| Developing ex. LDC | Saint Vincent and the Grenadines | 43,158 | 47.80 | 0.62 | 3.44 | 47.84 |
| LDC | Burkina Faso | 2,205,448 | 47.74 | 2.95 | 43.31 | 5.92 |
| LDC | Central African Republic | 180,000 | 46.33 | 0.11 | 46.28 | 7.12 |
| Developing ex. LDC | Zimbabwe | 3,633,950 | 45.65 | 11.13 | 26.06 | 16.65 |
| Developed | Iceland | 5,136,401 | 45.47 | 1.85 | 38.69 | 13.47 |
| Developing ex. LDC | Honduras | 8,027,967 | 43.73 | 3.29 | 7.40 | 44.04 |
| Developing ex. LDC | Ghana | 13,363,230 | 42.30 | 33.05 | 16.48 | 7.01 |
| LDC | Comoros | 21,638 | 42.21 | 0.00 | 3.53 | 54.26 |
| LDC | United Republic of Tanzania | 5,110,730 | 42.13 | 1.83 | 38.80 | 16.63 |
| Transition | Republic of Moldova | 2,268,999 | 40.96 | 1.24 | 3.71 | 53.74 |
| LDC | Rwanda | 570,381 | 39.98 | 4.90 | 44.87 | 9.89 |
| LDC | Madagascar | 1,608,477 | 39.26 | 2.76 | 21.96 | 35.29 |
| LDC | Djibouti | 110,109 | 38.59 | 10.98 | 18.64 | 21.19 |
| Developing ex. LDC | Grenada | 34,510 | 37.63 | 0.11 | 10.45 | 51.81 |
| Developing ex. LDC | Cameroon | 4,330,670 | 37.09 | 46.79 | 2.86 | 12.77 |
| LDC | Sierra Leone | 1,132,744 | 37.03 | 0.02 | 46.09 | 16.22 |
| LDC | Mali | 2,441,251 | 36.62 | 2.94 | 49.23 | 11.08 |
| Developing ex. LDC | Swaziland | 1,923,333 | 36.48 | 0.71 | 5.26 | 42.52 |
| Developing ex. LDC | Syrian Arab Republic | 5,333,333 | 35.78 | 29.02 | 3.04 | 32.02 |
| Developing ex. LDC | Brazil | 246,932,177 | 35.58 | 9.60 | 18.79 | 33.93 |
| Developing ex. LDC | Samoa | 68,158 | 34.99 | 0.04 | 1.82 | 56.53 |
| Developing ex. LDC | Guyana | 1,279,999 | 34.96 | 0.13 | 57.34 | 7.14 |
| LDC | Senegal | 2,571,123 | 34.90 | 19.05 | 13.37 | 32.11 |
| LDC | Liberia | 461,900 | 33.68 | 11.04 | 26.96 | 26.68 |
| Developing ex. LDC | Cuba | 5,637,970 | 33.66 | 9.65 | 24.18 | 22.82 |

| Status | Economy | Total all products | Agr. % | Fuels % | Ores % | Man. % |
|---|---|---|---|---|---|---|
| LDC | Myanmar | 9,782,583 | 33.39 | 39.04 | 18.24 | 9.32 |
| Developing ex. LDC | Ecuador | 23,717,395 | 33.33 | 57.36 | 2.10 | 7.10 |
| Developing ex. LDC | Saint Lucia | 172,030 | 32.93 | 31.46 | 2.19 | 33.42 |
| Developing ex. LDC | Antigua and Barbuda | 59,797 | 32.22 | 17.67 | 1.67 | 46.72 |
| Developing ex. LDC | Mauritius | 2,695,353 | 31.42 | 0.07 | 3.80 | 49.52 |
| Developing ex. Ldc | Turks and Caicos Islands | 23,876 | 30.42 | 0.21 | 10.47 | 36.69 |
| LDC | Togo | 1,242,908 | 29.75 | 9.12 | 24.81 | 35.19 |
| Developing ex. LDC | Sri Lanka | 9,795,315 | 29.35 | 0.37 | 5.15 | 65.08 |
| LDC | Lao People's Dem. Rep. | 2,241,387 | 28.77 | 17.06 | 39.49 | 14.48 |
| Developed | Latvia | 12,666,141 | 28.07 | 7.92 | 4.01 | 54.00 |
| LDC | Eritrea | 401,894 | 28.06 | 0.00 | 60.40 | 11.44 |
| Developing ex. LDC | Papua New Guinea | 6,276,719 | 27.80 | 17.37 | 51.82 | 2.71 |
| Developing ex. LDC | Barbados | 514,103 | 27.13 | 19.53 | 2.50 | 49.63 |
| Transition | Uzbekistan | 12,369,085 | 26.42 | 16.72 | 17.03 | 39.11 |
| Developing ex. LDC | Namibia | 4,466,135 | 25.59 | 1.27 | 50.51 | 22.35 |
| Developing ex. LDC | State of Palestine | 954,428 | 25.47 | 0.28 | 11.41 | 62.30 |
| LDC | Mauritania | 2,620,695 | 24.99 | 8.09 | 58.43 | 0.82 |
| Transition | Ukraine | 66,802,666 | 24.80 | 6.09 | 8.52 | 59.91 |
| Developing ex. LDC | Chile | 79,033,078 | 24.73 | 0.97 | 61.14 | 13.15 |
| Transition | Tajikistan | 1,236,131 | 24.47 | 2.50 | 54.44 | 12.62 |
| Developing ex. LDC | El Salvador | 5,379,454 | 24.41 | 2.27 | 2.79 | 68.99 |
| Developing ex. Ldc | Dominican Republic | 9,070,767 | 23.92 | 3.31 | 9.12 | 60.58 |
| LDC | Nepal | 892,929 | 23.67 | 0.00 | 4.02 | 72.27 |
| Developing ex. LDC | Costa Rica | 10,984,307 | 23.62 | 0.07 | 1.08 | 73.54 |
| Developing ex. LDC | Indonesia | 192,026,738 | 23.57 | 32.93 | 8.10 | 35.40 |
| Transition | Armenia | 1,405,444 | 23.56 | 5.70 | 47.00 | 23.44 |
| Developing ex. LDC | Niue | 20 | 22.87 | 0.47 | 12.97 | 59.06 |
| Transition | Georgia | 2,491,944 | 22.83 | 2.57 | 13.03 | 60.32 |
| Transition | Serbia | 12,582,095 | 22.34 | 4.18 | 8.56 | 63.35 |
| LDC | Mozambique | 3,909,279 | 21.72 | 33.73 | 36.30 | 6.83 |
| Developing ex. LDC | Marshall Islands | 56,400 | 21.67 | 2.11 | 0.22 | 75.70 |
| Developing ex. LDC | Jamaica | 1,634,589 | 21.56 | 22.74 | 43.45 | 11.87 |
| Developing ex. LDC | Pakistan | 25,026,109 | 21.44 | 2.89 | 1.87 | 73.40 |
| Developed | Denmark | 109,481,446 | 21.44 | 9.54 | 1.53 | 59.16 |

| Status | Economy | Total all products | Agr. % | Fuels % | Ores % | Man. % |
|---|---|---|---|---|---|---|
| Developing ex. LDC | American Samoa | 380,000 | 21.12 | 28.33 | 3.37 | 47.06 |
| Developing ex. LDC | Viet Nam | 114,489,233 | 21.06 | 10.79 | 0.87 | 67.00 |
| Developed | Cyprus | 1,972,759 | 21.06 | 8.83 | 9.82 | 51.87 |
| Transition | Kyrgyzstan | 1,887,744 | 20.01 | 15.01 | 19.37 | 43.12 |
| Transition | Montenegro | 530,232 | 19.87 | 18.59 | 42.42 | 19.12 |
| Developed | Greece | 34,383,426 | 19.68 | 36.57 | 8.02 | 33.48 |
| Developing ex. LDC | Morocco | 21,619,998 | 19.65 | 5.17 | 11.30 | 63.27 |
| Developed | Lithuania | 30,107,018 | 19.64 | 24.22 | 1.54 | 52.84 |
| Developing ex. LDC | Dominica | 34,675 | 19.29 | 0.02 | 8.15 | 72.53 |
| Developing ex. LDC | Thailand | 228,965,309 | 18.92 | 6.13 | 4.67 | 70.27 |
| Developing ex. LDC | Lebanon | 5,483,000 | 17.91 | 2.81 | 30.03 | 48.90 |
| Developed | Netherlands | 664,285,092 | 17.91 | 18.95 | 3.12 | 56.33 |
| Developed | Bulgaria | 28,125,419 | 17.50 | 14.65 | 17.40 | 47.95 |
| Developing ex. LDC | Anguilla | 20,455 | 17.22 | 6.19 | 3.50 | 68.23 |
| Developing ex. LDC | Peru | 44,484,651 | 17.03 | 11.87 | 59.77 | 11.32 |
| Developing ex. LDC | Jordan | 7,920,081 | 16.50 | 0.56 | 12.77 | 69.76 |
| LDC | Niger | 1,433,333 | 16.38 | 32.60 | 22.09 | 27.04 |
| Developed | Croatia | 12,553,512 | 16.37 | 13.38 | 6.03 | 64.03 |
| Developing ex. LDC | French Polynesia | 146,779 | 16.28 | 0.04 | 64.95 | 12.55 |
| Developed | Spain | 298,357,019 | 16.14 | 7.23 | 4.69 | 68.00 |
| Developing ex. LDC | Egypt | 29,926,284 | 15.71 | 34.18 | 8.95 | 40.62 |
| Developing ex. LDC | Bolivia (Plurinational State of) | 11,055,388 | 15.44 | 51.15 | 28.81 | 4.28 |
| Transition | TFYR of Macedonia | 4,241,362 | 15.37 | 5.77 | 6.18 | 72.63 |
| Developing ex. LDC | Malaysia | 227,652,638 | 15.07 | 20.13 | 2.93 | 61.38 |
| Developing ex. LDC | Panama | 15,278,272 | 14.88 | 19.85 | 5.39 | 55.79 |
| Developed | Australia | 259,273,801 | 14.74 | 27.50 | 42.28 | 11.72 |
| Transition | Bosnia and Herzegovina | 5,566,401 | 14.09 | 10.15 | 13.63 | 61.32 |
| Developed | Estonia | 16,838,848 | 14.03 | 11.99 | 3.69 | 65.69 |
| Developed | Portugal | 60,071,810 | 13.92 | 8.44 | 4.03 | 72.53 |
| Developed | Canada | 453,402,060 | 13.87 | 25.85 | 11.84 | 45.40 |
| Developed | France | 568,332,200 | 13.79 | 4.32 | 2.90 | 76.47 |
| LDC | Zambia | 9,653,223 | 13.55 | 1.23 | 71.08 | 13.19 |
| Developing ex. LDC | India | 309,219,803 | 13.35 | 19.46 | 13.01 | 51.87 |
| Developed | Poland | 189,122,104 | 13.09 | 4.88 | 4.89 | 77.04 |
| Transition | Belarus | 41,560,547 | 12.44 | 34.45 | 0.70 | 47.99 |

| Status | Economy | Total all products | Agr. % | Fuels % | Ores % | Man. % |
|---|---|---|---|---|---|---|
| Developing ex. LDC | Colombia | 58,683,001 | 11.57 | 65.53 | 6.13 | 16.75 |
| Developing ex. LDC | Northern Mariana Islands | 3,333 | 11.44 | 0.11 | 17.65 | 69.60 |
| Developed | Romania | 62,159,258 | 11.33 | 5.41 | 3.71 | 76.74 |
| Developed | United States | 1,534,432,239 | 11.21 | 9.01 | 6.83 | 64.09 |
| Developed | Ireland | 120,032,400 | 11.15 | 1.41 | 1.35 | 84.96 |
| Developing ex. LDC | Philippines | 51,338,540 | 10.98 | 3.11 | 6.57 | 72.71 |
| Developing ex. LDC | Turkey | 146,440,152 | 10.94 | 4.63 | 8.29 | 74.72 |
| LDC | Sudan | 5,576,359 | 10.85 | 54.65 | 31.53 | 2.96 |
| LDC | Cambodia | 7,930,124 | 10.49 | 0.00 | 2.50 | 86.72 |
| Developed | Belgium | 478,101,473 | 10.48 | 11.83 | 7.98 | 67.61 |
| Developing ex. LDC | Gabon | 9,650,038 | 10.45 | 78.69 | 6.45 | 4.41 |
| Developing ex. LDC | Tunisia | 17,304,958 | 10.19 | 15.50 | 1.62 | 72.57 |
| Developed | Luxembourg | 19,922,813 | 9.82 | 1.07 | 6.60 | 79.71 |
| Developing ex. LDC | Suriname | 2,518,776 | 9.60 | 9.31 | 62.73 | 4.18 |
| Developed | Hungary | 107,506,839 | 9.34 | 3.67 | 1.95 | 80.92 |
| Developed | Finland | 75,380,872 | 9.34 | 10.85 | 5.97 | 71.72 |
| LDC | Haiti | 833,091 | 9.27 | 0.00 | 1.91 | 82.84 |
| Developing ex. LDC | South Africa | 101,353,254 | 9.17 | 8.17 | 34.17 | 33.07 |
| LDC | Bhutan | 579,637 | 9.11 | 11.76 | 17.96 | 60.94 |
| Developed | Austria | 167,386,464 | 8.96 | 3.22 | 4.31 | 80.86 |
| Developing ex. LDC | Mongolia | 4,487,738 | 8.94 | 20.84 | 67.16 | 3.03 |
| LDC | Guinea | 1,432,912 | 8.72 | 34.96 | 53.53 | 2.33 |
| Developed | Sweden | 175,750,503 | 8.69 | 8.15 | 5.58 | 72.72 |
| Developed | Italy | 512,833,930 | 8.57 | 4.94 | 3.87 | 80.71 |
| LDC | Yemen | 9,000,000 | 7.41 | 86.71 | 2.21 | 2.47 |
| Developed | Norway | 158,584,366 | 7.06 | 68.42 | 5.53 | 15.77 |
| Transition | Albania | 2,082,549 | 6.69 | 24.47 | 13.35 | 55.03 |
| Developed | United Kingdom | 515,827,300 | 6.52 | 12.52 | 11.13 | 60.82 |
| Developing ex. LDC | Mexico | 366,778,138 | 6.44 | 14.23 | 5.55 | 72.87 |
| Developed | Germany | 1,452,344,484 | 6.36 | 2.59 | 3.66 | 82.37 |
| Developed | Slovakia | 81,263,479 | 6.16 | 6.00 | 2.90 | 84.86 |
| Developing ex. LDC | Guam | 44,927 | 6.04 | 11.67 | 20.53 | 21.93 |
| Developed | Czech Republic | 159,938,817 | 6.03 | 3.55 | 2.36 | 87.98 |
| Developing ex. LDC | Saint Kitts and Nevis | 44,295 | 5.82 | 0.02 | 0.89 | 83.70 |
| LDC | Bangladesh | 26,091,962 | 5.81 | 0.68 | 0.44 | 92.84 |

| Status | Economy | Total all products | Agr. % | Fuels % | Ores % | Man. % |
|---|---|---|---|---|---|---|
| Developed | Andorra | 103,107 | 5.76 | 0.00 | 0.53 | 87.47 |
| Developing ex. LDC | Tokelau | 114 | 5.63 | 0.09 | 2.78 | 86.14 |
| Developing ex. LDC | Korea, Dem. People's Rep. of | 3,820,000 | 5.21 | 40.94 | 16.40 | 36.97 |
| LDC | Sudan (...2011) | 8,981,723 | 5.19 | 81.97 | 12.25 | 0.57 |
| Developed | Slovenia | 33,680,960 | 4.99 | 5.25 | 4.03 | 69.37 |
| LDC | Timor-Leste | 20,013 | 4.98 | 88.13 | 0.23 | 3.24 |
| Developed | Bermuda | 12,485 | 4.94 | 32.47 | 1.41 | 43.01 |
| Transition | Turkmenistan | 15,833,333 | 4.93 | 88.00 | 1.12 | 5.82 |
| Transition | Russian Federation | 523,008,319 | 4.64 | 69.31 | 6.36 | 14.47 |
| Developing ex. LDC | China, Macao SAR | 1,009,287 | 4.59 | 0.46 | 7.28 | 80.65 |
| Developing ex. LDC | Bahamas | 929,167 | 4.58 | 66.22 | 2.49 | 23.07 |
| Developing ex. LDC | Aruba | 2,284,469 | 4.53 | 90.33 | 0.97 | 1.70 |
| LDC | Chad | 4,533,333 | 4.47 | 94.25 | 0.24 | 1.02 |
| LDC | Lesotho | 997,193 | 4.30 | 0.04 | 40.43 | 55.05 |
| Developed | Switzerland | 229,974,872 | 4.05 | 2.64 | 5.67 | 85.69 |
| Developing ex. LDC | Bahrain | 20,114,971 | 4.02 | 39.07 | 32.70 | 23.87 |
| Developing ex. LDC | United Arab Emirates | 343,333,333 | 3.89 | 57.22 | 16.18 | 22.29 |
| Developed | Malta | 4,041,828 | 3.83 | 40.79 | 1.08 | 53.16 |
| Developing ex. LDC | Nigeria | 114,547,010 | 3.82 | 93.93 | 0.57 | 1.61 |
| Developed | Israel | 65,906,056 | 3.78 | 1.41 | 30.53 | 63.90 |
| Developing ex. LDC | Iran (Islamic Republic of) | 104,830,788 | 3.51 | 68.18 | 4.90 | 14.16 |
| Developing ex. LDC | Montserrat | 3,395 | 3.45 | 0.06 | 28.87 | 62.96 |
| Developing ex. LDC | Congo | 10,666,667 | 3.38 | 86.59 | 4.34 | 5.62 |
| Developing ex. LDC | China | 2,052,059,316 | 3.26 | 1.58 | 1.45 | 93.62 |
| LDC | Dem. Rep. of the Congo | 6,400,000 | 3.10 | 14.50 | 77.25 | 3.81 |
| Developing ex. LDC | Oman | 51,575,743 | 3.09 | 71.70 | 4.64 | 15.47 |
| Transition | Kazakhstan | 87,633,159 | 3.03 | 72.47 | 13.21 | 11.29 |
| Transition | Azerbaijan | 32,881,754 | 2.80 | 94.29 | 0.61 | 2.19 |
| Developing ex. LDC | Singapore | 409,382,107 | 2.51 | 18.56 | 1.84 | 69.05 |
| Developing ex. LDC | Trinidad and Tobago | 13,565,631 | 2.38 | 63.60 | 1.96 | 32.06 |
| Developing ex. LDC | Korea, Republic of | 554,227,302 | 2.23 | 9.91 | 2.59 | 85.26 |

| Status | Economy | Total all products | Agr. % | Fuels % | Ores % | Man. % |
|---|---|---|---|---|---|---|
| Developing ex. LDC | China, Taiwan Province of | 303,782,016 | 2.19 | 6.80 | 2.87 | 87.41 |
| Developing ex. LDC | British Virgin Islands | 39,167 | 2.18 | 4.93 | 19.94 | 72.49 |
| Developing ex. LDC | China, Hong Kong SAR | 494,676,191 | 2.06 | 0.22 | 12.45 | 85.20 |
| Developing ex. LDC | Botswana | 6,486,918 | 1.99 | 0.52 | 90.75 | 6.59 |
| Developing ex. LDC | New Caledonia | 1,381,268 | 1.80 | 0.22 | 37.33 | 59.61 |
| Developing ex. LDC | Sint Maarten (Dutch part) | 144,760 | 1.55 | 0.82 | 10.69 | 5.46 |
| Developed | Japan | 778,949,530 | 1.40 | 1.99 | 3.72 | 88.16 |
| Developing ex. LDC | Nauru | 78,333 | 1.17 | 0.03 | 94.36 | 4.29 |
| Developing ex. LDC | Saudi Arabia | 376,343,850 | 1.06 | 84.99 | 0.63 | 13.23 |
| Developing ex. LDC | Venezuela (Bolivarian Republic of) | 91,573,796 | 1.02 | 83.27 | 2.56 | 13.09 |
| LDC | Equatorial Guinea | 14,500,000 | 1.01 | 95.14 | 0.19 | 3.45 |
| Developing ex. LDC | Algeria | 70,433,398 | 0.53 | 98.36 | 0.23 | 0.89 |
| Developing ex. LDC | Kuwait | 107,719,569 | 0.33 | 91.08 | 0.78 | 7.81 |
| Developing ex. LDC | Iraq | 89,055,799 | 0.25 | 98.74 | 0.35 | 0.65 |
| Developing ex. LDC | Cayman Islands | 24,160 | 0.14 | 0.58 | 0.56 | 96.40 |
| Developed | Gibraltar | 249,300 | 0.13 | 67.49 | 0.67 | 31.05 |
| Developing ex. LDC | Brunei Darussalam | 12,304,318 | 0.12 | 96.63 | 0.22 | 2.39 |
| Developing ex. LDC | Libya | 41,147,312 | 0.09 | 96.62 | 1.04 | 2.21 |
| LDC | Angola | 69,067,867 | 0.04 | 98.44 | 1.30 | 0.20 |
| Developing ex. LDC | Qatar | 128,549,429 | 0.03 | 89.27 | 1.35 | 6.44 |

Note: Merchandise trade by trading partner and product based on SITC, Rev.3. Country economic groups as used in UNCTAD statistics (http://unctadstat.unctad.org/EN/Classifications.html). Products groups include: Agr.: "Agricultural exports" (categories "All food items" (SITC 0 + 1 + 22 + 4) + "Agricultural raw materials" (SITC 2 less 22, 27 and 28)); Fuels: "Fuels" (SITC 3); Ores: "Ores, metals, precious stones and non-monetary gold" (SITC 27 + 28 + 68 + 667 + 971); Man.: "Manufactured goods" (SITC 5 to 8 less 667 and 68). *Developed and developing includes sovereign states and other territories.

SOURCE: DATA FROM UNCTADSTAT, MERCHANDISE TRADE MATRIX – PRODUCT GROUPS, EXPORTS IN THOUSANDS OF DOLLARS, ANNUAL, 1995–2013 (DATA RETRIEVED ON 16 FEBRUARY 2015).

APPENDIX 3

# Major Commodity Control Arrangements, by Product

| Arrangement | Scope | Nature | Participants | Entry into force and end date (including extensions) | Stabilisation mechanisms |
|---|---|---|---|---|---|
| **Coffee** | | | | | |
| "Convênio de Taubaté" or Agreement of the three Brazilian Coffee producing states (first 'valorisation scheme') | Unilateral | Producer/ exporter cartel | The three Brazilian coffee producing States (San Paulo, Rio de Janeiro and Minas Geraes). Brazil then accounted for over 80% of world coffee exports | 1906–1907 | Public stockholding scheme, involving public purchase and withdraw from circulation of coffee to maintain quotations above cost price. The scheme was funded by an export tax on coffee. |
| Coffee 'valorisation schemes' | Unilateral | Producer/ exporter cartel | Brazil – Federal Government | 1917–1920; 1921–1929; 1930–1937 | Public stockholding schemes and vast destruction of surplus stocks. |

 | DOI 10.1163/9789004350540_010

| Arrangement | Scope | Nature | Participants | Entry into force and end date (including extensions) | Stabilisation mechanisms |
| --- | --- | --- | --- | --- | --- |
| Inter-American Coffee Agreement | Regional/ plurilateral | Formally dual-interest ICA; in essence exporter cartel, but backed by the major consuming country | 14 Latin American coffee producing countries and the US | 1940–1947 | Export quotas: individual-country quotas for the exportation of coffee to the US, which the US agreed to enforce by import controls (the US also undertook to limit by quota the total entry for consumption of coffee produced in third countries); individual-country quotas for exports to the market outside the United States. |
| Mexico City agreement | Regional/ plurilateral | Producer/ exporter cartel | 7 major Latin American producing countries | 1957–1958 | Export quotas. |
| Latin America Coffee Agreement | Regional/ plurilateral | Producer/ exporter cartel | 15 major Latin American producing countries | 1958–1959 | Export quotas. |
| International Coffee Agreement | Regional/ plurilateral | Producer/ exporter cartel | 15 members of the Latin American Coffee Agreement, France and Portugal (1959) and Britain (1960) on behalf of their respective colonies. By 1960, 90% of world production | 1959–1962 | Export quotas. |

| | | | | | |
|---|---|---|---|---|---|
| International Coffee Agreement, 1962 | Multilateral | Dual-interest ICA | At its entry into force, 26 coffee exporting countries, representing 89.5% of world coffee export and 12 importing countries, accounting for 81.5% of world imports | 1963–1968 | Export quotas (monitored through certificates of origin and re-export); limitation of imports from non-members countries (to a quantity not in excess of their average annual imports prior of the entry into force of the Agreement); commitments to adjust production (to the amount needed for domestic consumption, exports and stocks) and regulate stocks. |
| International Coffee Agreement, 1968 | Multilateral | Dual interest ICA | Major exporters and importers | 1968–1976 (price control provisions suspended between 1973–76) | Patterned after ICOA 1962. |
| International Coffee Agreement, 1976 | Multilateral | Dual-interest ICA | Major exporters and importers | 1976–1983 | System of export quotas (exporting states), import restrictions from non-members (importing states) and domestic supply management. Export quotas: fixed (70% of the global annual quota, on the basis of average export volumes in 1968/69–1971/72) and variable parts (in proportion to verified stocks). The introduction, suspension and reintroduction of the quotas was automatically triggered by price |

| Arrangement | Scope | Nature | Participants | Entry into force and end date (including extensions) | Stabilisation mechanisms |
|---|---|---|---|---|---|
| | | | | | developments. Import restrictions: each member committed to limit its annual imports of coffee from non-member countries to average imports during 1971–74 or 1972–74. Supply management: commitments to control production and stocks. |
| International Coffee Agreement, 1983 | Multilateral | Dual-interest | Major exporters and importers | 1983–1994 (stabilisation provisions suspended in 1989) | Similar to the previous ICOA. |
| **Rubber** | | | | | |
| Voluntary restriction schemes | Unilateral | Producer/exporter cartel (private but publicly backed) | British estate companies in Malaya and the East Indies | 1917–1921 | Production restrictions. |

| | | | | | |
|---|---|---|---|---|---|
| Stevenson Scheme (compulsory restriction scheme) | Unilateral (colonial) | Producer/ exporter cartel | British Government (applied to Malaya and Ceylon, accounting for about 70 % of world rubber production) | 1922–1928 | Exports restricted on the basis of quotas for each estate. Out-of quota shipments hit by prohibitive export duties. Quotas automatically adjusted according to price changes. |
| Agreement for the Regulation of Production and Export of Rubber | Regional/ plurilateral (colonial) | Producer/ exporter cartel | Signed by France (obligations applying to French Indo-China), Britain (Ceylon, the Federated Malay States, the Unfederated Malay States, the Straits Settlements, the State of North Borneo, Brunei and Sarawak), India (Burma), the Netherlands (the Netherlands Indies) and the Kingdom of Siam – covering virtually the whole of world rubber production | 1934–1943 (economic clauses suspended since 1941) | Export quotas, periodically adjusted on the basis of estimated total demand; regulation of stocks and new planting; prohibition of the export of propagating material. |

| Arrangement | Scope | Nature | Participants | Entry into force and end date (including extensions) | Stabilisation mechanisms |
|---|---|---|---|---|---|
| International Natural Rubber Agreement on Price Stabilisation, 1976 | Regional/ plurilateral | Producer/ exporter cartel | Major natural rubber producing countries (Indonesia, Malaysia, Singapore, Sri Lanka, Thailand) | 1976–1979 | Buffer stock interventions to maintain prices within the stabilisation band. Floor and ceiling prices based on average RSS1 quotations on the Kuala Lumpur and Singapore markets. |
| International Natural Rubber Agreement, 1979 | Multilateral | Dual-interest ICA | Major rubber producers and consumers | 1980–1987 | International buffer stock (550,000 tonnes). Reference price periodically revised to reflect market trends. |
| International Natural Rubber Agreement, 1987 | Multilateral | Dual-interest ICA | Major rubber producers and consumers | 1988–1995 | Same as INRA 1979. |
| **Tea** | | | | | |
| Voluntary restriction schemes | Regional / plurilateral (colonial) | Producer/ exporter cartel (private) | The Tea Associations in India, Ceylon and the Dutch East Indies | Implemented in 1920 and 1930 | Output restrictions: Each tea company belonging to the Tea Associations in the producer countries committed to cut back output. |
| The International Tea Agreement, 1933–1938 | Regional/ plurilateral (colonial) | Producer/ exporter cartel (private, officially endorsed) | Tea Associations representing the majority of tea growers in India, Ceylon and the Netherlands East Indies. | 1933–1937 | Production and export restrictions:<br>– Export quotas, enforced by the Governments of the respective countries (all exports of tea subject to export licence); |

| | | | | | |
|---|---|---|---|---|---|
| | | | | | – Tea acreage regulations: prohibition of new planting and limitation of extension of new tea areas in the participating countries;<br>– Prohibition of exports of tea seeds and slips except under license and establishment of export quotas. |
| The International Tea Agreement, 1938–43 | Regional/ plurilateral (colonial) | Producer/ exporter cartel (private, officially endorsed) | Tea Associations representing the majority of tea growers in India, Ceylon and the Netherlands East Indies. In 1944 representatives of the Governments of Kenya, Uganda, Tanganyika and Nyasaland added to the International Tea Committee (agreement multilateralised) | 1938–1950 | Production and export restrictions:<br>– Export quotas (based on the maximum exports of tea from each of the producing countries in any one of the three years 1929, 1930 or 1931), administered through export licences;<br>– Prohibition of export from any of the producing countries of seeds, roots, stumps, cuttings, buds, and other propagating material;<br>– Limitations on replanting of tea and prohibition of new planting of tea. |
| International Tea Agreement of 8 May 1950 | Regional/ plurilateral (colonial) | Producer/ exporter cartel (private, officially endorsed) | Associations representing the majority of tea growers in India, Pakistan, Ceylon and Indonesia | 1950–1955 | Export quotas and tea acreage regulations. |

| Arrangement | Scope | Nature | Participants | Entry into force and end date (including extensions) | Stabilisation mechanisms |
|---|---|---|---|---|---|
| **Sugar** | | | | | |
| International Sugar Agreement (Chadbourne Plan) | Regional/ plurilateral | Producer/ exporter cartel (private, officially backed) | Sugar industries in Belgium, Czechoslovakia, Germany, Hungary, Poland, Yugoslavia, Cuba, Peru | 1931–1935 | Output and export restrictions: segregation and disposal of surplus stocks; fixed national export quotas; adjustment of national production to cover the export quota and home consumption. |
| Agreement concerning the Regulation of the Production and Marketing of Sugar | Multilateral | Dual-interest ICA | 22 countries, covering almost all the world trade in sugar | 1937–1942 | Import and export restrictions. Importers undertook to limit home production and imports of colonial preferential sugar to maintain the outlet on their markets for free market sugar. Members of the British Commonwealth exporters of preferential sugar to the UK undertook to limit those exports. Countries which were almost self-sufficient undertook not to export. Export quotas fixed for the free market suppliers. |

| | | | | | |
|---|---|---|---|---|---|
| International Sugar Agreement, 1953 | Multilateral | Dual-interest ICA | Major sugar importing and exporting countries (except Brazil & Peru). Sugar exports under preferential regimes not covered | 1954–1958 | Export quotas fixed for the free market suppliers (pro rata to the basic export tonnages for each exporter). Automatic reduction (or expansion) of export quotas when prices fell below (or exceeded) floor (or ceiling) levels. Supply management: in exporting countries, limits on carry-over stocks (not above 20% of basic tonnage; not below 10%). Import restrictions: importing members undertook not to import from third parties more than was imported from them in any of the three calendar years preceding the entry into force of the Agreement. |
| International Sugar Agreement, 1958 | Multilateral | Dual-interest ICA | Brazil and Peru joined. Sugar exports under preferential regimes not covered | 1959–1905 | Similar to ISA 1953: export quotas fixed for the free market suppliers; reduction/expansion of export quotas (to counter downward/upward price pressure). Import restrictions: to prevent non-participating countries from gaining advantage at the expense of participating countries, importing members agreed not to permit sugar |

| Arrangement | Scope | Nature | Participants | Entry into force and end date (including extensions) | Stabilisation mechanisms |
|---|---|---|---|---|---|
| | | | | | imports from non-participating countries as a group during any quota year of a total quantity of sugar larger than was imported from those countries as a group during any one of the three calendar years 1951, 1952, 1953. |
| International Sugar Agreement, 1968 | Multilateral | Dual-interest ICA | Sugar exports under preferential regimes not covered | 1969–1973 | Export quotas (adjusted to counter price movements). Importing members: limitation and prohibition of imports from non-members (limitation to the average quantities imported over the three year period 1966–68; prohibition if prices below a trigger level; undertook not to encourage further expansion of production). Exporting members: assurances and commitments in respect of supplies (release of stocks if price above trigger levels and priority to members for access to supplies). |

| | | | | | |
|---|---|---|---|---|---|
| International Sugar Agreement, 1973 | Multilateral | Dual-interest ICA | Sugar exports under preferential regimes not covered | 1974–1977 | Did not contain economic provisions (inability to reach agreement on basic export tonnages, prices, etc.). |
| International Sugar Agreement, 1977 | Multilateral | Dual-interest ICA | Sugar exports under preferential regimes not covered. The EC did to join. | 1978–1984 | Floor and ceiling prices defended through export quotas. Reduction and increase in quota levels were triggered by price movements. Suspension of quotas if prices below specified levels. Import restrictions: importing members undertook to limit imports from non-members to the average annual quantity over the four-year period 1973–76. |
| **Wheat** | | | | | |
| First International Wheat Agreement (Final Act of the Conference of Wheat Exporting and Importing Countries) | International | Dual-interest ICA | 9 major wheat exporters (Argentine, Australia, Canada and the United States of America; the “Danubian Countries” Bulgaria, Hungary, Romania and Yugoslavia, and the USSR) and 12 major importers | 1933–1934 | Production and export restrictions: export quotas and limitation of the acreage sown to wheat. Lowering of import tariffs in importing countries. |

| Arrangement | Scope | Nature | Participants | Entry into force and end date (including extensions) | Stabilisation mechanisms |
|---|---|---|---|---|---|
| International Wheat Agreement, 1949 (Second IWA) | International (multilateral) | Dual-interest ICA | Major exporting countries (including USA, Canada and Australia, but excluding USSR and Argentina) and 33 importing countries | 1949–1953 | Multilateral contracts (multilateral buying and selling arrangements within agreed price ranges). Producers and consumers were allotted individual export and import quotas. Producers were required to export quota-allotted quantities at or below a ceiling price. Consumers were required to purchase quota-allotted quantities at or above a floor price (guaranteed purchases and sales, at prices consistent with a set minimum and maximum). |
| Agreement revising and renewing the International Wheat Agreement, 1953 (Third IWA) | International (multilateral) | Dual-interest ICA | Not signed by Britain (max. price deemed too high): quotas accounted for only 25% of the 1956 world trade | 1953–1956 | Multilateral contract (broadly similar to IWA 1949 – adjustment of minimum and maximum prices). |
| International Wheat Agreement, 1956 (Fourth IWA) | International (multilateral) | Dual-interest ICA | Not signed by Britain (covered only about 20% of world exports) | 1956–1959 | Multilateral contract (broadly similar to previous Agreements (1949, 1953). |

| | | | | | |
|---|---|---|---|---|---|
| International Wheat Agreement, 1959 (Fifth IWA) | International (multilateral) | Dual-interest ICA | Britain re-joined; all major exporters joined, except the USSR | 1959–1962 | Terms of the multilateral contract revised: producers would meet collectively consumers' demand when prices at the maximum; consumers agreed to buy from producers a fixed percentage of their average imports at prices within the band (quotas inoperative). |
| International Wheat Agreement, 1962 (Sixth IWA) | International (multilateral) | Dual-interest ICA | USSR joined | 1962–1965 | Revised multilateral contract, as above (price band adjusted). |
| International Grains Arrangement 1967 (Wheat Trade Convention and Food Aid Convention) | International (multilateral) | Dual-interest ICA | Major exporters and importers | 1967–1971 (economic provisions suspended in 1969) | Revised multilateral contract. |
| **Cocoa** | | | | | |
| International Cocoa Agreement, 1972 | Multilateral | Dual-interest ICA | Major cocoa producers and consumers | 1973–1976 | Annual export quotas based on past production figures and buffer stock sales to maintain prices within a defined price band. Limitations of imports from non-members and commitment not to sell to/buy cocoa from non-members on terms commercially more favourable than for members. |

| Arrangement | Scope | Nature | Participants | Entry into force and end date (including extensions) | Stabilisation mechanisms |
|---|---|---|---|---|---|
| International Cocoa Agreement, 1975 | Multilateral | Dual-interest ICA | Major cocoa producers and consumers | 1976–1980 | Broadly similar to ICCA 1972 (export quotas and buffer stock interventions to maintain prices between a floor and ceiling level). |
| International Cocoa Agreement, 1980 | Multilateral | Dual-interest ICA | Large importers and exporters (the US and Côte d'Ivoire) did not participate | 1981–1986 | Buffer stock purchases and sales only (no quotas). Commitment not to sell to/buy cocoa from non-members on terms commercially more favourable than for members. |
| International Cocoa Agreement, 1986 | Multilateral | Dual-interest ICA | Major cocoa producers and consumers | 1987–1993 | Buffer stock purchases and sales only (no quotas). Commitment not to sell to/buy cocoa from non-members on terms commercially more favourable than for members. |

SOURCE: ICAS (SEE BIBLIOGRAPHY).

APPENDIX 4

# CAP Developments: An Overview

| | Milestones | Timeframe | Main features |
|---|---|---|---|
| **Price Support** | Creation of the CAP | 1962 | Price fixing, combined with border protection, in the form of a variable import levy, and with export subsidies.<br>(a) Price fixing. Setting of: – "Target prices", based on prices in areas of shortest supply; – "Threshold" border prices, or minimum import prices (threshold price + marketing costs = target price); – "Intervention prices", at which intervention agencies purchased surplus produce at guaranteed prices (open market purchases) or by other means (e.g. payment of the difference between the buying-in price and the selling price of the good).<br>(b) Variable import levy = Threshold price – c.i.f. price (most favourable quotations calculated for Rotterdam).<br>(c) Export subsidies (refunds) = World prices – intervention price.<br>Other sectoral regimes (e.g. oilseeds) essentially consisted of deficiency payments to the industry reflecting the difference between the price paid to the producer and the world price level. |
| | 1985/88 reforms | Marketing years 1985/86, 1986/87, 1987/88 | Setting of "stabilisers", i.e. ceilings on quantities guaranteed to receive support payments (maximum guaranteed quantities). In the form of: production quotas (milk); production-guarantee ceilings (oilseeds, cotton); processing-guarantee thresholds (fruit and vegetables); intervention thresholds (butter, powder milk, tomatoes). |

 | DOI 10.1163/9789004350540_011

| | Milestones | Timeframe | Main features |
|---|---|---|---|
| **"Coupled" Income support** | Mac Sharry reforms of 1992 | Agreed in 1992; gradually implemented from 1993/94 to 1995/96 | Shift from price support (product support) to income support (producer support): Substantive reduction (about 30% for cereals and 15% for beef) of guaranteed prices (target, threshold and intervention prices, notified as Amber Box support following the conclusion of the Uruguay Round). In return, farmers received "compensatory payments" (area and headage payments on the land sown to cereals and the number of beef cattle kept), subject to compulsory set-aside (requirement to withdraw land from production) and other accompanying measures (declared as Blue Box payments). |
| | Agenda 2000 reform | Agreed in 1992; gradually implemented in the period 2000/01–2006/07 | Price support further reduced (by 15% in two annual steps for cereals); partially compensated by increases in direct payments.<br>Rural Development Regulation (2nd "Pillar" of the CAP) |
| | Fischler reforms of 2003 | Agreed in 2003; gradually implemented (direct payments) in the 2005–07 period | "Decoupling" of area and headage payments with the creation of the Single Payment Scheme (SPS), a single annual payment based on a farmer's entitlement (based upon his historic pattern of receipts of area and headage payments ("historic model") or upon alternative methods ("regional model" / hybrid models)). SPS subject to "cross-compliance" conditions (compliance with good agricultural and environmental practices, etc.). Farmers could still receive "coupled aid" (based on production/prices) under specific support schemes. |

| | | | |
|---|---|---|---|
| | 2008 "Health Checker" | Agreed in 2008; gradually implemented during 2008–13 | Further decoupling for all payments as from 2012, except for some sectors (suckle cows, sheep and goat, and cotton premia). |
| **"Decoupled" and "conditioned" income support** | June 2013 reform | Adopted in 2013; effective as of 1 January 2014 (reformed direct payments as of 2015) | 1st pillar (direct payments and market support): – "Greening" of direct payments (30% linked to farmers' compliance with sustainable agricultural practices); – Removal of output restraints (dairy quotas would expire in 2015; end of wine planting rights for 2018; sugar quotas to be abolished by 2017); – Market (price) support as a targeted safety net.<br>2nd pillar (rural development): – "Greening" of the Rural Development programme (at least 30% to be allocated for organic agriculture, environmentally friendly investment, etc.); – Focus on competitiveness and innovation (financial incentives for setting up producer groups, short supply chains and cooperation (coupled with quality and branding); start up aid for young farmers; synergies between science and practice; risk-management tools). |

SOURCES: KEY DOCUMENTS AND COMMENTARIES RETRIEVED THROUGH EUROPA [EU'S WEB SITE] AGRICULTURE AND RURAL DEVELOPMENT PAGES, HTTP://EC.EUROPA.EU/AGRICULTURE/INDEX_EN.HTM.

APPENDIX 5

# US Farm Bills: A Snapshot

| Title (public law) | Main instruments | Policy focus |
|---|---|---|
| Agricultural Adjustment Act of 1933 (P.L. 73–10) | Price-support loans;<br>Acreage/production restrictions and processing taxes (later declared unconstitutional);<br>Market regulation through voluntary agreements with processors, producer associations, and other handlers of agricultural commodities. | Combination of price support, supply controls, and income support payments. |
| Agricultural Adjustment Act Amendment of 1935 (P.L. 74–320) | President given authority to impose import quotas when imports interfered with domestic price stabilisation. | Combination of price support, supply controls, and income support payments. |
| Agricultural Adjustment Act of 1938 (P.L. 75–430) | Mandatory price support (at 90% of parity) for corn, cotton, and wheat (through nonrecourse loans, parity payments and other instruments); permissive support for other products.<br>Mandatory acreage allotments and marketing quotas to keep supply in line with demand. | Combination of price support, supply controls, and income support payments. |
| Agricultural Act of 1948 (P.L. 80–897) | Mandatory price support (through any instrument or agency within or under the direction of the Department of Agriculture, by loans, purchases, or other operation). | Combination of price support, supply controls, and income support payments. |

 | DOI 10.1163/9789004350540_012

| | | |
|---|---|---|
| Agricultural Act of 1949 (P.L. 89–439) | Mandatory price support (loans, purchases, or other operations) extended to major non-basic commodities. | Combination of price support, supply controls, and income support payments. |
| Agricultural Act of 1954 (P.L. 83–480) | Set-aside and disposal programmes (Commodity Credit Corporation inventories and surplus commodities); Mandatory price support (at 82.5–90% of parity). | Combination of price support, supply controls, and income support payments. |
| Agriculture Act of 1956 (P.L. 84–540) | Acreage diversion programmes, with payments. | Combination of price support, supply controls, and income support payments. |
| 1965 Farm Bill – Food and Agricultural Act of 1965 (P.L. 89–321) | Milk marketing orders; Continued direct payment and diversion programmes for feed grains and cotton. | Combination of price support, supply controls, and income support payments. |
| 1970 Farm Bill – Agricultural Act of 1970 (P.L. 91–524) | Set-aside programmes and direct payments. | Combination of price support, supply controls, and income support payments. |
| 1973 Farm Bill – Agricultural and Consumer Protection Act of 1973 (P.L. 93–86) | Target prices and Deficiency Payments (crop-specific payment rates based on the difference between an established target price and the higher of the commodity loan rate or the national average market price for the commodity during a specified time period); Voluntary acreage controls. | Combination of price support, supply controls, and income support payments. |
| 1977 Farm Bill – Food and Agriculture Act of 1977 (P.L. 95–113) | Increased price and income support; Subsidised farmer-owned reserve programme. | Combination of price support, supply controls, and income support payments. |

| Title (public law) | Main instruments | Policy focus |
|---|---|---|
| 1981 Farm Bill – Agriculture and Food Act of 1981 (P.L. 97–98) | Previous programmes continued. | Combination of price support, supply controls, and income support payments. |
| 1985 Farm Bill – Food Security Act of 1985 (P.L. 99–198) | Minimum target price levels reduced. | Policy move in a market-oriented direction. |
| 1990 Farm Bill – Food, Agriculture, Conservation, and Trade Act of 1990 (P.L. 101–624) | Target prices frozen. | Policy move in a market-oriented direction. |
| 1996 Farm Bill – Federal Agriculture Improvement and Reform Act of 1996 (P.L. 104–127) | Fixed Production Flexibility Contracts (PFC), largely independent of current farm prices and production; Most product-specific payments and guaranteed prices in previous farm programmes eliminated (but nonrecourse commodity loans continued). | Policy shift: De-linkage between income support payments and farm prices. |
| 2002 Farm Bill – Farm Security and Rural Investment Act of 2002 (P.L. 107–171) | Support for wheat, feed grains, upland cotton, rice, and oilseeds through: Direct Payments (DPS) (fixed payments linked to historic planting and yields, decoupled from current production and prices); Counter-Cyclical Payments (CCP) (based on historical production, made when current effective commodity prices are below target prices); Marketing assistance loans.<br>A new dairy income support programme is introduced. | Price-related support reintroduced, deviating from the move towards greater market-orientation. |

| | | |
|---|---|---|
| 2008 Farm Bill – Food, Conservation, and Energy Act of 2008 (P.L. 110–234) | DPS;<br>Marketing Assistance Loans and Loan Deficiency Payments;<br>CCPS;<br>Average Crop Revenue Election (ACRE) program, alternative to CCPS. | Many of the commodity programmes introduced in previous farm legislation continued, with adjusted payment rates and eligibility; a new crop revenue election programme introduced. |
| 2014 Farm Bill – Agricultural Act of 2014 (P.L. 113–79) | DPS, CCPS, and ACRE replaced by the Price Loss Coverage (PLC) and the Agriculture Risk Coverage (ARC) programmes. PLC payments consist of deficiency (counter-cyclical) payments coupled to current prices (triggered when prices decline below statutory reference prices) but decoupled from current production (payments made on 85% of historical plantings). Under the ARC programme (revenue-based deficiency payment scheme, alternative to PLC), payments are tied to current prices and to a percentage of base acres. Marketing Assistance Loans and Loan Deficiency Payments are continued. Expanded federal crop insurance with subsidised insurance premium. | Reintroduction of "coupled" payments, tied to current price/output parameters. |

SOURCES: FARM BILLS RETRIEVED THROUGH HTTP://NATIONALAGLAWCENTER.ORG/FARMBILLS/; WTO US TRP SINCE 1995; KATHRYN L LIPTON ET AL., "MAJOR AGRICULTURAL AND TRADE LEGISLATION, 1933–96, APPENDIX III" IN *PROVISIONS OF THE FEDERAL AGRICULTURE IMPROVEMENT AND REFORM ACT OF 1996*, ED. FREDERICK J NELSON & LYLE P SCHERTZ (WASHINGTON, DC: ECONOMIC RESEARCH SERVICE, USDA, 1996).

# Bibliography

## 1 Legal Documents and Commentaries

### A *Intergovernmental Commodity Control Agreements*

Full text of treaties retrieved through United Nations Treaty Series Online Collection https://treaties.un.org/Pages/UNTSOnline.aspx?id=1. Text of early arrangements as collected in International Labour Office, *Intergovernmental Commodity Control Agreements* (Montreal, 1943). http://archive.org/details/intergovernmenta033428mbp.

#### i) Natural Rubber

International Natural Rubber Agreement, 1979 (with annexes). Done at Geneva on 6 October 1979. 1201 UNTS 191.

International Natural Rubber Agreement, 1987 (with annexes and procès-verbal of rectification of the authentic Arabic, Chinese, English, French and Russian texts). Concluded at Geneva on 20 March 1987. 1521 UNTS 3.

International Natural Rubber Agreement, 1994 (with annexes). Concluded at Geneva on 17 February 1995. 1964 UNTS 3.

#### ii) Coffee

Inter-American Coffee Agreement. Signed at Washington on 28 November 1940. 139 UNTS 159.

International Coffee Agreement, 1962 (with annexes). Done at New York, on 28 September 1962. 469 UNTS 169.

International Coffee Agreement, 1968 (with annexes). Open for signature at New York, from 18 to 31 March 1968. 647 UNTS 3.

International Coffee Agreement, 1976 (with annexes and official Russian translation approved by the Executive Board of the International Coffee Organization on 16 June 1977). Concluded at London on 3 December 1975. 1024 UNTS 3.

International Coffee Agreement, 1983 (with annexes). Adopted by the International Coffee Council on 16 September 1982. 1333 UNTS 119.

International Coffee Agreement, 1994, as extended until 30 September 2001, with modifications, by Resolution No. 384 adopted by the International Coffee Council in London on 21 July 1999. 2086 UNTS 147.

International Coffee Agreement 2001 (with annex). London, 28 September 2000. 2161 UNTS 308.

International Coffee Agreement 2007 (with annex, resolution and procès-verbal of rectification). London, 28 September 2007. 2734 UNTS 101.

### iii) Cocoa

International Cocoa Agreement, 1972 (with annexes). Concluded at Geneva on 21 October 1972. 882 UNTS 67.

International Cocoa Agreement, 1975 (with annexes). Concluded at Geneva on 20 October 1975. 1023 UNTS 253.

International Cocoa Agreement, 1980 (with annexes). Concluded at Geneva on 19 November 1980. 1245 UNTS 221.

International Cocoa Agreement, 1986 (with annexes). Concluded at Geneva on 25 July 1986. 1446 UNTS 103.

International Cocoa Agreement, 1993 (with annexes). Concluded at Geneva on 16 July 1993. 1766 UNTS 3.

International Cocoa Agreement, 2001. Geneva, 2 March 2001. 2229 UNTS 2.

International Cocoa Agreement, 2010. Geneva, 25 June 2010. 2871 UNTS.

### iv) Sugar

Agreement concerning the Regulation of Production and Marketing of Sugar (6 May 1937). Reprinted in: International Labour Office, *Intergovernmental Commodity Control Agreements* (Montreal, 1943), 26.

International Sugar Agreement. Done at London, on 1 October 1953. 258 UNTS 153.

International Sugar Agreement, 1968. Open for signature at New York from 3 to 24 December 1968. 654 UNTS 3.

International Sugar Agreement, 1973 (with annexes). Concluded at Geneva on 13 October 1973. 906 UNTS 69.

International Sugar Agreement, 1977 (with annexes). Concluded at Geneva on 7 October 1977. 1064 UNTS 219.

International Sugar Agreement, 1984 (with annexes). Concluded at Geneva on 5 July 1984. 1388 UNTS 3.

International Sugar Agreement, 1987 (with annexes). Concluded at London on 11 September 1987. 1499 UNTS 31.

International Sugar Agreement, 1992 (with annex). Concluded at Geneva on 20 March 1992. 1703 UNTS 203.

### v) Tea

The International Tea Agreement 1933–1938 (9 February 1933). Done on 9 February 1933. Reprinted in International Labour Office, *Intergovernmental Commodity Control Agreements* (Montreal, 1943), 47.

The International Tea Agreement 1938–1943 (25 August 1938). Reprinted in International Labour Office, *Intergovernmental Commodity Control Agreements* (Montreal, 1943), 52.

International Tea Agreement of 1950. Text in Interim Co-ordinating Committee for International Commodity Arrangements, *Review of International Commodity Problems 1950* (New York: United Nations, 1951) 54 (U.N. Doc. No. E/1907) (1951).

vi) Wheat

Final Act of the Conference of Wheat Exporting and Importing Countries (25 August 1933). Reprinted in International Labour Office, *Intergovernmental Commodity Control Agreements* (Montreal, 1943), 1.

International Wheat Agreement. Done at Washington, on 23 March 1949. 203 UNTS 179.

Agreement revising and renewing the International Wheat Agreement. Done at Washington, on 13 April 1953. 203 UNTS 242.

International Wheat Agreement, 1956. Formulated at the United Nations Wheat Conference which ended at London on 25 April 1956, and open for signature at Washington until 18 May 1956. 270 UNTS 103.

International Wheat Agreement, 1959. Opened for signature at Washington from 6 April 1959 until and including 24 April 1959. 349 UNTS 167.

International Wheat Agreement, 1962. Opened for signature at Washington from 19 April 1962 until and including 15 May 1962. 444 UNTS 3.

International Grains Arrangement 1967: (a) Wheat Trade Convention (with annexes). Opened for signature at Washington from 15 October 1967 until 30 November 1967; (b) Food Aid Convention. Opened for signature at Washington from 15 October 1967 until and including 30 November 1967. 727 UNTS 3.

International Wheat Agreement, 1971: (a) Wheat Trade Convention, 1971 (with annexes). Opened for signature at Washington from 29 March 1971 until 3 May 1971; (b) Food Aid Convention, 1971. Opened for signature at Washington from 29 March 1971 until 3 May 1971. 800 UNTS 45.

International Wheat Agreement, 1986: (a) Wheat Trade Convention, 1986 (with annex). Concluded at London on 14 March 1986; (b) Food Aid Convention, 1986. Concluded at London on 13 March 1986. 1429 UNTS 71.

## B *Havana Charter Documents*

### i) United Nations Conference on Trade and Employment, Fifth Committee (Inter-Governmental Commodity Agreements): Selected Documents, Summary Records and Reports

Draft Charter – Cuba: Proposed Amendment, E/CONF.2/C.5/3/Add.3, 5 December 1947.

Draft Charter – El-Salvador: Proposed Amendment, E/CONF.2/C.5/3/Add.8, 6 December 1947.

Draft Charter – Uruguay: Proposed Amendment, E/CONF.2/C.5/3/Add.12, 7 December 1947.
Draft Charter – Mexico: Proposed Amendment, E/CONF.2/C.5/3/Add.9, 6 December 1947.
Summary Record of the First Meeting, E/CONF.2/C.5/SR.1, 26 November 1947.
Summary record of the Second Meeting, E/CONF.2/C.5/SR.2, 28 November 1947.
Summary record of the Third Meeting, E/CONF.2/C.5/SR.3, 2 December 1947.
Summary record of the Fourth Meeting, E/CONF.2/C.5/SR.4, 3 December 1947.
Summary record of the Fifth Meeting, E/CONF.2/C.5/SR.5, 6 December 1947.
Summary record of the Sixth Meeting, E/CONF.2/C.5/SR.6, 10 December 1947.
Summary record of the Seventh Meeting, E/CONF.2/C.5/SR.7, 12 December 1947.
Summary record of the Eighth Meeting, E/CONF.2/C.5/SR.8, 13 December 1947.
Summary record of the Ninth Meeting, E/CONF.2/C.5/SR.9, 30 December 1947.
Summary record of the Tenth Meeting, E/CONF.2/C.5/SR.10, 31 December 1947.
Summary Record of the Eleventh Meeting, E/CONF.2/C.5/SR.11, 2 January 1948.
Summary record of the Twelfth Meeting, E/CONF.2/C.5/SR.12, 3 January 1948.
Summary record of the Thirteenth Meeting, E/CONF.2/C.5/SR.13, 6 January 1948.
Summary record of Fourteenth Meeting, E/CONF.2/C.5/SR.14, 21 January 1948.
Summary record of Fifteenth Meeting, E/CONF.2/C.5/SR.15, 9 February 1948.
Draft report to the Conference, E/CONF.2/C.5/W.5, 17 January 1948.
Report to the Conference, E/CONF.2/39, 9 February 1948.
Documents retrieved through GATT Documents 1946–1997 (http://www.wto.org/english/docs_e/gattdocs_e.htm); Stanford GATT Digital Library: 1947–1994 http://gatt.stanford.edu/page/home).

### ii) United Nations Conference on Trade and Employment: Final Act and Selected Preparatory Works

Report of the First Session of the Preparatory Committee of the United Nations Conference on Trade and Employment, E/PC/T/33, October 1946 ('London Report').
Report of the Drafting Committee of the Preparatory Committee of the United Nations Conference on Trade and Employment, E/PC/T/34, 5 March 1947.
Report of the Second Session of the Preparatory Committee of the United Nations Conference on Trade and Employment, E/PC/T/186, 10 September 1947 ('Geneva draft').
Reports of Committees and Principal Sub-Committees, ICITO I/8, September 1948 ('Havana Reports').
Havana Charter for an International Trade Organization, Havana, 24 March 1948. In United Nations Conference on Trade and Employment, Final Act and Related Documents, UN Doc. E/Conf.2/78 (1948).

Documents retrieved through GATT Documents 1946–1997 (http://www.wto.org/english/docs_e/gattdocs_e.htm); Stanford GATT Digital Library: 1947–1994 http://gatt.stanford.edu/page/home).

## C *GATT Documents (1954–55 Review Session, Working Party on Commodity Problems)*

Working Party on Commodity Problems Established by Decision of the CONTRACTING PARTIES on 22 December 1954 – Membership and Terms of Reference, L/301, 22 December 1954.

CONTRACTING PARTIES, Ninth Session, Interim Report of the Working Party on Commodity Problems, L/320, 1 February 1955 (including the annexed draft Special Agreement on Commodity Arrangements).

CONTRACTING PARTIES, Ninth Session, Summary Record of the Nineteenth Meeting, SR.9/19, 23 November 1954.

CONTRACTING PARTIES, Ninth Session, Summary Record of the Twenty-third Meeting, SR.9/23, 22 December 1954.

CONTRACTING PARTIES, Ninth Session, Summary Record of the Twenty-seventh Meeting, SR.9/27, 29 December 1954.

CONTRACTING PARTIES, Ninth Session, Summary Record of the Thirty-fourth Meeting, SR.9/34, 22 February 1955.

CONTRACTING PARTIES, Ninth Session, Summary Record of the Thirty-eighth Meeting, SR.9/38, 3 March 1955.

CONTRACTING PARTIES, Ninth Session, Final Report of the Working Party on Commodity Problems, L/416, 3 October 1955.

CONTRACTING PARTIES, Tenth Session, Summary Record of the Thirteenth Meeting, SR.10/13, 22 November 1955.

CONTRACTING PARTIES, Tenth Session, Summary Record of the Fourteenth Meeting, SR 10/14, 23 November 1955.

CONTRACTING PARTIES, Tenth Session, Summary Record of the Nineteenth Meeting, SR.10/19, 12 December 1955.

CONTRACTING PARTIES, Eleventh Session, Report of the Working Party on Commodity Problems, L/592/Rev.1, 20 November 1956.

Retrieved through: GATT Documents 1946–1997 (http://www.wto.org/english/docs_e/gattdocs_e.htm); Stanford GATT Digital Library: 1947–1994 (http://gatt.stanford.edu/page/home).

## D *UNCTAD and the NIEO*

UNCTAD (1st sess.). *Proceedings of the United Nations Conference on Trade and Development, Geneva, 23 March – 16 June 1964*, U.N. Doc. E/CONF.46/141 (1964), Vol. I, *Final Act and Report* and Vol. II, *Policy Statements*.

UNCTAD (2nd sess.). *Proceedings of the United Nations Conference on Trade and Development, Second Session, New Delhi, 1 February – 29 March 1968,* U.N. Doc. TD/97 (1968), Vol. I and Corr. 1 and 3 and Add. 1 and 2, *Report and Annexes.*

UNCTAD (3rd sess.). *Proceedings of the United Nations Conference on Trade and Development, Third Session, Santiago de Chile, 13 April to 21 may 1972,* U.N. Doc. TD/180 (1973), Vol. I, *Report and Annexes.*

UNCTAD (4th sess.). *Proceedings of the United Nations Conference on Trade and Development, Fourth Session, Nairobi, 5–31 May 1976,* U.N. Doc. TD/218 (1977), Vol. I, *Report and Annexes* and Vol. II, *Summary of Statements by Heads of Delegation and Summary Records of Plenary Meetings.*

Ministers of the Group of 77. *Declaration and Principles of the Action Programme of Lima,* U.N. Doc. TD/143 (12 Nov. 1971). Reprinted in UNCTAD, *Proceedings of the United Nations Conference on Trade and Development* (3d sess.), Vol. 1, Annex viii(F) 373, U.N. Doc. TD/180 (1973).

G77 and Non-Aligned Nations. *Manila Declaration and Programme of Action,* U.N. Document, TD/195, Nairobi, 5 May 1976. Reprinted in UNCTAD, *Proceedings of the United Nations Conference on Trade and Development* (4th sess.), Vol. I, Annex V, U.N. Doc. TD/218 (1977).

United Nations General Assembly. *Declaration on the Establishment of a New International Economic Order,* GA Res. 3201 (S-VI), U.N. GAOR, 6th special Sess., Supp. No. 1 (1974) at 3, U.N. Doc. A/9559 (1974).

United Nations General Assembly. *Programme of Action for the creation of a New International Economic Order,* GA Res. 3202 (S-VI), U.N. GAOR, 6th special Sess., Supp. No. 1 (1974), U.N. Doc. A/9559 (1974)).

United Nations General Assembly. *Charter of Economic Rights and Duties of States,* GA Res. 3281 (xxix), U.N. GAOR, 29th Sess., Supp. No. 31 (1974) 50.

United Nations General Assembly. *Integrated Programme for Commodities,* TD/RES/93(IV) (1976). In *Proceedings of the United Nations Conference on Trade and Development* (4th sess.), Vol. I, Part I.A.1, at 6.

## E *WTO*

### i) WTO Agreements

Final Act Embodying the Results of the Uruguay Round of Multilateral Trade Negotiations, Apr. 15, 1994, *The Legal Texts: The Results of the Uruguay Round of Multilateral Trade Negotiations* 2 (Cambridge, U.K.; New York, N.Y.: Cambridge University Press, 1999), 1867 UNTS 14, 33 ILM. 1143 (1994).

WTO Agreement: Marrakesh Agreement Establishing the World Trade Organization, Apr. 15, 1994, *The Legal Texts: The Results of the Uruguay Round of Multilateral Trade Negotiations* 4 (1999), 1867 UNTS 154, 33 ILM 1144 (1994).

General Agreement on Tariffs and Trade 1994, Apr. 15, 1994, Marrakesh Agreement Establishing the World Trade Organization, Annex 1A, *The Legal Texts: The Results of the Uruguay Round of Multilateral Trade Negotiations* 17 (1999), 1867 UNTS 187, 33 ILM 1153 (1994).

Agreement on Agriculture, Apr. 15, 1994, Marrakesh Agreement Establishing the World Trade Organization, Annex 1A, *The Legal Texts: The Results of the Uruguay Round of Multilateral Trade Negotiations* 33 (1999), 1867 UNTS 410.

Agreement on Subsidies and Countervailing Measures, Apr. 15, 1994, Marrakesh Agreement Establishing the World Trade Organization, Annex 1A, *The Legal Texts: The Results of the Uruguay Round of Multilateral Trade Negotiations* 231 (1999), 1869 UNTS 14.

### ii) Trade Policy Review Reports

WTO Secretariat. *Trade Policy Review: United States*, WT/TPR/S/200, 5 May 2008.

WTO Secretariat. *Trade Policy Review: India – Revision*, WT/TPR/S/249/Rev.1, 20 October 2011.

WTO Secretariat. *Trade Policy Review: China – Revision*, WT/TPR/S/264/Rev.1, 20 July 2012.

WTO Secretariat. *Trade Policy Review: The Philippines – Revision*, WT/TPR/S/261/Rev.2, 9 May 2012.

WTO Secretariat. *Trade Policy Review: Indonesia – Revision*, WT/TPR/S/278/Rev.1, 16 July 2013.

WTO Secretariat. *Trade Policy Review: New Zealand*, G/STR/N/4/NZL, 5 May 1999.

WTO Secretariat. *Trade Policy Review: Japan – Revision*, WT/TPR/S/276/Rev.1, 18 June 2013.

Retrieved through WTO Trade Policy Review page http://www.wto.org/english/tratop_e/tpr_e/tpr_e.htm).

### iii) Selected GATT and WTO Cases

GATT Panel Report, *Belgium Family Allowances*, G/32, adopted 7 November 1952, BISD 1S/59 [*Belgium – Family Allowances*].

GATT Panel Report, *EEC – Programme of Minimum Import Prices, Licences and Surety Deposits for Certain Processed Fruits and Vegetables*, L/4687, adopted 18 October 1978, BISD 25S/68 [EEC – Minimum Import Prices].

GATT Panel Report, *Canada – Administration of the Foreign Investment Review Act*, L/5504, adopted 7 February 1984, BISD 30S/140 [*Canada – FIRA*].

GATT Panel Report, *Japan – Restrictions on Imports of Certain Agricultural Products*, L/6253, adopted 2 February 1988, BISD 35S/163 [*Japan – Agricultural Products I*].

GATT Panel Report, *Canada – Import, Distribution and Sale of Alcoholic Drinks by Canadian Provincial Marketing Agencies*, L/6304, adopted 22 March 1988, BISD 35S/37 [*Canada – Provincial Liquor Boards (EEC)*].

GATT Panel Report, *Canada – Import Restrictions on Ice Cream and Yoghurt*, L/6568, adopted 5 December 1989, BISD 36S/68 [*Canada – Ice Cream and Yoghurt*].

GATT Panel Report, *Canada – Import, Distribution and Sale of Certain Alcoholic Drinks by Provincial Marketing Agencies*, DS17/R, adopted 18 February 1992, BISD 39S/27 [*Canada – Provincial Liquor Boards (US)*].

Appellate Body Report, *Japan – Taxes on Alcoholic Beverages*, WT/DS8/AB/R, WT/DS10/AB/R, WT/DS11/AB/R, adopted 1 November 1996, DSR 1996:I, p. 97 [*Japan – Alcoholic Beverages II*].

Panel Report, *Canada – Measures Affecting the Importation of Milk and the Exportation of Dairy Products*, WT/DS103/R, WT/DS113/R, adopted 27 October 1999, as modified by Appellate Body Report WT/DS103/AB/R, WT/DS113/AB/R, DSR 1999:VI, p. 2097.

Appellate Body Report, *Canada – Measures Affecting the Importation of Milk and the Exportation of Dairy Products*, WT/DS103/AB/R, WT/DS113/AB/R, and Corr.1, adopted 27 October 1999, DSR 1999:V, p. 2057.

Panel Report, *Chile – Price Band System and Safeguard Measures Relating to Certain Agricultural Products*, WT/DS207/R, adopted 23 October 2002, as modified by Appellate Body Report WT/DS207AB/R, DSR 2002:VIII, p. 3127 [*Chile – Price Band System*].

Appellate Body Report, *Chile – Price Band System and Safeguard Measures Relating to Certain Agricultural Products*, WT/DS207/AB/R, adopted 23 October 2002, DSR 2002:VIII, p. 3045 (Corr.1, DSR 2006:XII, p. 5473).

Panel Report, *Canada – Measures Relating to Exports of Wheat and Treatment of Imported Grain*, WT/DS276/R, adopted 27 September 2004, upheld by Appellate Body Report WT/DS276/AB/R, DSR 2004:VI, p. 2817 [*Canada – Wheat Exports and Grain Imports*].

Appellate Body Report, *Canada – Measures Relating to Exports of Wheat and Treatment of Imported Grain*, WT/DS276/AB/R, adopted 27 September 2004, DSR 2004:VI, p. 2739.

Panel Report, *Peru – Additional Duty on Imports of Certain Agricultural Products*, WT/DS457/R and Add.1, adopted 31 July 2015, as modified by Appellate Body Report WT/DS457/AB/R [*Peru – Agricultural Products*].

Appellate Body Report, *Peru – Additional Duty on Imports of Certain Agricultural Products*, WT/DS457/AB/R and Add.1, adopted 31 July 2015.

### iv) Official Commentaries and Indexes

*GATT Analytical Index – Guide to GATT Law and Practice* [online edition of the 1995 updated sixth edition, available at http://www.wto.org/english/res_e/booksp_e/gatt_ai_e/gatt_ai_e.htm].

*WTO Analytical Index: Guide to WTO Law and Practice* [online edition of the 2011 updated third edition, available at https://www.wto.org/english/res_e/booksp_e/analytic_index_e/analytic_index_e.htm].

*WTO Analytical Index: Supplement Covering New Developments in WTO Law and Practice (October 2011 – June 2015)* [online edition, available at https://www.wto.org/english/res_e/booksp_e/analytic_index_e/ai_new_dev_e.pdf].

worldtradelaw.net http://www.worldtradelaw.net/Worldtradelaw.net – WTO Case Law Index (Agriculture) (5 June 2015).

## 2 Secondary Sources

Abbott, John C. "Agricultural Marketing Boards in the Developing Countries." *Journal of Farm Economics* 49, no. 3 (1967): 705–22.

Abi-Saab, George. "Les sources du droit international: essai de déconstruction." In *Liber Amicorum Eduardo Jiménez de Aréchaga*, 29–49. Montevideo: Fundación de cultura universitaria, 1994.

Ackrill, Robert. *Common Agricultural Policy*. Sheffield: Sheffield Academic Press, 2000.

Akiyama, Takamasa, John Baffes, Donald Larson, and Panos Varangis. *Commodity Market Reforms: Lessons of Two Decades*. World Bank Regional and Sectoral Studies. Washington, D.C., 2001.

Akyuz, Yilmaz. "Managing Boom-Bust Cycles in Commodity Dependent Economies." Paper presented at UNCTAD, Global Commodities Forum, Geneva, 13 April, 2015.

Anania, Giovanni. *Agricultural Export Restrictions and the WTO: What Options Do Policy-Makers Have for Promoting Food Security?* International Centre for Trade and Sustainable Development, ICTSD Issue Paper 50. Geneva, 2013.

Anderson, Kym. "Understanding Government Interventions in Agricultural Markets." In *The Political Economy of Agricultural Price Distortions*, edited by Kym Anderson, 3–24. Cambridge: Cambridge University Press, 2010.

Anderson, Kym, ed. *The Political Economy of Agricultural Price Distortions*. Cambridge: Cambridge University Press, 2010.

Anderson, Kym, and Yujiro Hayami. *The Political Economy of Agricultural Protection: East Asia in International Perspectives*. Sydney; London; Boston: Allen & Unwin, 1986.

Avramović, Dragoslav. "Commodities in Nairobi." *Development and Change* 8, no. 2 (1977): 231–47.

Banga, Rashmi. *Impact of Green Box Subsidies on Agricultural Productivity, Production and International Trade*. Unit of Economic Cooperation and Integration among Developing Countries, UNCTAD. Background Paper No. RVC-11. Geneva, 2014.

Banga, Rashmi. "Greening of Subsidies and Food Security." Paper presented at UNCTAD, Global Commodities Forum, Geneva, 13 April, 2015.

Bargawi, Hannah, Elva Bova, Benno Ferrarini, and Susan Newman. "Low-Income Countries and Commodity Price Volatility." In *The Prospects of International Trade Regulation: From Fragmentation to Coherence*, edited by Thomas Cottier and Delimatsis Panagiotis, 452–82. Cambridge: Cambridge University Press, 2011.

Barrett, Christopher B., and Emelly Mutambatsere. "Marketing Boards." In *The New Palgrave Dictionary of Economics*, edited by Steven N. Durlauf and Lawrence E. Blume, 2d ed. London: Palgrave Macmillan, 2008.

Bauer, Peter Thomas. "The Working of Rubber Regulation." *The Economic Journal* 56, no. 223 (1946): 391–414.

Bauer, Peter Thomas. "A Review of the Agricultural Marketing Schemes." *Economica* 15 (1948): 132–50.

Bauer, Peter Thomas. "Origins of the Statutory Export Monopolies of British West Africa." *Business History Review* 28, no. 03 (1954): 197–213.

Beder, Sharon. "Trading the Earth: The Politics behind Tradeable Pollution Rights." *Environmental Liability* 9, no. 2 (2001): 152–60.

Bellmann, Christophe. "The Bali Agreement: Implications for Development and the WTO." *International Development Policy | Revue internationale de politique de développement*, no. 5.2 (2014).

Bennouna, Mohamed. "Le droit international relatif aux matières premières." *Collected Courses of The Hague Academy of International Law* 177 (1983): 103–92.

Benson, Todd, Nicholas Minot, John Pender, Miguel Robles, and Joachim von Braun. *Global Food Crises: Monitoring and Assessing Impact to Inform Policy Responses*. International Food Policy Research Institute, IFPRI Issue Brief 55. Washington, D.C., 2008.

Bergsten, C. Fred. "The Threat from the Third World." *Foreign Policy*, no. 11 (1973): 102–24.

Black, Julia, and David Rouch. "The Development of the Global Markets as Rule-Makers: Engagement and Legitimacy." *Law and Financial Markets Review* 2, no. 3 (2008): 218–33.

Bowers, Douglas E, Rasmussen D Wayne, and Gladys L Baker. *History of Agricultural Price-Support and Adjustment Programs, 1933–84: Background for 1985 Farm Legislation*. Economic Research Service, US Department of Agriculture, Agriculture Information Bulletin 485. 1984.

Braun, Joachim von, and Maximo Torero. *Physical and Virtual Global Food Reserves to Protect the Poor and Prevent Market Failure*. International Food Policy Research Institute, IFPRI Policy Brief 4. Washington, D.C., 2008.

Braun, Joachim von, and Maximo Torero. *Implementing Physical and Virtual Food Reserves to Protect the Poor and Prevent Market Failure*. International Food Policy Research Institute, IFPRI Policy Brief 10. Washington, D.C., 2009.

Brink, Lars. *Support to Agriculture in India in 1995–2013 and the Rules of the WTO*. International Agricultural Trade Research Consortium, IATRC Working Paper 14–01. 2014.

Broude, Tomer. "The Rule(s) of Trade and the Rhetos of Development: Reflections on the Functional and Aspirational Legitimacy of the WTO." *Columbia Journal of Transnational Law* 45, no. 1 (2006–2007): 221–61.

Brown, Christopher P. *The Political and Social Economy of Commodity Control*. London: Macmillan, 1980.

Brown, William Adams. *The United States and the Restoration of World Trade: An Analysis and Appraisal of the ITO Charter and the General Agreement on Tariffs and Trade*. Washington, D.C.: Brookings Institution, 1950.

Bruinsma, Jelle, ed. *World Agriculture: Towards 2015/2030: An FAO Perspective*. London; Sterling, VA: Earthscan, 2003.

Bürgi Bonanomi, Elisabeth. "Right to Food, Sustainable Development and Trade: All Faces of the Same Cube?" In *The Challenge of Food Security: International Policy and Regulatory Frameworks*, edited by Rosemary Rayfuse and Nicole Weisfelt, 70–91. Cheltenham: Edward Elgar, 2012.

Bürgi Bonanomi, Elisabeth. *Sustainable Development in International Law Making: International Food Governance and Trade in Agriculture*. Cheltenham: Edward Elgar, 2015.

Cafaggi, Fabrizio. *Rethinking Private Regulation in the European Regulatory Space*. European University Institute, EUI Working Papers, Law 2006/13. Fiesole, IT, 2006.

Cameron, James, and Kevin R. Gray. "Principles of International Law in the WTO Dispute Settlement Body." *International & Comparative Law Quarterly* 50, no. 02 (2001): 248–98.

Caney, Simon. *Justice Beyond Borders: A Global Political Theory*. Oxford; New York: Oxford University Press, 2006.

Canuto, Ottaviano. *The Commodity Super Cycle: Is This Time Different?* The World Bank, Economic Premise note series, no. 150. [Washington, D.C.], 2014.

Cashin, Paul, C. John McDermott, and Alasdair Scott. "Booms and Slumps in World Commodity Prices." *Journal of Development Economics* 69, no. 1 (2002): 277–96.

Chalmin, Philippe. "What Is the New Normal in Commodity Markets?" Paper presented at UNCTAD, Global Commodities Forum, Geneva, 13 April, 2015.

Charnovitz, Steve. "The Legal Status of the Doha Declarations." *Journal of International Economic Law* 5, no. 1 (March 1, 2002): 207–11.

Cheng, Fuzhi. *China: Shadow WTO Agricultural Domestic Support Notifications*. International Food Policy Research Institute, IFPRI Discussion Paper 00793. Washington, D.C., 2008.

Chimni, B.S. *International Commodity Agreements: A Legal Study*. London ; New York: Routledge Kegan & Paul, 1987.

Chinkin, Christine M. "The Challenge of Soft Law: Development and Change in International Law." *International & Comparative Law Quarterly* 38, no. 04 (1989): 850–66.

Clarfield, Kenneth W., and Metals Week. *Eight Mineral Cartels: The New Challenge to Industrialized Nations*. [New York]: Metals Week, 1975.

Coleman, Jules. "Efficiency, Utility, and Wealth Maximization." *Hofstra Law Review* 8, no. 3 (1980): 509.

Collier, Paul. *The Bottom Billion: Why the Poorest Countries Are Failing and What Can Be Done about It*. New York: Oxford University Press, 2008.

Committee on World Food Security. High Level Panel of Experts on Food Security and Nutrition. *Price Volatility and Food Security: A Report by the High Level Panel of Experts on Food Security and Nutrition of the Committee on World Food Security*. Rome: Secretariat HLPE c/o FAO, 2011.

Committee on World Food Security. High Level Panel of Experts on Food Security and Nutrition. *Social Protection for Food Security: A Report by the High Level Panel of Experts on Food Security and Nutrition of the Committee on World Food Security*. Rome: Secretariat HLPE c/o FAO, 2012.

Consultative Board to the Director-General Supachai Panitchpakdi. *The Future of the WTO: Addressing Institutional Challenges in the New Millennium*. Geneva: World Trade Organization, 2004.

Cordell, Dana. *The Story of Phosphorus: Sustainability Implications of Global Phosphorus Scarcity for Food Security*. Linköping University, Studies in Arts and Science, no. 509. Linköping, 2010.

Corea, Gamani. *Taming Commodity Markets: The Integrated Programme and the Common Fund in UNCTAD*. Studies in International Law. Manchester ; New York: Manchester University Press, 1992.

Coret, Alain. "Les accords internationaux relatifs aux produits de base: l'évolution depuis 1965." *Clunet* (1969): 575–609.

Cottier, Thomas. "Trade and Human Rights: A Relationship to Discover." *Journal of International Economic Law* 5, no. 1 (2002): 111–32.

Cottier, Thomas. "From Progressive Liberalization to Progressive Regulation in WTO Law." *Journal of International Economic Law* 9, no. 4 (2006): 779–821.

Cottier, Thomas. "Multilayered Governance, Pluralism, and Moral Conflict." *Indiana Journal of Global Legal Studies* 16, no. 2 (2009): 647–79.

Cottier, Thomas. *A Two-Tier Approach to WTO Decision Making*. NCCR Trade Working Papers, no. 2009/06. [Bern], 2009.

Cottier, Thomas. *Equitable Principles of Maritime Boundary Delimitation: The Quest for Distributive Justice in International Law*. Cambridge: Cambridge University Press, 2015.

Cottier, Thomas, and Manfred Elsig, eds. *Governing the World Trade Organization: Past, Present and Beyond Doha*. Cambridge: Cambridge University Press, 2011.

Cottier, Thomas, and Manfred Elsig. "Reforming the WTO: The Decision-Making Triangle Revisited." In *Governing the World Trade Organization: Past, Present and Beyond Doha*, 289–312. Cambridge: Cambridge University Press, 2011.

Cottier, Thomas, and Panagiotis Delimatsis. *The Prospects of International Trade Regulation: From Fragmentation to Coherence*. Cambridge: Cambridge University Press, 2015.

Cottier, Thomas, and Petros C. Mavroidis, eds. *State Trading in the Twenty-First Century*. Ann Arbor, MI: University of Michigan Press, 2000.

Cottier, Thomas, Joost Pauwelyn, and Elisabeth Bürgi, eds. *Human Rights and International Trade*. International Economic Law Series. Oxford; New York: Oxford University Press, 2005.

Cottier, Thomas, and Satoko Takenoshita. "Decision-Making and the Balance of Powers in WTO Negotiations: Towards Supplementary Weighted Voting." In *At the Crossroads: The World Trading System and the Doha Round*, edited by Stefan Griller, 181–229. Wien: Springer, 2008.

Cuddy, John D.A. "Compensatory Financing in the North–South Dialogue: The IMF and STABEX-Schemes." *Journal of World Trade Law* 13 (1979): 66–76.

Daintith, Terence, and Arthur Taylor Von Mehren. "Regulation." In *International Encyclopedia of Comparative Law: State and Economy*, edited by Terence Daintith and René David. Vol. 17, Part 10. Mohr Siebeck, 1997.

Dash, Anup. "Towards and Epistemological Foundation for Social and Solidarity Economy." Paper presented at UNRISD, Conference on the Potential and Limits of Social and Solidarity Economy, Geneva, 6 March, 2013.

Davis, Joseph S. "Experience under Intergovernmental Commodity Agreements, 1902–45." *Journal of Political Economy* 54, no. 3 (1946): 193–220.

Díaz Bonilla, Eugenio. "Price Volatility and Commodity-Dependent Countries." Paper presented at UNCTAD, Multi-year Expert Meeting on Commodities and Development, Geneva, 23 March, 2011.

Díaz Bonilla, Eugenio. *On Food Security Stocks, Peace Clauses, and Permanent Solutions after Bali*. International Food Policy Research Institute, IFPRI Working Paper. [Washington, D.C.], 2014.

Dimitri, Carolyn, and Anne Effland. "Milestones in U.S. Farming and Farm Policy." *AmberWaves*, June 2005.

Drache, Daniel. *The Short but Significant Life of the International Trade Organization: Lessons for Our Time*. University of Warwick, Centre for the Study of Globalisation and Regionalisation, CSGR Working Paper 62/00. Warwick, 2000.

DTB Associates. *Domestic Support and WTO Obligations in Key Developing Countries*. N.p., 2011.

DTB Associates. *Agricultural Subsidies in Key Developing Countries: November 2014 Update.* N.p., 2014.

"Ecuador's Economy: Banana Skins." *The Economist*, 25 April, 2002.

Effland, Anne B. *U.S. Farm Policy: The First 200 Years.* Economic Research Service/ USDA, Agricultural Outlook. 2000.

Ehlermann, Claus-Dieter, and Lothar Ehring. "Decision-Making in the World Trade Organization: Is the Consensus Practice of the World Trade Organization Adequate for Making, Revising and Implementing Rules on International Trade?" *Journal of International Economic Law* 8, no. 1 (2005): 51–75.

Elsig, Manfred. *Functioning of the WTO: Mapping the Challenges and Asking the Hard Questions.* E15 Expert Group on the Functioning of the WTO, Overview Paper. Geneva: International Centre for Trade and Sustainable Development (ICTSD) and World Economic Forum, 2014.

Elsig, Manfred *The Functioning of the WTO: Options for Reform and Enhanced Performance.* E15 Expert Group on the Functioning of the WTO, Policy Options Paper. Geneva: International Centre for Trade and Sustainable Development (ICTSD) and World Economic Forum, 2016.

Erten, Bilge, and José Antonio Ocampo. "Super Cycles of Commodity Prices since the Mid-Nineteenth Century." *DESA Working Paper 110.* New York, 2012.

Espa, Ilaria. "The Appellate Body Approach to the Applicability of Article XX GATT in the Light of *China – Raw Materials*: A Missed Opportunity?" *Journal of World Trade* 46, no. 6 (2012): 1399–1423.

Espa, Ilaria. *Export Restrictions on Critical Minerals and Metals.* Cambridge: Cambridge University Press, 2015.

Espa, Ilaria. "Designing Coherent and Equitable WTO Disciplines on Export Restrictions." Paper presented at UNCTAD, Global Commodities Forum, Geneva, 13 April, 2015.

FAO. *The State of Agricultural Commodity Markets 2009: High Food Prices and the Food Crisis. Experiences and Lessons Learned.* Rome: FAO, 2009.

FAO. *The State of Food Insecurity in the World 2009: Economic Crises. Impacts and Lessons Learnt.* Rome: FAO, 2009.

FAO, IFAD, IMF, OECD, UNCTAD, WFP, the World Bank, and WTO. *Price Volatility in Food and Agricultural Markets: Policy Responses.* N.p., 2011.

FAO, WFP, and IFAD. *The State of Food Insecurity in the World 2012: Economic Growth Is Necessary but Not Sufficient to Accelerate Reduction of Hunger and Malnutrition.* Rome: FAO, 2012.

Fawcett, James E.S. "The Function of the Law in International Commodity Agreements." *British Year Book of International Law* 47 (1970): 157–76.

Feichtner, Isabel. "The Waiver Power of the WTO: Opening the WTO for Political Debate on the Reconciliation of Competing Interests." *European Journal of International Law* 20, no. 3 (2009): 615–45.

Feld, Werner J. "Implementation of the European Community's Common Agricultural Policy: Expectations, Fears, Failures." *International Organization* 33, no. 3 (1979): 335–63.

Fennell, Rosemary. *The Common Agricultural Policy: Continuity and Change*. Oxford; New York: Clarendon Press, 1997.

[Finger, Joseph M.]. "Access to Supplies and Resources: Commodity Agreements – Comments by Joseph M. Finger." *American Society of International Law Proceedings* 71 (1977): 136–41.

Foltea, Marina. *International Organizations in WTO Dispute Settlement: How Much Institutional Sensitivity?* Cambridge: Cambridge University Press, 2012.

Footer, Mary E. "The WTO as a 'Living Instrument': The Contribution of Consensus Decision-Making and Informality to Institutional Norms and Practices." In *Governing the World Trade Organization: Past, Present and Beyond Doha*, edited by Thomas Cottier and Manfred Elsig, 217–40. Cambridge: Cambridge University Press, 2011.

Forssell, Sara. *Rice Price Policy in Thailand: Policy Making and Recent Developments*. Department of Economics at the University of Lund, Minor Field Study Series, no. 189. 2009.

Franck, Thomas M. "Minimum Standards of Public Policy and Order Applicable to Collective International Commodity Negotiations" *Collected Courses of The Hague Academy of International Law* 160 (1978): 395–436.

Franck, Thomas M. "Fairness in the International Legal and Institutional System: General Course on Public International Law." *Collected Courses of the Hague Academy of International Law* 240 (1993): 9–498.

Galtier, Franck, Bruno Vindel, and Peter Timmer. *Gérer l'instabilite des prix alimentaires dans les pays en developpement: une analyse critique des strategies et des instruments*. Paris: AFD, 2012.

Gariepy, Richard N. "International Commodity Agreements." *International & Comparative Law Quarterly* 25, no. 03 (1976): 677–84.

GATT, Consultative Group of Eighteen. *Agriculture in the GATT*. Note by the Secretariat. CG. 18/W/59/Rev.1. 20 January 1982.

Gerda, Blau. "International Commodity Arrangements and Policies." In *Proceedings of the United Nations Conference on Trade and Development*. Vol. III: 150. New York: United Nations, 1964.

"Ghana as Economic Model." *The Economist*, 25 April, 2002.

Gilbert, Christopher L. "International Commodity Agreements: Design and Performance." *World Development* 15, no. 5 (1987): 591–616.

Gilbert, Christopher L. "International Commodity Agreements: An Obituary Notice." *World Development* 24, no. 1 (1996): 1–19.

Gilbert, Christopher L. *International Agreements for Commodity Price Stabilisation: An Assessment*. OECD Food, Agriculture and Fisheries Papers, no. 53. Paris: OECD Publishing, 2011.

Gilbert, Christopher L. "International Commodity Agreements and Their Current Relevance for Grains Price Stabilization." In *Safeguarding Food Security in Volatile Global Markets*, edited by Adam Prakash, 202–30. Rome: FAO, 2011.

Glauben, Thomas, Ingo Pies, Sören Prehn, and Matthias Georg Will. *Alarm or Rather False Alarm? A Literature Review of Empirical Research Studies into Financial Speculation with Agricultural Commodities*. Leibniz-Institut für Agrarentwicklung in Mittel- und Osteuropa, IAMO Policy Brief 9e. 2012.

"Good, but Not at Election Time." *The Economist*, 25 April, 2002.

Goodwin, Geoffrey. "The OECD Industrialised Countries' Response." In *A New International Commodity Regime*, edited by Geoffrey Goodwin and James Mayall, 111–42. London: Croom Helm, 1979.

Goodwin, Geoffrey L., and James Mayall. *A New International Commodity Regime*. London: Croom Helm, 1979.

Gouel, Christophe. *Food Price Volatility and Domestic Stabilization Policies in Developing Countries*. National Bureau of Economic Research, NBER Working Papers, no. 18934. Cambridge, MA, 2013.

Gouel, Christophe. "Food Price Volatility and Domestic Stabilization Policies in Developing Countries." Paper presented at UNCTAD, Seventh Multi-year Expert Meeting on Commodities and Development, Geneva, 15 April, 2015.

Gray, John. *The Moral Foundations of Market Institutions*. London: Institute of Economic Affairs, Health and Welfare Unit, 1992.

Green, Robert C. *Program Provisions for Program Crops: A Database for 1961–90*. Agriculture and Trade Analysis Division, Economic Research Service, U.S. Department of Agriculture, Staff Report AGES 9010. Washington, D.C., 1990.

Griller, Stefan, ed. *At the Crossroads: The World Trading System and the Doha Round*. Wien: Springer, 2008.

Guy-Alain Emmanuel, Gauze. "Reform of the Cocoa Sector in West Africa." Paper presented at UNCTAD, Global Commodities Forum, Geneva, 13 April, 2015.

Häberli, Christian. "Food Security and WTO Rules." In *Food Crises and the WTO*, edited by Baris Karapinar and Christian Häberli, 297–322. Cambridge: Cambridge University Press, 2010.

Häberli, Christian. "Liberalising Trade and Investment in Agricultural Commodities: How Fast?" Paper presented at UNCTAD, Global Commodities Forum, Geneva, 31 February, 2011.

Häberli, Christian. "The Regulatory Framework for Multi-Stakeholder Commodity Partnerships." Paper presented at UNCTAD, Multi-year Expert Meeting on Commodities and Development (3d session), Geneva, 23 March, 2011.

Häberli, Christian. "Do WTO Rules Improve or Impair the Right to Food?" In *Research Handbook on the WTO Agriculture Agreement: New and Emerging Issues in*

*International Agricultural Trade Law*, edited by Joseph A. McMahon and Melaku Geboye Desta, 70–103. Cheltenam, U.K.: Edward Elgar, 2012.

Häberli, Christian. "The WTO and Food Security: What's Wrong with the Rules?" In *The Challenge of Food Security: International Policy and Regulatory Frameworks*, edited by Rosemary Rayfuse and Nicole Weisfelt, 191–216. Cheltenham: Edward Elgar, 2012.

Häberli, Christian. "Le blocage des réformes dans la politique agricole suisse et ses répercussions internationales." *La Vie Économique. Revue de Politique Économique* 4 (2012): 27–30.

Häberli, Christian. "Right to Food and Right to Water: Même Défi ?," Paper presented at the W4W 2d Interdisciplinary Colloquium on Water, Vital Need and Global Justice (2e Colloque Interdisciplinaire "Eau, besoin vital et Justice Globale"), Geneva, 20 March, 2012.

Häberli, Christian. "God, the WTO – and Hunger." In *Poverty and the International Economic Legal System*, edited by Krista Nadakavukaren Schefer, 79–106. Cambridge: Cambridge University Press, 2013.

Häberli, Christian. *Ethiopia's Food Reserve Policies and Practice*. NCCR Trade Working Papers, no. 2013/02. [Bern], 2013.

Häberli, Christian. *After Bali: WTO Rules Applying to Public Food Reserves*. FAO Commodity and Trade Policy Research Working Paper, no. 46. Rome: FAO, 2014.

Hager, Michael L. "Commodity Agreements and the Developing Countries: A Collective Bargaining Approach." *The International Lawyer* 7, no. 2 (1973): 309–25.

Hallam, David. "Developments and Challenges in Agricultural Commodity Markets: Situation and Outlook." Paper presented at UNCTAD, Multi-year Expert Meeting on Commodities and Development, Geneva, 23 March, 2011.

Haque, Irfan ul. *Commodities under Neoliberalism: The Case Of Cocoa*. G-24 Discussion Paper Series, no. 25. Geneva: United Nations, 2004.

Held, David. "From Executive to Cosmopolitan Multilateralism." In *Taming Globalization: Frontiers of Governance*, edited by David Held and Mathias Koenig-Archibugi, 160–86. Oxford: Polity Press, 2003.

Helgason, Agnar, and Gisli Palsson. "Contested Commodities: The Moral Landscape of Modernist Regimes." *The Journal of the Royal Anthropological Institute* 3, no. 3 (1997): 451–71.

High Level Panel of Eminent Persons on the Post-2015 Development Agenda. *A New Global Partnership: Eradicate Poverty and Transform Economies through Sustainable Development*. New York: United Nations Publications, 2013.

Hilf, M. "Power, Rules and Principles: Which Orientation for WTO/GATT Law?" *Journal of International Economic Law* 4, no. 1 (2001): 111–30.

Hoekman, Bernard. *Proposals for WTO Reform: A Synthesis and Assessment*. The World Bank, Policy Research Working Papers, no. WPS5525. 2011.

Horlick, Gary N., and Kristin Heim Mowry. "The Treatment of Activities of State Trading Enterprises under the WTO Subsidies Rules." In *State Trading in the Twenty-First Century*, edited by Thomas Cottier and Petros C. Mavroidis, 97–119. Ann Arbor, MI: University of Michigan Press, 2000.

Howse, Robert, and Tim Josling. *Agricultural Export Restrictions and International Trade Law: A Way Forward.* International Food and Agricultural Trade Policy Council, IPC Position Paper. 2012.

Huchet-Bourdon, M. *Agricultural Commodity Price Volatility.* OECD Food, Agriculture and Fisheries Papers, no. 52. Paris: OECD Publishing, 2011.

ICCO. *Outline of a Cocoa Supply Chain Management Programme.* Document EX/130/9, 17 August, 2006.

IFAD, and UNEP. *Smallholders, Food Security, and the Environment.* Rome: IFAD, 2013.

"India Surges Ahead of Pakistan in 2012–13 Basmati Rice Exports to the EU." *Oryza.com*, 21 May, 2012.

Institute for Agriculture and Trade Policy. *Grain Reserves and the Food Price Crisis: Selected Writings from 2008–2012.* [Minneapolis]: IATP, 2012.

Interim Co-ordinating Committee for International Commodity Arrangements. *Review of International Commodity Arrangements.* E/CA/2. United Nations, 16 September, 1947.

International Food & Agricultural Trade Policy Council. *High Food Prices and Food Price Volatility: What Role for Policy?* IPC Alert. 4 April, 2011.

International Labour Office, ed. *Intergovernmental Commodity Control Agreements.* Montreal, 1943.

International Rubber Regulation Committee, and Andrew McFadyean. *The History of Rubber Regulation, 1934–1943.* Published by G. Allen and Unwin, for the International Rubber Regulation Committee, 1944.

IOSCO. *Report on Trading of OTC Derivatives.* FR03/11, February 2011.

Irwin, Douglas A., Petros C. Mavroidis, and Alan O. Sykes. *The Genesis of the GATT.* The American Law Institute Reporters' Studies. Cambridge: Cambridge University Press, 2008.

Irwin, Scott H., and Dwight R. Sanders. "Index Funds, Financialization, and Commodity Futures Markets." *Applied Economic Perspectives and Policy* 33, no. 1 (2011): 1–31.

Irwin, Scott H., and Dwight R. Sanders. "Testing the Masters Hypothesis in Commodity Futures Markets." *Energy Economics* 34, no. 1 (2012): 256–69.

Jabbari, David. "From Criticism to Construction in Modern Critical Legal Theory." *Oxford Journal of Legal Studies* 12, no. 4 (1992): 507–42.

Jacks, David S. "From Boom to Bust: A Typology of Real Commodity Prices in the Long Run." National Bureau of Economic Research, NBER Working Papers, no. 18874. 2013.

Johnson, Harry J. *Economic Policies toward Less Developed Countries*. Washington, DC: The Brookings Institution, 1967.

[Johnston, Charles R. Jr.]. "Access to Supplies and Resources: Commodity Agreements – Remarks by R. Johnston, Jr." *American Society of International Law Proceedings* 71 (1977): 129–33.

Jones, William O. "Food-Crop Marketing Boards in Tropical Africa." *The Journal of Modern African Studies* 25, no. 3 (1987): 375–402.

Kahn, Kabir-ur-Rahman. *The Law and Organisation of International Commodity Agreements*. The Hague: Martinus Nijhoff, 1982.

Karapinar, Baris. *Export Restrictions and the WTO Law: 'Regulatory Deficiency' or 'Unintended Policy Space'*. NCCR Trade Working Papers, no. 2010/11. [Bern], 2010.

Karapinar, Baris. "Export Restrictions and the WTO Law: How to Reform the 'Regulatory Deficiency.'" *Journal of World Trade* 45, no. 6 (2011): 1139–55.

Karapinar, Baris. "Defining the Legal Boundaries of Export Restrictions: A Case Law Analysis." *Journal of International Economic Law* 15, no. 2 (2012): 443–79.

Keck, Alexander, and Patrick Low. *Special and Differential Treatment in the WTO: Why, When and How?* WTO Economic Research and Statistics Division, Staff Working Paper ERSD-2004-03. [Geneva], 2004.

Khor, Martin. "WTO Food Fight Before and at the Bali Ministerial." *South Bulletin* 78 (2014).

Kibola, Hamisi S. "Stabex and Lomé III." *Journal of World Trade* 18, no. 1 (1984): 32–51.

Kishore, Avinash, P.K. Joshi, and John Hoddinott. "India's Right to Food Act: A Novel Approach to Food Security." In *2013 Global Food Policy Report: Overview*, edited by Andrew Marble and Heidi Fritschel, 29–41. Washington, D.C.: International Food Policy Research Institute, 2014.

Kissack, Robert. "Crisis Situations and Consensus Seeking: Adaptive Decision-Making in the FAO and Applying Its Lessons to the Reform of the WTO." In *Governing the World Trade Organization: Past, Present and Beyond Doha*, 241–62. Cambridge: Cambridge University Press, 2011.

Klein, Kenneth. "International Commodity Agreements." *Georgia Journal of International & Comparative Law* 6 (1976): 275–307.

Knudsen, Odin, and John Nash. "Domestic Price Stabilization Schemes in the Developing Countries." *Economic Development and Cultural Change* 38, no. 3 (1990): 539–58.

Kohen, Marcelo G., and Jesko Langer, eds. *Georges Abi-Saab. Le développement du droit international. Réflexions d'un demi-siècle*. Vol. I. Geneva: The Graduate Institute Publications, 2013.

Konandreas, Panos. "Global Governance: International Policy Considerations." In *Safeguarding Food Security in Volatile Global Markets*, edited by Adam Prakash, 329–60. Rome: FAO, 2011.

Konandreas, Panos, and George Mermigkas. *WTO Domestic Support Disciplines: Options for Alleviating Constraints to Stockholding in Developing Countries in the Follow-up to Bali*. FAO Commodity and Trade Policy Research Working Papers, no. 45. Rome: FAO, 2014.

Krueger, Anne O. *The Political Economy of Agricultural Pricing Policy*. Vol. 5, *A Synthesis of the Political Economy in Developing Countries*. Baltimore: Johns Hopkins University Press, 1992.

Krueger, Anneo O., Maurice Schiff, and Alberto Valdés, eds. *The Political Economy of Agricultural Pricing Policy*. Vol. 3, *Africa and the Mediterranean*. Baltimore: Johns Hopkins University Press, 1991.

Lake, David A., ed. *The International Political Economy of Trade*. The Library of International Political Economy 1. Aldershot Hants: Edward Elgar, 1993.

Lamy, Pascal. "Letter to Dr de Schutter and Attached Comments." 14 December, 2011. https://www.wto.org/english/news_e/news11_e/agcom_14dec11_e.htm#letter.

Lang, Andrew, and Joanne Scott. "The Hidden World of WTO Governance." *European Journal of International Law* 20, no. 3 (2009): 575–614.

Liapis, Pete. *Structural Change in Commodity Markets: Have Agricultural Markets Become Thinner?* OECD Food, Agriculture and Fisheries Papers, no. 54. Paris: Organisation for Economic Co-operation and Development, 2012.

Lines, Thomas. *The Potential Establishment of Emergency Food Reserve Funds*. UNCTAD Special Unit on Commodities Working Paper Series on Commodities and Development, Discussion Paper 3. Geneva, 2011.

Lipton, Michael. "Staples Production: Efficient 'Subsistence' Smallholders Are Key to Poverty Reduction, Development, and Trade." Paper presented at UNCTAD, Global Commodities Forum, Geneva, 18 March, 2013.

Lipton, Kathryn L., and Susan L. Pollack. "Major Agricultural and Trade Legislation, 1933–96, Appendix III." In *Provisions of the Federal Agriculture Improvement and Reform Act of 1996*, edited by Frederick J Nelson and Lyle P. Schertz. Washington, D.C.: Economic Research Service, USDA, 1996.

MacBean, Alasdair I., and Duncan Nguyen. "International Commodity Agreements: Shadow and Substance." *World Development* 15, no. 5 (1987): 575–90.

Mahiou, Ahmed. "Declaration on the Establishment of a New International Economic Order." United Nations Audiovisual Library of International Law, 2011.

Mahler, Vincent A. "The Political Economy of North–South Commodity Bargaining: The Case of the International Sugar Agreement." *International Organization* 38, no. 04 (1984): 709–31.

Maizels, Alfred. *Commodities in Crisis: The Commodity Crises of the 1980s and the Political Economy of International Commodity Policies*. Oxford: Clarendon Press, 1992.

Marble, Andrew, and Heidi Fritschel. *2013 Global Food Policy Report: Overview*. Washington, D.C.: International Food Policy Research Institute, 2014.

Marceau, Gabrielle. "A Call for Coherence in International Law: Praises for the Prohibition against 'Clinical Isolation' in WTO Dispute Settlement." *Journal of World Trade* 33, no. 5 (1999): 87–152.

Marceau, Gabrielle. "WTO Dispute Settlement and Human Rights." *European Journal of International Law* 13, no. 4 (2002): 753–814.

Martin, Will, and Maros Ivanic. "The Food Price Crisis, Poverty and Agricultural Trade Policy." In *Food Crises and the WTO*, edited by Baris Karapinar and Christian Häberli, 25–48. Cambridge: Cambridge University Press, 2010.

Matthews, Alan. *Food Security and WTO Domestic Support Disciplines Post-Bali*. ICTSD Programme on Agricultural Trade and Sustainable Development. Geneva: International Centre for Trade and Sustainable Development, 2014.

Mayer, Jörg. *The Growing Interdependence between Financial and Commodity Markets*. UNCTAD Discussion Papers, no. 195. Geneva, 2009.

McCorriston, Steve, David H. Hemming, Julien D. Lamontagne-Godwin, Janice Osborn, Martin J. Parr, and Philip D. Roberts. *What Is the Evidence of the Impact of Agricultural Trade Liberalisation on Food Security in Developing Countries? A Systematic Review*. London: EPPI – Centre, Social Science Research Unit, Institute of Education, University of London, 2013.

McIntyre, Beverly D., Hans R. Herren, Judi Wakhungu, and Robert T. Watson. *Agriculture at a Crossroads: International Assessment of Agricultural Knowledge, Science, and Technology for Development – Global Report*. Washington, D.C.: Island Press, 2009.

Meadows, Donella H, Dennis L. Meadows, Jørgen Randers, and William W. Behrens III. *The Limits to Growth: Report for the Club of Rome's Project on the Predicament of Mankind*. New York: Universe Books, 1972.

Meier, Gerald M. "UNCTAD Proposals for International Economic Reform." *Stanford Law Review* 19, no. 6 (1967): 1173–216.

Meléndez-Ortiz, Ricardo, Christophe Bellmann, and Jonathan Hepburn. *Agricultural Subsidies in the WTO Green Box: Ensuring Coherence with Sustainable Development Goals*. Cambridge: Cambridge University Press, 2010.

Meredith, David. "State Controlled Marketing and Economic 'Development': The Case of West African Produce during the Second World War." *The Economic History Review* 39, no. 1 (1986): 77–91.

Meredith, David. "The Colonial Office, British Business Interests and the Reform of Cocoa Marketing in West Africa, 1937–1945." *The Journal of African History* 29, no. 2 (1988): 285–300.

Metzger, Stanley D. "Developments in the Law and Institutions of International Economic Relations: UNCTAD." *American Journal of International Law* 61, no. 3 (1967): 756–75.

Minot, Nicholas. *Transmission of World Food Price Changes to Markets in Sub-Saharan Africa*. International Food Policy Research Institute, IFPRI Discussion Paper 01059. Washington, D.C., 2011.

Mohanty, Samarendu. "Thailand's Rice Mortgage Program." *AsiaSentinel*, 27 September, 2011.

Mohanty, Samarendu. "Why Does Everyone Hate the Thai Rice Mortgage Scheme?" IRRI blog entry. 5 November, 2012. http://irri.org/blogs/sam-s-rice-price-and-market-blog/why-does-everyone-hate-the-thai-rice-mortgage-scheme.

Monke, Jim, Randy Alison Aussenberg, and Megan Stubbs. "Expiration and Extension of the 2008 Farm Bill." Congressional Research Service Report, December 2013.

Montemayor, Raul. *Public Stockholding for Food Security Purposes: Scenarios and Options for a Permanent Solution*. International Centre for Trade and Sustainable Development, Issue Paper 51. Geneva, 2014.

Murphy, Sophia. *Grain Reserves: A Smart Climate Adaptation Policy*. Institute for Agriculture and Trade Policy, 2010.

Murphy, Sophia. *Trade and Food Reserves: What Role Does the WTO Play?* Institute for Agriculture and Trade Policy, 2010.

Musselli, Irene. "La régulation des cours et des marchés des produits de base: vers une nouvelle architecture internationale?" *Journal Du Droit International*, no. 3 (2012): 903–38.

Musselli, Irene. *Farm Support and Trade Rules: Towards a New Paradigm under the 2030 Agenda*. UNCTAD, Policy Issues in International Trade and Commodities, Study Series, no. 74. Geneva, 2016.

Nappi, Carmine. *Commodity Market Controls*. Lexington, Mass.: D.C. Heath, 1979.

Narayanan, Sudha. *The Balance: The National Food Security Act vis- à -vis the WTO Agreement on Agriculture*. Indira Gandhi Institute of Development Research, 2013.

Nelken, David. "Is There a Crisis in Law and Legal Ideology?" *Journal of Law and Society* 9, no. 2 (1982): 177–89.

Newbery, David M.G., and Joseph E. Stiglitz. *The Theory of Commodity Price Stabilization: A Study in the Economics of Risk*. Oxford: Clarendon Press, 1981.

Niek Koning, Muriel Calo, Roel Jongeneel. *Fair Trade in Tropical Crops is Possible*. North South Centre, North–south Discussion Paper 3. Wageningen, The Netherlands, 2004.

OECD. *Multifunctionality: Towards an Analytical Framework*. Paris: OECD Publishing, 2001.

OECD. *Evaluation of Agricultural Policy Reforms in Japan*. Paris: OECD Publishing, 2009.

OECD. *Agricultural Policies in OECD Countries: At a Glance*. Paris: OECD Publishing, 2010.

OECD. *An Assessment of Commodity Agreements for Commodity Price Stabilisation*. TAD/CA/APM/WP(2010)36/FINAL, 19 May, 2011.

OECD. *Export Restrictions in Raw Materials Trade: Facts, Fallacies and Better Practices* (OECD, 2014).

OECD, and FAO. *OECD-FAO Agricultural Outlook 2011–2020*. OECD Publishing and FAO, 2011.

Osmańczyk, Edmund Jan. *Encyclopedia of the United Nations and International Agreements*. 3d ed. New York and London: Routledge, 2003.

Paarlberg, Robert. "Agricultural Policy Reform and the Uruguay Round: Synergistic Linkage in a Two-Level Game?" *International Organization* 51, no. 03 (1997): 413–444.

Paarlberg, Robert. "The Political Economy of American Agricultural Policy: Three Approaches." *American Journal of Agricultural Economics* 71, no. 5 (1989): 1157–64.

Pattanayak, Subhrendu K., Brooks M. Depro, and Tayler H. Bingham. *Economic Analysis of the Rubber Tire Manufacturing MACT, Final Report*. U.S. Environmental Protection Agency, August 2000.

Pauwelyn, Joost. "The Role of Public International Law in the WTO: How Far Can We Go?" *The American Journal of International Law* 95, no. 3 (2001): 535–78.

Pauwelyn, Joost. "How to Win a WTO Dispute Based on Non-WTO Law? Questions of Jurisdiction and Merits." *Journal of World Trade* 37, no. 6 (2003): 997–1030.

Pauwelyn, Joost. "Human Rights in WTO Dispute Settlement." In *Human Rights and International Trade*, edited by Thomas Cottier, Joost Pauwelyn, and Elisabeth Bürgi, 206–31. Oxford: Oxford University Press, 2005.

Pellet, Alain. "Article 38." In *The Statute of the International Court of Justice: A Commentary*, edited by Andreas Zimmermann, Christian Tomuschat, and Karin Oellers-Frahm, 677–792. Oxford: Oxford University Press, 2006.

Perugini, Cristiano. "Who Bears the Burden of Common Agricultural Price Policy? The Distributive Effects of Market Price Support in the Agricultural Sector." *Rivista internazionale di scienze sociali* 112, no. 4 (2004): 471–93.

Petersmann, Ernst-Ulrich. "GATT Law on State Trading Enterprises: Critical Evaluation of Article XVII and Proposals for Reform." In *State Trading in the Twenty-First Century*, edited by Thomas Cottier and Petros C. Mavroidis, 71–96. Ann Arbor, MI: University of Michigan Press, 2000.

Petersmann, Ernst-Ulrich. "Human Rights and International Trade Law: Defining and Connecting the Two Fields." In *Human Rights and International Trade*, edited by Thomas Cottier, Joost Pauwelyn, and Elisabeth Bürgi, 29–94. Oxford: Oxford University Press, 2005.

Petrick, Martin. "The Co-Evolution of Semantics and Policy Paradigms: 50 Years of Europe's Common Agricultural Policy." *Intereconomics: Review of European Economic Policy* 43, no. 4 (2008): 246–52.

Pincus, John A. "What Policy for Commodities?" In *Readings in International Economic Relations*, edited by Finn B. Jensen and Ingo Walter, 453–65. New York: Ronald Press, 1966.

Pindyck, Robert S. "The Cartelization of World Commodity Markets." *The American Economic Review* 69, no. 2 (1979): 154–58.

Prakash, Adam, ed. *Safeguarding Food Security in Volatile Global Markets*. Rome: FAO, 2011.

Raban, Ofer. "The Fallacy of Legal Certainty: Why Vague Legal Standards May Be Better for Capitalism and Liberalism." *Boston University Public Interest Law Journal* 19, no. 2 (2010): 175–91.

Rangarajan, L.N. "Commodity Conflict Revisited: From Nairobi to Belgrade." *Third World Quarterly* 5, no. 3 (1983): 586–609.

Rashid, Shahidur, and Solomon Lemma. *Strategic Grain Reserves in Ethiopia: Institutional Design and Operational Performance*. International Food Policy Research Institute, IFPRI Discussion Paper 01054. Washington, D.C., 2011.

Ravenhill, John. "What Is To Be Done for Third World Commodity Exporters? An Evaluation of the STABEX Scheme." *International Organization* 38, no. 03 (1984): 537–74.

Rayfuse, Rosemary, and Nicole Weisfelt. *The Challenge of Food Security: International Policy and Regulatory Frameworks*. Cheltenham: Edward Elgar, 2012.

Reinhart, Cannen M., and Peter Wickham. *Commodity Prices: Cyclical Weakness or Secular Decline?* IMF Staff Papers, vol. 41, no. 2. 1994.

Reynolds, Amy. "Recent Developments and New Challenges in Commodity Markets, and Policy Options for Commodity-Based Inclusive Growth and Sustainable Development." Paper presented at UNCTAD, Multi-year Expert Meeting on Commodities and Development, Geneva, 15 April, 2015.

Reynolds, Paul D., and Paul Donovan Reynolds. *International Commodity Agreements and the Common Fund: A Legal and Financial Analysis*. New York: Praeger, 1978.

Richter, J.H. "Agricultural Policy in the European Common Market." *Journal of Farm Economics* 43, no. 3 (1961): 637–42.

Rijsberman, Frank R. "Water Scarcity: Fact or Fiction?" *Agricultural Water Management* 80, no. 1–3 (2006): 5–22.

Ritson, Christopher, and David Harvey, eds. *The Common Agricultural Policy*. 2d ed. New York: CABI Publishing, 1997.

[Rogers, William D.]. "Access to Supplies and Resources: Commodity Agreements – Comments by William D. Rogers." *American Society of International Law Proceedings* 71 (1977): 141–42.

Rothstein, Robert L. *Global Bargaining: UNCTAD and the Quest for a New International Economic Order*. Princeton: Princeton University Press, 1979.

Rowe, John Wilkinson Foster. *Primary Commodities in International Trade*. Cambridge: Cambridge University Press, 1965.

Ruggie, John Gerard. "International Regimes, Transactions, and Change: Embedded Liberalism in the Postwar Economic Order." *International Organization* 36, no. 02 (1982): 379–-.

Sampson, Gary P., and Richard H. Snape. "Effects of the EEC's Variable Import Levies." *Journal of Political Economy* 88, no. 5 (1980): 1026–40.

Schachter, Oscar. "International Law in Theory and in Practice: General Course in Public International Law." *Collected Courses of the Hague Academy of Internatioanl Law* 178 (V 1982): 9–396.

Schachter, Oscar. "Just Prices in World Markets: Proposals De Lege Ferenda." *The American Journal of International Law* 69, no. 1 (1975): 101–09.

Schultz, Theodore W., ed. *Distortions of Agricultural Incentives*. Bloomington: Indiana University Press, 1979.

Schwarzenberger, George. "The Principles and Standards of International Economic Law." *Collected Courses of the Hague Academy of Internatioanl Law* 117 (1966): 1–98.

Seo, S., Robert Mendelsohn, Ariel Dinar, Rashid Hassan, and Pradeep Kurukulasuriya. "A Ricardian Analysis of the Distribution of Climate Change Impacts on Agriculture across Agro-Ecological Zones in Africa." *Environmental & Resource Economics* 43, no. 3 (2009): 313–32.

Sharma, Ramesh. *Food Export Restrictions: Review of the 2007–2010 Experience and Considerations for Disciplining Restrictive Measures*. FAO Commodity and Trade Policy Research Working Papers, no. 32. Rome: FAO, 2011.

Sharma, Ramesh, and Panos Konandreas. *WTO Provisions in the Context of Responding to Soaring Food Prices*. FAO Commodity and Trade Policy Research Working Papers, no. 25. Rome: FAO, 2008.

Silva, José Graziano da, Mauro Eduardo Del Grossi, and Caio Galvão de França. *The Fome Zero (Zero Hunger) Program: The Brazilian Experience*. Ministry of Agrarian Development, 2011.

Singh, Harsha. "We Need an Open and Predictable Trading System to Address Price Volatility." Paper presented at the International Food and Agricultural Trade Policy Council, Barcelona, 26 May, 2010.

Slayton, Tom. *Rice Crisis Forensics: How Asian Governments Carelessly Set the World Rice Market on Fire*. Center for Global Development, CGD Working Paper 163. Washington, D.C.: 2009.

Smith, Alistair. "Rethinking Price – The Heart of the Matter." Paper presented at the World Banana Forum, FAO, Rome, December 2009.

Sorel, Jean-Marc, and Valérie Boré Eveno. "Article 31: Convention of 1969." In *The Vienna Conventions on the Law of Treaty: A Commentary*, edited by Olivier Corten and Pierre Klein, vol. I: 804–37. Oxford: Oxford University Press, 2011.

South Center. "The WTO's Bali Ministerial and Food Security for Developing Countries: Need for Equity and Justice in the Rules on Agricultural Subsidies." Report drawn upon discussions in two Expert Group Meetings held in 2013 on the Multilateral Trading System Organised by the South Centre in the preparation of the WTO's 9th Ministerial Conference in Bali in December 2013.

Special Raporteur on the Right to Food (Olivier de Schutter). *Mission to the World Trade Organization*. A/HRC/10/5/Add.2. 4 February, 2009.

Special Raporteur on the Right to Food (Olivier de Schutter). *Countries Tackling Hunger with a Right to Food Approach*. Briefing Note 1. 2010.

Special Raporteur on the Right to Food (Olivier de Schutter). *The World Trade Organization and the Post-Global Food Crisis Agenda: Putting Food Security First in the International Trade System*. Activity Report. November 2011.

Special Raporteur on the Right to Food (Olivier de Schutter). *From Charity to Entitlement: Implementing the Right to Food in Southern and Eastern Africa*. Briefing Note 05. 26 June, 2012.

Special Raporteur on the Right to Food (Olivier de Schutter). *Interim Report of the Special Rapporteur on the Right to Food*. A/68/288. 7 August, 2013.

Special Raporteur on the Right to Food (Olivier de Schutter). *Final Report: The Transformative Potential of the Right to Food*. A/HRC/25/57. 24 January, 2014.

Steger, Debra, ed. *Redesigning the World Trade Organization for the Twenty-First Century*. Waterloo, ON.: Wilfrid Laurier University Press, 2009.

Stevens, Christopher. *The Future of Special and Differential Treatment (SDT) for Developing Countries in the WTO*. Institute for Development Studies, IDS Working Paper 163. Brighton, Sussex, 2002.

Stocker, Thomas F., Dahe Qin, and Working Group I Technical Support Unit, eds. *Climate Change 2013: The Physical Science Basis: Working Group I Contribution to the Fifth Assessment Report of the Intergovernmental Panel on Climate Change*. Cambridge: Cambridge University Press, 2014.

Swinnen, Johan F.M. *Agricultural Protection Growth in Europe, 1870–1969*. The World Bank, Agricultural Distortions Working Paper No. 80. Washington, D.C., 2009.

"Symposium on Efficiency as a Legal Concern Introduction." *Hofstra Law Review* 8, no. 3 (1980): 485.

Talbot, John M. "Where Does Your Coffee Dollar Go? The Division of Income and Surplus along the Coffee Commodity Chain." *Studies in Comparative International Development* 32, no. 1 (1997): 56–91.

Teubner, Gunther. "Substantive and Reflexive Elements in Modern Law." *Law & Society Review* 17, no. 2 (1983): 239–85.

"Thai Rice. Less Paddy Power. Populist Politics Mess up Thailand's Biggest Crop." *The Economist*, 14 July, 2012.

"Thailand Rice Mortgage Program Could Continue Indefinitely, Says Commerce Minister." *Oryza.com*, 28 October, 2013.

"The EEC's Farm Policy." *The Economist*, 1 April, 1978.

The World Bank. *World Development Report 1983*. New York: Oxford University Press, 1983.

The World Bank. *World Development Report 1985*. New York: Oxford University Press, 1985.

The World Bank. *World Development Report 2008: Agriculture for Development*. Washington, D.C.: The World Bank, 2007.

The World Bank. *Responding to Global Food Price Volatility and Its Impact on Food Security*. DC2011-0002, 4 April 2011. The World Bank, April 2011.

The World Bank, and FAO. *The Grain Chain Food Security and Managing Wheat Imports in Arab Countries*. Washington, D.C.: The World Bank, 2012.

The World Bank, FAO, and IFAD. *Improving Food Security in Arab Countries*. Washington, D.C.: The World Bank, 2009.

Thomas, Lines. *Supply Management: Options for Commodity Income Stabilization*. Winnipeg, Manitoba: International Institute for Sustainable Development, 2007.

Tielu, Apelu, and Ivan Roberts. "Farm Income Support: Implications for Gains from Trade of Changes in Methods of Support Overseas." *ABARE Current Issues* 98, no. 4 (1998): 1–8.

Timmer, Peter. *Getting Prices Right: The Scope and Limits of Agricultural Price Policy*. Ithaca: Cornell University Press, 1986.

Timmer, Peter. "Food Price Policy: The Rationale for Government Intervention." *Food Policy* 14, no. 1 (1989): 17–27.

Timmer, Peter. "Getting Agriculture Moving: Do Markets Provide the Right Signals?" *Food Policy* 20, no. 5 (1995): 455–72.

Tomuschat, Christian. "International Commodity Agreements." In *International Encyclopedia of Comparative Law*, edited by Ernst-Ulrich Petersmann, Christian Tomuschat, and Albert Bleckmann. Vol. 17, *State and Economy*, Chap. 25, *Universal Economic Organizations*: 47–73. Mohr Siebeck, 1997.

Tozer, Bruce. "Outcomes of the Public-Private Initiative on Commodity Market Volatility." Paper presented at UNCTAD, Global Commodities Forum, Geneva, 18 March, 2013.

Trachtman, Joel P. "The Domain of WTO Dispute Resolution." *Harvard International Law Journal* 40 (1999): 333–77.

*Trade Liberalization and the Right to Food. Video Debate between Pascal Lamy and Olivier De Schutter.*, 2009. http://www.wto.org/english/forums_e/debates_e/debate14_e.htm.

UK HM Treasury, and Department for Environment, Food and Rural Affairs (Defra). *A Vision for the Common Agricultural Policy*. London: HM Treasury, 2005.

UNCTAD. *A Survey of Commodity Risk Management Instruments*. UNCTAD/COM/15/REV.2. 6 April, 1998.

UNCTAD. *Intergovernmental Producer-Consumer Cooperation in Commodities in Mid 1990s: A Handbook on International Commodity Agreements, Arrangements and Study Groups*. Geneva: United Nations, 1998.

UNCTAD. *Overview of the World's Commodity Exchanges*. UNCTAD/DITC/COM/2005/8. 2006.

UNCTAD. *The Global Economic Crisis: Systemic Failures and Multilateral Remedies*. Geneva: United Nations, 2009.

UNCTAD. *Trade and Development Report 2009*. Geneva: United Nations, 2009.

UNCTAD. *Policy Actions to Mitigate the Impact of Highly Volatile Prices and Incomes on Commodity Dependent Countries, and to Facilitate Value Addition and Greater Participation in Commodity Value Chains by Commodity-Producing Countries*. TD/B/C.I/MEM.2/14. 2 February, 2011.

UNCTAD. *Price Formation in Financialized Commodity Markets: The Role of Information*. New York; Geneva: United Nations, 2011.

UNCTAD. *Least Developed Countries Report 2015: Transforming Rural Economies*. Geneva: United Nations, 2015.

UNCTAD, and CFC. *Global Crises and the Commodity Dependence of the Least Developed Countries: Impacts, Challenges and the Way Forward*. UNCTAD/ALDC/MISC/2011/6. 28 April, 2011.

UNHCR. *Climate Change, Natural Disasters and Human Displacement: A UNHCR Perspective*. 23 October, 2008.

United Nations. *The Future We Want*. Outcome Document of the United Nations Conference on Sustainable Development. Annexed to the General Assembly Resolution 66/288 of 27 July 2012.

United Nations. *The Road to Dignity by 2030: Ending Poverty, Transforming All Lives and Protecting the Planet: Synthesis Report of the Secretary-General On the Post-2015 Agenda*. New York, 2014.

United Nations Interim Co-ordinating Committee for International Commodity Arrangements. *Review of International Commodity Arrangements*. Geneva: United Nations, 1947.

United States, Congressional Budget Office. *Background Paper: Commodity Initiatives of Less Developed Countries: U.S. Responses and Costs*. Washington, D.C., 1977.

US Department of Agriculture. *Guidelines for Fruit, Vegetable & Specialty Crop Marketing Orders*. 25 January, 1982.

USDA Foreign Agricultural Service. *Thailand. Grain and Feed. Cabinet Approval of Rice Mortgage Scheme 2008*. GAIN Report TH8095. 13 June, 2008.

USDA Foreign Agricultural Service. *Indian Cabinet Approves National Food Security Bill 2013*. GAIN Report IN3037. 11 April, 2013

USDA Foreign Agricultural Service. *Vietnam Grain and Feed Annual 2013*. GAIN Report VN3016. 3 April, 2013.

Valentini, Laura. *Justice in a Globalized World: A Normative Framework*. Oxford: Oxford University Press, 2011.

Valluis, Bernard. "Policy Actions About Agricultural Commodity Market Volatility." Paper presented at UNCTAD, Multi-year Expert Meeting on Commodities and Development, Geneva, 23 March, 2011.

Varangis, Panos, and John McIntire. *Reforming Côte d'Ivoire's Cocoa Marketing and Pricing System*. The World Bank, Policy Research Working Papers, no. WPS2081. Washinton, D.C., 1999.

Vastine Jr., J. Robert. "United States International Commodity Policy." *Law and Policy in International Business* 9 (1977): 401–77.

Vivero Pol, José Luis. "Food as a Commodity, Human Right or Common Good? Implications for Hunger Eradication." Paper presented at UNRISD, Seminar Series, Geneva, 9 April, 2013.

Warwick Commission. *The Multilateral Trade Regime: Which Way Forward?* Nottingham, U.K.: University of Warwick, 2007.

WFP. *World Hunger Series: Hunger and Markets*. London: Earthscan, 2009.

Wickizer, Vernon D. "The Smallholder in Tropical Export Crop Production." *Food Research Institute Studies* 1, no. 01 (1960): 49–99.

Wight, Brian, and Adam Prakash. "The Fallacy of Price Interventions: A Note on Price Bands and Managed Tariffs." In *Safeguarding Food Security in Volatile Global Markets*, edited by Adam Prakash, 231–41. Rome: FAO, 2011.

Wijkström, Erik, and McDaniels Devin. *International Standards and the WTO TBT Agreement: Improving Governance for Regulatory Alignment*. WTO, Economic Research and Statistics Division, Staff Working Paper ERSD-2013-06. Geneva, 2013.

Wilcox, Clair. *A Charter for World Trade*. New York: Macmillan, 1949.

Williams, Gavin. "Marketing Without and With Marketing Boards: The Origins of State Marketing Boards in Nigeria." *Review of African Political Economy* 12, no. 34 (1985): 4–15.

Williamson, John. "What Should the World Bank Think about the Washington Consensus?" *World Bank Research Observer* 15, no. 2 (2000): 251–64.

World Food Programme. *World Hunger Series: Hunger and Markets*. London: Earthscan, 2009.

Wright, Brian. *International Grain Reserves and Other Instruments to Address Volatility in Grain Markets*. The World Bank, Policy Research Working Papers, no. 5028. Washington, D.C., 2009.

Zimmermann, Andreas, Christian Tomuschat, and Karin Oellers-Frahm. *The Statute of the International Court of Justice: A Commentary*. Oxford: Oxford University Press, 2012.

# Index

www.ingramcontent.com/pod-product-compliance
Lightning Source LLC
LaVergne TN
LVHW010624300926
849162LV00001B/53
* 9 7 8 9 0 0 4 3 1 4 2 3 8 *